ISRAEL

FODOR'S MODERN GUIDES

are compiled, researched and edited by an international team of travel writers, field correspondents and editors. The series, which now almost covers the globe, was founded by Eugene Fodor.

OFFICES
New York and London

Editorial Staff for Fodor's Israel:

Editor:	RICHARD MOORE
Area Editor:	DIANNE NICHOLSON LAWES
Editorial Contributors:	ROGER COSTER JR., JORAM KAGAN, JERILYN ROGIN, ARNOLD SHERMAN, AVIAD YAFEH
Photographs:	DOUGLAS DICKINS, ISRAEL GOVERNMENT TOURIST OFFICE
Maps:	ALEX MURPHY

FODOR'S

ISRAEL
1981

FODOR'S MODERN GUIDES, INC.

Distributed by

DAVID McKAY COMPANY, INC.
New York

**All the following Guides are current (most of them also in
the Hodder and Stoughton British edition).**

CURRENT FODOR'S COUNTRY AND AREA TITLES:

AUSTRALIA, NEW ZEALAND AND SOUTH PACIFIC	INDIA
AUSTRIA	IRELAND
BAJA CALIFORNIA	ISRAEL
BELGIUM AND LUXEMBOURG	ITALY
BERMUDA	JAPAN AND KOREA
BRAZIL	JORDAN AND HOLY LAND
CANADA	MEXICO
CARIBBEAN AND BAHAMAS	NORTH AFRICA
CENTRAL AMERICA	PEOPLE'S REPUBLIC OF CHINA
EASTERN EUROPE	PORTUGAL
EGYPT	SCANDINAVIA
EUROPE	SOUTH AMERICA
FRANCE	SOUTHEAST ASIA
GERMANY	SOVIET UNION
GREAT BRITAIN	SPAIN
GREECE	SWITZERLAND
HOLLAND	TURKEY
	YUGOSLAVIA

CITY GUIDES:

LONDON	ROME
PARIS	WASHINGTON, D.C.

FODOR'S BUDGET SERIES:

BUDGET EUROPE	BUDGET GERMANY
BUDGET TRAVEL IN AMERICA	BUDGET ITALY
BUDGET CARIBBEAN	BUDGET MEXICO
BUDGET BRITAIN	BUDGET SPAIN
BUDGET FRANCE	BUDGET JAPAN

USA GUIDES:

USA (in one volume)	NEW YORK
CALIFORNIA	NEW ENGLAND
COLORADO	FLORIDA
HAWAII	MIDWEST
FAR WEST	OUTDOORS AMERICA
ALASKA	PENNSYLVANIA
SOUTHWEST	SUNBELT LEISURE GUIDE
SOUTH	

SPECIAL INTEREST SERIES:
CIVIL WAR SITES

EDITORS' FOREWORD

Though Israel is a relative newcomer to the modern family of nations, it also is the land where many of man's early attempts at civilization were made, where monotheism found its first foothold, and where the basics of Western ethics were born. Not surprisingly, the land has, for centuries, drawn scholars, historians, archeologists and pilgrims. Only a few decades ago, such adventurers needed solid determination, enduring strength and abiding faith to handle the awkward treks to holy and historical sites. Often they traveled by camel or donkey, or rode motor vehicles across rough roads and paths, then carefully edged on foot into barely accessible areas. It was not uncommon for them to be beset by bandits, mosquitoes, assorted digestive troubles and relic rogues.

Things are very different today mostly because modern Israelis are probably the world's greatest biblical history buffs, intensely anxious to learn everything that ever happened in this land. Exciting ancient sagas are part of every schoolchild's study and archeology is, without doubt, a favorite hobby of the average citizen. With the caution of experimental scientists Israelis have covered the land millimeter by millimeter to ascertain what occurred where, and when. Many events related to the Bible have been substantiated by recent discoveries which have also unearthed important, sometimes previously unknown, pre-biblical information, sites and artifacts. Large and small museums are scattered about the country, and each historical or religious site is easy to reach, well-tended and clearly marked in several languages. Even "traditional" and legendary sites are marked and explained. You can visit these places alone, armed only with this book; hire a private guide, or join a tour group. And you can have confidence that all guides today have been licensed only after passing extensive in-depth courses sponsored by the Israel Government Tourism Administration.

In the new air-conditioned Holy Land you can ride streamlined buses on the roads once walked by the Apostles or scuba-dive in the waters of Eilat, Israel's peephole on Asia and Africa, where King Solomon received the Queen of Sheba. You'll also find sun-worshipers, in ever-increasing numbers, who come for holidays in the year-round good climate and to enjoy the plethora of outdoor activities, including golfing at Caesarea, one-time capital of Roman Palestine. The spa areas attract many health addicts, and beauty-oriented tourists indulge in packs and baths of that Dead Sea mud so fondly favored by Cleopatra.

Other travelers are more interested in places like the Kennedy Memorial in Jerusalem, only a stone's throw away from any number of sites of Persian, Hellenic, Israelite, Roman, Christian, Arabic or Turkish significance. The graves and battle locales of 20th-century wars and battles also attract their share of visitors.

Inevitably, in a country as volatile as Israel, it is difficult to keep up with the current state of affairs. This is especially true of the Sinai region, now returning to Egyptian rule. As we go to press the availability of this area for tours and the status of hotels in, for example, Sharm-el-Sheikh, is uncertain. It would be difficult for a daily newspaper and it is even more difficult for an annually revised guide. But, within these limitations, we have tried to provide as much purely practical information as we can, and as much background color and coverage, so that our readers will feel, especially while planning their trip, that they have some idea of what Israel is like today.

We would like to express our appreciation to all the personnel of the Israel Government Tourism Administration for its valuable help in the preparation of this guide. We are indebted to Mr. Lee Silverman, Advertising and Public Relations Manager for El Al in Great Britain, for much assistance, and to Joram Kagan. We are also extremely grateful to Dianne Nicholson Lawes who revised this edition.

Errors are bound to creep into any guide. When a hotel closes or a restaurant's chef produces an inferior meal, you may question our recommendation. Let us know, and we will investigate the establishment and the complaint. Your letters will help us to pinpoint trouble spots.

Our addresses are:

in the U.S.A., Fodor's Modern Guides, 2 Park Ave., New York, N.Y. 10016;

in Europe, Fodor's Modern Guides, 1-11 John Adam Street, London WC2.

CONTENTS

CONTENTS

Supplements

FACTS
AT YOUR
FINGERTIPS

FACTS AT YOUR FINGERTIPS

Planning your trip

Devaluation in some European countries with consequent rising taxes and costs throughout and possible inflationary trends to come, make accurate budgeting long in advance an impossibility. Prices mentioned throughout this book are indicative only of costs at the time of going to press (mid-1980). Keep a weather eye open for fluctuations in exchange rates, both when planning your trip and while on it.

WHAT WILL IT COST. Naturally, all costs will depend on how you travel to Israel, the accommodations you choose, your side-trips, entertainments, incidentals, purchases, and so forth. However, for elementary calculation and a rough idea of expenses involved, you can plan according to these four categories: *De Luxe, Comfortable, Economical,* and *Student.*

Tourists in the *De Luxe* category would opt for first-class plane travel to Israel, then the daily per person tab could run as high as $75–175 and include the best hotels, chauffeur-driven or rented cars, rounds of nightclubs and such.

For the *Comfortable* category, economy air travel would start the trip, and the per person daily expenses would run $50–75 which would cover good hotel rooms (with private baths), good restaurants, drive-yourself cars and a restricted round of entertainments.

The *Economical* tourist travels overland by *sherut* or bus and buys excursion air travel, and may even hitch-hike, as well as use buses. In Israel, this economy-minded visitor stays in comfortable hotels, but has showers instead of baths in the room; eats in good, reliable restaurants that always are crowded because of their reasonable prices; travels in the country via bus, *sherut* or train; watches TV in the hotel lobby or takes in an occasional movie as entertainment—which allows a daily per person rate of $30–40.

The *Student* category involves camping out, staying at Youth Hostels or hotels not recommended by the Israel Government Ministry of Tourism because they lack minimum standards most Westerners require; eating quick meals at cafés and snack bars; traveling internally by hitch-hiking mostly, and using student organizations to receive international student fares for inter-continental

3

and local transportation. This *budget* budget can run as low as $20–25 daily, per person, within Israel.

Typical One-Day First-Class Budget

	IS
Room in 4–5 star hotel, taxes and service included	($22–78) 250
Lunch in restaurant	50
Half-day sightseeing trip by bus	60
Taxi	20
Movie	10
Cigarettes	8
Drinks: 1 beer, 1 cup of coffee	60
Miscellaneous	30
Dinner with drinks	100
Approximate total for one day:	588

Typical One-Day Economical Budget

	IS
Room in 2- or 3-star hotel, taxes and service included ($7–38)	113
Lunch in restaurant	25
Half-day sightseeing trip by bus	40
Movie	10
Cigarettes	5
Drinks: 1 beer, 1 cup of coffee	4
Dinner in restaurant	40
Approximate total for one day:	237

Not included: The local tour programs, cost of car rental, theaters, nightlife, souvenirs and other purchases. All these expenses depend so much on individual preferences, it is impossible to strike an "average."

MONEY. In 1980 Israel returned to the shekel. The reason was in part a desire to reaffirm links with the past and to boost the ailing economy psychologically by means of reference to an ancient and historic currency and partly the result of pragmatic economic thinking. The new currency is extremely flexible and, being devised on a "new one equals ten old" basis, allows "cancellation" of small units that should, if predictions are right, save some IS15 million every year.

The shekel (equivalent to 10 lira and 1000 agorot in the old currency) is available in bank notes of IS1, IS5, IS10, IS50 and IS100. There are four coins; one new agora (aluminum), five new agorot (aluminum), 10 new agorot (bronze) and a half-shekel (copper-nickel) which equals 50 new agorot.

As this edition goes to press (mid-1980) the US dollar equals about IS5 and the pound sterling IS12. However, this is bound to change soon as Israel's inflation-fighting measures have a built-in devaluation factor, so we strongly advise you to re-check rates of exchange at a bank both before and during your trip. Generally, the devaluation of the shekel will be linked to the rise and fall of the dollar, but while dollar prices will probably change only slightly, shekel rates will soar. For this reason, many official tourist prices are quoted in dollars.

Note: Principal international credit cards, such as American Express, Diners Club International, Visa, Eurocard and Master Charge, are accepted by most Israeli hotels, restaurants and shops, as are traveler's checks. Foreign currency or State of Israel bonds can be exchanged at banks into local-currency traveler's checks or bank checks.

Visitors may bring into Israel any amount of Israeli or foreign currency in cash or traveler's checks and take out any amount of foreign currency. Foreign currency is exchangeable only in authorized banks, but all services and purchases may be paid for in the following freely exchangeable currencies: US dollars, Canadian dollars, pounds sterling, Swiss, Belgian and French francs, Danish, Swedish and Norwegian crowns, Dutch florins, German and Finnish marks, Italian lire and Austrian schillings. When leaving Israel, you may reconvert into foreign currency up to $3,000 or the equivalent.

Financial Benefits for Tourists

Tourists who pay in foreign currency—for accommodations, food and drinks at their hotel, regular tours, car hire, driver-guides, flights within Israel—are exempt from local taxes which would normally add an extra 28% to their bills, including 12% Value Added Tax. However, tourists are not exempt from taxes on other tourist services, on tickets to parks and places of interest or when eating outside their hotel. However, you will receive a refund, at your port of departure, for VAT paid on goods purchased with foreign currency at shops listed by the Ministry for Industry, Trade and Tourism. There are also discounts, ranging from 5% to 30%, for goods purchased at shops bearing Ministry emblems. (All hotel guests pay 15% service charge.)

 TIPPING. Tipping used to be frowned upon in Israel in the good old days, and tips would be haughtily refused. Now the sad truth is that it's the tourists themselves who have helped to foster the system. Still, the outstretched palm is less in evidence than in many other countries. *Cafés, restaurants and hotels* are required by law to add 15% to the bill, which sum is distributed to the entire staff, but people usually tip 10–15% more today, anyway. In *cafés* and any but the better or more fashionable restaurants, there is no need to add a further tip. After an elaborate meal in a *first-class restaurant,* an additional 10–15% tip will be appreciated. In *hotels,* tip the porter and chambermaid between IS3–4, depending on service rendered; 10% on room service. Other personnel can be tipped if they perform special services—doormen, etc., IS3–5.

Taxi drivers and *ushers* in theaters and motion-picture houses are not tipped. *Hairdressers* and *barbers* expect a 10% tip. *Porters* at Haifa port and David Ben-Gurion Airport receive a salary, but it is customary to pay IS5 minimum per luggage cart. At *churches* and *tourist sites* where no admission charge is paid, pay the attendant between IS3–10.

 WHEN TO GO. Though the Bible declares: "To everything there is a season, and a time for every purpose under the heaven," in the Land of the Bible tourism is a year-round thing, encompassing every season. Most folk visit Israel for fun in the sun, or for religious or idealistic purposes, and many combine both reasons and enjoy an "inspiring" Mediterranean vacation. The greatest masses of tourists hit Israel between April and mid-October, and during special religious seasons, so these peak times are more expensive in travel fares and hotel rates. To avoid the extra tariffs, and the jostling crowds of non-natives, plan for a trip between October and April—but bypass the winter religious holidays.

If the weather is a determining factor for your trip, you can pick almost any time of the year, for the Holy Land is blessed with a temperate clime that's often compared to the French and Italian Rivieras, and Florida or southern California in the USA. Generally, there are sun-drenched summers and mild, balmy winters; however, the weather also offers sharp contrasts that depend as much, and sometimes more, on the geography as on the season. While some tourists ski the snow-crested peaks of Mount Hermon, others scuba dive throuth clear Red Sea Gulf waters to stare at marine life in almost-unbelievable varieties of kind and color. During the same winter season, folk can be sitting (unsinkable) on the waters of the Dead Sea while—45 minutes away—Jerusalemites are shivering in a chill wind.

For a touch of the "exotic," there's a scorching, dry desert wind called the *hamseen* that blows in from the east in the spring and end of summer. Its name means "fifty" in Arabic, and some Arabs say it blows 50 days a year in parts of the Arabian lands. In Israel, thank goodness, the hamseen comes and goes and lasts about 2–3 days at a time.

Geographically, Israel links Asia and Africa, but naturalist/purists add Europe and claim three continents meet, with four climate zones: Mediterranean (warm, humid and semi-humid), Irano-Turanian Steppe and Arabo-Saharan Desert (semi-arid, arid and extremely arid), plus small tropical oases scattered here and there. As the land is primarily desert and wilderness, most of the weather combines warm to hot days with cool nights. The coastal plain and northern regions have much of the "typical" Mediterranean weather; winter's mild along the plain, with occasional blusterings predominantly along the shore, but there's snow sometimes in the mountains between November and March.

There *is* a rainy season. In the Red Sea Gulf port of Eilat, and in the Negev's Beersheba, this season respectively averages from 10 to 37 days annually, and produces average yearly totals of one to eight inches rainfall. But that's down south. Usually, it rains hardest in the Upper Galilee region and along the Mediterranean Coast, with some places getting as much as 30–40 inches average annual downpour during some 65 days a year. Yet, between April and October, the rain is rare anywhere in the country.

After a fleeting interlude of springtime that's spectacular for its riots of wild flowers, the summer countryside takes on a pervasive earthy coloration, punctuated by green fields and airy forests. During the long stretch of summer, the heat can be sweltering and the mercury can climb over 104°F in some places, but even then, the coast gets fresh sea breezes and the hill country nights are clear and cool. Even the hottest months have been called "entirely bearable" along the Mediterranean coastal and mountain regions, and it's worth noting that most of Israel's deep-South towns make air-conditioning a "must" for tourist facilities, as well as most homes and buildings. In key spots, temperature ranges (in °F) are as follows:

	January	July
Jerusalem	45–60	67–83
Tel Aviv	48–66	72–88
Haifa	50–63	72–83
Tiberias (Sea of Galilee)	54–70	78–98
Eilat	52–72	84–104

 KEEPING THE CALENDAR STRAIGHT. If you plan your Israel trip to coincide with a certain festival or holiday, do give some very special pre-traveling attention to the calendar . . . er, calendars! Calendar dates in Israel can get slightly out of kilter unless you keep reminding yourself that at least two systems, the Gregorian and the Hebrew, are in daily use, plus the Moslem and the Julian. Newspapers, for example, always show two dates, one of which, the Gregorian, you'll recognize. The other date belongs to the Hebrew calendar, based on the Israelite era. The latter is reckoned from the arbitrarily (and mythically) assigned date of the creation of the universe, generally accepted as 3760 B.C.

SPECIAL EVENTS. Now that you know about the Jewish calendar, it's time to learn something about the great religious festivals that punctuate it, without of course overlooking all the Christian and Moslem observances.

Note: The Ministry of Industry, Trade and Tourism has full lists of all holidays, festivals and such, and all holy sites as well—yours for the asking, but too long to print in detail here. However, here is a general list.

On **January** 1 (Tebet): New Year's Day services in Catholic and Protestant churches, followed by Epiphany on January 6 (Twelfth Night), celebrated in the Catholic church only. Second Sunday after Epiphany, Franciscan pilgrimage from Nazareth to Cana. On the 7th and 8th, Christmas for the Christians of the Eastern Churches, and on January 14, their New Year.

The Armenian Christmas and the Eastern Christian Epiphany fall in January-**February.** A delightful custom is *Tu B'Shevat,* the New Year of the Trees, or Jewish Arbor Day, occurring in the last half of Shevat (around late January). On this occasion, school-children plant thousands of saplings on the hillsides and the ceremonies are accompanied by singing and dancing.

Tel Hai Day falls at the end of Adar (beginning of **March**) and commemorates the *kibbutz* that was defended against Arab attack in 1920 by Joseph Trumpeldor and his comrades at the cost of their lives. On this day, young people from all over Israel make a pilgrimage to Tel Hai in tribute to these pioneer heroes. The *Feast of Purim* in Feb. or March commemorates Esther's rescuing of the Babylonian Jews from the danger with which Haman threatened them. The Book of Esther is read in the synagogues, costumed merrymakers dance in the streets, and the high point of the day is the festive Purim meal.

The time-honored custom of *Mishloah Manot,* the exchange of gifts between neighbors and friends, is ever popular, and hotel guests are not overlooked at this time. On March 25, there is a pontifical mass in the Church of the Annunciation in Nazareth. The Moslem festival of *Id-el-Adha* usually falls in March.

Good Friday and Easter are celebrated in all the Christian churches. Around the same time, the Jewish Passover is also celebrated, commemorating the Exodus of the Jews from Egypt. Services begin with the *First Seder Evening,* during which the story of events of the Exodus is narrated. Ceremonies are held in all the main hotels and in the *kibbutzim.* Although this is primarily an occasion for family gatherings, the Israeli Government Tourist Office can sometimes arrange for visitors to attend services in a *kibbutz.* The next day is the first day of Passover *(Pesach).* Passover is celebrated with only one seder evening in Israel. Only Jews *visiting* Israel need keep a second seder there. For visitors, there are services in the principal hotels.

Kibbutz Ein Gev holds its traditional Music Festival during **April.** At the end of Nisan religious services are held in the synagogues in memory of the victims of Nazism *(Yom Hashoa).* April is also the month for the *Flower Show* at Gan Ha'em on Mt. Carmel, Haifa.

A week after Yom Hashoa there is a memorial day for the soldiers who fell in the battle for Israel's independence. The next day is *Independence Day,* and dancing Israelis fill the streets till late at night. Reserve hotel accommodations far in advance for this.

Israel's labor movement celebrates May Day, **May** 1. About this time comes the Festival of *Nebi Shu'eib,* the picturesque 3-day *Festival of the Druse,* held at the Horns of Hittin, near Lake Tiberias (Sea of Galilee). This celebration commemorates the Biblical character Jethro, father-in-law of Moses and the holy man of the Druse. Also in Iyar, about the beginning of May, the *Lag Ba'omer,* a traditional pilgrimage to the tomb of Rabbi Shimon Bar Yochai, generally considered to be the author of a celebrated mystic work, the *Zohar.* Thousands of people flock to his tomb on Mount Meron, near Safad, and dance around a gigantic bonfire. In the month of Sivan **(May-June)** there is the

Shavuot, or the Feast of Weeks (Jewish Pentecost), commemorating the handing down of the Ten Commandments to Moses. The celebration has an agricultural significance going back to Biblical times, when tillers of the soil brought their first fruits to the Temple in Jerusalem. It is marked by singing, dancing, and theater performances in farm settlements and in the schools. Around the same time of year there is the Christian Pentecost (Whitsuntide), celebrated in the Western and Eastern churches.

On June 24, at Ein Kerem, the birthplace of John the Baptist, the church of St. John of the Mount holds special services. The 20th day of Tamuz is the anniversary of the death of Theodor Herzl, the founder of Zionism.

The second half of **July** is marked by a festival in honor of the Prophet Elijah at Mt. Carmel (Haifa), and there is a Catholic procession to the statue of Our Lady of Carmel. July and **August** (the month of Av) bring the great annual music and drama festival, the *Israel Festival,* featuring world-famous orchestras and soloists. Concerts are held in Jerusalem, Caesarea, Tel Aviv, and Haifa, among other places. The ninth day of Av commemorates the destruction of the First Temple (587 B.C.) and of the Second Temple (A.D. 70); this is called *Tish'a Be'av,* a fast day. In August, a pilgrimage takes place to King David's tomb on Mt. Zion in Jerusalem. Also in August, every three years, there is the *Zimria,* the international choral festival. On August 6, for the Festival of the Transfiguration, there is a pontifical mass in the Franciscan Church on Mt. Tabor. August 15 is the Feast of the Assumption, with a pontifical mass in the Church of the Dormition on Mt. Zion.

In **September-October** the 1st and 2nd days of Tishri are the Hebrew New Year, or *Rosh Hashanah,* followed on the tenth day of the same month by the most solemn of all the Jewish religious festivals, *Yom Kippur,* the Day of Atonement, observed with fasting and prayer. *Succot,* or Feast of the Tabernacles, begins a few days later and lasts for one week. This is a harvest festival as well as a religious anniversary recalling the temporary homes of the Children of Israel during their wanderings in the wilderness. On this occasion each family builds a booth-like structure covered with greenery and decorated with flowers, fruits, and bright illustrations, where they gather and enjoy their meals. Succot is a good time to be at a kibbutz guest house, since the settlements give this agricultural holiday special attention. The day following the end of the Succot is the *Simhat Torah,* or the Rejoicing of the Law. On this day the reading of the Pentateuch (Torah) is completed in the synagogues and immediately begun anew. Worshipers sing and dance in the streets while holding aloft the Scrolls of the Law. At the same time of the year there is an informal sports event called the Three-Day March, which is a pilgrimage to Jerusalem. The marchers camp and picnic along the way. Individuals or groups interested in participating can get information about it from their local Israeli Tourist Office. Many visitors of all ages and nationalities have taken part in past years, averaging 15,000 marchers each year.

In **October-November** (Heshvan), the Kinneret Festival takes place at Ein Gev on the shores of Lake Tiberias. In **November-December** (Kislev), there is a commemoration of the victories of Judas Maccabaeus over Antiochus Epiphanes, who had tried to convert the Jews by force to paganism (in the 2nd century B.C.), and of the rededication of the Temple that followed. This is *Chanukah,* the Feast of Light, which lasts eight days; lights are kindled on the eight-branched candelabrum beginning on the evening of the first day with one light and adding a new light on each successive evening. *Id-el-Fitr,* the three-day Moslem festival which marks the end of the month-long fast of Ramadan, usually falls in November.

On December 8 the Festival of the Immaculate Conception is held, with religious services in the Church of the Dormition on Mt. Zion. On Christmas Eve and Christmas Day there are services in the Catholic and Protestant churches, and notably a midnight mass on December 24 at Nazareth and Bethlehem.

 HOW TO GO. Free travel folders and detailed information can be obtained from Israel Government Tourist Offices (IGTO), as under:

USA. 352 Fifth Avenue, New York, NY 10001. (212) 560-0650.

5 South Wabash Ave., Chicago, Ill. 60603, (312) 782-4306.

6380 Wilshire Bd., Suite 1700, Los Angeles, Calif. 90048, (213) 658-7462.

795 Peachtree St., Atlanta, Georgia. 30308, (404) 873-1470.

Canada. 102 Bloor St. West, Toronto, Ontario M5S IM8, (416) 964-3784.

Great Britain. 59 St. James's St., London SWIA ILL, (01) 493-2431.

In Israel. *Acre,* Khan-el-Umdan, Old City; *Arad, Magen* David Bldg.; *Ashkelon,* Commercial Center, Afridar; *Beersheba,* Beit Tnaut Hamoshavim; *Bethlehem,* Manger Sq.; *Eilat,* New Commercial Center; *Haifa (Town),* 18 Herzl St.; *(Port),* Shed No. 12; *Jerusalem (West),* 24 King George St.; *(East)* Jaffa Gate; *David Ben-Gurion Airport,* Terminal Bldg.; *Nahariya,* Egged Bus Stn., Sderot Ga'Aton; *Natanya,* Kikar Ha'atzmaut; *Nazareth,* Cassanova St.; *Safad,* Municipality Bldg.; *Tel Aviv,* 7 Mendele St.; *Tiberias,* 8 Alhadess St.; *Ramallah,* Al Muqhta, Al Muqhtaribin Square.

TRAVEL AGENTS. The more you investigate the choices available for traveling to Israel, the more you may be amazed at their number and variety. Then you'll find that one of your first decisions will be whether to plan everything by yourself, or get a little help from your friendly travel agent. Even the most experienced traveler can profit by using the services of a travel agent, whose specialized work is not, after all, expensive. The services he renders you, such as reserving plane tickets, hiring and booking hotel rooms, etc. will be repaid him in the form of commissions. Agents are entitled to mark-ups, if they plan your whole trip for you.

Among the many **American** travel agencies offering tours or individual ticketing to Israel, the following are prominent.

American Express, American Express Plaza, New York 10004.

American Travel Abroad Inc., 250 W. 57th St., New York 10019.

Arkia Israel Airlines, 575 Lexington Ave., New York 10022.

Catholic Travel Center, 761 South Atlantic Blvd., Los Angeles, Calif. 90022.

Command Travel, 6 East 45 St., New York, NY 10017.

Eastours Scholastic Journeys (senior citizen and student tours), 1140 Ave. of the Americas, New York 10036.

El Al Israel Airlines, 850 Third Ave., New York, NY 10022; offices also in Atlanta, Baltimore, Boston, Chicago, Cleveland, Detroit, Houston, Los Angeles, Miami Beach, Philadelphia, San Francisco, St. Louis and Washington, DC, USA, and in Montreal and Toronto, Canada.

Foreign Tours, 1140 Ave. of the Americas, New York 10036.

Kwik Travel Services, 2726 W. Peterson, Chicago, Ill. 60659.

Maupintour, 900 Massachusetts St., Lawrence, Kansas 66044.

Nili Tours Inc., 18 E. 48th St., New York 10017.

Sharon Travel Associates, 18 E. 48th St., New York 10017.

Unitours/Club Universe, 8 S. Michigan Ave., Chicago, Ill. 60603.

Wilcox World Tours, 214 NW Bank Bldg., Asheville, N.C. 28801.

There are many **British** travel agents who operate tours to Israel. Here is a small selection:

Club Méditerranée, 62 South Molton St., London W1.

Pennworld Ltd., 10 Broad St., Hereford HR4 9AG.

Serenissima, 2 Lower Sloane St., London SW1W 8BJ.

Slade Travel, Slade House, 397 Hendon Way, London NW4 3LE.

Sundowners Ltd., 8 Hogarth Place, London SW5 0QT.

Sunquest Holidays Ltd., 43–44 New Bond St., London W1Y 9HB.

Thomson's Holidays, Greater London House, Hampstead Rd., London NW1 78D.

PILGRIMAGES. A pilgrimage to the Holy Land is no more the long, exhausting, and peril-fraught adventure that it once was. Instead, nowadays it's a deeply moving experience, a fascinating journey, one that's relatively easy and not so expensive. However, without losing sight of its purpose, you can also make your visit to the Holy Shrines an occasion for rest and relaxation. Persons who travel alone or who are left to their own devices run the risk of overlooking many interesting things that they have no way of knowing about unless they are advised by competent guides. Even if the rugged individualist may not be attracted, organized group tours still offer certain undeniable advantages, including the bringing together of people with similar tastes and backgrounds, the providing of lectures and material on specific sites visited, participation in liturgy and in Biblical evocations at the places touching on Jesus' life, etc. However, you can ask IGTO for a list of all churches and Holy Places of all denominations, with services scheduled, plus a list of holidays, and use this on your own, or as an "extra" on a guided tour. Christian research libraries may be visited, too.

The Israel Tourism Administration has an official *Pilgrimage Committee,* (IPC), with Mrs. Haya Fischer as director. Aside from tours and fellowship sessions, IPC offers receptions, lecture/film series, open forums, special awards and medals, etc. All pilgrims can receive a beautiful Pilgrimage Certificate. Arrangements can be made for Jordan River baptism too. Write IPC, Jerusalem, POB 1018, or ask at any IGTO.

Staying in a Christian Hospice can be a special and rewarding adventure for the pilgrim, and the charges are minimal. (See page 27.)

Among Holy Land tours promoted by airlines are those packaged by American operators *Atlas International Tours,* 2 W. 45th St., New York 10036, *Eastours Inc.,* 1140 Ave. of the Americas, New York 10036, *Tower Travel Corp.,* 380 Madison Ave., New York 10017 and *Sharon* (see above). *The Catholic Travel Office*—1019 19th St., Washington, D.C. 20036—also operates pilgrimage programs to Israel.

Eastours Inc. (see above), run special 10- to 14-day *bar mitzvah* tours which include a visit to an Israeli family with a son of bar mitzvah age, the ceremony, guided visits, etc.

In Great Britain, the following agents arrange pilgrimages: *Orientours,* Kent House, 87 Regent St., W1, *Peltours,* 156 Oxford St., W1, *W. F. & R. K. Swan Ltd.,* 237 Tottenham Ct. Rd., W1, and *Bales Tours Ltd.,* 16 Coventry St., W1, all in London.

Religious organizations which arrange tours (or their agents) include *Spes,* 31 Great Smith St. SW1, *Inter-Church Travel Ltd.,* 125 Pall Mall, SW1, both in London, and *Pilgrimair,* 22 Norman St., St. Leonards-on-Sea, Sussex. Tours are about 15 days' duration and include travel by air, full board accommodation in good hotels, excursions and guides.

STUDENTS. *Israel's Student Tourist Association* (ISSTA) has a very active no-age-limit program for visiting students and young people, students seeking travel advice and for holders of the International Student Card, available for $2 in the USA from CIEE, 205 East 42 St., New York, NY 10017; in the United Kingdom, from the Travel Department, National Union of Students Travel Service, Compass House, Lypiall Rd., Cheltenham and from AAS, 139 Kensington High St., London W8; in Canada from AOSC, 44 St. George St., Toronto, Ont., or TOURBEC, 112 Ouest, Rue St. Paul, Suite 500, Montreal, Quebec. (All members of International Student Travel Conference (ISTC)). With current, dated, signed, full-time student ID (no plastic cards) you can get ISC at any ISSTA office. Some of the discounts include free or greatly reduced admission at museums. There are also discounts on some public transport and at many hotels, restaurants, tours, nightclubs etc. The *Federation of International Youth Travel Organizations* (FIYTO) offers concessions to holders of the YIEE *(Youth International Educational Exchange)* Card. This is recognized in Israel; details from ISSTA or IGTO.

Hotel rooms can be booked through ISSTA in central Tel Aviv and Jerusalem at special low rates that include breakfast. Best to book in advance by mail.

Through ISSTA you can also buy tickets for unlimited travel around Israel (except Sinai); 2 weeks for $40; 3 weeks for $50; 4 weeks for $60. It's also a good idea to ask about ISIS international student travel insurance.

ISSTA offers students a variety of low-cost package tours around the country. For example, a 9-day tour covering all areas costs $299 (1980 prices). A 5-day Sinai Safari is $208; leaving from Jerusalem, the tour goes to the Negev, Eilat, Bedouin settlements in Sinai and also crosses over to Santa Katarina in Egypt. The cost includes meals, sleeping bag, mask and snorkle and guide. Each year ISSTA offers a new variety of tours within Israel and overseas. Their current booklet (apply at any ISSTA office upon arrival) has the details. For those who want to work on a kibbutz, ISSTA organizes something called the International Student Work Camp. There's also a Student Archeological Dig, as well as special ISSTA camping programs.

Another ISSTA feature is the student flights, on a charter basis, from Europe and the USA. Savings of 50% are available on flights from every major European city for Israel. If you are planning to visit Europe before Israel and would like to know the student charter flight-schedule, write for a book called *Traveling Student* (in USA) or *Student Traveler* (in UK), at addresses above. All flights are via established European charter airlines, usually on Caravelles or Comet 4B's. There are Student Travel Services in the major European cities.

ISSTA Offices in Haifa, Beit Hakranon, Herzl St. 16/20, Room 245; in Jerusalem, 5 Eliashar St. (02) 231418; in Tel Aviv (Head Office), 109 Ben Yehuda St. (03) 247164. Students can receive mail at all three. All letters should be addressed to ISSTA Poste Restante.

Americans can go to high school in Israel for one or several years, full-time, with full US accreditation. Apply *World Zionist Organisation,* Dept. of Education and Culture, 515 Park Ave., NY, NY 10022.

Hai-Fun—a new, unique program, co-sponsored by Technion Student Association and Haifa Tourism Development Association, invites foreign students to a fun stay on Mt. Carmel Technion Campus. Mix with students here, Q-A sessions (politics, etc.), sports, tours, dances, lots of cultural-social activities. Details from Students House, Technion City, Haifa. A similar program is operated by Miki Schlosser; details from POB 33594, Haifa.

 TRAVEL DOCUMENTS. To enter Israel, you must be able to show a valid passport issued by the duly appointed authority in your country. Most Arab lands will not allow visitors to enter their countries directly from Israel (Egypt and Jordan are exceptions). And some Arab lands can make difficulties if you have an Israeli visa in your passport. For this reason, the Israeli Government will, on request, give you a separate visa card. This can be carried in your passport while in Israel and discarded when you leave. If you wish, however, you may find it convenient to visit Israel only after visiting any Arab countries on your itinerary.

The British "Visitor's Passport" is *not* valid for Israel: the conventional 10-year type is essential. Citizens of the United Kingdom do not require visas.

Citizens of the United States and Canada receive Entrance Visas free of charge at the port of entry. These are valid for 3 months from their issuing date, and usually can be renewed for additional three-month periods without much difficulty after 3 months of consecutive residence in Israel. Renewals are obtainable at any of the 17 district offices of the Ministry of the Interior.

Addresses in the three main cities are as follows:

Jerusalem: Generali Blvd., 1 Rehov Shlomzion Hamalka.

Tel Aviv: Shalom Tower, 9 Ahad Ha'am St.

Haifa: Government Bldg., (opposite Town Hall).

Health Certificates. An international certificate of vaccination against smallpox is required except by tourists who have been resident more than 14 days in Europe, the US or Canada immediately prior to arrival in Israel—provided those places are free from smallpox.

Pets. If you plan to bring your dog or some other pet into Israel, don't forget that all-important veterinary certificate, and have your dog vaccinated against rabies (this should be stated on the certificate).

Note: Pets from European or North American countries can enter Israel without wait; animals from Africa and Asia will be quarantined.

 MEDICAL SERVICES. No one plans to get sick or have an accident when vacationing, but everyone knows it can happen, and so it's a good idea to know something about what you'll do if anything happens to you in a foreign land. In Israel, you're in luck, for the country has an overwhelming number of fine medical doctors, clinics and hospitals that offer excellent medical services on an internationally-high standard.

Tourists may go to all emergency wards and all first-aid centers, and local folk are especially good about helping you get to the nearest one—either taxi drivers or regular motorists, and bus drivers have even been known to abandon fixed routes and wheel their vehicles to a clinic to deliver a patient. All areas have centers marked by the red star of David on a white field, symbol of *Magen David Adom*, equivalent to Red Cross. For **emergency medical service,** telephone 101 (very efficient). **Emergency dental treatment** is available at the Tel Aviv branch of the *Israel Dental Association's First Aid Clinic,* 49 Rehov Bar Kokhba, Tel Aviv (03) 284649.

Since Israel manufactures many drugs and medicines, you can choose from these or from foreign imports at pharmacies throughout the country. Even nights, holiday periods and Sabbath hours, when all else closes, at least one emergency duty pharmacy is open in every town and city, and it's listed in the English-language newspaper, *The Jerusalem Post.*

There also are many private doctors, as well as dentists, and their office visit fees range from IS 50–60 up. If you prefer, call your local embassy or consulate for recommended names. (Note: many visit Israel especially for cosmetic surgery.)

Wheel chairs may be rented by tourists, with 1–2 days' notice, from Alyn Orthopaedic Hospital for Crippled Children, Rehov Shmayahu Levin, Kiryat

Yovel, Jerusalem (deposit IS450; pay $5 per day), telephone 02-412251, or contact Mifalai Arye, New Industrial Center, 76 Rehov Shesh, Tel Aviv (deposit IS500, pay minimum IS45 monthly fee), telephone 03-33050.

Ambulances display the emblem of the *Magen David Adom,* the red star of David on a white field.

Aside from this, you may well want to investigate these services:

International Association for Medical Assistance to Travellers (IAMAT) offers you a list of approved English-speaking doctors who have had postgraduate training in the US, Canada or Gt. Britain. Membership is free: the scheme is worldwide. An office call costs $15, a hotel call is $20, a holiday or weekend call is $25. For information, apply in the US to Suite 5620, 350 Fifth Ave., New York 1001; in Canada, 1268 St. Clair Ave. W., Toronto. A similar service is provided by *Intermedic,* 777 Third Avenue, New York, NY 10017. There is an initial membership charge of $6 per person, or $10 per family, and the subsequent fee schedule is about twice that of IAMAT's.

Europ Assistance Ltd. provides its members with unlimited help. There are two plans: one for travelers using tours or making their own trip arrangements, the second for motorists taking their cars abroad. Multi-lingual personnel staff a 24-hour, seven-days-a-week telephone service which brings the aid of a network of medical and other advisors to assist in any emergency. Special medical insurance is part of the plan. Basic price: £3.00 per person. Write to Europ Assistance Ltd., 252 High St., Croydon CRO INF; for details phone 01-680 1234. **Note:** this service is only available to British citizens and, in Israel, is limited to non-motorists.

 WHAT TO TAKE. Casual is the key word for proper attire in Israel. Summer calls for slacks with open-neck, tie-less shirts for men, and breezy resort styles for women. All kinds of jeans are popular and fashionable for males, females, all ages and all year, and usually are great for touring. Safari suits, casual suits, pant-suits and the like are recommended, and most tourists want something dressy for nights at clubs, discos or concert halls.

Both men and women wear open sandals and shorts (usually short-shorts) around town and touring; the kaftan and other long robes are at home in Israel; bikinis are preferred swimming outfits, though all types of beachwear are seen.

Israel's immigration from more than 70 lands, plus constant tourism means almost every kind of national style can be seen on the streets, plus designer clothes and fashion fads, so visitors can rely on individual style preference and feel at ease always. Note: some exclusive eateries have jacket/tie dress codes.

Summer travelers will be significantly more comfortable in 100% cotton, despite the fact that the miracle blends are more convenient, and this is especially true for any close-fitting garments under or outer. Men's drip-dry shirts are fine, but as a rule, all fabric selections should "breathe" in this climate. For summer mornings and evenings, bring a jacket, shawl or sweater, as it's chilly in many areas.

Winter tourists will want a raincoat (for rain or chill) and men will find most local businessmen don neckties with suits or jackets for this season. Leather and suede are popular winter fabrics, though often only as jackets, and some people enjoy wearing furs. Wool suits and sweaters are good winter choices, and boots are popular for all ages.

All tourists should bring comfortable shoes, since touring translates into a lot of walking. It's best to bring two pair and alternate daily, to save foot soreness.

All tourists—especially summertime travelers—should bring gear to protect them from Israel's strong sun: hats, sunglasses, at least one longsleeved shirt. (All these are available in Israel, plus lotions, etc.) Women will likely want scarves to protect hair from fairly constant breezes.

Note: For visits to holy shrines, monasteries, churches and synagogues, special dress is required. Men should pocket a skullcap for synagogues, or knot a handkerchief at all corners and use this instead. Women often will need to cover their heads, shoulders, arms and legs (no shorts allowed, but slacks are OK).

Soap is supplied in better hotels, but often missing elsewhere, so bring along several small bars, or a soap case for purse or bag. Foreign cosmetics, toiletries and such are available, but at super prices that include heavy import taxes; same goes for foreign alcohol, tobacco, etc. Camera buffs should check *Photography* and *Customs* in this chapter, then stock up on film. People who want to take gifts to Israelis should also check *Customs*.

LEARN HEBREW. Before your trip, try the one-day language course at the New School, 66 West 12th St., New York 10011, where they claim to teach you sufficient Hebrew for typical travel situations. Held on a Friday, the cost is $50 and the course is offered several times yearly.

Or, if you would rather learn Hebrew *in* Israel, ask the *World Zionist Organization,* Department of Education and Culture, 515 Park Ave., New York 10022, for details of their intensive 8-week summer course. Or write Ulpan Akiva, Nethanya, Israel. Another idea is to write the Ministry of Tourism or your nearest IGTO, requesting the amusing booklet, *Hebrew With A Smile.*

 WHAT TO DO. Various travel agencies in Israel offer half-day or longer tours, all conducted by expert official guides. Assorted itineraries have been set up by the *Travel Agents' Associations* in conjunction with the Israel Government Tourism Administration. Though some of the larger tours can be started in a number of the larger cities, the majority start only in Tel Aviv, Jerusalem, Haifa or Eilat. For names of leading tour operators, check through the next few pages, particularly under *Special Interest Holidays.*

Weekly/monthly tours. Minimally priced or free, these are sponsored by the Ministry, municipalities or organizations, and IGTA can supply precise days, hours, starting points and such, for you to tour: Bar Ilan University, Druse Villages, En Hod Artists' Village, City of Jerusalem, Givat Ram University Campus, Hadassah Medical Center and Chagall Windows, Knesset (Israel's parliament), American Mizrachi Women's Institutions, Mount Scopus University Campus, ORA Organization-Handweaving For Blind, ORT Institutions (rehabilitation and special education), Pioneer Women/Moetzet Hapoalot Institutions (work with women and children), Sharre Zedek Hospital and New Medical Center underway, Technician Campus, Weizmann Institute of Science, WIZO Institutions, Yad Veshem (Martyrs' and Heroes' Memorials), ZOA's Agricultural and American High School, Tel Aviv University, and Yeshiva High School, Bnei Akiva.

Sound and Light tours are also regularly scheduled in Yaffa, Jerusalem and Masada. *Walking tours* are popular features in many municipalities, and they usually focus on a particular quarter or religious shrines, synagogues and churches.

Regular Happenings throughout Israel. The actual list is almost endless, but these are particularly pointed out for tourists and IGTA has all details about the following types of events: community singing, chamber music, special exhibitions, play-readings, dinner club (ZOA), modern dance, opera, English theater, children's theater, children's concerts, bridge and duplicate bridge evenings and contests, chess club activities including competitions, international folk dancing evenings, carillon concerts, Russian immigrant concerts and art exhibits, art film club evenings, hikes and hiking events, ethnic music festivals, ethnic traditional festivals (see *Calendar* and *Holidays* this section), symphony concerts, ballet, pantomime, recorded music evenings, French theater, Yiddish theater, philatelic exhibitions, arts and crafts fairs, open house at social clubs, bazaars, book fairs, street art shows, and so forth.

Jews and non-Jews are invited to celebrate the Sabbath with two programs, *Oneg Shabbat* welcomes the Sabbath on Friday evenings, and *Melaveh Malka* ushers out the Sabbath on Saturday evenings. Both usually include a program of songs, a lecture and refreshments, and are scheduled by IGTA.

IGTA branches in Israel can also help you join in the following activities: *Meet the People, Meet Your Professional Counterpart,* and *Meet the Artist.* If you're interested, you can be invited to the home, office or studio of English-speaking Israelis with backgrounds similar to your own.

Folklore Evenings. No visit to Israel is complete without at least one evening of folk dancing and singing. You will become acquainted with the time-honoured, picturesque customs and costumes of communities from all parts of the world, notably with those of the Middle East, and you will be introduced to the spirit of contemporary Israel as expressed in its singing and dancing. Some of the *kibbutzim* have their own folk-groups. Similar performances are to be seen in all areas and cities, practically the year round. For exact dates and places ask at any IGTA office.

Tree planting. By planting a tree in Israel you can help to embellish the countryside and enrich the land. In so doing, you perform an act recommended in that Book of Books, the Bible. Contact the *Jewish National Fund,* 41 Shapiro St., Tel Aviv, (03-287111). Go on a free "Planters' Tour" or mail $7 and they plant it, but you still get a certificate and emblem.

SPECIAL INTEREST VACATIONS. There are many opportunities for tourists of all ages to plan for a holiday in Israel and indulge their hobbies at the same time. In fact, a family can make a "separate/together" trip, with members of the family spending part of their time doing their own thing. Here are a few of the many possibilities:

Summer Camps for Ages 5–18. Throughout the land, summer camps cater to youth in different age groups, and offer a great variety of programs designed to mix young people from Israel and abroad. Though foreign campers seldom speak Hebrew, they find few problems communicating by song, dance and other camp activities, and many Israeli youngsters speak at least smatterings of other languages—English being most frequent. Quite often, friendships made in these camps are kept up through correspondence, and it becomes an enriching experience far beyond the summer days.

One of the best-known is *Garin's Summer Camp,* located near Natanya in Moshav Udim, overlooking the Sharon Plain and close to the Mediterranean. Here, children 6–14 are accepted and placed in groups of 10–15 for supervised activities, including crafts, riding, sports and scouting. Special tours of Israel are arranged for groups of foreign kids, helping them acquire a first-hand insight into its history. Directors Manya and Michael Garin have operated the camp for nearly twenty years. Details are available from the camp office (6 Rachel St., Tel Aviv, Israel) or from any IGTO abroad.

Other recommended camps include: *Camp Shomrom,* Meir Shfeyal Youth Village (near Netanya) or 31 Brandeis St., Tel Aviv; season runs from July 1 to Aug. 1 and they accept kids from 10 to 17; there are Hebrew classes, arts, crafts, trips, sports and it costs about $1,200 for the entire season. *Camp Eretz,* Kfar Mordechai, near Gedera; season runs from July 6 to Aug. 15 and they accept kids from 8 to 14; there are all the above activities and the cost comes to about $20 per day. *YMCA,* King David St., Jerusalem; this is a day camp; the season runs from July 1 to Aug. 29 and they accept kids from 6 to 12; here too there are Hebrew classes and all sorts of other activities; the cost is $50 for a 2-week session.

Young People's Bar Mitzvah & Bat Mitzvah Ceremonies. The IGTA Youth and Student Department helps make all necessary arrangements for boys and girls to experience these Jewish religious coming-of-age ceremonies in Israel. The traditional favorite site is the Western Wall (last remnant of the Second Temple and Judaism's most sacred site). After the ceremony, the Ministry presents the boy with a prayer shawl, the girl with a set of Sabbath candle holders, and both with special certificates.

The ceremony now also takes place at Masada, scene of one of the most important episodes in Jewish history. Here, arrangements are made by various religious organizations (IGTA will help make contacts), and the service is held in the ancient synagogue of Masada, excavated together with other parts of the former fortress, several years ago. Applications must be made well in advance for either location.

Also, *Shromrom Camp* has a Bar Mitzvah program for boys aged 12–14, featuring ceremonies at the Wall.

Congresses or Conventions. You might find your peers or professional counterparts are meeting or holding seminars while you're in Israel. Or perhaps a gourmet group is presenting symposiums, and you'd like to go. To find out, check with the Conventions Division, Ministry of Industry, Trade and Tourism, 24 King George Street, Jerusalem (telephone 02-237311), or with your nearest IGTO overseas. A periodic publication lists all. You might even make your holiday a business trip.

Archeological digs. If you're 18–35 and interested in doing a bit of digging at any of the ten ancient sites throughout the country, write the Youth and Student Division, Ministry of Tourism, PO Box 1018, Jerusalem. All the digs are for a minimum of two weeks and you'll have to shovel, haul, clean, attend lectures, and perhaps at the end of it receive an academic credit. **Note:** the prefix *tel* on a town or area name indicates an archeological mound.

Underwater Adventures. Many people visit Israel strictly for the underwater delights along the Mediterranean and in the Red Sea Gulf, where fantastic marine life is found. Tours and Safari programs are planned for these diving buffs, and special details are yours by writing firms listed under "Underwater Sport," or through travel agents. Note: *The Red Sea Diver's Guide* is a book that lets you plan your own underwater tour; available at shops in Israel or direct from the publisher ($13): Red Sea Divers Ltd., 32 Ben Yehuda St., Tel Aviv. The book features diving site details and maps, underwater photos, index of fish and invertebrates, etc.

University Studies. For internationally accepted academic credit, or for personal enjoyment, many tourists combine Holy Land trips with courses or seminar studies at Israel's universities, special colleges and learning institutions. Subject matter is highly varied, as are course lengths and fees, so inquire at IGTO or write directly to Israel's Ministry of Education & Culture, Jerusalem.

Experience Kibbutz/Moshav Life. There're two programs that allow you to live a while on a kibbutz with other visitors who are curious about experiencing kibbutz life firsthand. The Volunteer program, for men and women between 18 and 35, has a one-month minimum duration, and participants do agricultural, industrial and other types of work in return for room, board, linens, work clothes, insurance and so forth. There's also a several-month program that divides participants' days between work hours and classes for studying Hebrew. Information about both programs can be obtained from IGTO abroad or from the Youth and Student Division, PO Box 1018, Jerusalem.

The Moshav Experience is a new group tour from Shomrom Tours, 62 Ben Yehuda St., Tel Aviv. For ages 18 to 35, it offers programs that combine tours around Israel with 18 to 22 days living and working on a moshav. In 1980, the price was from $119 to $220.

Hot Springs and Spas. The Tiberias Hot Springs, on the shores of Lake Tiberias, have been known for their therapeutic properties since biblical times. Modern bath and treatment facilities, plus medical clinics, draw international crowds either to relax or get relief from rheumatic, skin and female ailments (see

Galilee chapter). En Nun Springs, with mineral drinking waters, amid the ruins of ancient Migdal, 4 miles north of Tiberias, and El Hamma (Hammat Gadar) thermo-mineral springs 12 miles southeast of Tiberias, have similar programs. At the Dead Sea are similar baths (see Negev chapter), especially for skin and scalp treatments. With such demands for these places, and others not yet poshly developed, Israel has opened a Health Resorts Authority, 68 Hapalmach, Jerusalem, (02-64251).

Nature Lovers Israel. The Nature Tours Department, Society for the Protection of Nature in Israel (7 Narkiss St., Tel Aviv, tel. (03) 223688), organizes a number of extremely popular tours of varying length that scout out the surprising abundance of wild life in Israel. (There are more than 3,000 different types of plants, 400 different birds and over 100 different species of mammals and reptiles.) The society manages to keep costs down to a minimum and tour fees are very reasonable. The SPB has tour coordinating centers in Jerusalem, Haifa, Beersheba, Upper Nazareth and Eilat and for $10 a year you can become a member and receive their quarterly magazine. Write for details.

National Parks and Sites. These include places like Megiddo (Armageddon), Masada, Qumran, Caesarea, which are run by the National Parks Authority, 3 Rehov Het, Hakirya, P.O.B. 7028, Tel Aviv, (03-252281). Here tourists can buy a 14-day ticket for visits to all sites and parks, for only $4.

Desert Touring. There's nothing quite like the fantastic experience of traveling through the Judean Wilderness, Negev Desert, or Sinai in specially equipped vehicles with "desert rat" guides who know the flora, fauna, historical sites, and local monks and Bedouin! These trips can last one day or one week, and a variety of them are offered by several firms. The two best-established are recommended, and you can write them directly, or book through your travel agent: *Neot Hakikar,* 28 King David St., Jerusalem, (02) 221624, and *Johnny's Desert Tours,* Commercial Center, PO Box 261, Eilat (059) 76777. (Both cover the country.)

How to Reach Israel

FROM NORTH AMERICA

BY AIR. Sixteen scheduled airlines fly regularly to Tel Aviv's busy airport: *Air France, Alitalia, British Airways, El Al, KLM, Olympic, Sabena, Swissair, SAS, TWA, Austrian Airlines, Lufthansa, Cyprus Airways, Turkish Airlines,* and *Tarom.*

Each airline charges the same fares and the only true difference from one carrier to the next (apart from the nationality of the stewardesses) is the system of "direct" and "non-direct" flights between New York and Tel Aviv. A direct flight is when an airline stops en route at London or Rome, for example, discharges and picks up passengers and then continues right on to the destination. Non-direct means landing at a European city, getting off the plane, waiting two or three hours for the connecting flight to Tel Aviv (but see Bonus Stopovers, below), boarding the flight, and worrying whether your baggage made the plane-transfer with you. The best advice is to check with a travel agent and see which airline and flight schedule best fits your needs. El Al is the only international carrier offering non-stop New York-Tel Aviv service.

Fares. The variety and complexity of airline fares today is truly staggering and all air travelers would do well to consider the situation carefully well in advance of their trip.

The two basic fares from New York to Tel Aviv are first class and economy. At press time they cost $3,104 and $1,978 return in high season respectively. Frankly they are expensive and not really justified in terms of better service or conditions. Even if you have paid the full economy fare, you are treated in exactly the same way as somebody traveling on the much less expensive Excursion and APEX fares. And it is no secret, as more and more people take advantage of low-cost fares, that the service provided by the airlines has become sloppy, whatever the glossy advertisements may proclaim to the contrary. Even in first class you are not immune. It is standard airline practice to transfer passengers to the first class cabin if it is not full and is unbalancing the trim of the aircraft. So whilst Excursion and APEX fares have their limitations (you must book a specified number of days in advance and cannot transfer your ticket) the lower price makes them increasingly attractive. At press time, New York-Tel Aviv in high season was $1,321 for Excursion and $1,036 for Apex. Both, of course, are return fares.

Charter flights also venture to Israel, though they were prohibited until recently. Regulations today, however, are much more liberal and services are expanding. Though they are available mainly from Europe, they also originate from the USA. *Nesher Charter Flights* operates two weekly DC 10s between New York and Tel Aviv.

A final word of warning; though it is strongly recommended that all air travelers shop around carefully before their trip, bear in mind that travel agents, for all their expertise, are not in all circumstances the tourist's best friend. Not only can they too be bewildered by the enormous variety of fares, but they receive a commission from airlines for all tickets they sell. The more expensive the ticket, the larger their commission. So it is imperative to compare prices if you want to be sure of getting a good deal.

 BY SEA. There are no regular maritime communications to speak of between North America and Israel. Americans wishing to join a Mediterranean cruise which includes Israel must fly to Europe or sail to a European port. Chandris operates cruises from Venice, which call at Haifa. Address: *Chandris, Inc.,* 666 Fifth Ave., New York 10019. *Epirotiki Lines* also features occasional cruises from Piraeus (Athens) to Haifa. Information is available from them at 608 Fifth Ave., New York 10020. Out of New Orleans, Houston or Galveston, *Lykes Bros. Steamship Co. Inc.* features four sailings a month to Eastern and Western Mediterranean. Haifa is a port of call. For information and rates, contact Lykes Bros. Steamship Co. Inc., Lykes Center, 300 Poydras St., New Orleans, La. 70130. For freighter information, contact *Air and Marine*

Travel Service, 501 Madison Ave., New York, NY 10022; *Pearl's Freighter Tips,* 175 Great Neck Road, Great Neck, NY 11201; *Freighter Travel Club,* Box 12693, Salem, Oregon 97309 or *Traveltips Freighter Travel Association,* 40–21 Bell Blvd., Bayside, NY 11361; or consult *Ford's Freighter Travel Guide,* Box 505, 22030 Ventura Blvd., Woodland Hills, Calif. 91364.

FROM GREAT BRITAIN

BY AIR. There is a daily direct service between London and Tel Aviv operated by *British Airways* and *El Al.* For the most part, travelers from other parts of Britain and Eire have to transfer at London. The standard first class and economy fares on this route are exceptionally high. First class return at presstime was £1,040 and economy £696. Excursion fares at £461 are still high, particularly as the booking restrictions do not make them particularly convenient. The APEX fare (£193 at presstime) certainly represents the best deal available on scheduled flights, though you must book at least three weeks in advance. The very best deals, however, are on charter flights, with prices starting from around £170 return. Check the advertisements in the Sunday papers, the magazine *Time Out* and the *Times, Daily Telegraph* and *Guardian* for details as these vary all the time.

BY SEA. There is no direct sea route from the UK to Haifa, but there are several fly/cruise inclusive trips which include Israel in their itinerary. *Costa Line* have regular weekly summer sailings from Genoa. *Paquet French Cruises* includes Haifa as a port of call on fall cruises out of Toulon, France. Tour operators featuring fly/cruise packages include Exprinter International of New York and Continental Express of Beverley Hills, Calif.

Arriving in Israel

BY AIR. Israel now has two international airports; David-Ben Gurion International Airport near Lod which has been in operation for many years and which still handles the bulk of the traffic entering and leaving the country, and Etzion Airfield, near Eilat.

Arriving Tourists. The first thing to expect is waiting, possibly for quite a time, to clear passport and visa inspections, to gather your luggage, and to find transportation. The clever traveler will wait with as little luggage and paraphernalia as possible, and if he or she is loaded down with many small items, buying one huge tote-bag can make the whole trip much easier. Just be sure it'll fit under your airplane seat.

As soon as you clear the passport check, grab a luggage cart and look for the sign above baggage conveyors that indicates your flight. Instead of merely waiting for bags to be unloaded, you might visit the Information Desk here, and pick up brochures, maps and folders about Israel or from representatives of IGTA and other local services and agencies. You can page or be paged from here, ask about telephones or for any special advice. If you need a doctor or special help, ask. You even can book a place to stay from here (see page 24).

When your baggage arrives, if it seems damaged, file a claim immediately at the office in the same area as luggage pick-up. Otherwise, load it on the cart and head for the Customs—wheeling your own cart.

Within reasonable limits, all personal effects may be brought in duty-free. In fact, often tourists aren't even requested to open their bags for inspection. If you have nothing to declare, you can pass directly through the Customs' *Green Line*.

"Nothing to declare" includes clothes and personal items, a reasonable quantity of camera film, up to ¼ liter of perfume or cologne, 2 liters of wine, 1 liter of other alcoholic beverages (liqueurs, etc.), ½ lb. of tobacco products or 250 cigarettes, 3 kilos of food (1 kilo each, maximum) for personal use. You may also bring in, on a temporary import basis, one still camera, one motion picture camera, binoculars, a typewriter, sporting gear, a transistor or other portable radio. Be sure to go through the *Red Line* and declare any tools or implements of your trade or profession, plants, fresh meat, drugs, fresh fruits or other foods, animals, television sets, any items that might be considered pornographic, and any arms.

Tourists may bring in gifts with a value of up to $75 duty-free. Certain gifts may be brought in without an import license, but may be subject to duty. Be sure to check first with an office of the Israel Government in your country.

Note: All Customs allowances apply only to those over 17 years of age.

If, for some reason or another, you have some waiting time at the terminal before going to your hotel, browse through the shops: newsstand, barber shop, car rental desks, etc. You can find gifts for your friends, relatives or you, and have a coffee or light snack at the refreshment stand. If you're really hungry, there's a restaurant just a flight of stairs away (go outside to find them).

Transportation from Airport. If you have no special transport arranged, you can *rent* a car here, or grab the *El Al* bus that serves every arriving and departing El Al plane, running every half-hour, approximately, and takes passengers to its Tel Aviv bus station ($1 one-way) where you can switch for local buses or taxis. The El Al bus is blue, white and green. Rented cars can be left here on departure. *Egged buses* also ply to and from the airport and Tel Aviv, between 5 A.M. and 10.30 P.M. These buses run every 15–30 minutes, depending on the time of day, for an IS2.80 fare, one-way. Service stops at dusk on Fridays and holiday eves. There's an Egged bus each hour to and from Jerusalem, 7.30 A.M. to 6.30 P.M. for IS9.60 and a 75-minute bus linking the airport and Haifa for IS10.40 from 5.30 A.M. Two daily buses make the round to and from Beersheba, for IS1.20.

Jerusalem Sherut Service (see *Traveling in Israel*) has all-hours airport service, plus door-to-door delivery. Jerusalem service is also provided by *Nesher and Migdal Jerusalem taxi companies,* which meet every plane arriving or leaving the airport, day and night, except on the Sabbath and Yom Kippur.

Taxi fares to and from the airport are controlled by the State Ministry of Transport, and a sign outside the Customs Exit will keep you up-dated on the latest official rates. Do check the sign first, then agree on the fare before entering the taxi. If you agree to pay the driver the required fee, he cannot refuse to carry you or your luggage. When other passengers join at your consent, the overall fare remains the same. Additional bags have a small charge each. The rates when this book went to press can help you estimate your budget, and here are a few samples (all either to, or from, the airport): Ashkelon, IS10.20 (between 5.30 and 21.00; higher rates all other hours); Beersheba IS17; Eilat, IS58; Haifa, IS17.50; Herzliya hotels. IS5; Jerusalem, IS9; Nahariya, IS23; Tel Aviv/Jaffa, IS3.75; Tiberias, IS23.

Staying in Israel

HOTELS. The Ministry of Tourism checks and grades Israel's tourist hotels, granting ranks of 1 to 5 stars. The more stars a hotel rates, the more comfortable, luxurious and varied its facilities. Of course, there are hotels that have *no* rank—because they fail to meet minimum Ministry standards for serving international tourist trade. An independent tourist can cut his costs by finding such hotels, but there's always risk: no towels or soap, less than fresh cleanliness, and perhaps less than "respectable" clientele. For that reason, we list only those establishments sanctioned by the Ministry. Some 1- to 5-star hotels have year-round rates, but most have high and low seasonal prices, with high season running April-October (though this can vary), and encompassing most special religious holiday seasons.

Examples of minimum-maximum rates for *Deluxe* 5-star hotels are $28–78, single, and $22–45 per person in double occupancy rooms. *Comfortable* category 4-star rooms run $19–55 for a single and $13–36 per person for double rooms. For the 3-star hotel, the price range for singles is $12–38, for doubles, per person rates go from $11–28. *Economical* tourists will find the lower-priced 2-star hotels often have private bath, or shower, and w.c. (especially in smaller towns), and even the 1-star hotels frequently are air-conditioned, though their rates are only $7–9 for one, and from $14–16 per person, in a double-occupancy room.

Reservations. It's best to book months in advance for Israel's high season—April-October—and for religious holiday seasons. Book through your travel agent, or write to *KAL Holiday Services Ltd.,* 28 Rehov Gordon, Tel Aviv, 222042, which offers a total vacation service.

Airport Accommodation Service. The Israel Government Tourism Administration Office at the Information Desk at Flight Arrivals (open 24 hours a day) will book you into a hotel. There is a $1 fee plus a $7 deposit per person.

HOLIDAY/RECREATION VILLAGES. These seashore villages—all on the Mediterranean Coast or the
Red Sea Gulf—accommodate both Israelis and foreign
guests, in equal numbers. Housing is usually in small
two-bed cabins and bungalows, though these can be thatched or of wood, bricks,
stone . . . ranging from adequate to enchanting and cooled by sea breezes to
powerful air-conditioners and humidity regulators. The emphasis is always
casual living and sun plus water sports: skin-diving, underwater fishing, sailing
and boating, swimming. Though each village has its own distinctive atmosphere,
most of them are alike in that they're open only between April and October. For
special religious holiday seasons, their rates usually climb a bit.

Club Ashkelon, at Ashkelon Beach on the Mediterranean, and **Red Rock
Hotel Club,** on the Red Sea Gulf at Eilat, are "French Villages" that concentrate on offering "total vacations"—for each presents tourists with full facilities
for water sports, horseback riding, tennis, disco' dancing, plus live music and
entertainment, and tours of the region as well as of the country. Both have
superb French and Israeli cooking. Not geared to handle children under 6, and
singles come either with group tours or during July and August and Jewish
holiday seasons. Ashkelon rates, per person in a double room, run $30–45 a day,
single daily rates are $38–53, with breakfast; August and Jewish holidays are
higher. Red Rock charges approximately $27–30 (double) and $39–43 (single).
(No dogs allowed.) Write direct, or reserve through *Histour* travel agencies.

Club Méditerranée: Arzhiv, near Nahariya, and near Eilat, on the Red Sea,
offering a range of facilities and sports, including swimming, sailing, riding,
desert trips, dancing and nightclub. Offices of the *Club Méditerranée* are located
in the USA at 40 West 57th St., New York 10019, and at 8009 Via de Ventura,
Scottsdale, Arizona 85258; in Canada, at 2 Place Ville Marie, Suite 459, Montreal, P.Q.; in Great Britain, 5 South Molton St., London W1; in Israel, 78 Rehov
Frishman, Tel Aviv; in France, 75 Pl. de la Bourse, Paris 2; in Belgium, 50 Rue
Ravenstein, Brussels. Write for details.

LESS EXPENSIVE VILLAGES have rates that run from $13–25 daily for
one, and from $8–15 daily, per person in double-occupancy rooms. These in-
clude:

Kayit Veshayit Shore Resort, near Caesarea, has 55 rooms with shower, a
self-service snack-bar/restaurant, sports facilities and programs of evening entertainment 6 nights a week. For information, write: Kibbutz Guest Houses, 100
Rehov Allenby, Tel Aviv, or to the resort, Kibbutz Sdot Yam. Open March-
October. Singles $23, doubles $16.

Dor Beach Village, near Haifa. Handsome beach on sheltered bay. 75 partly
air-conditioned rooms with showers. Also 27 family apartment units at $55 per
unit. Restaurant and evening entertainment. Visitors invited to kibbutzniks'
homes. Friday evenings. Reserve months ahead for July and Aug. Address: Dor
Beach.

Green Beach, on coast near Natanya. Excellent beach, huge pool, sports,
nightclub. The Swiss cuisine is kosher. Singles $17, doubles $13. 150 rooms with

bath or showers. 4-bedded rooms suitable for students or young people at reduced rates.

Sun Bay, Eilat. Lagoon Beach on the Red Sea. 99 hexagonal bungalows, also camping. Open all year. Recently renovated. Boasts rock gardens and palms, riding, diving etc.; partly air-conditioned. Singles $19, doubles $12.

Neviot Village, Nueiba, Sinai. 85 air-conditioned rooms with showers, fantastic beach with a Bedouin village next door. Skin-diving center, tennis, desert tours, restaurant. Half-board rates (minimum): $27–36; add $9 for full board.

DiZahav is the name of another village, and also the name of another oasis along the Sinai coast—often called *Dahab*. Its 42 air-conditioned rooms have showers; fees run $16–21; for room in the 30 bungalows, it's $11–14; add $8 for half-board or $15 for full board. Red Sea gulf water sports; centers for diving, sailing, surfing; Desert Tours operation; Bedouin and camels, private beach, restaurant, night club.

Tel Aviv area has the **Maccabia Village** in Ramat Chen, where the international Maccabia Games (something like a Jewish Olympics) are held and accommodated every four years. (1981 is one of those years). There's a heated pool, tennis courts, and telephones in the 103 air-conditioned rooms, shower or bath, and all rooms are centrally heated. There's a kosher restaurant. Singles $21–25, doubles $13–15; dorms with 16 beds are $8 per bed.

In the Jerusalem region, the **Judean Hills Recreation Center** is located in the Jerusalem Forest, and offers 40 rooms, 34 showers and 6 baths, central heating, swimming, tennis and a kosher restaurant. Triple occupancy rooms $1.50 less per person; doubles $13.50; half-board $6; full board $10.

Ein Gedi Holiday Village, on the Sea of Galilee, has 92 rooms, air-conditioned, plus private beach, self-service restaurant, pool, TV room, gardens and all the extras of Ein Gedi Kibbutz which operates it. Singles $13–17; doubles $10.

KIBBUTZ GUEST HOUSES. These range from 2- to 4-star hotels, and certainly offer an extremely comfortable—if somewhat distant—way of observing the kibbutz cosmos. All charge according to grade and have bright, clean, comfortable rooms, and modern, new dining rooms. Most have swimming pools and all provide regular slide, film, lecture and tour programs on kibbutz life. There is no roughing it attached to staying in these kibbutz accommodations. Some 16 out of the 225 kibbutzim have these guest houses and each is located in a rural or scenic part of the country. The majority are in the Galilee.

Most of the kibbutz guest houses are open year-round; rates are $12–27 per person. Two are 4-star, with the same space for about $18–29 per person, all season. Half-board and full-board rates on request.

You will find many of the kibbutz guest houses listed in our *Israel Town by Town* section which follows. If you need further information or wish to make reservations, the kibbutzim have formed a liaison organization: *Kibbutz Rest & Guest Houses,* POB 1139, 100 Allenby St., Tel Aviv.

YOUTH HOSTELS. Age doesn't make much difference in Israel's youth hostels, for folks of all ages stay here. Many have single, family, igloo and bungalow accommodations, plus the usual dormitories, of course. Many are air-conditioned, with swimming and sports, playgrounds and cafés. All serve some meals; some have facilities for you to cook. Write *Israel Youth Hostel Association,* POB 1075, 3 Dorot Rishonim, Jerusalem, open 9–2 except Sat. Contact them for real bargain "Israel on the Youth Hostel Trail" tours for individuals of all ages, year round, including accommodation and breakfast at 25 Youth Hostels, unlimited Egged Bus travel (except in Tel Aviv and Sinai areas); half-day guided Egged tours, free entrance to parks and archeological sites, maps, etc. Buy the tour from abroad or in Israel.

Overnight rates for members are $2.80; non-members pay $3.80. In family rooms (4 beds), it's $3.40–4.50. Breakfast is about "mandatory" at $1.20 and $1.30; and a real bargain. Hot meal or fish lunch is $2.50–3, light dinner is $1.60–1.80. Air-conditioning is 0.50. Note: Youth Hostels are usually open only between 7–9 A.M. and 5–11 P.M., and to stay in your room during the day, pay another .35. These prices are scheduled to change before 1981. Bear in mind also that prices are always high in Sinai.

For the membership card that allows better rates than for non-members, check the *American Youth Hostels, Inc.,* National Campus, Delaplane, Virginia 22025; in Canada, *Canadian Youth Hostels Assn.,* 333 River Rd., Vanier City, Ottawa, Ont.; in Britain, *Youth Hostel Association,* Trevelyan House, 8, St. Stephen's Hill, St. Albans, Herts. If you don't have one go to the Jerusalem Hostel office and get one.

Note: We have included some details of youth hostel locations in our section *Israel Town by Town* which follows. For complete list and details, write *IYHA.* Hostels in Israel can be dormitory, family bungalows, huts, modern cubes, etc., and they are scattered all over the country, urban and rural.

Vouchers for bed/breakfast can now be bought in dollars (5 for $15) at main hostels.

CHRISTIAN HOSPICES. Some 30 Christian hospices throughout the country provide room and board at low rates. Preference is given to pilgrimage groups, but when space is available almost all hospices will accept the general tourist, Christian and non-Christian. The average costs are minimal. A room and 3 meals ranges from approximately $7–24 per person; bed only rates, $8–10; bed and breakfast from $3.50 to $17. Half-board and full-board range from $8–20.

Located in West and East Jerusalem, Haifa, Mount Tabor, Nazareth and Tiberias, they vary greatly in size and accommodations, but all offer tourists unique Holy Land experiences. For complete list and particulars, write to your local IGTO (see p. 10).

CAMPING. Bungalows, thatched huts, cabins and caravan trailers, or tents—all are camping accommodations in Israel! Bring your own gear and pay a daily rate of $2.50–3.50. Children under 13 pay $1–1.50. Electricity use for air-conditioning or refrigerator is $3.50; $3.50–4.50 rents tent and bed (with sheets and blanket); beds in 3–4 person cabins and bungalows are $5–7.50 per person daily. A fully equipped trailer caravan rents for $24 (4 beds) and $30 (6 beds) daily. Another $2 daily gives you extra lights or a personal fridge box. Price depends on season: lowest during "off" season; higher in July/August and holidays; highest on weekends and eves of holidays. Charges slightly higher in Eilat. There are discounts of 5–10% for members of the *Israel Camping Union.*

Certain camps sell fresh produce and other groceries—even souvenirs! All provide complete sanitary facilities, kitchen sinks, showers, telephones, post office, first aid, electricity for your equipment, and space for your car and trailer. Camps are guarded, lighted at night. Advance reservations advisable, especially for July, August. Address: *Israel Camping Union,* POB 53, Nahariya. Also ask details of ICU Package Programs: minimum 14-days with airport reception/departure service, tent/cabin/room/accommodation choice, bus/rental car/mini bus tour choice, many extras. All are excellent buys.

 FOOD AND DRINK. We are paying quite a lot of attention in this edition to the all-consumingly interesting subject of what to eat and where. In a later chapter we outline the kind of food that is available. Here we give a few useful points and then launch into a tour of some of Israel's more intriguing eating spots.

Like any developed country, Israel offers a wide variety of eating places, with prices to match the quickie streetside snack bars, the truly elegant dining establishments, and all that comes in between. Here are some approximate prices:

Restaurant prices. $3.50 for a plain continental breakfast. $5 for a full Israeli-style breakfast. Lunch in a top-quality restaurant can be $15 and up; in a moderate-price restaurant, $8–10; at a lunch counter or snack bar, $3–5. Dinner, in a top restaurant, will average $20, without extra drinks, etc. A cup of coffee costs from IS4–8, depending on the café's location. A bottle of beer costs about the same. Wine is from IS15 a bottle in restaurants. Hotel restaurant food is usually kosher, ordinary restaurants differ.

Note: These are average minimum-maximum prices; appetites and selection can make big differences. For example, most restaurant lunches and dinners include a first dish or soup, main meat or fish dish, dessert, beverage and coffee or tea. But a *specialty* first dish can run IS20 and up, by itself, in moderate-to-luxury restaurants, etc. All restaurants must now by law post menus outside, so diners can check costs and offerings before being seated; lunch and dinner menus and/or prices often vary greatly at the same eatery. Restaurants catering to tourists must have menus in two languages (Hebrew plus either French or English) and may also use Arabic as a third. All prices must be in Israeli shekels, but may also appear in US dollars. Remember that local taxes and VAT will be added to the bill, adding another 28%, and always check to see if service is included before tipping.

POLLUTION REPORT The fabled Mediterranean is in trouble—its pollution edges ever nearer the critical point, and countries that it touches obviously are not doing enough about this problem. Conferences have been held with little actual results, and as the waters of this almost-landlocked sea lap the shores, they bring three major pollutants: oil, sewage and industrial waste. No country is free of this, and Israel—at the far end of the Mediterranean—receives a heavy backwash. However, the Israeli government has launched a national program, at an estimated £30 million, to combat sewage pollution, and the city of Tel Aviv, alone, spends almost £500,000 annually to keep its seashore clean. All this money and effort still doesn't produce pollution-free beaches, but it helps tremendously. When pollution occurs, swimming is prohibited and the beach is closed until clear. Nevertheless, with a choice of over 63 official bathing beaches on the Mediterranean coast, 12 along Lake Tiberias and 2 in Eilat, water-sports addicts are unlikely to feel deprived. Also, the Red Sea gulf (Eilat to Sharm-el-Sheikh) is a Nature Preserve, as are other areas.

Note: Wherever you swim along the Mediterranean coast, it's a good idea to wear old beach shoes and swimming gear—bits of tar abound and are difficult to remove, even with turpentine. Further, most of the Mediterranean coast is rocky, even if the beach itself happens to be sandy.

 SPORTS. Israelis are outdoor people, and most of their sporting activities take advantage of the country's good weather. The participant sports are listed here, but Israel also has spectator sports—with soccer and basketball at the top of all lists. Ticket agencies in all cities and towns can tell you what's happening while you're in town, and sell you seats.

Note: The *Maccabia Games* (Jewish Olympics) are held every four years in Maccabia Village, a suburb of Tel Aviv. 1981 is one of those years and the games are scheduled to run from July 6 to 16. Some 3,000 youngsters from 30 different countries are expected to compete.

Water-Sports. Israel offers a variety of water-sports: swimming, underwater fishing, skin-diving, casting with fishnets, water-skiing, surfing, wind-surfing (big at Tel Aviv Marina, in Tiberias and Eilat) sailing, angling, etc. There are plenty of good *swimming* spots along the coast, but the Mediterranean can be treacherous and even the most expert swimmers must respect the warning notices that are posted. Many municipalities, hotels and *Kibbutzim* have pools. *Underwater-fishing* is particularly good sport in several places along the Mediterranean coast and in Lake Tiberias.

You will enjoy *net-fishing* off the beaten track, at Moshav Michmoret, near Natanya. And try *water-skiing* on Lake Tiberias and at Eilat, *surfing* and skiing at Ashkelon, *sailing* along the Mediterranean, Tiberias and Eilat shores. Don't miss the *wind-surfing* at Eilat and other places. Watch for the International

Wind-surfing Championships in Nahariya in 1981, or learn yourself at Tel Aviv Marina for $28–61.

Scuba diving. There are nearly 20 diving centers in Israel and Sinai, including Eilat, Dizahav, Ophira, Akhziv, Caesarea, Haifa, Ashkelon, Jaffa and Tel Aviv. All give lessons as well as rent equipment. They can all supply full information about diving in the Gulf and along the long Mediterranean coast line. For a complete list of these centers, write *The Federation for Underwater Activities in Israel,* Tel Aviv Port, Tel Aviv (03-457432), or check with IGTA or IGTO.

The best place for scuba diving is the Gulf of Eilat, which includes the Sinai coast line from Eilat itself to Sharm-el-Sheikh, and has the highest international recommendation (three stars) for underwater sports from the World Underwater Sports Federation in Paris.

All diving centers operate wherever diving is possible. Underwater tours are available too, some covering several sites elaborately via car and boat travel; others include photography and archeological dives.

Sailing. Haifa's *Carmel Yacht Club* welcomes sailing addicts, and its members are more than happy to invite you aboard their sail boats. The season lasts all year and the goings-on are especially lively on Saturdays and holidays. Club-house at Kishon Port. Regattas once a month or more, particularly during the summer. For details write to the Club. Motor boats and sailboats for 2–4 persons can be rented at Israel's many water-sports areas. In fact, you can invest 10 hours and about $25 and learn to sail one. All waterfronts have marinas, Tel Aviv's being especially attractive and well-situated on the hotel strip—a good place to watch international yachts come and go, or the annual regatta. Fine sailing conditions prevail most of the year. You can also charter yachts here for about $80–130 for 12 hours. (Tourists who plan to sail to Israel in their own yachts should dock first at Haifa or Ashdod to clear customs.)

Horseback Riding. The French vacation village located at Ashkelon keeps 12 horses; you can take lessons in horsemanship, or go off on pleasant ambles around the countryside. The Club also organizes one-day horseback excursions. The *Rose of Galilee Ranch* (Vered Hagalil), on the Tiberias-Safad highway, has 10 horses, and organizes one- and two-day outings for groups of from 4 to 10 people, guides and picnic lunches provided. One excursion retraces Jesus's footsteps to the Mount of the Beatitudes. Rates range from IS20 for an hour's riding through IS100 for a day's trail riding with lunch to IS120 for a day's riding with kibbutz or Bedouin-camp overnight. Advance booking is advisable.

You will likewise find horses for hire in Tiberias, Nahariya, Natanya, Beersheba and Herzliya. Look for *Herod's Stables,* Dan Caesarea Hotel; *Havat-Hadar Riding Center,* Rishon-le-Zion; *Sun Bay Hotel Riding Center,* Eilat—for riding, touring, lessons. In Tel Aviv at *Gordon's Riding & Sport Club* (near the Ramat Aviv Hotel). Near Natanya, *Einhorn Ranch,* Moshav Udim, and *Green Beach (Hotel) Riding Center* in Natanya. *Neve Noy Riding School* is in Beersheba, Rehov Keren Kayamet. Arad's *Abir Riding School* is in both Arad and Beersheba, and *The Riding Center of Israel,* Ganei Yehuda.

Tennis—Golf—Hunting. Tennis is an ever-growing sport here, with championship leagues and courts found in most municipalities, many hotels, and Tel

Aviv Country Club, of course. An impressive *Israel Tennis Center* opened in 1976, in Ramat Hasharon, outside Tel Aviv. Welcomes locals, tourists; hosts big international matches. For details, write or call (03) 485222.

Israel's only golf course is at Caesarea (18 holes).

For potential hunters, the most interesting is perhaps the boat-hunting in the Hula Valley north of Lake Tiberias. Since it takes almost two months to get permission to import a hunting rifle—and there are all sorts of other formalities —it is simplest to hunt with the *Israel Hunters Association*, 83 Nahlat Benhamin St., Tel Aviv. The season is from 1 Sept. to 31 Mar.

Snow Skiing. The *Israel Ski Club* centers on Mount Hermon, where the highest peaks soar over 9,000 feet above sea level. Open daily. Snow from December-April. All equipment needed can be rented, for adults and young-sters. There are chair lifts to tyro or pro runs, cafés and restaurants high and low, plus a ski school, first-aid station—even a ski patrol. Check weather and security before going. For all details, even accommodations, write to: *Hermon Ski Site,* Moshav Neve Ativ, Mobile Post, Ramat Hagolan, Israel.

Walking and Hiking. Outings on foot are one of Israel's favorite pastimes. Some folk walk just to stretch their legs, but most Israelis combine walking with another national passion: getting to know the land intimately, its ancient sites, geography, flora and fauna. The Society for the Protection of Nature plans many short and long walking-hiking tours. There also are regular walking tours of most cities, plus popular annual events like the *March Around Jerusalem,* the *International Sea of Galilee Marathon* (an International Amateur Athletics Federation event), *Race Around Mount Tabor,* the *Night March in the Negev,* etc. International participants, individuals and groups, often take part in these events, and if such a fancy strikes you, merely check with IGTO or IGTA for all details and dates, or write to the National Committee for the Friends of Nature, POB 4142, Haifa, for its annual calendar of outings. Addresses of branches are: Mrs. H. Saenger, 7 Arlorosoff St., Tel Aviv; Miss T. Schlesinger, St. Martin 13, Jerusalem; Hapoel, 21 Hechalutz St., Haifa and Friends of Nature, POB 4475, Haifa. Marches, races and swim competitions also open to tourists include many organized by *HaPoel Sports Organization* (8 Rehov Ha'Arba, POB 7170), and by *Maccabi Sports Organization,* 68 Ibn Gevirol—both in Tel Aviv: write for particulars.

Hang gliding. This popular and spectacular sport has many devotees in Israel. For details of action around the country, call or write the *Wings Office,* 134 Ben Yehuda St., Tel Aviv, (03) 233490. Or write Arnon Har Lev, 124 Rehov Balfour, Tel Aviv, who can supply information about the *Agur Hang Gliding School and Club,* Bat Yam. They give lessons for beginners (tuition consists of 5 3-hour classes; cost $100 and all equipment supplied). More experienced hang gliders can hire equipment from them, but you must be able to produce an authorized hang gliding certificate of competence.

Cycling. To join a bicycling bunch of tourists, contact *Israel Cyclists Touring Club,* POB 339, Kefar Saba, Israel. Itineraries set from 8–14 days for groups, plus special arrangements for individuals and 3–5 persons. A unique, healthy way to see the Promised Land. (Also contact *Ya-Alat,* Eilat, for *Rent-A-Bike* touring.)

 CLOSING TIMES. The Sabbath, or seventh day of the week, is Israel's day of rest. It begins theoretically with the appearance of the first star in the Friday evening sky. Actually, everything begins to shut down around 1 P.M. on Friday, with a few food shops remaining open until 3 P.M. This may seem a bit early, but remember, people need time to get home, cook for that night and the morrow (religious Jews never cook on the Sabbath), change clothes and get to synagogue before dusk. Normal activities resume, at least in part, some 27 hours later. Since Israel uses the biblical calendar and its religious holidays are therefore movable feasts, it is impossible to list specific dates for the Jewish New Year, the Day of Atonement, the Harvest Festivals, Passover, Independence Day, etc. (See section on *Main Holidays and Religious Celebrations.*)

Business hours are generally as follows:

Israel Govt. Tourist Office, Sunday through Thursday, 8 A.M.-6 P.M. (5 P.M. in winter), Friday from 8 A.M. to 3 P.M. (2 P.M. in winter). Exception: the IGTO in Nazareth and Bethlehem where they are open on Saturdays and closed on Sundays.

Stores and shops: Sunday through Thursday, 8 A.M.-1 P.M. and 4-7 P.M., Fridays and holiday eves 8 A.M.-3 P.M. Business offices: 8 A.M.-3 P.M. Fridays and holiday eves, 8 A.M.-1 P.M. Banks: Sunday through Thursday, 8.30 A.M.-12.30 P.M. and 4-5.30 P.M. Fridays and holiday eves, 8.30 A.M.-noon. (Under a new regulation, Israeli banks are now closed on Wednesday afternoons.) Post office hours 8 A.M. to 6 P.M., some branches open until 8 P.M.; Fridays, 8 A.M. to 2 P.M.

Note: Department stores are usually open during lunch hours.

Never on Saturday. Public transportation stops on Friday about an hour before the onset of the Sabbath—except in Haifa, Nazareth and East Jerusalem —and starts again after nightfall on Saturday. Theaters and motion-picture houses close. (As a result there's a terrific rush on Saturday nights to attend a play or a movie.) Although the museums, zoos and such stay open, they don't sell tickets; you must buy them ahead of time. If you're driving a car, you have to be careful on Saturdays of things other than mere traffic; if your route takes you through certain orthodox, deeply religious areas, such as the Mea Shearim area in Jerusalem, for example, you can run into real trouble with the local residents, who don't appreciate having their Sabbath disturbed by motor vehicles.

It is considered a violation of the Sabbath to smoke even an innocent-looking cigarette in certain restaurants and most hotels. There's usually a sign to remind potential offenders: don't disregard this warning, at the risk of being discourteous to Orthodox Jews.

CONVENIENT CONVENIENCES. Public lavatories in Israel are generally disappointing by Western standards. First, you should know to keep pocket-size tissues with you at all times, since many toilets lack paper. Secondly, many also lack soap and/or towels, so pre-moisturized towelettes are very handy. Next, many restaurants and cafés have toilets somewhere "out back," through an alley, etc., and to get directions, do not ask where you can "wash your hands" or where the "ladies' or gents' " room is—the waiters will not understand. They will understand the word "toilet" and perhaps know "WC" as well. Toilets are marked usually with "OO" and are for both male and female use; some are marked in English, or by "WC." The ones in most gasoline stations are to be avoided if at all possible; the ones in older bus stations are also unbearable. Tourists' best bets are those in hotels (the bigger, the better, and don't worry about whether or not you're staying there), good restaurants, department stores, new-looking bus stations, and air terminals. But wise travelers will *never* forget that pack of tissues!

ENTERTAINMENT. A whole chapter is devoted to cultural events and museums throughout the land, and nightclubs are listed with specific cities and towns. However, visitors may also want to visit the *Wax Museum* in Tel Aviv, *Safari Land* outside Tel Aviv, the *Biblical Zoo* in Jerusalem and other zoos around the country. There're regular *auctions* of antiques and assorted items, and *fair grounds* in major regions.

Movie Houses are often called Israel's favorite entertainment places. You'll find them everywhere, showing the latest local and international films, plus the oldies but goodies. Few movie houses feature continuous performances. For the more popular films it's necessary to reserve seats in advance (seats are numbered, as in regular theaters). Shows usually start at 4.30, 7.15 and 9.30 P.M., but it's wise to check on the hour. Foreign films are always shown in their original languages. For non-English-language films, subtitles are in Hebrew and English; for English-language films, subtitles are in Hebrew and French.

TELEVISION is available in all hotel lobbies, and some hotels offer it in the rooms for an extra charge. And it can be fascinating to watch local programming of Israel, and Jordan (picked up in most areas). For English broadcasts, check the English-language newspaper, *The Jerusalem Post,* which lists packaged USA and British programs of both channels. **Radio** offers a wide choice of Israel broadcasts, plus those of several other nearby countries. English news can be heard on the Voice of Israel, the BBC and the Voice of America—check *The Jerusalem Post* for details.

NEWSSTANDS. All over Israel, they're plentiful and well-stocked. Many British and continental newspapers are on sale the day following publication, and the *International Herald Tribune* is flown in daily. *The Jerusalem Post* is the only paper in English—one of Israel's 24 dailies in 11 languages. Magazines, periodicals and books from around the world are usually found at newsstands and places like *Steimatsky's,* the largest chain of book shops.

BABY-SITTER SERVICE. Check with IGTA and your hotel. Many towns and hotels offer tourists child care services, even nursemaids by day.

ELECTRICITY. Israel has AC, 220 volts, 50 cycles. Many luxury hotels have bathroom sockets for USA 110 volt-60 cycle electric shavers.

 MAIL. The post office emblem is a white deer on a blue background. Mail-boxes, which aren't too plentiful, are at least colored bright red and usually set against a wall or along the edge of the sidewalk. In addition to being sold at the post offices, stamps can also be bought at hotels and all shops displaying the white deer emblem; the sign is often accompanied by a few words in Hebrew, sometimes in English and French. Sample postal rates are as follows:

Airmail Overseas destinations: Postcards, to Europe and Egypt IS1.30; elsewhere, IS1.50. Airmail letters (first 10 grams), to Europe and Egypt IS2.10; to North and Central America: IS3.20; to South America, Australia and New Zealand: IS3.60. Aerogram letters are sold for IS1.90 to any destination and there are some new illustrated ones.

Hints for Philatelists: Certain post office branches have special services just for you. In Tel Aviv, at 2 Pinsker Street and 27 Allenby St.; Jerusalem, 19 Yafo Street; Haifa, Hanevi'im Street. In addition, there are many stamp shops: try the Stamp Center at 94 Allenby St., Tel Aviv.

The Director of Philatelic Services, Ministry of Communications, Jerusalem, issues a book, *How to Collect Israel Postage Stamps,* which is available directly from the Ministry, or from IGTA. There're also frequent philatelic exhibitions IGTO can tell you about.

 TELEPHONES. You can make telephone calls from any grocery store or drugstore, and, of course, from cafés. The charge for a call is IS1.20, approximately. Telephone booths are few and far between. For local calls you need a token (these are sold at post offices and kiosks). Tokens *(asimonim)* cost about half a shekel, but some booths take coins. The phone directory is published in Hebrew and English.

Israel has radio-telephone service with over 100 countries, including overseas direct dialing. For placing foreign-country calls, dial 18. Israel time is 7 hours ahead of US Eastern Standard Time. Thus, if you want to talk to New York at 9 in the morning, call at 4 P.M. Tel Aviv time. There is of course telegraphic service with virtually every country in the world. Public telex, on a cash basis, is available at Jerusalem's Central Post Office.

Note: You are warned not to make long-distance phone calls from your hotel room without checking very carefully what the cost will be. Hotels add $1.50 surcharge for credit-card calls, and up to $7 plus 20% tax on other overseas calls. They also charge more for local calls than public telephones.

 PHOTOGRAPHY. Israel's stunning landscapes and picturesque inhabitants make it truly a Promised Land for camera fiends. However, there is one caution to be heeded: always bear in mind that there are certain religious communities whose members resent having their pictures taken. These include certain Orthodox Jewish sects and many women among the Moslems and the Druse. Your discretion in this respect will be appreciated.

Israel is blessed with an abundance of camera and photo-supply shops run by experts in their field who do first-rate developing and enlarging of black-and-white-film. Color film can be processed in Israel. Film is expensive, and the visitor will do well to bring a supply with him (see *Customs*). As there is lots of light, medium-speed film is fine for Israel. Climatic conditions vary, of course, with the regions and seasons. For best results with your pictures, remember that Israel in the springtime and summer is subject to the same contrasts that you will find in all warm and/or hot countries: heat and humidity in the coastal areas, heat and dryness in the interior and the Negev.

Protect your camera against the sun and heat. Don't take pictures between noon and 3 P.M., particularly in the summertime. In the Negev, don't take color shots in the early morning or late afternoon: the result will most likely have a reddish overtone. Bring along a fine, soft brush and a chamois cloth: the dust is always with us, especially in the Negev.

Note: Those once-in-a-lifetime holiday films are vulnerable to the X-ray security machines on airports. At some, such as London's Heathrow, extra-powerful equipment is used; on most the machines are of the "low-dose" type. Both can cause films to be "fogged," and the more often the film passes through such machines, the more the fog can build up.

Warning notices are displayed sometimes, and passengers are advised to remove film—or cameras with film in them—for a hand check. But many airport authorities will not allow hand inspection and insist that all luggage pass through the detection devices.

There are two steps you should follow. First, ask for a hand-inspection whenever you can. Second, buy one or more *Filmashield* lead-laminated bags, which are manufactured by the American SIMA Products Group. These will protect films from low-dosage X-rays, but should not be relied on against the more powerful machines. The bags are also available in Britain.

KILOMETERS INTO MILES. This simple chart will help you to convert to both miles and kilometers. If you want to convert from miles into kilometers read from the center column to the right, if from kilometers into miles, from the center column to the left. Example: 5 miles = 8.0 kilometers, 5 kilometers = 3.1 miles.

Miles		Kilometers	Miles		Kilometers
0.6	1	1.6	37.3	60	96.6
1.2	2	3.2	43.5	70	112.3
1.9	3	4.8	49.7	80	128.7
2.5	4	6.3	55.9	90	144.8
3.1	5	8.0	62.1	100	160.9
3.7	6	9.6	124.3	200	321.9
4.3	7	11.3	186.4	300	482.8
5.0	8	12.9	248.5	400	643.7
5.6	9	14.5	310.7	500	804.7
6.2	10	16.1	372.8	600	965.6
12.4	20	32.2	434.9	700	1,126.5
18.6	30	48.3	497.1	800	1,287.5
24.8	40	64.4	559.2	900	1,448.4
31.0	50	80.5	621.4	1,000	1,609.3

TIME. Israel is seven hours ahead of New York time (six hours ahead of New York's Daylight Savings Time); two hours ahead of Greenwich Mean Time.

Traveling in Israel

BY AIR. If you don't feel like spending six hours driving from Eilat back to Tel Aviv, or four hours driving from Tel Aviv to the Dead Sea, then take an *Arkia* plane. Arkia, Israel's domestic airline, links Tel Aviv with Jerusalem, the Galilee (at Rosh Pina), the Dead Sea (Sodom), Beersheba and Mitzpe Ramon in the Negev, Eilat at the Gulf, Santa Katarina and Sharm-el-Sheikh in Sinai. Several flights daily make the rounds from these destinations; sample one-way fares from Tel Aviv are: Eilat—$46; Rosh Pina—$22; Mount Sinai—$100. Kids fly at half-fare rates.

Arkia offices in Israel are: in Tel Aviv, 88 Hashashmonain St.; in Jerusalem, Tefahot Building, 9 Heleni Hamalka St.; in Haifa, 4 Ibn Sinai St.; in Eilat, at the air terminal; in Beersheba, 31 Herzl St.; in Rosh Pina, at the airport. There's also a USA office at 575 Lexington Ave., New York, NY 1002. Arkia also operates charters to and from abroad.

Air Tours. *Arkia* has many good tour programs that let you see more of Israel in a shorter time. For folk who take the increasingly popular charters to Eilat, Arkia does an intensive 1-day Jerusalem tour combining air and land travel, lunch, guided trips to sights and sites—and all for $115. A 2 day trip to Santa Katarina and Sharm-el-Sheikh, with an overnight stay in a 4-star hotel, works out at $299. In May, June and July, a 4-day, 3-night stay in a 4-star Eilat hotel. Including breakfast and roundtrips flights from Tel Aviv or Jerusalem, the cost is $116. This is part of their Budget Plan, which entails sleeping two to a room. Arkia have also introduced a 1-day trip to Cairo from Tel Aviv which takes in all the main sights, including the world-famous Egyptian Museum, where you'll see the fabulous Tutankhamun displays, and the Great Pyramids. The cost of $280 includes both flights and lunch and dinner. But be warned; this is an exhausting day. For details on further tours, contact your travel agent.

Kanaf/Arkia, Inland Air Charter Company flies 9-seat executive aircraft, tours Eilat and Santa Katarina Monastery, and offers the monastery plus Sharm-el-Sheikh. One-day in Eilat, from Jerusalem or Tel Aviv, with food, tours, etc., runs $96; the Galilee tour is $45. Also half- and one-day "Flightseeing" tours of Israel—interesting, moderately priced. Contact Arkia.

Other firms licensed by Israel's Transport Ministry, Civil Aviation Department, to charter planes for private trips and air tours include: *Masok Helicopters and Air Services, Ltd.,* 97 Sderot Rothschild, Tel Aviv; *Ma'of Airlines, Ltd.,* 34 Itzhak Sade, Tel Aviv; *Shahaf Air Services Ltd.,* 6 Peta Tikvah, Tel Aviv; *Elrom,* Dov Airport, Tel Aviv, and *Chim Avir,* 97 Rothschild, Tel Aviv.

Note: all but the last are also licensed for *aerial photography.*

 BY TRAIN. Train travel is the cheapest means of transportation, but rail links only a small portion of the country, and the travel is also the slowest way of getting about—but this usually is compensated by the scenic routes, especially the Tel Aviv-Jerusalem trip. The fastest trip is between Tel Aviv and Haifa. Other cities linked by rail are Natanya, Hadera, Acre, Shave Ziyyon, Nahariya, Bene Berak, Binyamina. Parking facilities, bus links everywhere.

Israel's nationalized railways (only one class) have diesel engines and modern rolling-stock, although the coaches are not heated in winter. Stations usually are jammed with crowds on Friday afternoons and before and after holiday periods, so try to avoid getting caught in such rushes. Examples of regular one-way fares from Tel Aviv: to Jerusalem, IS6.70, to Haifa, IS9. The Haifa/Jerusalem is IS1.32, one-way. (Eight new luxury coaches now run the Tel Aviv/Haifa rails—for an extra fee.) Students with proper international cards get discounts. Seat reservations: IS1–2. Children under 4 ride free; ages 4–9 pay half-fare; students and senior citizens enjoy 25% discount. Light refreshments served on all trains; buffets at major stations.

 BY BUS. Israel has a highly efficient network of city and inter-urban public bus services, usually featuring quite modern equipment that frequently includes air-conditioning. Each city and town has a central bus station where you can get local buses, or start trips for any point in Israel—via express and/or way-stop routes.

The rush hours, holiday periods, and Sabbath eves bring the most dense crowds, which you will find either fascinating or totally exasperating. Generally, stations close and bus transport stops before dusk on Fridays, resuming service

Saturday nights—Haifa is the exception, and that's for local service only. Interurban travel is a good way to observe the cosmos of Israeli society, as well as a usually fast means of getting around.

The bus companies are cooperatives, and the driver usually owns part of his line or comes from a kibbutz that does. The bus driver is one of Israel's national characters, noted not only for having one of the largest salaries, but also for his general free-wheeling verve and casual demonstration of expert gear manipulation. He also usually speaks several languages and is often a university graduate.

Both *Egged* and *Dan* operate public buses that cover the entire land, and *United Tours* has a shuttle service from the Herzliya resort-hotel area through Tel Aviv. Samples of Egged's regular prices are: Haifa-Tel Aviv, IS1.04 (Express, IS1.19); Jerusalem-Tel Aviv, IS1.98; Jerusalem-Eilat, IS3.88. There's also *Run-About Tickets,* good on all Egged buses except within Tel Aviv or in Sinai area—tourists just present passports at any Egged Tours Office, and pay (foreign currency only) $25 for 7 days, $45 for 14 days, $52 for 21 days, or $60 for 30 days of unlimited bus travel.

Arab-owned/operated buses also ply parts of the Israel-administered areas, and it can be an interesting experience to try a short trip on one.

Note: Highly volatile petrol prices may cause all transportation costs to skyrocket before this edition gets to press.

BUS TOURS. For touring parts or all of Israel—from half-day to 7-day jaunts, you can't beat the prices and service offered by *Egged Tours. Egged-YaAlat Tours,* and *Dan Tours.* All operate modern, luxury motor coaches with expert drivers and experienced, multi-lingual and government-licensed guides. They have offices in every town or city, and you'd best book well in advance for most tours. Many trips are year-round, but others are slated only from 1 April through the first of August, September or November. Some combine with internal air travel, and most offer hotel pick-up service. Most tours, and prices, are the same, from each company.

Depending on the tour, discounts range from 10% to 20% for children under 12, honeymooners and students. Even without discounts, the fares are very reasonable. From Tel Aviv, 2 days in Jerusalem/Bethlehem/Hebron is $96; two days in Eilat for $106; two in the Galilee/Golan for $96. The circular 8 day excursion leaves weekly, covers the country and includes food plus overnights from Tiberias to Eilat, Tel Aviv to the Dead Sea. It costs $425, including half-board and overnight stays in 4- and 5-star hotels. You can join all tours from most towns and cities. For more details contact your travel agent or write Egged-Dan Tours, 59 Ben Yehuda St., Tel Aviv, or Dan Tours, 5 Bograshov St., Tel Aviv.

Note: Bus tours to Egypt (Cairo, Memphis, Giza etc.) operate regularly and are very popular. Prices range from about $210 for 4 days, including first class hotel. They are well worth looking into. There are shorter and longer tours available too.

BY CAR. Car Hire Israel's local and international agencies rent cars at prices varying about 10% from one firm to another. Sample standard rates range from $14– 47 a day, with insurance sometimes charged separately (about $5) plus 15 to 50 cents per km. However, there are also unlimited mileage rates and special weekly rates that are more economical. Assorted taxes and fees, totaling nearly 30%, are paid by Israelis, but waived for tourists who pay by credit card or in foreign currency. Be prepared to leave a deposit of $250–500, plus estimated mileage charges.

There's usually quite a selection of vehicles to choose from ranging from Volkswagens to Fords, Chevrolets, Opels, Peugots, Jeeps and even minibuses.

To rent a car in Israel, you must have a valid license from your own country, or an international driver's license, and be over 21.

Israel's Ministry of Transport has approved the following self-drive car hire companies:

Tel Aviv. *A. Zamir,* Sherutei Rehev, 4 Rehov Hamikzoah; *Eretz (71) Rent-a-Car Ltd.,* Railway Station, Rehov Arlozorov; *Hertz Rent-a-Car (Israel) Ltd.,* 10 Rehov Carlebach and 81 Hayarkon St., also at Hilton and Sheraton hotels; *ITS Rent-a-Car (Avis) Ltd.,* 89 Hamasger St., also at 75 Hayarkon and in Hilton, Plaza and Moriah Hotels; *Kopel (Self-Drive) Ltd.,* 252 Hayarkon; *Ramtours Ltd.,* 32 Rehov Hayarkon; *Segev Tours Ltd.,* 108 Derekh Petah Tiqwa; *Sholam Drive Yourself Ltd.,* 9 Rehov Schnitzler; *Siyur Vetiyul Drive Yourself,* 5 Rehov Shalom Aleichem; *Sun Tours Drive Yourself,* 8 Rehov Bograshov; *Zohar,* 112 Hayarkon St., *Inter-Rent/Dollar,* 160 Hayarkon St.

Ben Gurion Airport. *Hertz, ITS (Avis), Inter-Rent/Dollar.*

Benek Bera. *Champion (VW) Rent-a-Car,* 27 Baruch Hirsch St. and Old Herzlia Rd.; *Intercar,* 18 Rehov Modinn; *Zohar,* 102 Rabbi Akiva St.

Jerusalem. *Inter-Rent & BAT,* 14 Shlomzion Hamalka; *Hertz,* 27 Salahdin St. and 18 King David St.; *Kopel,* 8 King David St.; *Zohar,* 178 Jaffa Rd. and 22 King David St.; *ITS (Avis),* 20 Haatzmaut Rd., 3 Levontin St. and at the Dan Carmel Hotel; *Inter-Rent,* Champion Motors, North Razel St., Shemen Beach.

Eilat. *Gindi Rent-a-Car, Hertz* and *Yankele Rent-a-Car* are all in the new Commercial Center; *ITS (Avis)* at Eilat Airport; *Inter-Rent,* Laromme Hotel; *Kopel,* Eilat Center; *Zohar* at the Hotel Bel.

Acre. *Nativ Haifa Ltd.,* 18 Gibborei Sinai.

Ashod. *ITS,* Pan Lon Bldg., 2 Rogozin St.

Natanya. *Hertz,* 8 Haatzmaut Sq., *ITS (Avis),* 1 Ussishkin St.; *Sharet Tours and Transport Ltd.,* 3 Rehov Ahad Ha'am; *Sverdlov Ltd.,* 54 Rehov Herzl; *Tamir,* Beit Itzak (near Natanya); *Kopel,* 10 Kikar Haatzmaut.

Nahariya. *ITS,* Kikar Ha'Iria, Gaaton Ave. 19.

Ophira. *ITS* at the airport.

Beersheba. *Hertz,* New Rasco Center; *ITS (Avis),* Derech Hevron; *Tel Tours,* 93 Hahisttadruth; *Inter-Rent,* VW Beersheba, Hevron Rd.

Herzlia-on-Sea. *Hertz,* Sharon Hotel; *Kopel,* Kikar Shalit.

Rehovot. *Hertz,* 207 Herzl St.

Rosh Pina. *Hertz,* "Delek" Gas Station.

Sharm-el-Sheikh. *Hertz Center,* Aqua Marine Club.

Tiberias. *ITS (Avis),* Rehov Elhadiff, Sonol Station.

Note: Many of these firms deliver to hotels and airports all over the country. In Israel, as elsewhere, Hertz and Avis both offer "rent it here, leave it there" options.

Temporary Import. Tourists may bring cars and other vehicles into Israel on a temporary import basis. A vehicle ferry operates between Haifa and other Mediterranean ports. Check IGTA for latest details, forms.

Motoring and Highways. For all their advances in other fields, Israelis in general are pretty wild drivers. So watch out. "Defensive driving" is the best rule, as the cars around you are liable to do anything. Israel's private car population has risen from several thousands to 300,000 in less than one generation. Remember your own road courtesy—you'll be safer that way.

You can pick up good *maps* of Israel at any Government Tourism Office or buy more detailed maps at any stationery store.

Israel has some 2,500 miles of main *roads* and they're improving every year. Most of the Tel Aviv-Jerusalem road is a four- to six-lane highway, except for a portion going through the Latrun bulge. What was once an arduous two hours' drive is now a smooth, safe one-and-a-quarter-hour trip. The same goes for the Tel Aviv-Haifa highway, which can now be negotiated in little more than an hour.

Secondary roads are also in pretty good shape and some of the most scenic routes, such as Acre-Safad and Rosh Hanikra-Metulla, have had the frameshaking jolts taken out of them.

Specifics. Traffic moves on the right side of the road, cars pass on the left. Right-hand priority at intersections unless otherwise indicated. Speed limit: 80 km. an hour on highways (exc. where indicated 90 km.), 50 km. in towns (unless otherwise indicated). All signals and special indications are in Hebrew, Arabic, and English. Don't be surprised at certain intersections to see the red lights turned on in every direction. They all change to green in due time and in turn. Distances are all given in kilometers. The right of way belongs to the main highway *in all cases.* Doctors' cars, instead of the familiar caduceus, display the emblem of the Red Star of David on a white ground. The wearing of seat belts is compulsory.

In frontier zones, don't try to act smart by driving your car beyond the yellow signpost marked "Frontier—Danger."

Road signs and markers, once pretty scarce, have proliferated and the chances of your getting lost on the road are pretty slim. However, Americans may get quite confused trying to figure out Israel's "International Road Signs," which actually conform to the European system. It is as well to carry a card listing them where you can glance at it while driving.

Gasoline. Israel has plenty of filling stations, so there's no excuse for letting your tank get down to its last drop. Beware of the Sabbath, though, when some stations close, so fill up on Friday. Also, consider carrying along a small jerrican of, say, one extra gallon for emergencies (although passing drivers and Israelis in general are friendly and accommodating). You'll notice three names of gasoline that may sound unfamiliar: Paz=Shell; SONOL=Socony Vacuum; and DELEK is an Israeli firm.

Filling stations usually have two kinds of fuel, Super (Octane R 94), and Normal (Octane R 83). Current prices in 1980 were Normal, IS3.25 per liter; Super, IS3.45 per liter; oil runs about IS4.50 per quart. No tipping is expected.

If you're not used to driving in hot climates, remember to carry along a container of water and check the water level frequently.

DISTANCES IN ISRAEL, BY ROAD:

	Kilometers	Miles
Jerusalem-Tel Aviv	71	44
Jerusalem-Haifa	161	100
Jerusalem-Beersheba	121	75
Tel Aviv-Haifa	97	60
Tel Aviv-Ashkelon	60	37
Tel Aviv-Beersheba	107	66
Tel Aviv-Eilat	342	212
Tel Aviv-Tiberias	134	83

BY TAXI. The taxi services in Israel fall into three categories, all quite different. They are: **Taxi Cabs.** Regulated by the Ministry of Transport, taxi service is found in all towns and cities, and fares are fixed by meters or by printed brochures or sheets issued by the Ministry. Most popular vehicle is the Mercedes, though many vintage-model automobiles also are operated. Since fares are constantly changing as the shekel devalues and as gasoline prices soar, it's safest to tell you that a short trip in town can run about IS10–20, and tipping is optional. For inter-city or suburban trips, know the fee before you start—ask to see it written in the book, if in doubt. Inter-urban fares are regulated, but high; 1980 samples appear on page 24. By law, the driver cannot refuse to convey any passenger willing to pay the required fee, and he also must carry your luggage (about a half-shekel fee for each for all but first bag). Taxi stands are marked by blue square.

Sherut Taxis. Israel has an extremely useful institution in the form of *sherut* (service) taxis. In the big cities you'll also see meter taxis; but these don't interest us. We're talking about the *sherut* taxis, which spend their time quite literally "in service." They're a hold-over from earlier times when transportation was in scant supply. The *sherut* is designed to be shared by several persons: it's generally an American car with its interior remodeled or a firetruck-red minibus. The fares and distances covered were set up when the *sherut* first went into service. These taxis commute between a city and its suburbs. They can also take you from one city to another. Although rates run higher than bus fares for equivalent distances, you can't call your trip to Israel complete unless you've had at least one ride in a sherut. Fares are more on Fridays and holiday eves, and from 11.31 P.M. to 4.59 A.M., with day samples as follows: Jerusalem-Tel Aviv: IS20.80;

Jerusalem-Beersheba: IS14.50. You can hail them at any point along the way. Identifying mark: a white panel in the window with the taxi's destination written . . . in Hebrew, alas!

Sheruts also ply through Judea and Samaria, in the West Bank. A ride from Jerusalem will cost about IS5 to Allenby Bridge, IS1 to Ramallah, IS2.50 to Hebron or Jericho. More at night, naturally. Expect about 25% and each suitcase is an extra IS.30.

Taxi Chauffeur-Guides. The big taxis that sport the official "tourist" emblem are approved and regulated by the Ministry of Tourism. Drivers of these taxis are quite competent guides authorized to conduct you on a regular sightseeing tour, complete with commentaries and explanations of points of interest. Such chauffeur-guides take annual refresher courses in order to keep up to date. They are specially selected, trained, and supervised, and the rates they charge are official ones. The cost is $112–130 a day (small or large car) for 10 hours, up to 200 kilometers. This covers four tourists; add another $25–31 for the driver to stay overnight, and 38 cents for each extra kilometer. For each half hour after 6 P.M., add $7. All cars are air-conditioned luxury models.

Leaving Israel

 CHECKING-IN FORMALITIES. El Al Israel Airlines' passengers have a special baggage check-in service the night before their flights. This can save you lots of time, as it means you can arrive at the airport only one hour in advance, rather than two hours before your plane departure. Take your bags in person, as messengers with them will not be accepted. Your luggage will be checked by El Al's super-security personnel, and your ticket validated. Be sure to have IS42, age 2 and up, for airport tax. The service is available only at these two El Al offices: Jerusalem, 12 Rehov Hillel and Tel Aviv, Ben Yehuda Street at Shalom Aleichem corner. It is available all nights until 11.30 except Fridays and holiday eves. Saturday nights it's open from 7 to 10 P.M. If you take advantage of this service, the next morning you can stroll past the waiting crowds of fellow passengers, and go directly upstairs to passport control.

Before entering the departure hall, you may be frisked (yes, frisked!) and all your hand luggage may be searched. Again, it's El Al security force doing its job, and though you may be taken aback, do not be offended—it's done for your protection and safety!

The departure hall covers a huge area that includes rows of seats for waiting, a café and restaurant, a bank for exchanging money and lots of shops for Duty Free buying before your flight. These are well supplied with local and international merchandise covering the usual range of goods. If you've bought Duty Free items within Israel—under the plan whereby you save 15–30% if the shop delivers them to your flight—you will receive them at Bank Leumi Le-Israel, in the departure hall. Be sure to have your receipts with you and handy. This is also where VAT refunds will be made if you've kept proper records.

CUSTOMS ON RETURNING HOME. If you propose to take on your holiday any *foreign-made* articles, such as cameras, binoculars, expensive timepieces and the like, it is wise to put with your travel documents the receipt from the retailer or some other evidence that the item was bought in your home country. If you bought the article on a previous holiday abroad and have already paid on it, carry with you the receipt for this. Otherwise, on return home, you may be charged duty (for British residents, VAT as well) a second time on the same article.

Americans who are out of the United States at least 48 hours and have claimed no exemption during the previous 30 days are entitled to bring in the following items duty free. These values have recently been changed under the new customs law, which became effective on November 2, 1978. Americans are now able to bring in $300 worth of purchases duty-free (up from $100). For the next $600 worth of goods beyond the first $300, inspectors will assess a flat 10% duty rather than hitting you with different percentages for various types of goods. For the next $600 worth of goods above the duty-free $600, there will be a flat duty of 5%. The value of each item is determined by the price actually paid (so keep your receipts). All items purchased must accompany the passenger on his return; it will therefore simplify matters at customs control if you can pack all purchases in one holdall. Every member of the family is entitled to the exemption, regardless of age, and the allowance can be pooled.

Not more than 200 cigarettes, or one carton, may be included in your duty-free exemption, nor more than a quart of wine or liquor (none at all if your passport indicates you are from a "dry" state or are under 21 years old). Only one bottle of perfume that is trademarked in the US may be brought in, plus a reasonable quantity of other brands.

Do not bring home foreign meats, fruits, plants, soil, or other agricultural items when you return to the United States. To do so will delay you at the port of entry. It is illegal to bring in foreign agricultural items without permission, because they can spread destructive plant or animal pests and diseases. For more information, read the pamphlet *Customs Hints,* or write to: Quarantines, US Dept. of Agriculture, Federal Center Bdg., Hyattsville, Maryland 20782 for leaflet No. 1083.

Antiques are defined, for customs purposes, as articles manufactured over 100 years ago and are admitted duty-free. If there's any question of age, you may be asked to supply proof.

Smaller gifts may be mailed to friends (but not more than one package to one address). There should be written notation on the package "Unsolicited gift, value under $25." Duty-free packages, however, cannot include perfumes, tobacco and liquor.

If your purchases exceed your exemption, list the most expensive items that are subject to duty under your exemption and pay duty on the cheaper items. Any article you fail to declare cannot later be claimed under your exemption.

British citizens returning direct from Israel, and also for goods bought in a duty-free shop on ship, at airport or on a plane have these allowances:

200 cigarettes (or 100 cigarillos, or 50 cigars or 250 gr. tobacco); 1 liter of strong spirits (or 2 liters of other spirits or fortified wines) plus 2 liters of still table wine; 50 gr. perfume and 0.25 liter toilet water; gifts to the value of £28.

If you have only the permitted quantities described above, you can go through the "Nothing to Declare" gates at the airport or harbour.

Canadian residents may, after 48 hours away, bring back duty-free articles worth $50 on a verbal declaration. After 7 days out of Canada they are entitled to an exemption of $150 a year, plus 40 ounces of liquor, 50 cigars, 200 cigarettes and 2 lb. of tobacco. Personal gifts should be mailed as "Unsolicited Gift—Value Under $15." For details, ask for the Canada Customs brochure, "I declare."

 **DUTY FREE** is not what it once was. You may not be paying tax on your bottle of whiskey or perfume, but you are certainly contributing to somebody's profits. Duty-free shops are big business these days and mark-ups are often around 100 to 200%. So don't be seduced by the idea that because it's duty free it's a bargain. Very often prices are not much different from your local discount store and in the case of perfume or jewelry they can be even higher.

As a general rule of thumb, duty-free stores on the ground offer better value than buying in the air. Also, if you buy duty-free goods on a plane, remember that the range is likely to be limited and that if you are paying in a different currency to that of the airline, their rate of exchange often bears only a passing resemblance to the official one.

THE
ISRAEL SCENE

PROPHETS, KINGS AND WARRIORS

The Saga of Israel's Early History

Many people visit today's Israel as pilgrims to the Land of the Bible, hoping to trace the footsteps of Abraham, Moses, Joshua, David, Solomon or Jesus. They want to see where ancient battles raged, where kings fell and heroes were made, where miracles were wrought.

Most pilgrims—be they Jewish, Christian, Moslem, Druze, Bahai or any of the many other sects that hold this land holy—will find the Bible an excellent guide and reference to most holy and historical places in Israel. Whether or not Jewish scripture and Christian gospels are accepted as literal or divinely inspired, they do present the most detailed record available of the ancient peoples and happenings in this land. Scientific estimates of man's origins range from 600,000 to 2,500,000 years ago, and though no one expects to pinpoint the Garden of Eden, it is reasonable to suppose that hundreds of thousands of years were needed for Adam's descendants to multiply over the world.

Stories of floods and divinely-wrought cataclysms are found in mythologies of many ancient peoples, including the Babylonians and Sumerians. The Bible story of The Flood features Noah, the righteous man spared to keep mankind alive. Unfortunately, his sons' sons were less righteous, and the Bible tells how Ham, Japhet and Shem became proud and sinful, then how God destroyed the Tower of Babel they were building and scattered them to far-off places, from whence they repopulated the world. Of particular biblical interest is Shem's descendant, Terah, who lived in Ur, in a land the Bible calls Chaldea (also known as Sumer, a part of Mesopotamia in what now is Iraq).

The Patriarchs

Though archeology proves men farmed, raised livestock, had tools, lived in cities, could read and write and travel long distances for trade or war, most of the world's population was still nomadic in the days of Terah. One of these nomads was Abraham of Ur, Terah's son, who heard a divine voice telling him to move with his family to Canaan. Heeding God's command, sometime around 2,000 B.C., Abraham left the Euphrates valley, taking Lot with him.

After wandering throughout Canaan, Abraham was at the edge of the Negev desert when, according to the Bible, he drew water from a well and made an oath at an oasis called Beersheba, now a bustling city. Lot settled in Sodom on the banks of the Dead Sea. In time, God tested Abraham by asking him to sacrifice his son, Isaac. Abraham's willingness prompted God to halt the execution. The incident led to the covenant between God and man: in exchange for a belief in one God (monotheism), symbolized by the covenant of circumcision, God promised that Abraham's children would become a great nation. About the same time, God destroyed the cities of Sodom and Gomorrah with an earthquake and fire because of their evil ways. The story tells how two angels led out Lot and his wife; but against the angels' instructions, Mrs. Lot looked back and was turned into a pillar of salt. (Today guides will point out a salt pillar they claim is Mrs. Lot.)

The times were patriarchal. Abraham's son Isaac inherited the clan leadership; his son Jacob received the mantle from him. Semi-nomadic, living in tents, herding goats, the clan sought to make its way in the land of Canaan. A beloved young son Joseph, with a coat of many colours, aroused his older brothers' jealousy and was sold into slavery, whence, in the Egyptian royal palace, he became an interpreter of dreams and finally a man of great power. Then, due to a famine, Joseph's father, Jacob, along with his family, migrated to Egypt.

The Exodus

The story of how the Israelites grew numerous and finally were enslaved in Egypt in the province of Goshen, of their exodus from the land of captivity under the leadership of their brilliant teacher Moses, and their return to the Promised Land, is repeated each year in the Passover dinner, the *seder*. Apart from the obvious symbolism of a dispersed, enslaved people struggling for freedom and their own homeland, it is also a dramatic story—there were plagues visited upon Pharaoh and the people of Egypt, pursuing armies, the waters of the Red Sea parting, divine revelations and the hardships endured during a 40-year desert migration (Moses wanted the old people with their slave mentality to die out before he stormed into Canaan with hardened desert warriors). The time in Egypt and the Exodus homeward is thought to have occurred about 1,400–1,200 B.C. During this period, God delivered the Ten Commandments to Moses—the "thou shalt" and "thou shalt not" laws. The Book of Leviticus and the Book of Deuteronomy elaborated these laws into a codification that touches on every aspect of man's social, religious and economic behaviour. From this time on, the people of Israel were set apart; they must live by these laws.

Tribes and Judges

Moses died at the border of Canaan before he could enter the Promised Land. Joshua took his place. Having crossed the Wilderness of Zin and skirted the enemy's defenses, Joshua's armies advanced from the east, from Moab, in what is now Jordan. Spies were sent into Canaan to ascertain the enemy's strength. Joshua's forces defeated one king after another. Most spectacular was the battle of Jericho, when the walls came tumbling down to the blast of trumpets. (The ruins of ancient Jericho may be visited in the Dead Sea Region, Administered Territories.) Ranging north of the Sea of Galilee, Joshua's forces crushed Jabin, King of Hatzor. (The conquest of Canaan corresponds fairly well to the facts as confirmed by modern excavations. A museum at a kibbutz near Hatzor today reveals evidence of Hatzor's destruction during the Canaanite period.) With the country secured, it was divided up among the twelve tribes of Israel—Asher, Naphtali, Zebulon, Isaachar, Menasseh, Ephraim, Gad, Dan, Benjamin, Judah, Reuben, Simeon. After Joshua's death, the tribes were led by a series of Judges, or princes, who were actually heroes emerging at times of military crises.

The Book of Judges has little to do with justice and the law: it is mainly an account of Israelite military actions. Gideon fought the Midianites near Mount Gilboa. In the Valley of Jezreel, now verdant and fruitful, Deborah the Prophetess inspired the armies under Barak to defeat the Canaanites—at the River Kishon, near Megiddo. (Judges v recounts the famous battle in the book *Song of Deborah.*) In these many wars, God is seen helping to bring military victories to the Children of Israel as a reward for piety and righteousness.

As time passed, Israel's enemies gained strength: the Hebrews were dealt a series of defeats by the Philistines, a people who had immigrated from Crete and Cyprus and settled along the southern coast of Canaan —at Gaza, Ashkelon, Ashdod, Ekron and Gat. In 1050 B.C., the Israelites suffered a disaster. At the Battle of Shiloh, the Philistines swept through the defending tribes and captured the sacred Ark of the Covenant (I Samuel iv. 5). The demand for a king was made to the prophet Samuel: as matters stood, the loose tribal federation was unable effectively to oppose the organized Philistine armies.

Kings

Reluctantly, Samuel agreed, and for the first time since Joshua the tribes had a single ruler. Anointed by Samuel around 1025 B.C., Saul unified the tribes' military power and started to turn back the Philistine advance. David, whose defeat of a Philistine giant on a hillside near Jerusalem had been a big morale-booster, went on to succeed Saul. (The site of the David-Goliath confrontation, the Valley of Elah, is 20 minutes from modern Jerusalem.) His military campaigns were even more successful. He utterly defeated the Philistines, the Moabites, and the Edomites. Israel's territory now extended throughout Canaan into what is now Syria and Jordan. David also recaptured Jerusalem from the Jebusites and made the city his capital.

When the Ark of the Covenant was brought to Jerusalem, it marked the beginning of Jerusalem as a great religious center. A period of reforms, peace and prosperity accompanied David's forty-year rule. The reign of his son, Solomon, was even more magnificent in its luxury and display. The first Temple was built in Jerusalem, the mineral resources of the country were tapped, trade, diplomacy, and royal treaties were undertaken.

But Solomon also instituted forced labor, a military draft, and collected huge taxes under a new system that cut across old tribal lines. Upon Solomon's death, discord erupted: not only did Syria and Edom revolt, but the entire kingdom was split in two; the Kingdom of Judah was formed in the south and the Kingdom of Israel in the north. In a few short years the empire built by David and Solomon disintegrated as the two kingdoms rocked under a series of assassinations and violent shifts in monarchy.

Trouble with Baal

II Kings describes the internal wars, invasions, and the rapid succession of kings. In the Northern Kingdom, a period of relative calm accompanied the reign of Omri (876 B.C.), who founded the new Israelite capital of Samaria. He won victories over the Moabites and the princes of Damascus, and allied himself with the powerful Phoenicians through the marriage of his son, Ahab, to Jezebel, daughter of the Sidonian king. But the era of stability in the Northern Kingdom was brief: the prophet Elijah stirred up the people to the point of rebellion, by protesting against Jezebel's efforts to have them worship the pagan god, Baal. At a spot on Mount Carmel, in what is now Haifa, he found the priests of Baal and threw them over a cliff. A revolution followed, and another blood bath. Jehu ascended the throne. It was not until the reign of his grandson, Jereboam II (786–746), that some measure of peace returned. But the prophecies of Amos proved correct: sinful Israel would be destroyed by God's righteous wrath—in 721 B.C. the Assyrians destroyed Samaria and deported more than 20,000 Israelites.

The Southern Kingdom, Judea, held out a little more than a century longer, largely through an alliance that King Hezekiah struck with Egypt and Ethiopia (even while the prophet Isaiah warned the king of the consequences of such an alliance). In proportion to the way they transgressed and sacrificed children to both Baal and God, the Israelite military defeats grew more and more disastrous. Finally, the Babylonians went on the march, defeating the Egyptians, the Assyrians, and then capturing Judea in 597 B.C. The invading king, Nebuchadnezzar, killed the Judean king, Zedekiah, and plundered and then destroyed Solomon's Temple. The invaders took many captives, and tens of thousands of Israelites were carted off to Babylon.

The Prophets

The admonitions by Elijah and Elisha against the worship of pagan gods mark the beginning of the Prophets' period. In the north, Amos and Micah inveighed against forsaking God's commandments and the commission of impiety. In the south, the prophet Isaiah observed the fall of the Northern Kingdom, and foresaw the same fate for Judea. From Jerusalem, the capital, he prophesied the doom of a people who would not change their ways. But Isaiah also forsaw a "returning remnant" of Israelites, a better time to come when a great kingdom would be restored under a Messianic leadership, a time without war or troubles when "nations would forge swords into ploughshares."

Jeremiah, who was born near Jerusalem in 645 B.C., lived through the period of final catastrophe. Perhaps the most flamboyant of the great prophets, he intentionally provoked the authorities with his stern accusations and dire warnings. He told the Jerusalem crowds that God would destroy the Temple, and the crowds nearly killed him on the spot. Official Judea accused him of treason and put him away in a deep cistern so he wouldn't weaken the army's morale. Jeremiah's prophecies went a step further than simply forecasting the impending disaster. He envisaged a new Davidic-type Messiah who would restore Israel to greatness. And when this time came, the sins of the Jews having been punished and forgiven, there would be a new order: children would no longer suffer for their father's sins; each would carry the burdens of his own sins.

The essence of the prophetic teachings were quite radical for the times: sacrifice and ritual were valueless; higher, individual moral standards were needed; the priests should not be heeded; Jews must set an example for mankind wherever they live. The reward for all this would be a new world in which Israel could live as an untroubled nation. (Already some interesting fulfillment is seen in that the Mosaic Laws have become a basis for the Judeo-Christian culture of later days.)

Exile

The deportation of the Israelites of Babylon (present-day Iraq) did not involve all the population but mostly the élite and leadership, while the farmers remained to work their land. And in some way, it was not totally disastrous, for new prophets carried on the earlier themes— Ezekiel and others, known and unknown to modern scholars. A different type of religion began to develop. God's chosen people were not confined to observing their religion in one particular place. Synagogues and religious assemblies evolved for the first time. Prayers and devotions replaced ritual and sacrifice. These new ideas, developed during Babylonian captivity, were later to assure the Jewish people's survival: the basics of the religion were exportable anywhere the people went.

The Babylonian Empire succumbed to the Persians. As it turned out, relatively enlightened men ruled Persia in the sixth and fifth centuries B.C., and as a result the Jews of Persia enjoyed a modest prosperity. Israelite leaders persevered until finally Syria agreed to grant Judea a measure of political autonomy.

It was around this time of revolt and regeneration—168 B.C.—that the Book of Daniel was written. The only one of Israel's apocalyptic prophets, Daniel envisaged a time when the "beasts," i.e. the great powers which oppressed Judaism, would be overthrown. After a final judgment, a mysterious "Son of Man" would appear who would establish everlasting dominion over all nations. At the end of all things, said Daniel, there would be a general resurrection of the dead.

These were new ideas in Judaism; to some, they represent a questionable appendage to the Old Testament; to others, they are a foreshadow of events to come less than two centuries later.

The Romans

Israel's freedom was lost again in 63 B.C. when Roman legions, under Pompey, conquered Jerusalem. In 40 B.C., the Romans appointed Herod "king." Herod set about building and rebuilding all over Judea. Although he rebuilt Jerusalem, he transferred the capital to his new, cosmopolitan seashore capital of Caesarea, which has been partially excavated. Herod the Great died in the year 4 B.C.—the same year, most scholars agree, when Jesus was born. Herod's sons then divided up the country among themselves; Judea and Samaria were ruled by Archelaus, "the Procurator," Herod Antipas was Tetrarch of Galilee; Philip presided over the northeast provinces, which extended into what is now Syria and Jordan.

The Coming of Christianity

In the first century B.C., many Jewish holy men and priests went about the country proclaiming the coming of a Messiah—the "savior" who would deliver the people from Rome's tyrannical, evil rule. Hadn't the prophets written of a Messiah? Isaiah called him a "suffering servant". Daniel even linked his "Son of Man" to ideas of a final judgment and resurrection of the dead, reward and punishment to be meted out, and a leader whose kingdom would be final. Basing expectations on both prophecy and legend most Jews then thought in terms of a Messiah who would restore in some striking way the greatness of Israel as a physical, political entity. After all, Judaism always had encompassed the political, civil, and physical behavior of adherents, as well as the spiritual.

Other Jews, however, came up with something different: the concept of spiritual rebirth of the Jewish nation. They wrote of it in great detail—though their writings were destined to remain hidden until a 20th-century shepherd stumbled across ancient jars containing parchments that became known as the Dead Sea Scrolls. Excavations in the area where they were discovered (Qumran, and nearby sites along the Dead Sea shores) revealed more scrolls, dating from 200 B.C. to A.D. 70, plus the remains of communities where those who penned the scrolls lived and worked. Scholars seem to concur in referring to these communities as strongholds of a pious esoteric movement within Judaism: the Essenes. A monastic community bound together by a covenant, their scrolls explain the divinity of a Messiah, a "teacher of righteousness" who had died at the hands of the "Sons of Darkness" (see the writings at the Shrine of the Book, Israel Museum, Jerusalem). They also tell how the Essenes broke with Jerusalem's religious establishment and withdrew to the Judean Wilderness to prepare for the coming of the Messiah, and of their religious community; its "New Covenant" of a baptism ritual, and ceremonials for eating together in conditions of ritual purity—which some theologists identify with those of Christianity's Last Supper. Altogether, what has been learned of the Essenes bears phenomenal resemblance to early Christianity.

The religion, Christianity, focuses on the life of "Joshua ha Messiah" which, after being translated into the language of the land at that time (Greek), and then into others, evolves into "Jesus the Christ" in English. The life of Jesus is recorded in four gospels: Matthew, Mark, Luke and John. These biographers may differ on certain details, and each has his own emphasis, but for the most part they offer a cohesive portrait, beginning with birth in Bethlehem near Jerusalem—a birth marked by the heavenly sign of a special star. Luke and Matthew trace Jesus's genealogy to the royal house of David, one of the families, according to Jewish tradition, from which the Messiah would come. The infant Jesus, they explain, was whisked away in Egypt at an angel's instruction, because Herod was slaughtering all possible "messiah-children" in the Bethlehem area. Later, Jesus's family settled in Nazareth, in the Galilee region. Then, aside from a visit to Jerusalem's Temple, at about the age of bar-mitzvah, little is recorded of Jesus's adolescence and early manhood.

When approximately 30, Jesus met John the Baptist (the Immerser), and was baptized by John in the Jordan River, near both Jericho and Qumran's Essene communities. Afterwards, Jesus took up the life of a teacher, travelling to various synagogues but concentrating mainly at Capernaum (near modern Tiberias on the Sea of Galilee), where the first disciples were gathered: fishermen Simon, Andrew, James and John.

Soon drawing great crowds, Jesus preached the unique message that the Kingdom of God was imminent and the end of the present age was at hand; that one should not rebel against Roman rule but, rather, return good for evil; seek humility and turn the other cheek for, at the final judgement, rewards will go to the meek, the humble, the righteous.

Jesus found himself at odds with the two major religious parties of his time—the Sadducees and the Pharisees. The Sadducees—the priestly aristocracy that controlled the Temple—were angered when he attacked the Temple services as corrupt and predicted that the Temple would be utterly destroyed. The Pharisees, whose religious life was centered on the Law, the Torah, and on the scrupulous observance of all its precepts (particularly those regarding tithing and purity), were provoked by Jesus's claim that the Law would be superseded, and that the minutiae of purity and tithing were of little account in the eyes of God.

Rome allowed the Jewish community full authority in its own religious matters, so the community leaders, having heard Jesus's new interpretations of the Law of Moses, figured they might catch the Nazarene violating religious law. If so, they could book a religious case against the preacher and silence Jesus's dangerous words. But all the most diligent spies, with all their clever traps and baiting, could "find no fault" in Jesus's adherence to Jewish law. Jesus continued preaching, while quandary and fear beset Jewish leadership, and Rome rumbled about plots to overthrow its rule.

The New Testament records how things came to a head when Jesus, enacting Zachariah's messianic prophesy by entering Jerusalem at Passover astride an ass, was hailed with palm branches and greeted with ovations as the long-expected Messiah. Heading for the Temple, Jesus smashed vendors' tables there, drove out money-changers, then debated with priests and officials who challenged those acts. Later, on the slopes of the Mount of Olives with the disciples, Jesus prophesied the Temple's destruction, and a time of terrible suffering that would end with a trumpet call, the dead rising from their graves, and the day of final judgement.

Foreseeing coming death, Jesus sat down to celebrate Passover supper with the disciples, announcing that one of them would be the betrayer. At this, the Last Supper, Jesus enacted a ritual which the disciples were to perpetuate. Breaking bread, Jesus told them to eat it, saying "This is my body." Pouring wine for them to drink, He said, "This is my blood." This ritual would form and seal a new covenant, a new testament.

Following supper Jesus was indeed betrayed by a follower, and taken first to the high priests, then to Pilate and Rome's authority. His execution, according to Roman punishment for criminals, was by crucifixion. The gospels tell how, three days after burial, Jesus's body was missing from its sealed tomb. They tell how the Christ reappeared, as a man of flesh and blood, to the disciples; how they watched Christ's ascent into heaven, after receiving instructions to spread the good news that the true Messiah had come, had died as a willing sacrificial victim to atone for man's sins, so eternal life could belong to all who believed; how Christ would return and establish the new Kingdom of God.

After the death of Jesus, the disciples preached the gospel of Christ. But it was through a citizen of Rome, Paul, that Christianity really spread throughout the Mediterranean world. On a trip to Damascus, Paul (Greek-and-Roman education, but an observing Jew, a Pharisee) had a vision, reminiscent of Abraham's encounter with God two thousand years before. The experience converted Paul to the "Christian sect of Judaism," and he set out, with his companions Silas and Timothy, on his long missionary journeys, to convert others. It was Paul who changed Christianity from a Jewish sect into a separate religion: faith in Christ was the simple key—man would not come to know God through the Torah, he explained, but only through belief in Christ. Ideas of salvation from sin plus immortality had great appeal to oppressed masses all over the known world. The Pauline interpretation of Christ became the essence of the new religion.

Inextricably meshed into the saga of the land of Israel, two of the world's major religions found birth, and grew to create thinking that would mold much of the development and future of the world. A third great religion, Islam, would find birth in the Judaeo-Christian monotheism, centuries later. Then it, and its sibling religions, would be labeled leaders of a dance of diplomacy, despotism and death—all for possession of this "holy" earth, even into modern history. But all that's in the future, for at this point in the historical story, Christianity has just come to light.

The Roman Occupation

All available evidence indicates that the occupying Roman forces were unaware of the significance of the event that occurred on that Passover in Jerusalem. The sons of Herod and the subsequent Roman procurators were having their troubles with the Palestinian population. (The Romans first called the land Palestine, changing the name from Philistina, the area on the Mediterranean coastline occupied by the Philistines.) The Roman abuses became more and more flagrant and, in A.D. 66, rebellion finally broke out. Initially the rebels met with success, until the emperor Nero, alarmed by the defeat of the Roman forces, dispatched the tough and experienced general Vespasian with a considerable army to deal with the situation. Vespasian set about subduing the country, and by A.D. 68 was at the gates of Jerusalem. When Vespasian was elevated to the imperial throne, his son Titus assumed the conduct of the war. He pressed the seige of Jerusalem with great vigour, but such was the fanaticism of the defenders that the city resisted him for about two years. The end was inevitable: in August A.D. 70 the last stronghold was stormed and the Temple was destroyed.

Thousands of Jerusalemites were led off to slavery in Rome, but small bands of rebels continued to fight the Romans. Acts of hopeless daring and courage occurred. In A.D. 70, a group of Zealots at Masada, a desert stronghold overlooking the Dead Sea, held out against the attacking legions for 1–3 years; finally, rather than surrender and become slaves, the garrison committed mass suicide. In A.D. 132, Simon Bar Kochba led a rebellion that achieved short-lived success when Jerusalem was recaptured. But the Emperor Hadrian, at the height of his power, quelled the rebellion in A.D. 135, and destroyed Jerusalem. He rebuilt it and gave the ancient capital the name Aelia Capitolina, decreeing that no Jew could set foot in the city.

By this time, Judea was devastated. The remaining Jews were concentrated in the Galilee, where a Jewish intellectual life took root. Under the leadership of Rabbi Yehuda Ha-Nasi, the oral commentaries on the law were first codified into the Mishna. For the next few centuries Tiberias was to remain Judea's center of learning, culminating, in the fifth century, in the compilation of the Talmud. But the majority of Jews were at this time in the Diaspora, outside Israel: most of them, along with the greatest centers of scholarship, were in Babylonia.

The sect that the Romans of the first century considered just another new superstition grew to engulf the entire Mediterranean world in the next two centuries. At the same time, the Roman Empire began to crumble: the army's morale weakened, the colonial populations withdrew their support, and a deep corruption in the social structure in Rome itself further hastened the Empire's downfall.

In 325, with Christianity everywhere, the Roman Emperor Constantine encouraged the new religion, and it became the official religion of the land. Pilgrims flocked to Palestine, burning down synagogues wherever they found them and persecuting the Jews who were now viewed by the Christians as infidels. Under the reign of Julian the Apostate, who sought to stamp out Christianity, the Jews were shown greater consideration; Julian even promised to rebuild the Temple after his return from a campaign against the Persians—from which he was destined not to return. A few years later, the Roman Empire split apart. The Western part was ruled from Rome, the Eastern half from Byzantium (later Constantinople and Istanbul). Palestine fell into a deep sleep under the domination of the Eastern Empire.

Meanwhile, much was happening nearby which would affect Jews, Christians—the whole world.

Islam Enters the Scene

At the turn of the 7th century, the vast Arabian peninsula had hordes of marauding Bedouin, dabs of agricultural settlements, and a few settled communities within walled towns. Of these towns, Mecca and Medina were prosperous, and though Mecca was somewhat larger, both boasted some 20,000 population. Mecca was also the religious center of the local polytheistic religion, which focused on pilgrimage to the Kaaba, a small square temple made from ancient black stones and incorporating a meteorite cornerstone linked with Judaism's Father, Abraham. The temple was a sanctuary from tribal feuds, and a place where feuds were abandoned annually, for purposes of worship.

In Okaz, near Mecca, was a market where locals and visitors gathered to refresh themselves and listen to the latest poets. The Arabic language was a uniting feature among all tribes, and making verses appears to have been the chief art form of the day. One of the most popular poets was 40-year-old Mohammed, an orphan who lived with his grandfather, of the House of Hashem, tribe of Qoraish, in Mecca. His verses weren't of love, camels, ancestors or princely patrons. He spoke of one God. Some historians say his life and travels among Christian and Jewish communities helped him develop his Arabized form of monotheism, and that it was perhaps some time before Mohammed realized he was preaching a new religion. At any rate, his verses were so perfect that all who heard them recognized "divine inspiration"—for Mohammed was no trained poet, yet he surpassed all other artists. He had to be a Prophet.

Mohammed made converts, and soon came up against the Kaaba guardians. Medina then invited the Prophet to seek refuge in its town, to become the lawgiver, judge and arbitrator for its diverse factions. Sending his followers ahead, finally accompanied only by his father-in-law, Abu Bakr, Mohammed went to Medina in A.D. 622—and here the Moslem era begins, dating from this year of the *Hejira* (literally "emigration," but also called the "abandoning," i.e. of idolatry).

In Medina, Mohammed broke totally with all forms of Judaism and Christianity, ordaining Friday as the day for congregational prayer. He preached that Abraham's spiritual heritage had passed to Ishmael, son of Hagar, rather than to Isaac, explaining how Ishmael's sons then peopled the deserts to become known, eventually, as the "Arabs." Mohammed's new religion was called Islam (surrender), and was essentially a lay religion. It had no apostolic succession, no hierarchy, no sacraments nor ordained priesthood. Even the *ulema*—who teach, guide and regulate Islam—cannot control it, and are only laymen, themselves. (Much later, after a split within Islam, a Sunnite class of *ulema* set up a hierarchy of judges, muftis and theologians, under the Ottoman Turks.)

It was also in Medina that Mohammed became a warrior, a military leader. In A.D. 630, with 10,000 warriors backing him up, the Prophet entered Mecca and promptly smashed all the Kaaba's idols (one is reminded of Abraham, who supposedly did the same thing in Ur, at his father's home). Mohammed then made Mecca his religious capital, recognized the Kaaba's holiness and tie with Abraham, and transferred the direction for prayer from Jerusalem to Mecca. Medina remained his political capital and Islam, the theocracy, grew to encompass religion, state and culture.

Within a mere 11 years, the Prophet had brought a large proportion of the Arabian peninsula under his theocratic rule. The doctrine of *jihad*—holy war—had been introduced, with motivation for conquest being the "opening" of a path for Allah and Islam. Should one of the "faithful" fall in battle, he was "assured immediate entry to Paradise," a much more worldly afterlife than conceived by Jews or Christians.

The more conquests, the more converts, and the path of conversion was relatively simple. To be Moslem, one needed to testify that " . . . there is no god but Allah, and Mohammed is the messenger of Allah." The other four of Islam's Five Pillars include praying five times daily, annual fast from dawn to dusk during Ramadan month, pilgrimage to Mecca at least once in a lifetime, and the giving of alms to the poor.

The conquests spread outside the peninsula after Mohammed's death (A.D. 632) when Abu Bakr held and wielded the "Sword of God" as the first Caliph. His short reign ended two years later, and Omar-ibn-al Khattab started a 10-year Caliphate. Omar became one of the greatest figures in Moslem or Arab history, finally destroying the Persian Empire and occupying Iraq, and taking Syria and Egypt from the Byzantine Empire. The Omar-led desert warriors took Damascus, Jerusalem, Alexandria—and kept on "opening" paths. By decree of Omar, the "faithful" warriors became a subsidized military caste, allocated annual pensions from imperial revenues and spoils of conquest. It was also during Omar's Caliphate that the Koran was finished—though Abu Bakr had been the original one to commit the oral verses to writing and assembly into a single volume. Thus the Koran, with the Sharia (Islamic law), and precepts and practice of the Prophet, supplied Moslems with religion and rules for living and government. Only much later did a split occur between Sunnites (those who followed custom) and the Shiites (partisans of the Prophet's son-in-law, Ali).

Islam on the March

In the 7th century, peoples in the eastern world fell under the new ruler—Mohammed—whose religion, Islam, marched across the entire East and very nearly engulfed the West as well. His successors, the Caliphs, rendered the Jews much more humane treatment than they had received under the Byzantines.

Under Islam, Jerusalem became a holy city again: Moslems decided that Mohammed was transported to heaven (they'll show you the footprint the Prophet left) from the rock some believe was Abraham's altar, now inside the gilded Dome of the Rock (Mosque of Omar), which was built in A.D. 650 on the site of Solomon's Temple, to initiate a Moslem pilgrimage to Jerusalem (in competition with Mecca).

The 400 years under Moslem rule was a golden age for the Jews: Arab mathematics, science and architecture flowered while Europe stagnated. Jewish scholars and scientists made substantial contributions to this period. The most famous was Moses Maimonides, a Spanish-born physician and philosopher.

The Arab (Saracen) Empire gave way in 1071 to the advance of the Seljuk tribes, Turkish warriors who persecuted both Jew and Christian and conquered all of Persia and Asia Minor.

In the West, Rome was repeatedly sacked by barbarian tribes. Occasionally, the Popes benefited from these invasions and converted the invaders to the Christian faith. Often, these newly baptized pagans were irritated because the Jews clung to their faith.

Jews suffered purges and hatred that led to further wandering, but during the first thousand years of their exile, they experienced no major mass expulsions or attacks—these would come later. As the end of the first millennium of Christianity drew to a close, Europe sank more and more into the Dark Ages of superstition and illiteracy. Empires were cut up and appropriated to the rule of many princes and Church bishops.

The East profited from this paralysis of the West during the 11th century. In 1009, Caliph Hakim destroyed the Church of the Holy Sepulcher. This time, rumor accused the Jews: they must have counseled the accursed caliph. Travelers returning from Spain reported that Jews and Moslems were thick as thieves down there. In 1012, the caliph of Egypt brought indignation to a crescendo by pillaging Jerusalem and expelling its Christian priests, along with Judaism's leaders.

The Crusades

Never before, nor since, has the Christian world united in such an undertaking. In terms of time, it spanned nearly four centuries. In terms of culture it embraced nearly all peoples of the then Western world and many of the little-known Mid-East. This was the Crusades. The goal of this Herculean effort was to occupy and wrest from Moslem control Palestine—the Holy Land—the geographical region now primarily occupied by the State of Israel.

The Crusades began in earnest when a monk of the Order of Cluny from Auvergne, Eude de Chatillon, became Pope Urban II in 1088. His primary wish, in the expanding Western world, was to strengthen the position of the papacy and to put an end to the Byzantine Schism, the split between East and West centers of the Church. Although Palestine was in the hands of the Moslem "infidels," the claim that the sacred places of Christianity were inaccessible to pilgrims was not exactly accurate, and the Pope knew this.

In the fall of 1095 Urban II issued his famous appeal for a Crusade in the belief that by uniting a pilgrimage to the Holy Land with a war against the infidels, Jerusalem could be reconquered while simultaneously liberating the Eastern Christians from the yoke of the Turks. There followed a veritable migration of warriors—migrations which would last until the middle of the 15th century and carried on by a spirit of conquest and personal gain equal, if not superior, to their religious zeal.

Preceded by a popular crusade under Peter the Hermit, which was dispersed in Anatolia, all of Christianity took part in the First Crusade. From July of 1096 until May of 1097, four armies streamed to the Levant to meet in Constantinople. Then, divided into two echelons— one under Bohémond, the other under Godfrey de Bouillon—they took two years to rout the Turks and secure Antioch before continuing to Jerusalem, whose formidable walls they first saw on June 7, 1099. Only after massive assault and bloodshed did they liberate the Holy Sepulcher a month later.

Jerusalem conquered, it needed government, and several of the leaders vied to rule. The matter finally was decided when Baudouin, brother of Godfrey de Bouillon, Duke of Brabant, forced Daimbert, the Archbishop of Pisa and an adroit ecclesiastical Machiavelli, to crown him king in Bethlehem, on Christmas Day, 1100. Having curbed the overzealous archbishop and identified Jerusalem with a royal title, Baudouin spent the next ten years conquering Palestine, capturing all Egyptian-held ports except Tyre and Ashkelon, and establishing his reign over Galilee, which Tancred had conquered.

Organization of the Latin States

The territory of the Kingdom of Jerusalem covered an area much larger than the 7,200 square miles occupied by present-day Israel. The Kingdom occupied all the coastal cities from Beirut to Ashkelon (which was not taken until 1153), included all of the interior as far as the Jordan, and even passed the boundary to the river in the principality of Tiberiad and the province of Beyond-Jordan. The Negev Desert was also under Latin control. The expansion of the Franks would not be curbed until the capture of Damascus by Saladin in 1174. In the north, three other Christian and Latin states had been established, similar in structure to the Kingdom of Jerusalem: the county of Tripoli (beyond the present frontier of Lebanon), the principality of Antioch (Antakya in present-day Turkey), and the county of Edessa in Syria.

Great orders of knighthood were born in Jerusalem: the Templars, the Hospitalers of St. John of Jerusalem and, later, the Teutonic Order. Supported by independent funds sent from Europe, these knights and their sovereigns enjoyed a great deal of autonomy—a situation from which they did not neglect to profit.

Despite this, secular knights remained subject to orders of the king, who was commander-in-chief of the armed forces in time of war, and whose approval was needed for appointments of all ecclesiastical dignitaries. Being Guardian of the Holy Sepulcher conferred incontestable moral authority on the king, giving him an advantage over the Latin states of Tripoli and Edessa.

At this time, the ruling class numbered only several thousand Westerners, primarily French nobility and clergy, who reigned over a mixed world of natives, immigrants, Moslems, Jews and Christians who quickly adopted towards each other an attitude of tolerance—the only one which could have worked under the circumstances. This kind of peaceful coexistence never failed to amaze new arrivals from Europe who often expected to earn their salvation by killing off the greatest possible number of Infidels.

To conquer is one thing; to remain, something else again. The major political problem was already evident: would a Christian state survive in the midst of a Moslem world?

The Caliphs of Baghdad and Cairo were only mildly interested in these realms and, when it served their interest, they didn't mind establishing temporary alliances with the Franks. Unfortunately, the Franks did not understand the importance of reaching an accommodation with their neighbours. They did not see that the most essential thing was to prevent the Moslem states from doing precisely what they eventually did: uniting in a *jihad*—a holy war—which would signify the end of the Christian kingdoms. Zangui, the Atabeg of Mossul, attacked and captured Edessa in 1144. Although he died two years later, his son Nureddin pursued the holy war. The Franks never dreamed of forming a defensive alliance while the Moslems still lacked an alliance of their own.

The Second Crusade

When Edessa fell, Pope Eugene III issued a call to arms and the kings of Europe led the next Crusade. After encounters with the Turks, the armies of French and German sovereigns joined at Jerusalem. Louis VII committed a strategic error, however, by not attacking Aleppo and diverting the Moslems who had taken Edessa. Another tactical and political error was made in 1148, when Crusaders attacked Damascus, forgetting that its independence had protected Jerusalem from Nureddin, who was tirelessly trying to unite all Moslems in a holy war. This disaster cost the Franks all the prestige previously won in the eyes of the Turks, and led to Damascus eventually opening its doors to Nureddin.

Though Baudouin III, Jerusalem's King from 1143–1163, had taken the Egyptian fortress of Ashkelon, it meant little. During the reign of Amaury I (Baudouin III's brother), Nureddin's general, Saladin, re-established the authority of an Abbasid Caliph at Cairo, and the Moslems of Iraq, Syria and Egypt achieved political unity. The menacing shadow of *jihad* fell squarely across the Kingdom of Jerusalem and the Latin states of the East.

When Nureddin died in 1174, Saladin consolidated Islamic forces, carefully avoiding a provocation of the Franks. By forming clever alliances with the maritime Italian cities, he simultaneously succeeded in setting Byzantines and Franks at loggerheads with one another.

The three remaining Latin states—Jerusalem, Tripoli and Antioch— were fortified as well as any on earth and, militarily speaking, would have been safe against any surprise if their rulers had only possessed political common sense. But their internal wrangling brought Jerusalem to the brink of civil war.

In a battle within sight of the Lake of Tiberias and near a double spur named after the locality of Hittine, Saladin cut an army of desert-weary Franks to bits. Nothing remained to prevent Saladin from marching on Jerusalem. He entered the city on October 2, 1187. In the entire kingdom only the fortresses of Belvoir and Tyre continued to resist. In Jerusalem itself, wealthy Franks were able to buy their freedom and leave the country. Jews and Christians submitted without too much discomfort to a tolerant Moslem domination.

The Third Shock

Saladin's conquest of Jerusalem was the direct cause of what came to be the most remembered of all the Crusades: the Third Crusade (1189–92), preached by Pope Clement III and led by colorful men, including the English King Richard the Lion-Heart, Philip II (Philip Augustus) of France and Frederick Barbarossa of Germany. Frederick drowned accidentally in the River Cydnos while en route to the Holy Land and his troops returned home. Richard and Philip cordially loathed each other. Richard held vast lands in France, a situation scarcely pleasing to Philip.

Philip arrived within sight of St. Jean d'Acre (Acre, to the north of Haifa) in April of 1191. Richard, who had tarried long enough to put Cyprus in his pocket, arrived two months later. Guy of Lusignan, King of Jerusalem from 1186 to 1187 when he was defeated by Saladin, was released in 1188 on renouncing the throne, and promptly laid siege to Acre. When Richard arrived, Lusignan received his support.

After a memorable siege marked by heroic sacrifices on both sides, the three kings succeeded in taking the city. Thus, Acre became the principal city of the amputated Kingdom of Jerusalem and remained so for more than a century, thanks to the commerce carried on principally by Italian traders.

Philip, feeling his task was done, returned to France. Once home he hoped to make off with the French holdings of Richard, after having promised to do nothing of the kind. Richard, meanwhile, wasn't about to let go of a good thing and thus reconquered all the ports south of Acre: Haifa, Caesarea, Arsuf and Jaffa (a southern suburb of present-day Tel Aviv). Lusignan, once again renouncing his claim to the throne of Jerusalem, was granted Cyprus by Richard in 1192, and his descendants ruled there until 1474.

The disaster of Tiberias was wiped off the slate. Richard further succeeded in extracting from the Arabs the right of Christian pilgrims to visit the Holy Sepulcher. Unable to retake Jerusalem, his actions nevertheless gave the kingdom a stay of execution for another hundred years. Innumerable legends are woven around Richard the Lion-Heart, in Palestine as well as in the West. It is accurate to say that war was never absent from Richard's spirit . . . but he knew only one way to wage war, and that was by means of action. Saladin waged it in two ways: by action and policy. He was Richard's superior as a statesman.

The Ways of God

The results of the Third Crusade had been judged disappointing in Europe. Under the impetus of the great and combative Pope Innocent III, the Count of Champagne (Thibaut IV) embarked from Venice on the Fourth Crusade (1202–4). Seeing that the Crusades were short of funds, the Doge Enrico Dandola pressured the Frankish troops into taking Zara on the Dalmation coast (present-day Zadar). Events following this Crusade were even less pleasant.

Alexis, the pretender to the Byzantine throne, promised to pay all the debts of the Crusaders, and led the French and the Venetians before Constantinople. The people revolted against the Crusaders, who in turn sacked the city in such thorough fashion that it was unable to recover until it fell into the hands of the Ottomans more than 200 years later.

It was one vast squaring of accounts between the Latins and the Byzantines; but all Christianity would later have to pay the price.

Shaken, Innocent III and his successor Honorius III dispatched a fifth crusade under the leadership of Jean de Brienne. His purpose was to lay siege to the city of Damietta in Egypt, hoping to gain a valuable pawn which could be traded off for the return of Jerusalem. He failed.

Success was achieved by the Germanic Emperor, Frederick II, who not only had his own ideas on the rights of the papacy but in addition controlled a lot of land in Italy—a situation the popes did not particularly appreciate. After marrying Yolande (Isabelle II, 1212–1228), who was due to inherit the Kingdom of Jerusalem, Frederick departed on the Sixth Crusade.

He won the return of Jerusalem, Bethlehem, Nazareth, Sidon (Scyda, in present-day Lebanon), Lydda (Lod, in Israel) and many other holy places for a period of ten years. For his efforts he received a severe scolding from the papacy: "One does not negotiate with the Moslems—one kills them," and his Italian possessions fell victim to the papal wrath. Indeed, the popes had quietly taken to preaching the necessity of a crusade against their personal adversaries. Nevertheless, Frederick had himself crowned King of Jerusalem in 1229.

Internal power struggles undermined the Franks and in 1244 Jerusalem once more fell into the hands of the Infidels (Turks in the pay of Egyptians). In one year, nearly all of Palestine and Damascus had fallen beneath the sway of Sultan Ayoub of Cairo.

The Seventh Crusade followed, led by Louis IX of France. Almost an exact replica of the Fifth, the Crusaders again tried in vain to take possession of Damietta in hopes of trading it for Jerusalem.

After Louis IX's return to France, Egypt became the dominating power in whose hands lay the destiny of Latin interests in the East. In 1260 the Mongols thrust toward Baghdad, Aleppo and Damascus. In a decisive battle at Ayn Djalout near Nazareth, Mameluke Sultan of Egypt, Qutuz, and his general Babar defeated the Mongols under the command of the Nestorian general Kitboga. This battle was of crucial importance to the religion of Islam, in particular, and to world history in general. It not only preserved Islam in Western Asia, but also killed any feeble hopes for the Christianization of the Mongols—they adopted Islam because it impressed them as being the religion of the strong.

The battle of Ayn Djalout—Goliath's Well—marked the decline of the Latin and Christian states in the East. The Sultan declared war against them, even against Acre, which previously had refrained from opposing him. He recaptured Caesarea, Haifa and Arsuf in 1265. The fortress of Safad fell in 1266; Jaffa, the Château de Belvoir and Antioch followed in 1268.

Louis IX had wanted to mount an eighth crusade to stop Babar but his brother, Charles of Anjou, King of Sicily, who occupied Acre from 1277 to 1286, opposed any military action directed toward the Holy Sepulcher. He was afraid that his personal plans might be hampered. Since Charles enjoyed good relations with the Sultan of Cairo, he persuaded his brother Louis rather to make war in Tunisia, where he met his death.

Conflicts among the Italian colonies and the chivalric orders of the Templars and the Hospitalers made things more and more difficult for the royal power. The last Latin fortress in the East fell between 1271 and 1303. Now that Louis IX was dead, Babar had a free hand. He captured the last three châteaux remaining to the Franks: Safita, the Crac des Chevaliers (between Safita and Homs in Syria) and Montfort, in the north of Israel. Tripoli fell to Sultan Qalawoun in 1289 and his son, Khalil, took Acre in 1291. Tyre, Haifa and Atlit (Château Pèlerin) quickly followed.

The dynamic flame which had illuminated and sustained the First Crusade had burned out. The knights were now fighting all along the coasts of the Baltic Sea. The Hundred Years War in France, the Reconquista in Spain, the Ottoman thrust into Central Europe—all contributed toward turning the attention of the West away from the Holy Land.

The rise of nationalism, the decline of feudalism and an era of exploration combined to push the crusading ideal far out of mind. With the Kingdom of Jerusalem now but a memory, Palestine was destined to remain under Moslem domination until the 20th century.

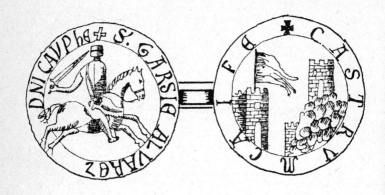

FROM EXILE TO RETURN

A Chronicle of Intolerance

The Roman dispersion forced large segments of the Jewish population to leave their homeland and start a long march through history—always strangers in strange lands. Their descendants fell mainly into two categories: those who headed north into Europe, and those who moved into other countries of the Middle East.

While the beginnings of the Diaspora (the period of wandering) are frequently dated to the reaction of Rome's legions against the Jewish uprisings, this is not strictly accurate. Long before Rome, many Jews of the Holy Land had been exiled to other lands—Babylonia, for one example.

When the Arabs arrived in Morocco in the 7th century, they found large Jewish communities that had existed there from time immemorial. In their dispersion, however, the Jews managed to keep their identity; they lived in communities apart from others, with synagogues as their centers.

Early Emigrations

The Jewish community in exile was forced to organize as a group in order to practise its religion. At first it was the Jews who rejected equal citizenship rights that would have subjected them to obligations incompatible to their faith. They were fierce monotheists living among pagans. However, this did not prevent them from participating in public life to a certain extent. Julius Caesar exempted Jews from obligations that they could not accept on religious grounds. That started people talking. The man who had to do a dirty piece of work to replace a "conscientious objector" ended with a grudge against this whole community of foreigners. Among the upper classes, the same feeling of hostility appeared: rich families contributed towards the maintenance of pagan temples, but the monotheistic Jews did not share the expense.

At this time, the rulers of Rome, while not exactly encouraging the spread of Judaism, did not persecute the Jews wandering throughout the empire. These were the days in which Christians were the target of the wrath of Rome and, while many Christians were Jews, the Romans took pains to persecute on the basis of religion rather than place of birth or national origin.

Paradoxically, hostility toward the Jews grew with the progress of Christianity in the Western world. The first Christian missionaries preached in the synagogues and many were natives of Palestine. Gradually, as more and more of the world of Rome abandoned its pagan beliefs for those of Jesus, it would be the Jews who would end up in the minority.

The Scapegoat Syndrome

With hostility increasing wherever they roamed and settled, some Jews segregated themselves from non-Jews, while others tried to integrate with the culture of Christian lands. For example, English Jews approached Richard the Lion-Heart to wish him success in his Crusade to Palestine.

Unfortunately, the well-intentioned action had the opposite effect on the Bishop of London who denounced the Jewish community as "these dogs" who had dared "to enter a Christian Church." There followed perhaps the first large-scale purge of the Jews in the Western world: fires, pillaging of Jewish homes, massacres of the people. Worst of all was the carnage in York where, besieged for six days in a fortress, Jews committed suicide there rather than surrender to their persecutors.

The ultimate failure of the Crusaders only heightened the popular anti-Jewish sentiments of the people. Frustrated in the loss of the Holy Land, many sought a scapegoat. The Jew was a convenient one.

As the killings of Jews became more common, so did the attempts to justify the actions of the Christians. A hodge-podge of fantasies, bred by ignorance and superstition, and featuring the "Devil," fascinating and terrifying, were rife in the land. As a sign of the times, the Hebrew word *shabbat,* meaning "rest day," took on the connotation of a witches sabbath presided over by Satan himself.

Three Charges

Three main charges were leveled at the Jew. The first, "ritual murder," involved the fable that the blood of a Christian child was necessary in the practice of Jewish religious rites, just as it was thought to be needed for sorcerers' magic recipes. The second charge, "profaning the Host"—the thin, unleavened wafer used in the Communion of the Mass—stemmed from the ignorance and superstition that drenched much of medieval Europe, when most people were unable to comprehend most daily natural occurances, let alone an alien faith or culture. Believing the Host to be the one defense against all manner of magicians, witches and alchemists who schemed to make life unbearable by creating plagues, droughts and earthquakes, the European figured all agents of Satan naturally wanted to seek, sieze and destroy the Host. The only non-Christian member of his society was the Jew, so the Jew must be after the Host. The fact that the wafer was nothing more than a wafer to the Jew never occurred to the fearful Christian.

The third charge, "universal Jewish conspiracy to destroy Christianity by poisoning wells," can be traced to the Black Plague which wiped out a quarter of Europe's population in the mid-14th century. Originating in Asia, the epidemic spread death over the Continent, then crossed the Channel and made ghastly inroads into the British Isles. Everywhere, its spread was encouraged by deplorable sanitary conditions. The Jews, whose religion made them obey old precepts based on hygienic concepts, got off more easily than their neighbors—ergo, Satan must have been protecting them. Tens of thousands of Jews were thus tortured and murdered.

Soon, individuals and nations alike were blaming every catastrophe, cataclysm, disease and war on the Jews.

As if this weren't enough for the wandering Jews to contend with, they were also held in contempt for the practice of usury, or money lending. This, in the eyes of many Christians, was their greatest sin, for the church has long preached against this practice, forbidding it to its members. At that time, however, it was one of the few occupations available to the Jew, who was barred already by society from entering any of the professions or powerful trade guilds.

The Sephardim

Meanwhile, in Spain, there existed a co-existence of Christian, Jew and Moslem that could have served as an example for the world. All worked together to further the glory of the country. They prepared a golden age in Spanish history. Christians were converted to the faith of Mohammed and Moslems were baptized. The Jews, as long as they were not persecuted, were permitted to remain Jews.

Scholars, philosophers and poets wrote in Hebrew and Arabic. The Jews broke out of the Talmudic straight-jacket; the Christians and the Arabs became interested in the Jewish holy books, and learned Hebrew Philosophy. Poetry and art were openly discussed on religious and secular levels in an atmosphere of complete freedom of thought and expression.

When Prince Henry the Navigator (1394–1460) created his famed academy at Sagres in Portugal two centuries later, Christians, Arabs and Jews were still to be found side by side in this think tank of exploration and astronomy.

In the 15th century, Ferdinand married Isabella, joining the crown of Castile to that of Aragon. They reigned hand in hand, doing their utmost to deserve their name as the "Catholic kings." In 1492, the last bastion of Islam fell before their onslaught, and the Moslems left Granada. That same year, the Catholic kings expelled from a unified Spain all Jews unwilling to be baptized. In terms of that era the Jews were treated generously: they had three months to sell or give away their goods and they could take out anything except gold or silver.

To Wander Again

The Iberian peninsula had been an ancient homeland for the Jews. Tradition held that their first settlements went back to the days of Solomon; they supposedly founded Toledo. However, the edict ended the largest, freest and most prosperous Jewish community in all Europe.

In despair, the Jews emigrated to countries bordering the Mediterranean. Italy, Turkey and the Balkans took them in. A few plodded north and asked the Netherlands for hospitality. Others were allowed to enter Portugal. In 1498, Portugal imitated her big sister, Spain; the Jews were expelled and had to move on, occasionally over the seas to that New World that did not yet bear the name America.

Jews were not actually forced to become expatriates. For centuries, religious oppression and the Inquisition had periodically offered them a choice between conversion, death or expulsion.

Renaissance in Western Europe

In France and England, after the roving massacres of the Crusades, Jews in cities established their own quarters, separate from those of Christians. Those living in the country came to join them, fleeing isolation that threatened to cost them their lives. Until then, Jews had served as intermediaries between Europe and Asia. But from now on, Christians would trade directly with the Orient. Three occupations remained open to the Jews: they could be craftsmen, small shopkeepers or money lenders. And the last of these activities, obviously reserved for the rich, was authorized only upon payment of special taxes.

In 1306, Philip the Fair drove the Jews out of Paris, confiscating their possessions. His son, Louis X, known as *le Hutin* (quarrelsome), called them back because, he claimed, "the cry of our people demands this."

Next, the Jews were confronted with temporary residence permits which they could renew only by paying exorbitant sums. Finally in 1394, Charles VI issued his edict expelling Jews perpetually from France. Only a few communities were to subsist in the independent provinces of Provence and Avignon. A hundred years earlier, England's 16,000 Jews had been hit by a similar measure. There, too, they were given three months to "dispose" of their possessions.

The 16th century witnessed efforts by men to rediscover ancient Greek philosophy. Human thought broke out of the molds imposed on it. Western Europe rushed to the statutes left by ancient civilizations; love of art and beauty swept away the last restrictions and the Vatican even founded a museum. But the hope brought by the Renaissance and its humanism seldom affected the Jew.

The transplanted Sephardim tried to adapt to their new mode of life. Their Ashkenazim brethren settled in new lands, their main center now in Germany. There, they were under the authority of lords or the emperor to whom they paid fees for the right to exercise the only occupations allowed them. Always it was the same: craftsmen, small shopkeepers or money changers. Most of the time, they were forced to wear distinctive dress that was purposely ridiculous.

In 1348, the plague came in from Asia. Certainly, the Jews must have been poisoning the wells. Two thousand of them were burned alive in Strasbourg. In Cologne, Mainz, Worms and Frankfurt, thousands of Christians spared by the Black Death slaughtered thousands of Jews who also had survived. Roads were filled with fugitives heading east.

In Eastern Europe

Fleeing eastward, the Jews found a new home, and a relatively liberal charter, under Polish Prince Boleslaus. Although again relegated to the role of money lenders or small shopkeepers, they were allowed to administer their own communities and enjoyed the protection of the authorities. Soon large communities developed at Poznan, Cracow and Lvov. Vitold, the duke of nearby Lithuania, followed the Polish example.

In 1563, after conquering the city of Polotsk and probably recalling this subversive movement of half a century earlier, Ivan the Terrible ordered that all Jews—men, women, children and the aged—should be thrown into the river "except those who shall receive baptism."

Things grew even worse in 1648. Chmielnicki led the Ukrainian Cossacks in a revolt against their Polish landlords. For three years, the Jews were caught in the middle. This blood had hardly dried before an uprising by Cossack peasants, the *Haidamaks,* broke out. Again, the revolt was directed against feudal lords and priests with the Jews added for good measure.

Assimilation, Pogroms

About this time, the "good Jew" made his bow in Central Europe as the *Hofjude,* the Court Jew, born out of the choice confronting the average petty prince in Germany. Caught between the desire of his people to return to the tranquil times they had enjoyed before the Thirty Years' War and his own urge to keep up as lavish a court as Versailles, and also caught between his own determination to rule and his obligations to the nobles, he adopted a half-way approach: he hired a Jew to do the work and serve as a buffer. It was not a bad solution. The Hofjude found the right tone needed to appease any appearance of anger among courtiers. Most important of all, he could not offend them.

The privileges enjoyed by the court Jew as an individual could be revoked without notice. His fortunes depended solely upon the good-will of his employer and the skill with which he obeyed him. The Hofjude simply carried out suggestions approved by his master. All he could do was advise. Naturally, as soon as a Jew was in such a position, his co-religionists began to breathe more easily.

Slowly, the Jews returned and discreet communities appeared again. Gradually, life for the Jew resumed nearly normal proportions as this period of relative calm spread from Germany to the Austro-Hungarian Empire.

Some 100,000 refugees—Ashkenazim from the north and west, Sephardim coming up from the south—settled in two Turkish-dominated provinces that were to be integrated later into the primitive kingdom of Rumania. They also went to Bulgaria.

In Russia and Poland squires valued Jews as intermediaries and money lenders, while peasants valued the goods Jews brought from remote lands, and the credit and services they rendered. Though squire and peasant benefited from the Jews in their society, this was easily forgotten when wine and beer flowed, and great sport was made of beating Jews with knouts, flails, sword or pitchfork. The death of a single Jew was only an everyday incident; the murder of several Jews, with women and girls first raped and then slit open, was given the honor of a new word: this was a *pogrom*.

One would think that, with such a history of oppression, the Jews would have disappeared from the world—or at least would have been almost universally united. In fact, frequently a non-Jew is heard to say that what they most admire about the Jew is his sense of solidarity. Such was not the case.

The east was the territory of the Ashkenazim; the Mediterranean and the Balkans were reserved for the Sephardim. Wherever they met, first in Rumania and Holland and then just about everywhere, a social and religious break soon appeared between the two.

Emancipation and Modern Anti-Semitism

Jewry was split once more during the 18th century. The French Revolution finally "officially" emancipated the Jews in the west. Russia, however, after the partitioning of Poland, subjugated them even more.

In Central Europe, Joseph II, son of the great Maria Theresa, issued the Patent of Tolerance in 1782 which incorporated Jews into Austro-Hungarian society.

In France, the Revolution wiped out all differences between various religions with a stroke of the pen. In a celebrated plea Abbé Gregoire told the National Assembly after it had adopted the Declaration of the Rights of Man: "Fifty thousand Frenchmen are going to bed tonight as serfs. Do what is needed so that they may wake up tomorrow as free citizens." The count of Clermont-Tonnerre summed up general opinion when he said: "We grant nothing to the Jewish people and everything to the Jewish citizen."

Ever since Cromwell, Jews had been allowed to return to England (1655). But they were emancipated only in the 19th century. Great families had enjoyed civil rights for a long time but not political rights. For example, if they were elected as municipal councilors or Members of Parliament, they obviously could not take an oath which obliged them to state: "I swear by the faith of a Christian." The debate over the abolition of this compulsory oath lasted some thirty years and ended only in 1858. In 1874, Disraeli, a Jew, became prime minister and was instrumental in the building of the British Empire during the years of Queen Victoria.

Meanwhile, the Jews continued to filter back into almost all sections of central Europe. Those advanced ideas spread by the Encyclopedists in France began to put intellectuals on the side of natural defenders of minorities, education freed minds from theological domination. After the French Revolution, Napoleon's armies forced conquered nations to adopt the measures of tolerance voted in France. But at an individual level, hostility remained rooted in men's hearts: it had been there too long to be wiped out overnight. As for the Jewish communities, they had good reason to continue to be wary of their neighbors. The ghettos retained their walls.

As the spiritual pressure of Western liberalism began to build up, the barriers that were still hampering Jewish emancipation fell one after another. The 19th was a century that knew passports only as an exception. Many men traveled to the United States, earned enough to pay their family's passage and, once everyone was reunited, began to work like demons. They were saved. Still most stayed behind.

Turning away from the Talmudic *yeshivoth,* Jewish children went to primary and secondary schools, then to universities in some cases. Stymied in the East by quotas, students hunted diplomas wherever they were accessible. Unfortunately, mob fury was raging once more in these countries. At Bucharest and Jassy in Rumania in 1866, and in other cities in 1870 and 1873, pogroms left Jewish communities in mourning. In Russia, a decree by Nicholas I in 1827 ordered that Jews had to serve twenty-five years in the army. This measure was intended to encourage them to be converted. His successor, Alexander II, eased the lot of the Jews somewhat when he abolished serfdom in 1861. The civil service began to allow them to enter its ranks.

Then the rebirth in Germany of the old ritual murder myth and the trials at Xanten in 1892 and Konitz in 1900 lit the fuse of the powder keg once more and stirred new pogroms. Vienna elected an anti-Semite its mayor. Nor did western Europe differ: the Dreyfus affair rocked France at the end of the 19th century. But Europe had yet to experience Adolf Hitler.

Society continued to oppose what it termed, either openly or secretly, the "Jewish invasion." Before the Third Reich, there were 16 million Jews in the entire world out of a total population of two-and-a-half-billion.

The idea began to take hold that the Jew aimed at gaining a foothold in affairs that would allow him to take over the world. But the Jew has never profited from anything except the feeling that he wasn't wanted. He was always condemned to flee again and again from the antagonism of his old fellow countrymen . . . and his new ones.

He knew that he would never have time to take his time. He knew that, sooner or later, he would need money to buy freedom and life for himself and his family. There you have feelings and sensations that put wings on a man.

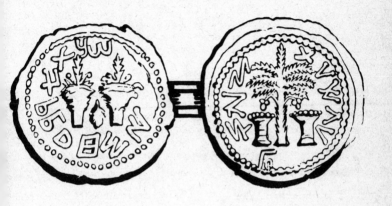

THE ONCE AND FUTURE
HOMELAND

From Aspiration to Achievement

by
AVIAD YAFEH

All through the Diaspora, the centuries following the final defeat of the ancient Hebrews by the Romans, until the founding of the State of Israel, the idea of a return to Zion remained strong in Jewish thought.

Zion was the name of the Jebusite stronghold in Jerusalem. When David captured the city, he made Zion a symbol of the city. In the times that followed, the word came to symbolize "the promised land," long promised but never attained.

77

The return to Jerusalem, in spirit or body, has permeated Jewish prayer and conservation all these years. 'If I forget thee, O Jerusalem, let my right hand lose its cunning'.

In all the dispersion and exile, wherever the Jews wandered they always prayed to return one day to Jerusalem. Also, in every generation there were large and small groups of exiled Jews who actually returned, or tried to return, to re-establish their families and join the Jewish communities of Palestine—for there never was a period when Jews have not lived in their ancestral country.

Though the continuation of Jewish communities in their holy land remained uninterrupted, for 2,000 years none of the land could be governed by its own inhabitants, as one foreign conqueror after another came to seize rulership. Centuries of this left a deep scar across the face of the land itself. With no durable central government and no strong local population interested in the country's welfare, the land was laid waste. Trees were hacked away to build military fortresses, but new ones never planted. The soil eroded and rocks studded the mountains and hills; swamps seeped to cover many plains and valleys. The population shrank accordingly.

Commentary on the conditions prevailing towards the end of the 19th century comes from the American author Mark Twain, whose memoirs note how sad was the view of the practically empty holy land: only a few Bedouin here and there, a few Jewish communities concentrated mainly in the holy cities, and a very few Arabs, as well. Yet it was precisely at this period of time that the prayers, dreams, hopes and expectations of the exiled Jews began to find reality. The slow movement for return to Palestine took on new impetus. It was the age of enlightenment in Europe, the time of the modern nationalistic movements that united Italy and Germany and strengthened the central rule in the other countries. In this fermenting philosophical era, modern Zionist ideas were developed. Jews also tried to organize, along the contemporary lines of thinking, a movement to rebuild the devastated and empty homeland they had been forced to leave thousands of years earlier.

Among the first teachers of modern Zionistic thinking was Moses Hess, a German-born socialist Jew who wrote *Rome and Jerusalem.* The Jewish masses in Russia were strongly impressed also by *The Eternal People,* a book by Peretz Smolenskin, a Russian Jew. Smolenskin prophesied that the Hebrew language was a great binding force on the Jewish people and that Palestine could again flourish as a center for Jewish culture.

An Ideal Form

The ideas began to take root. A group formed by Rabbi Mohilever, called *Hovevei Zion* (Lovers of Zion), launched the first actual immigration to Palestine. A group of Russian students, calling themselves *Bilu,* started a settlement there. By 1882, there were agricultural settlements at Petach Tikva, Mikvei Israel, Rishon Le-Zion, Rosh Pina, and Zichron Ya'akov.

Judah Pinsker, a Russian doctor, upon seeing his fellow Jews slaughtered in the Odessa pogrom, denounced all ideas about Jews assimilating into Russian society. He produced a book, *Self-Emancipation,* in which he warned of the wide prevalence of anti-Semitism throughout Europe. He wrote that Jews never had and never would escape anti-Semitism by moving from one country to the next. Complete territorial independence was the only answer, Pinsker wrote.

It was at this time that Theodor Herzl, born into a well-to-do Jewish family in Budapest, was writing drawing-room comedies and popular newspaper articles. On assignment from his newspaper in Vienna, *Neue Freie Presse,* Herzl went to France to cover the Drefus Affair.

There, confronted first-hand with an unyielding French attitude towards Dreyfus in particular and all Jews in general, Herzl realized the depth of the prevailing anti-Semitic atmosphere.

Out of this experience arose Herzl's *Der Judenstaat* (The Jewish State), published in 1896 and perhaps the most influential of all the early Zionist books. That same year, there were some 4,000 pioneer settlers in Palestine. The area had an overall Jewish population of 30,000 to 40,000.

Herzl assumed leadership of the growing movement and in 1897 convened the First Zionist Congress in Basel, Switzerland. Plans for mass migration were discussed and what had long been a dream began to assume the properties of a reality. The aim of the new Zionist movement was "to create for the Jewish people a homeland in Palestine secured by public law." Herzl traveled back and forth across Europe—meeting important citizens, diplomats, royalty and businessmen—to rally support for the movement. He spoke to the Turkish Sultan, the Kaiser, and the Tsar's minister.

In his zeal Herzl very nearly agreed to a British suggestion for setting up a new Palestine in Uganda. But the desire was a return to Zion, and such other valuable sites as Cyprus and the Sinai desert were declined. Before he died, he wrote another book, *Old New-Land,* a prophetic novel, in which he envisioned what Israel would one day be.

In writing of a new city called Haifa, he prophesied that "huge liners rode at anchor" and at "the top of the mountain there were thousands of white homes and the mountain itself was crowded with imposing villas. . . . A beautiful city had been built close to the deep blue sea" and "a serpentine road" led "to Mount Carmel."

The picture he drew proved to be amazingly accurate. Today, in Haifa port, through which hundreds of thousands of immigrants have passed, a sign bearing Herzl's words reminds each new wave of Zionists: "If you wish, it will not be only a dream."

Organizations were formed to buy land from the Turkish and Arab land-owners. Here and there, patches of rocky soil, barren for more than fifteen centuries, became the property of the Jewish National Fund. Using all the new agricultural techniques of the time, the settlers began to rejuvenate the soil, and soon where before there had been sand and rock there were the beginnings of pastures, orchards and vineyards. Between 1880 and the start of World War I, about 100,000 settlers arrived in Palestine.

The British Pledge

On November 2nd, 1917, the British government published the Balfour Declaration in which it pledged to "use their best endeavours to facilitate the establishment in Palestine of a national home for the Jewish people." Recognition was also given to "the historical connection of the Jewish people with Palestine."

The League of Nations in July of 1922 approved the Palestine Mandate and held Great Britain responsible "for placing the country under such political, administrative and economic conditions as will secure the establishment of the Jewish national home."

The British found a country still mostly denuded of vegetation, eroded and rocky and mostly deserted by its population. Only some 400,000 Arabs lived in the whole of Palestine, and 80,000 Jews. The Jews were the majority in Jerusalem, and they were also settled in the other holy cities (Tiberias, Hebron and Safad), as well as in the few agricultural communities established since modern Zionism began at the end of the 19th century.

It was a strange phenomenon that, as the exiled Jewish people never was able to develop its own potential until it resettled in its own country, the same seemed true for the land itself. The holy land had become more and more barren while the Jews were dispersed all over the world, whereas when their resettlement began, the land became revitalized.

As Jewish migration back to Palestine continued, the Jews were very careful to purchase every piece of land they wanted to settle, and for this they established special fund-raising organizations like the Jewish National Fund and the Jewish Foundation Fund, which were the arms of the World Zionist Organization and the Jewish Agency. The swamps and plains were the cheapest land the Jews could buy from the Arab land-owners, who preferred living in hilltop villages. This type of land was also the easiest to resettle without arousing the Arab neighbors. At least this was true at first, before the Jews proved they could drain the swamps—even though many of them were struck by malaria and were sick, incapacitated for life, or died in the process.

A new boom in economy swept Palestine and, in turn, attracted more people. Arabs came from neighboring countries into the regions settled by Jews. Other Arabs moved down from the mountains into the newly established Jewish centers. Laborers came from the nearby Arab countries—at first to earn a little money and then return to their villages, but later on they came to stay, to live beside the Jews. And the Jewish immigration continued rising.

It was no easy task to absorb the mass of Jewish newcomers without prejudicing the interest of the country's inhabitants, especially as the Arabs kept pouring into Palestine as well. Economically, of course, the Arabs benefited by the Jewish influx; culturally (in the broad sense), they definitely did. But greed and jealousy often stimulate hostility quicker than hard work, and troubles bagan sprouting up here and there.

Between Two Fires

Notwithstanding the vision of the League of Nations' decision, the Colonial Office in London was confronted with day-to-day problems. On one hand, in matters of technical purpose, they cooperated with the Jewish communities. Together, they expanded the Haifa harbour, built roads, developed public works and water supplies and so forth. But at the same time, the British found themselves facing writhing unrest in Palestine, and they had to try to tackle it.

The British gave way to Arab pressure. Trans-Jordan was exempted from the mandate's provisions for a Jewish national home, thereby shutting off most of the territory from immigration and land development. Then, as Jewish efforts created more opportunities to absorb new immigrants, the administration set up all kinds of stumbling-blocks to quiet Arab agitation. Laws concerning taxes and agriculture were now geared to discourage settlement.

In 1936 a Royal Commission concluded that, although a sovereign Jewish state was a necessity, its territory must be limited to about five per cent of the area that had originally been granted. Although adopted, this proposal left the administration uneasy and, in the end, British officialdom realized that the plan looked absurd.

It was then that a serious blow was dealt the fledgling country. World War II was fast approaching and to sway Arab powers away from the Rome-Berlin Axis, the British government published its White Book which reduced immigration to 75,000 over a five-year period.

Jewish dissatisfaction increased when the high commissioner was given power to forbid the transfer of Jews in certain regions and to create within ten years the conditions for establishing a Palestinian government based on the country's "present population." At the time, it was two-thirds Arab.

Over half of the territory of Palestine was closed off to Jews. In the remaining areas heavy restrictions were imposed on the acquiring of land by the Jewish Agency. With immigration just about shut off, Palestinian Jews themselves were condemned to little more than minority status in their "national home."

The Mandate Commission of the League of Nations declared the White Book incompatible with the task assumed by Great Britain in Palestine, a task that Britain herself had defined. The White Book was denounced in Parliament by Winston Churchill and other Conservatives and by all the leaders of the Labor Party, but with no result.

The White Book's psychological effect on the settlers was that Arab turbulence had been rewarded and Jewish patience penalized. They felt that all efforts of the past could not now be used to rescue German Jews from Nazi persecutions.

Still the Palestine Jews decided to maintain a truce toward England, even though many felt that the barriers raised by the British on the coasts of Palestine constituted a death sentence for the hundreds of thousands being hunted down by the Nazis.

The Jews just waited. They helped Great Britain in her war effort; fought in her armies.

When World War II ended, it was expected that, at the least, Palestine would be allowed to take in the survivors of the Nazi death camps. But Ernest Bevin, then Britain's Foreign Secretary, was handling the "Palestine problem," and so the restrictive White Book policy was maintained.

On Oil and Terrorism

England was concerned about her oil supplies and her relations with the Arab world proved an overriding consideration in dealing with all phases of the Palestine situation.

After this became clear, bitterness drove the Jewish population of Palestine into action—*Aliyah Beth* was launched, the illegal immigration of Jewish concentration camp survivors. Ships carrying clandestine emigrants ran the British blockade. In this atmosphere it was not surprising that clashes broke out; even less so that they eventually led to an armed resistance.

The resistance movement took several forms, ranging from the official position which avoided head-on conflict and preached negotiation while secreting Jewish refugees into the country, to the terrorism of extremist groups.

The Wanderer Takes Root

Being unable to own land in their dispersion of 2,000 years, and being deprived of the freedom to toil lovingly in their homeland, the Jews returning to Palestine started eagerly to develop and cultivate the country.

Palestine is a strange and difficult country to develop. The early Zionists used to say that if you forgot the land for one day, it would forget you for months. It is a land that must be cultivated very carefully in order to bear fruit and sustain its people. Half the area of Palestine is either rocky mountain where nothing can be grown, or deserts that include the Negev and the Judean Wilderness. Although the country is very small, roughly the size of Massachusetts, and more than half of it uncultivable, the *main* problem early settlers faced was lack of water. (It's still a problem!) There's not enough water even to irrigate the half of land that can be cultivated. The pioneering Jewish farmers became world-known experts in making the most of every drop of water in the country. They tapped all known water sources—rivers, springs, underground waters and rain waters—so that this precious life-giving element could be used to revive the country that had been neglected for centuries.

Of course, cultivation and development needed more than water, it also required simple hard work. Seven million trees were initially added to a country that was almost treeless. The swamps were drained with eucalyptus trees and with trenches and canals. Eroded mountains were tilled in contours to preserve soil from erosion, and to add beauty. Soon, the swamps, the mountains, and even the deserts were in bloom.

The agriculture of the new settlements flourished. It was possible mainly because the Jewish-Zionist settlers worked the most difficult areas in groups, founding joint ventures in several forms—like the kibbutz system, which is collective ownership of the land, or the moshav system, where each settler owns a private home, small garden and yard, animals for husbandry and such, but collectively joins in ownership of machinery and equipment, and in the marketing of produce and products. As these farmsteads thrived, it became known that the visitor to Palestine could immediately distinguish a Jewish settlement from an area either deserted for centuries or inhabited by Arabs, by the color of the terrain. Green dominated everywhere one walked in Jewish settlements, while the rest of the land remained brown, dun or yellow.

Jewish Self-Rule

Zionist settlers brought along a lot of know-how, energy, and European standards of living and education that far exceeded Middle-Eastern life styles. The Jews soon realized they simply could not be satisfied with the results of schools established by the British Mandate in the same system used to set up schools for the "natives" of many underdeveloped countries they ruled.

The Jews were the first to pay taxes to the Mandate government but, simultaneously, they established a self-rule and paid additional taxes to the Jewish Community Council. Through this council, they then founded the independent school system which they thought necessary, and it soon had very high standards. Side by side with this step, they started establishing new universities, the first three being the Hebrew University in Jerusalem, the Haifa Technion School of Engineering, and the Weitzman Institute of Science and Research in Rehovot (near Tel Aviv).

The machinery of self-rule later began being used more and more to protect the interests of Jewish settlers, and to establish governing bodies for Jewish communities and settlements which were, in turn, under the overall jurisdiction of the British Mandate government.

The British Give Up the Mandate

At the end of April 1946, an Anglo-American study commission published its report. It rejected the White Book unconditionally and recommended that 100,000 persons be admitted during the following year. In addition, its conclusions stressed the need to lift restrictions on the acquisition of unused land, previously limited to one-twentieth of the available territory. The Palestinian State could not be more Jewish than Arab nor more Arab than Jewish: its government would have to make an internationally guaranteed pledge to protect and preserve the interests of the three major religions. Finally, the government would be required to make efforts to close the gap between Jewish and Arab living standards.

Clement Attlee, then British Prime Minister, said neither yes nor no. As a first condition, he demanded that "the illegal armies in Palestine be dissolved and all arms surrendered." Practically speaking, this was a clear-cut refusal. How could arms be surrendered when the Arabs were openly receiving rifles while the Jews had to run a thousand-and-one risks to procure them? Even if a majority of the Jews were willing to trust England, it was unrealistic to expect extremist groups, totally free of any official influence, to accept such terms.

The truce observed during the commission's inquiry was broken. Acts of violence and terrorism ravaged the country, followed by reprisals that called out revenge in turn.

Great Britain stuck to her guns, imposing curfews, searching houses, imprisoning, sentencing and hanging terrorists. To maintain order, the army and the police were given almost unlimited powers.

In February, 1947, British proposals were rejected by both Jews and Arabs. England then took the case to the United Nations on the grounds that her Mandate had become unworkable and that the obligations contracted with the two communities could not be reconciled.

The Mandate Abolished

Two months later, the United Nations sent a new commission to Palestine, composed of delegates of eleven nations. Its report recommended putting an end to the British Mandate and granting Palestine independence as soon as possible. In its conclusion, the report called for partition of the country and an economic union between the two States, one Jewish and one Arab.

The delegates from Iran and India added a so-called minority plan calling for a federal State. It was this partition plan that was adopted by the United Nations General Assembly on November 29, 1947, by a vote of 33 to 13. A commission of five nations was set up to supervise the operation. But the UN was unable to stop what happened after that. As the British civil and military authorities pulled out, chaos erupted on all fronts.

Independence and War

On May 14, 1948, the day the British left, David Ben Gurion proclaimed the independence of the State of Israel. Already there was fighting throughout the country. But the following day, May 15, five armies—representing the military might of over 40 million Arabs—swarmed across Israel's borders and attacked the 650,000 settlers. Many lines buckled and by May 20 the Old City of Jerusalem was in Arab hands. The Arab command predicted the fighting would be over in a week and the Jews would be driven into the sea. The invading forces were the regular armies of five Arab States, fighting in opposition to the resolution of the United Nations, and attacking Jewish forces that previously had been active only in the defense of their own small settlements.

The Jewish defenders proved that miracles also happen in the 20th century. They had no alternative but to fight the best they could; so fight they did, to win the war. Israel's brief, violent war with the Arab countries is one of the great dramas of modern times.

Twice, truce was agreed between the invading armies and the defending forces, through United Nations mediation. But the truces did not last long, and fighting resumed. Jews tried very hard to defend all their settlements and people and, for political tactical reasons, to retain control of all the territories allotted to them by the UN Partition Plan. As they had to keep close contact with each other, all the previously discussed ideas of "kissing points" and "meeting places" between the Jewish State-to-be and the Arab State-to-be were abolished, and direct communication was forged between all Jewish points in Palestine. Jerusalem, Tel Aviv, Jaffa, Haifa and the Galilee (and eventually the Negev) came into Jewish hands and the attacking armies of Arabs were repulsed and forced to retreat.

The tide of battle had changed. In the Galilee, the Syrian armies had been thrown back across the borders. As November became December, Israeli forces pursued the retreating Egyptians out of the Negev and into their own territory.

The war was over. In the first months of 1949, Israel signed separate armistice agreements with Egypt, Jordan and Lebanon and Syria. A peace conference with the Arabs, scheduled for Lausanne, failed to materialize.

First Years of Independence

The establishment of the State of Israel was not, in itself, the only goal for the Israelis or for the Jews of the world who rushed to live in the new State. The real goal had been to establish a home for the Jews who were scattered all over the world, so they could cease wandering from nation to nation, unwanted by residents of those countries. While reestablishing the Jewish identity and independence of the Jewish Home, the aim was to found it on a sound basis of justice and equality. In building a new country out of nearly nothing, the pioneers wanted more than to make it bloom with produce and people, they wanted to do all this via equal opportunity and equality between the races, religions, sexes and cultures. It's no wonder, therefore, that among the first laws passed by the young State were the Law of Return, the Law of Compulsory Education, the Law of Land Authorities.

The Law of Return gave the right to every Jew who wished or needed to immigrate, to do so as if he were returning to his Home. Except in the case of criminals, the State has no right to stop immigration of Jews. This law, and the deep impression within world Jewry about the fact that at long last a Jewish State existed, caused masses of Jews to pour into the country. From the concentration camps and elsewhere, the remnants of Nazi terror came, joining those who had tried to reach Palestine during the British Mandate, but were not allowed further than the barbed-wire camps in Cyprus. Others who came were hundreds of thousands of Jews who had lived for centuries under Moslem rule in North Africa and Middle-Eastern Arab countries.

In the first three years of independence, more than a quarter-million Jewish immigrants had arrived in Israel. Before the first decade of independence was over, the Jewish population of Israel had doubled the 650,000 total of those living in Palestine at the end of the British Mandate. Soon the number passed the one-million mark, then the two-million mark. Absorbing the masses of immigrants was an enormous job, especially since it necessarily was done simultaneously with the task of strengthening and building a new army to defend the country.

Yet with vision and trust in their future, Israelis tightened their belts again and again, lowered their standard of living, and absorbed the millions of newcomers. This policy proved, in the long run, even a good economic investment. The immigrants were not taken to the population centres, but were sent to distant regions, first residing in poor transitional camps and later establishing themselves as new cities, towns, agricultural settlements and so on. New industries were established and Israel's economy has shown something quite interesting: the larger the immigration, the more jobs exist, and only when there were years of slow immigration were there any signs of unemployment. The country exported under $50 million in goods in its first years of existence, but after 20 years, exports passed the $1-billion point, and then that figure nearly hit $7-billion recently.

Soon, the first immigrants became the oldtimers, absorbing newer immigrants and making the deserts bloom even more. Over 100 million trees were planted during the first 15 years of statehood alone, with the number constantly rising. The landscape of the country changed in other ways as well—to blend ancient holy sites, archeological ruins and the most modern communities.

With all this, Israel developed itself as a modern democracy with a parliament (the Knesset), free and equal national and local elections, freedom of the press, and such. The Israelis continuously tried to weld the distant past of ancient Jewish independence and cultural genius, as exemplified by the Bible, to the recent past of the Nazi Holocaust, and the efforts of others to exterminate the Jewish spirit and the Jews themselves. Defense may have been paramount, but Jewish heritage could not be forgotten for it had an important role in shaping the "Purpose" for existing. The Hebrew language, dead and unspoken for centuries, was revived and became the language of the land and the medium through which cultures of dozens of Jewish tribes from many countries of dispersion could be mixed into one national culture, reborn and reshaped on its own ancient soil, while still preserving the diversity of the countries of origin of the immigrants.

Compulsory education between the ages of 5 and 15 became another tool for raising the standards of most immigrants from backward lands (and the State keeps trying to increase this so as to supply educational facilities to all from the age of two years through the completion of high school). Educational facilities gradually became extended by seven universities, colleges and scientific institutes, all to help forge a most modern and advanced nation out of what had been, only a few years earlier, a barren land.

The Sinai Campaign and the Six-Day War

In the seven years following the armistice, Israel's borders were constantly violated. The worst situation was near Gaza, on the Egyptian frontier. In October and November, 1956, Israel staged the massive Sinai Campaign—and seized and destroyed all Egyptian military installations throughout the Sinai desert. In three days, the Israeli forces were at the Suez Canal. At the same time the Anglo-French expedition bombed Port Said and prepared to occupy the Canal Zone. Pressure from the United States and Russia forced all the invading armies to leave.

Israel departed, but only after securing a United Nations pledge to guard the Gaza Strip and to station an outpost at the Gulf of Tiran, which had been captured from the Egyptians. In this latter case, Israel won the right of free and unharassed passage through the Gulf of Aqaba to the port of Eilat so that she could trade with Africa and the East.

Eleven years after, in May, 1967, the Middle East began to smolder again. Syria was stepping up its campaign against Israel. Egypt began bringing troop concentrations up along the Israeli border.

Shortly after, Nasser demanded the withdrawal of the UN garrisons in the Gaza Strip and Sinai. To the amazement of everyone, probably including Nasser himself, the troops were called back by the UN. On May 22, nevertheless, he declared the Tiran Strait closed to Israeli shipping, thus sealing Israel's gateway to Africa and Asia.

In a war lasting less than a week, Israel defeated the armies of Egypt, Jordan and Syria; in a Six-Day War, it changed the map and destiny of the Middle East. When the smoke of battle cleared, Israel found almost a million more persons under its jurisdiction and some 26,000 square miles added to its administrative territory.

The Aftermath

No one could have expected the Syrian and Egyptian forces to be able to resume hostilities. But massive aid refilled their arsenals. With all this new strength the Egyptians started a war of attrition across the Suez canal, that went on for more than two years. The US intervened and, as a direct result, Israel's National Coalition Government fell in August, 1970, leaving Golda Meir to establish another Cabinet. Temporary peace returned to the fronts and Egypt's new President, Anwar Sadat, stressed a new Egyptian position: closer to the US and world moderates.

In October, 1973, Sadat launched his massive surprise assault across the Suez Canal while the Syrians simultaneously attacked from the Golan Heights. This surprise attack that took Israel unguarded was the most dangerous period for the survival of Israel. In a few days, Israel had miraculously managed to reorganize its forces, stop the aggression and turn over the cards to hit back and win a great military victory. But the result of the "Yom Kippur" War—so called because Egypt attacked on the holiest day of the Jewish year, Yom Kippur—was nevertheless disastrous for both sides. Not least was the unbearable cost of over 3,000 Israelis killed on the battlefields, and many more wounded—compared with the toll of the 1948 War of Independence, the *first* war, which cost twice the number of lives, but lasted six months.

A danger of world war emerging from the Middle East war forced the United States and Soviet governments to look for ways to halt the aggression. Arab leaders, mainly Sadat, realized that even massive Russian arms and the advantage of complete surprise attack had not conquered the Israelis. This made them ready to accept American intervention and mediation. During four years little progress was made, although Israel continuously called on Arab world leaders to enter negotiations for peace.

Then, in the fall of 1977, Egyptian President Anwar Sadat became the first Arab leader to accept the offer by recognizing the State of Israel and visiting Jerusalem at the invitation of Prime Minister Menachem Begin. There was cheering throughout Israel and, when Begin later visited Cairo, throughout Egypt. World hopes were high that a lasting peace would result from these contacts between leaders of both lands. Hopes soared in March, 1979, when Begin and Sadat signed the Israel-

Egypt peace pact (the Camp David Peace Treaty) at a formal White House ceremony in Washington, D.C., with mediating U.S. President, Jimmy Carter, as witness.

That treaty is the cornerstone of more comprehensive peace agreements in the area. Though there is tremendous risk involved, according to Jewish statesmen, Israel has agreed on systematic withdrawal from the Sinai Peninsula by 1982, and is now discussing with Egypt the future autonomy of the Judea-Samaria district and the Gaza Strip. The U.S. continues to act as a partner but not a party in these talks. Israel agreed to such far-reaching concessions with hopes that other Arab countries would join the process to help establish comprehensive peace for the region. To date, however, neither Jordan nor the Palestinians have been willing to participate, much less other Arab lands. In a special July, 1980, U.N. General Assembly session, a proposal for the formation of a P.L.O.-led Palestinian state was overwhelmingly approved by third-world countries and the Soviet bloc, though Western nations voted against it or abstained. The following day, Israel's Government passed a long-debated bill establishing West and East Jerusalem as the land's "united and indivisible" capital, which caused a furor.

Despite this, the normalization in relations between Israel and Egypt has progressed enormously and steadily. Embassies have been exchanged and an infrastructure is being laid for cooperation on political, social and economic levels. Today, rather than pointing to the differences between Israelis and Arabs, much is being said about their similarities: related cultures and languages, shared regional problems, similar ancient roots and even many overlapping religious elements. Hopefully, the future will strengthen these mutual qualities. Tourism is lending a hand here. Israel has had open-bridge policies since 1967, and business went on as usual between Israel and Jordan even during the 1973 war. Tourism has grown through the years, with an average of more than 150,000 Arabs from neighboring lands visiting Israel each year, and the average growing annually. Now that Israelis may visit Egypt, several border crossing points are kept busy constantly. (See *Border Areas* chapter for more details.)

THE ISRAELI WAY OF LIFE

Struggle, Dedication and Nervous Exhaustion

by
ARNOLD SHERMAN

Author of ten published books on such diverse subjects as family humor in Israel, aviation, war and poetry, Mr. Sherman moved to Israel from America some years ago. His articles appear regularly in the United States, Europe and Israel. He lives in a fishing moshav north of Netanya.

Living in Israel is like navigating through a minefield. Your sanity, perhaps even your life, depends on agility, resourcefulness and sense of direction. There is no latitude for deviation or meanderings, and so nerve endings are perpetually frayed and your temper is only a few degrees under boiling.

In other areas of the world, people alter places. In Israel, places change people. One of Joshua's spies expressed a sentiment that many Israelis would agree with today: "This is a land that devours its inhabitants." The statement may seem radical, but it contains a nucleus of hard fact—perhaps not in the pejorative sense of physically self-destructing, but in a more pragmatic framework of totally consuming energies and activities.

Israel is an amorphous blend of struggle and dedication. A civilian is simply a soldier who has been furloughed home for ten or eleven months. An automobile represents a good deal more than a chassis and four wheels. It is a 350% (tax) offering to the Treasury. Hebrew is not merely a resurrected, Semitic language. It is a semantic commitment which requires patience, stolidness and a large dollop of masochism. In a land of educated people, teaching is about as thin as a laser beam. Israel is a socialist entity operating in an ambience of competition and private enterprise. It is a land where it may not be nobler to be a plumber than a doctor, but where the plumber's remunerations are certainly more discernible.

You don't have to be superman to live in Israel, but you have to be tough. Callousness is not an *a priori* requisite for financial and emotional success, but a calloused approach is the inevitable byproduct of the struggle. Often we Israelis sit around and wonder what is happening to us. We came here to live a Jewish life in an independent country. Those of us who emigrated from the West did so through our own volition. No one forced or cajoled or threatened us to leave. And yet here we are watching our children learn about the innards of the M16 when they should be studying Spinoza or isolating viruses. We long for an honest life and yet create fiction out of income tax statements. We seek a modicum of peace and yet, once every two weeks, someone slams a gun into our hands and we prowl our villages and communities through the long nights. We are very egalitarian—except when it affects our pocketbooks.

We secretly think that we have a mission onto the world and yet we have become the most xenophobic of all peoples, conditioned to believe that we are conspicuously alone. We are a proud people with huge achievements in our short/long history. And we are also paranoics convinced that *Götterdämmerung* is right around the corner.

In short, we are Israelis. We have our own way of life which has evolved because of the contingencies faced daily. We are neither better nor worse than any other people, but we are different and we are learning to live with and accept that difference. There are fewer hangups these days and less false pride. We are not characters out of the novel *Exodus* and we are not the meek products of a ghetto. We are a nation; and the expression of that nationhood will be found in a number of distinctive areas.

The Sabra Syndrome

One cause of our controlled lunacy is our children. Sabras (native-born Israelis either in fact or through adoption) set the standards for the rest of us—and these are mighty strange standards indeed.

Sabras expose our weaknesses, ridicule the values we so assiduously shepherded across the sea, blush over our Hebrew, wince at our accents. They blame us for not fighting Hitler more heroically even if we were just children during World War II. They think a tie is a sign of utter decadence and find the words "thank you" and "please" beyond the realm of expression. They blame us for all the shortcomings in the Knesset, suggesting they will boot our backsides when the senility grows a bit more pronounced. They are generally good kids who are taught independence in tandem with waddling. They don't smirk or giggle about sex, and the few instances of local drug addiction are regarded with incredulous wonderment. For the Sabras, heavy drinking means two bottles of beer and a teacher is either a pal or a misfitted emissary of the Gestapo. Nearly everything they learn is directly involved with Israel, so Julius Caesar is brushed off in an hour while Theodor Harzl warrants a month. Knowing every track and gully in the country, they're hardpressed to locate Cuba or the Virgin Islands on a world map. It's an insular sort of existence which prepares them for the vicissitudes of a rough and ready life.

With a population of 3.7 million, about one of every three Israelis is in some form of school. This makes for a young population and a youthful impetus. No one questions the power and prerogatives of youth in Israel. The young are all-pervasive and omnipresent.

When the State was declared a reality in 1948, there were 600,000 Jews residing in the land, only part of whom were actually born in Israel. Since then, the country has been inundated by waves of Jewish immigration—from the Middle East, the Mahgreb, Eastern Europe. What emerged was the anomaly of the Sabra being a minority in his own land. Natural birth never could keep up with the unnatural and unscheduled flow of newcomers.

But what the Sabra lacked in numbers, he made up in charisma. He was the natural outgrowth of the land; proud, hearty, unbowed and totally comfortable living in a Hebrew environment. He was the product of kibbutz and moshav. He fought in the Jewish Brigade and stormed Arab ramparts during the War of Independence. He wore his Judaism easily, tailoring it to the specifications of the Mediterranean. He had no problems with Hebrew because he was bottle-fed the language. But most of all, he was confident. He had absolutely no doubts that Israel was his land, that he was part of a four-thousand-year-old chain.

The Sabra generation is chafing with impatience and inexorably moving toward power. This phenomenon can be discerned in every aspect of Israeli life.

When the Israeli army was created in 1948 out of such diverse elements as the Haganah, the Palmach, the Irgun and the Stern factions, there was heavy reliance on volunteers and experts from abroad. Some of these men were mercenaries and adventurers; others were idealists. But the one thing they were *not* was Israeli. The situation today is totally different. The overwhelming majority of key officers are Sabras and, naturally, so is the rank and file. It is a young army where youthful officers are either promoted quickly or retired quickly. Usually both. The military is the strongest and most salient bastion of the young Israeli.

But the Sabra is moving into leadership in other areas as well. The collective communities forming the backbone of the country's hinterland were the realizations of East European aspiration and perspiration. Now nearly all the flourishing kibbutzim and moshavim are run by the young, with the older generation either having died off or retired from the scene.

When I first arrived in Israel more than a dozen years ago, the prototype of an Israeli politician was very middle-aged, passionately socialistic and dominantly East European. It was painfully obvious that he preferred Yiddish to Hebrew and *kneidlach* to *felafel*. Even during the recent tenure of Golda Meir, fifteen of her 24 ministers were of Russian or Polish origin. And of course to balance off these lopsided figures and placate the large numbers of Oriental and eastern Jews, most of the remaining representations were allocated because of ethnic considerations. The impatient Sabra was kept on a taut leash.

The situation has now changed dramatically, with Sabras more and more obvious on the political leadership level. Many of those now foremost on the scene are as indigenous to this Mediterranean landscape as the desert acacia. In effect it is a new era and a new generation for Israel. The present young leaders of government, army, commerce and industry are totally comfortable in their powerful positions. If there is a second language in the Knesset, it is English and not Yiddish. Israel is now in a transitional period, and the generation that was groomed for leadership has begun to come into its own.

Language of Frustration

When I was inducted into the Israeli army at the ripe age of 34 I discovered that, despite two academic degrees and a lifetime of writing, I was being listed as an illiterate. Someone dictated a passage of the Bible which I was expected not only to transcribe but to understand, and I sublimely failed both tests. It was an indication of things to come.

Hebrew in Israel is not only a language, it is a commitment. You can manage without it easily—if you refrain from speaking to anyone under 30, relegate yourself to hotel areas, or locate students desperately anxious to learn English or French. Otherwise, expect a certain degree of incomprehension. The resurrection of the Hebrew language after a 2,000-year sleep was no mean feat, and the language's importance and intrinsic beauty are hammered into the heads of the young as soon as their brain cells congeal. With immigrants arriving from over 100 different countries, Israel without Hebrew would not be Israel.

The whole thing actually began with a fellow named Eliezar BenYehuda who is considered the "father" of modern Hebrew. Arriving in Palestine in 1881, he devoted his life to Hebrew letters, established a school for Hebrew, prepared a dictionary and issued a weekly in the strange, problematic language. Since then, the Semitic idiom has been restored to its biblical glory, give or take a few new-fangled introductions like "radio" for radio and "telephone" for telephone. Because of its almost mathematical construction, reestablishing the ancient language has had its light moments. So a train is really a variant of a chariot and a kite is an "aphifon" because its root "oof" characterized flight. There are endless other examples, the language having been carefully reconstructed on the twin pedestals of logic and need.

Despite the fervor of Hebrew, however, every Israeli youngster should speak at least a smattering of English—theoretically at least, for it is a required subject from grade-school up. The problem is that the Sabra is somewhat embarrassed about speaking English and, more often that not, he feigns ignorance unless forced into a corner or confronted by a Brooklyn aunt.

Since most Hebrew words are constructed and configured from relatively simple roots, this sublimely logical language allows an inventiveness which would drive Daniel Webster up the wall. Yiddish, once a fairly reliable form of communication, has been more or less eclipsed by now. The younger generation knows a few words, but few youngsters are really able to communicate in what was once the cultural heritage of European Jewry.

While Hebrew is the uncontested lingua franca of the young, the tempo of immigration determines the other assorted sounds which percolate through the thoroughfares of the country. During the brief period of large-scale Russian immigration, the Slavic nuance suddenly appeared in most large cities and Cyrillic lettering mushroomed in stores and supermarkets. French was imported by Moroccan and Tunisian Jews. Many of the 30-year veteran German Jews still tenaciously hang on to their old idiom and one commonly repeated joke deals with two of these citizens, perched on the seashore, who hear the screams of a drowning man: "*Hotsilu, hotsilu*" (save me, save me)! One former-German turns to the other and says, "He should have learned swimming instead of Hebrew."

In my own home, although we speak mostly English, my older daughter proved her sabradom by failing English in her matriculation exams, and her younger sister has resisted English literature for as many years as she has been in school. "It's ridiculous," the young moppet explained. "Who speaks English anyway?"

To end on a happy note for the 3-billion, 497-million non-linguists who have never learned the language of the Bible: Israelis are an accommodating people and while their English syntax leaves much to be desired, their accents heavy and their vocabularies rusted by non-use, they will invariably emerge with a more comprehensible language the moment they have unequivocally determined that you really are not proficient in their own unique form of expression.

The Army

If a single common denominator exists in the zany land of Israel it is the ubiquitous presence of the world's most amazing citizen army. Unlike any other military force in the world, it permeates every aspect of the country's national life. With the exception of the ultra-orthodox and the severely handicapped, everyone serves and continues serving.

Zahal (the Israel Defense Forces) traces its origins to a time long before the creation of the modern Jewish State, but its contemporary importance transcends its main mission of defending the country from attack. A land of immigrants from varying backgrounds and cultures, Israel utilizes its armed forces to create a coherent, homogeneous nation out of a diversified citizenry. Recruits who never knew the Hebrew language emerge from Zahal three years later speaking, reading and writing Hebrew. Boys of Yemenite origin mix with youngsters whose parents emigrated from Poland. History is taught in tandem with the intricacies of firing a mortar accurately. Shy girls are transformed into capable women. Atheists bed down beside Yeshiva students. The army is a way of life for nearly every Israeli.

Training for the army begins before the army. Youngsters have their first taste of military life while they are still in high school. At the age of 18, males are mobilized to Zahal for a period of three years while most unmarried girls are drafted for a two-year period. Women, except when they are officers, are released from reserve duty as soon as they are mothers, but paternal considerations have no effect on the tenure of males—they generally serve an average of 45 days a year in the reserves until they reach age 55. After that, there is the home defense guard for male and female volunteers.

Because of its fundamentally civilian nature, Zahal is the most informal military apparatus in the world. Officers are called by their first names, saluting is unusual, and only the vaguest dichotomies exist throughout the ranks. It is an army whereby a professor serves under his student and a machinist orders the shop foreman, and where emergency mobilization is 110% because retired soldiers refuse to be retired. There is great pride in Zahal because it is the reflection of the best that Israel has to offer. Outwardly, Israel's soldiers don't look very spiffy—in fact, they appear downright sloppy at times. It would be a mistake to underestimate the potency of the force because of relaxed discipline.

The Israeli army is truly Israeli and not merely Jewish. The Druse and Circassian minorities are recruited (except for girls) just like their Jewish fellow citizens. A number of Bedouin tribes have volunteered for compulsory conscription and, while there are not many of them, Arabs can join Zahal if they so wish. As a matter of fact, a high percentage of the country's border police are Druse and the lingua franca among them is Arabic.

Country Versus City

Israel is that rare land where the country cousin thumbs his nose at his big-city relation whom he regards as misguided at the best and pathetic at the worst. With 229 settlements and only about 102,000 members, the country's kibbutzim provide Israel with a totally disproportionate number of ministers, members of Knesset, high-ranking army officers, pilots and paratroopers. They are the unquestioned élite and, believe me, it is not easy for an Israeli to admit that he is inferior to anyone—much less another Israeli.

Israel is comprised of three major forms of settlement. The overwhelming majority of people live in cities or suburban areas and most of this density will be found along the coastline—from Haifa in the north to Ashkelon in the south—and around Jerusalem. Tel Aviv and its satellite enclaves alone account for about half a million people. These city dwellers are an urban, sophisticated lot faced with the same ecologies as Parisians, Londoners and New Yorkers. Their streets are safer than most other places; they can commute with relative ease; supermarkets, cinemas and cafés abound. But they are also crowded quarters of the world. Free space is at a minimum. Cleanliness is not always what it should be. Saturday at the beach represents a struggle for a foothold of sand. City people are more constrained by their environment, less comfortable in the open spaces, more irritable and ulcer-prone than their agrarian counterparts.

Between the two spectra—city and kibbutz—lies the domain of the moshav. Unlike kibbutzim, where all is collectively owned and life is highly regimented, the 352 moshavim are an admixture of collective endeavour and private living. Homes and gardens belong to the individuals, although tracts are communally farmed and small industries are joint enterprises. The price of joining a kibbutz is community acceptance; a moshav usually requires some form of investment. Individual freedom on a kibbutz is secondary to the needs of the commune; moshavniks are fiercely protective of their private and family rights. While kibbutzniks form 3% of the population, moshavniks number 135,000, or 31% of Israel's population.

The kibbutz is a unique product of Israel and, if you will forgive the expression, it is the only type of voluntary communism which really worked. A person stays on a kibbutz because he or she wants to, not because he or she is compelled. In order to attract and keep members, kibbutzim maintain one of the country's highest living standards—replete with swimming pools, recreational facilities, libraries, concert halls, coffee shops, discotheques. Young married couples receive more spacious apartments than their veteran parents. Trips to Europe and America are organized on a rotation basis. On the other hand, however, the kibbutzniks do work hard and their freedom is strictly regulated by what is good and acceptable to the community.

Like everything else in the country, pragmaticism and a few dollops of idealism dictated the complexion and viability of the kibbutz enterprise. The first kibbutz was established at Degania, along the Sea of Galilee, in 1909, and kibbutzim have been proliferating through the country ever since. In those early and difficult days, the commune was the ideal settlement plan for the isolated Jewish communities—which were precariously struggling to survive in an alien and hostile environment. The kibbutz also expressed the political and social sentiments of a pioneering generation which had fled the oppressions of Tsarist Russia.

Today, unlike the moshavim which are still mainly agricultural, the kibbutzim are drifting more and more toward light industry, and even tourism, in order to find useful employment for a generation of oldsters who can no longer be employed in rigorous farming activities, yet who still thrive on the kibbutz ideal of each member doing his share.

So Israel provides a little of everything for everybody. You can be an idealistic member of a kibbutz, a private farmer, an urban sophisticate. Each reflects a difference in temperament and living standard. And together they form Israel.

The Oriental Flavor

The demographic map of Israel today shows that some 25% of the Jewish population of Israel was born either in Europe or the Americas; almost 20.4% was born in Asia and Africa (mainly Arab countries); and nearly 54.2% are Israel-born Sabras. Most illuminating is that only about one quarter of Israeli Jews were born in the Western countries, while the majority were born in Israel or other Middle Eastern lands— the Oriental Jews constitute more than half the local Jewish population.

Israel is paradoxical, enigmatic and often self-contradictory—and so when we state that this is a Jewish land we mean, in effect, that ours is a land with a Jewish majority. About 16% of the population, nearly 600,000, are non-Jews and they run a gamut to include Druse who have fought and bled for the country since its inception, to Maronite Christians, Bedouin nomads, flourishing Moslem communities that are a credit to the co-existence which has traditionally existed in the land. During the 1973 Yom Kippur War, Arabs donated their blood so that Jews could live, Greek Orthodox priests prayed for Middle Eastern peace, Circassians distinguished themselves on all fronts.

After some 30 years of steady evolution and change, Israel has become a nation which combines the traits of both east and west. Our local food is almost wholly Arab—keeping in mind that more than half our Jewish population originated in Arab countries. Arab students study in all our universities and when the first Bedouin doctor graduated from medical school, it was a moment of great Israeli rejoicing.

Even a modern-day Doctor Pangloss would have to admit that problems still exist, that integration is not complete and co-existence is not exactly a synonym for total national unity, but the direction is the right one and the signs are clear. In the meantime, the welding of east and west continues, two cultures are proclaiming a unique expression of their own, and distrust and suspicion are being eroded by daily contact. What is emerging is a proud, new country with a fervent desire for peace.

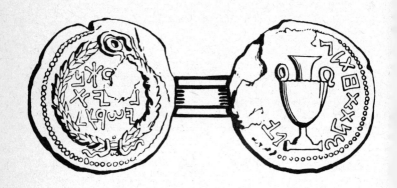

CREATIVE ISRAEL

A Blend of Cultures

by
DIANNE NICHOLSON LAWES

In Israel creativity is expressed as parts of many life styles—each struggling for at least a toe-hold in what may eventually evolve into a uniquely Israeli culture. So far, however, no such thing exists. Creative Israel stews in the mixed languages and symbolisms of the whole world. Immigrants and their offspring carry over childhood-learned tastes and techniques, adopting them to the exhumed language—Hebrew—then adapting them in tandem with daily security/economic stresses.

There is constant artistic stimulation when so much confronts and intermingles in the name of culture. And it becomes more and more difficult to define standards of local artistic achievement—especially since more than half today's population stems from Middle East culture patterns, and Israel's establishing Eastern European influence sways under the Oriental impact. Nevertheless, persistent furores of creative activity produce an interestingly wide range, which is matched only by the nation's enthusiastic response and appreciation. This could easily be called a nation of culture addicts.

Bible Basics and Official Encouragement

It's a mammoth task to mold a common culture from the diverse acquired preferences of Israel's people. The Bible has been the main answer. After all, Israel was "revived" as the Bible Land, and all its people share the great cultural heritage of the biblical Children of Israel—a treasure carefully guarded during ancient wars and long exiles. So, youngsters here are nursed on the Bible, studying it from the day they enter compulsory pre-kindergartens throughout school years. Every Independence Day, Israeli and foreign youth fiercely compete in the officially sponsored International Bible Contest.

Meanwhile, this youth-oriented nation does everything budgets allow to introduce young people to fundamentals of culture. Schools have free government-subsidized afternoon groups for music instruction, choir, drama, dance, ceramics, art, gymnastics and reading skills. The Ministry of Education and Culture also sponsors a professional traveling Children's Theatre, and many other grass-roots projects— often focusing on communities through the centres for adult culture and education maintained throughout the country.

Each municipality, regional council and local community also underwrites special cultural events and programs, even the labor unions do it. Israel Defense Forces participate, too—with bands, orchestras and touring entertainment units. IDF's radio station is quite popular, and some of the best TV musical productions are put together by, and star, IDF entertainment corps members.

The Kibbutz Movement gets into the act as well, by sponsoring events within kibbutzim, and by encouraging kibbutzniks' creative endeavours with lessons here and abroad, and allowing talented members regular work-free hours to devote to artistic expression. You can sample a bit of kibbutznik cultural fare via the Ichud Kibbutzim Choir, with tours here and overseas, and the Israel Chamber Orchestra—50 per cent of its members are kibbutzniks. And you can visit the Kibbutz Movement art gallery on Gordon Street, Tel Aviv.

It's really impossible to list all the privately funded cultural activities in Israel, but one organisation deserves special note: the Jerusalem Foundation. Rich with minority groups, Jerusalem has special cultural needs. Many of its residents have no traditions of participating in organized cultural events. So the Foundation, supported by world-wide philanthropists, and recruiting donated services of artists such as Frank Sinatra and Danny Kaye, provides a program that takes every school child to a theatrical performance, a concert, and the Israel Museum at least once a year. Plays have been chosen from the works of Shalom Aleichem, Egyptian playwright Tewfik El Hazin and others, and concerts have been given by the Jerusalem Chamber Ensemble and various Arabic musical companies. Theatrical entertainments prepared by Arab youth groups for East Jerusalem have been sponsored, and Kurds, Armenians, Moroccans and others each have had week-long cultural activities and exhibitions. The Foundation also supports a program for Jewish/Arab youth in the Israel Museum. Then, with the Jerusalem Municipality, the Foundation helps organize an annual festival for a month each spring, featuring music, dance and drama by Israeli and international artists.

Local demand for subsidized arts programs gives the impression that Israelis are eager to enrich their own cultural preferences by absorbing as much as they can of everyone else's. What makes the real situation so exciting is that each group also retains its own communal traditions, and celebrations offer visitors the best opportunities for sharing in these unique activities. Check *Special Events* in *Facts at Your Fingertips,* and try to arrange your trip to coincide with some special event.

Television and Radio

Most local feasts and fasts are featured on non-commercial, government-owned Israel Television, Jerusalem. Originally an education channel, its first telecast was the 20th Anniversary Independence Day Parade in Jerusalem, 1968. Today, its annual Christmas Eve Bethlehem broadcast is seen live here and abroad—thanks to satellite linkage that began in 1973, when daily war coverage brought Israel Television world praise.

The single-channel, black/white broadcasts divide programming into Hebrew and Arabic, with half the schedule still reserved for educational purposes. Then come kiddie shows, followed by news, discussion and game shows, documentaries, sports magazines, American and European shows, and films from just about everywhere. Many Israelis install special antennae to receive Jordan Television, which offers English news (Arab-style), color telecasts and more English-language thrillers and dramas.

On radio, *Kol Yisrael* (Voice of Israel) provides tourists with a means for sampling Israel's cultural make-up. Five regularly scheduled programs (stations) include broadcasts in Russian, Romanian, Georgian, Persian, French, Hungarian, Yiddish, Ladino and Moghrabi. Lively batches of music, interviews, and "how to" shows keep Israelis tuned-in all day, but hourly news rivets their attention. Twice daily you can join this local custom, when English news is aired. Or you can sample FM stations with light and classical music, the Israel Arabic Station, IDF's station, broadcasts from surrounding countries and from the BBC, Voice of America, etc. Another popular station is Abie Nathan's Voice of Peace, transmitted round-the-clock to Israel and Arab lands from his ship in the Mediterranean, featuring "peace talk shows" (mostly in English), contemporary music, USA-style disc jockeys.

Music

It's everywhere, a big part of life, and all its forms are available and appreciated. Youngsters love pop, and Israeli rock groups often are rightfully accused of imitating British/American trends. But the sounds are good—good enough to win first place in the 1978 and 1979 Eurovision Song Contests! One group—Lakat Kiveret—distinctly blends Israeli folk sounds, Oriental themes and rock beat, and created a rock opera *Siporray Poogy* (Poogy Tales).

In contrast, fine sacred music is regularly presented in several places; a popular Country-Western/Mountain group (USA immigrants) twangs and sings in Hebrew; and first-class jazz groups appear in Tel Aviv's Tzavta Club, Jerusalem's Khan, and other places. Dizzy Gillespie sat in at the Tel Aviv Barbarim Students Club (near Rehov Hamasger) when visiting Israel, and other musicians found here have played around the world.

Yet it's only fair to admit that classical music dominates the scene, with every town and village sporting groups, ensembles and orchestras. Its popularity permeates all age-income-origin levels. *Note:* Israel holds the world *per capita* record for season subscription to a philharmonic orchestra: the Israel Philharmonic Orchestra. Travelling the land, IPO presents some 230 concerts annually, attended by about 60,000 people; by popular demand it's played army posts from Sinai to Quneitra, following Israel's five military campaigns.

Arturo Toscanini conducted its inaugural concert, but IPO was founded in 1936 by Bronislaw Huberman. Today, its home is Tel Aviv's 2,700-seat Mann Auditorium, and more than half its members were born and trained here. IPO makes annual world tours. IPO's musical adviser since 1968 has been Zubin Mehta—appointed Musical Director of the New York Philharmonic in 1976. Impressed by the young people's IPO support, Mehta initiated three programs, with "talk-ins" afterwards: Music Viva series of pre-baroque, contemporary and avant-garde music; IPO concerts at universities, and the Youth Concert series. Music marathons, another hit with young Israelis, are the brainchild of Lukas Foss—chief conductor and musical director of the Jerusalem Symphony Orchestra. These events present hour after hour of non-stop music by a single composer.

Hundreds of other orchestras and classical groups exist, and special mention is due to the active Haifa Symphony Orchestra, and the chamber orchestras of Holon, Beersheba, Ramat Gan and Natanya. Their performances, as well as those of IPO and JSO, are well worth a tourist's time.

Isaac Stern is very involved in Israeli musical life, and his project is to continue bringing international musicians to Jerusalem's *Mishkenot Shena'anim* centre, where they work with Israelis. Pablo Casals helped launch this center, which has welcomed a long list of top musicians. Outstanding among hundreds of other music centers, here, the Targ Center in Ein Karem, outside Jerusalem, features "Meet the Artist" orchestral series twice monthly, and slates frequent workshops giving young musicians a chance to work with masters.

Jewish Soul Music, based on Hasidic melodies and offered up by IPO clarinetist Giora Feidman, has gained a large following, while Uri Segal and Moshe Atzman are earning excellent reputations here and abroad as guest conductors, and IPO's Mordechai Rechtman is called "one of the finest bassoonists of modern times" by Zubin Mehta.

Israeli composers are active, too, with a 700-member association and works that run the gamut of styles. *Masada* and *Ashmedi* are operas by Joseph Tel (b. 1910); *Ein Gev* is by Odeon Partos (b. 1907); the Song of Songs oratorio is by Mark Lavry (1903–67), and *Jerusalem* by M. Seter.

Frequently performed here, Israeli composers' operas are sometimes included in the season of the National Opera, founded in 1947 by Edis de Phillipe. Based in Tel Aviv, it presents a wide range of operatic works, and recently added lighter repertory productions (*Showboat, Merry Widow, Die Fledermaus,* etc.).

So much activity inspires many musical events. The Israel Festival of Music and Drama is the largest and most lauded. Founded in 1961, it encompasses the annual Ein Gev Festival (at Kibbutz Ein Gev on Galilee's shore), which features foreign and local dance and musical artists. The Israeli Festival of Music and Dance flourishes each July/August in Jerusalem, Tel Aviv and Caesarea, presenting superb theater, dance and music by Israelis and overseas groups (such as the Royal Ballet, Greek Art Theater, the Amadeus Quartet, etc.). Jerusalem is also the site of Sacred Music Week each December; the annual Jerusalem Festival, and the Zimriya: International Assembly of Choirs in Israel, which also holds concerts in other key cities. In nearby Bethlehem, there is an annual tradition for choirs from all over the world to assemble and sing, during the Yule season and particularly on

Christmas Eve. Each spring, the Arthur Rubinstein International Piano Masters Competition holds forth in Tel Aviv. In late summer, look for Haifa's International Folklore Festival.

Dance

When foreigners think about dance in Israel, they possibly visualize kibbutzniks cavorting across productive fields, singing and dancing the *hora* (native folkdance). Though kibbutzniks do dance a lot, the vision is less than accurate. All Israelis dance a lot, whenever there's reason or excuse. However, the hodge-podge effect holds true, for they dance in most conceivable fashions, including the ever-popular Western forms. Every municipality and settlement has a folkdance group and several holidays inspire street-dancing. Children study folkdancing in school, and some have outside lessons in ballet, ethnic or modern dance. Kibbutz dining halls often become dance halls on Saturday nights, about the same time that urbanites amass at popular discos or hotels with dance bands. Those bands, by the way, usually have members from assorted backgrounds, and must be able to switch easily from pop or waltzes to polkas, rock or Oriental rhythms to meet the dancers' demands.

Of professional dance companies, Inbal is unique in the world—presenting traditional dances of Yemenite Jews. Founded in 1949, and always enlarging its repertoire, it draws from biblical and Oriental themes and collects rave reviews here and overseas.

Modern dance performances are always packed with young Israelis, some being hard-core devotees who later discuss the relative merits of artists and companies. The three leading groups include Batsheva Company, which had America's Martha Graham as artistic director when it was founded in 1964, and the Bat Dor Company. Both perform works by local and international choreographers, touring Israel and abroad. Efrati Dance Theater, circa 1973, was formed by dancer/choreographer Moshe Efrati, who's also famous for teaching mime to deaf mutes.

Frankly, classical ballet hasn't found its feet in Israel, but local fans insist Valery and Galina Panov could provide the base of a company that would gain huge support. Meanwhile, classes exist here and there, and there's heavy attendance when foreign companies stage annual productions (the Royal Ballet, Merce Cunningham Company, Stuttgart Ballet, etc.).

Theater and Film

Israel's National Theatre, Habimah, began as a studio in Stanislavski's Moscow Art Theatre in 1918. The "method" master taught and supported the young company and assigned his protegé Vakhtangov to direct its players in *The Dybbuk*—a landmark in theater history. Today, Habimah no longer adheres strictly to "method," but still reveres its Moscow studio founding. Next in prestige is Cameri, Tel Aviv's Municipal Theater, founded in 1944. Several younger companies—all government-subsidized—include the Haifa Theater and Jerusalem's Khan Company (most members under 35).

Most of these groups present a mixed fare of well-known classics by Shakespeare, Molière and Chekov, plus assorted contemporary plays by Eugène Ionesco, Arthur Miller and Neil Simon, generally emphasizing international works; The Haifa Theater seams to be the only one stressing plays dealing with current Israeli reality. Local playwrights do exist, however. (Ironically, Israel Eliraz's plays—staged successfully in London, New York, Paris and Brussels—haven't found much support here. Eliraz also wrote the libretti of three Joseph Tel operas—the operas were acclaimed for both music and text in Hamburg, New York and Munich, but caused no clamor at home.) Tel Aviv is usually full of sure-hit Israeli comedies, almost always privately produced, and Israelis enjoy frequent touring companies from abroad. Experimental, avantgarde works are rarely attempted locally, except occasionally by Tel Aviv's Tzvata Club or Jerusalem's Khan—which together constitute Israel's closest kin to New York's Off Broadway or London's fringe theaters. Though *Hair* and a few other shows have featured un-costumed casts here, nude theater's never caught on in Israel; neither have period plays.

For an evening of Israeli theater, try Shakespeare in Hebrew, or a production of Israel's hottest new playwright. If you're after more international flavor, look for overseas theater groups visiting Israel about once a year—Britain's Royal Shakespeare Company—you name it. Just be sure to book advance tickets.

Israelis are film freaks! Until 1968—when local TV was introduced —they were the biggest filmgoers, *per capita,* in the world, averaging a minimum of 23 annual trips to the cinema. They still rank among the world's top movie fans, and clamor to ticket agents to buy advance tickets for Saturday night flicks. Many cinemas screen three daily shows of international and local films (fear not, all Hebrew films are subtitled in English and French). When drive-in cinema arrived in Tel Aviv, it gave Israelis a chance to combine at least two passions: automobiles and movies. And relatively new Cinematheque (Jerusalem,

Tel Aviv, Haifa) was the first of the film clubs designed to cater to Israelis' hunger for classics and avant-garde movies.

Since 1970, Israel has established itself as a base for foreign and local film production. Directors Otto Preminger, Norman Jewison and Michael Cacyoannis are among those who have been impressed by the land's many location possibilities and technical facilities. Israel has its own Film Festival, and participates in the annual Cannes and Berlin Festivals, plus the Vienna Biennale. Locally produced *Sallah Shabbati* and *The Policeman* both won the Golden Award; *The House on Chelouche Street* was nominated for a 1974 Academy Award. Israel's Public Arts Council awards prizes annually to three original film scripts, funds a "Cinema for Youth" project which screens quality films for teenagers and runs workshops for young people interested in film making. Israeli universities go further, offering academic courses in film.

The Printed Page

Israel ranks as one of the world's top two nations in publishing, according to the number of different book titles printed annually compared with population figures. Each spring brings National Book Week —sponsored by the 100-member Book Publishers Association—which sets up stalls in every small community and big city, so thousands of Israelis can browse through and purchase new books. Old books are popular (and cheaper) too, with growing numbers of used-book shops as witness. Every two years, the Jerusalem International Book Fair attracts some 100,000 locals, plus some 750 international publishers. At one opening ceremony, Israel's only literary award is presented— the Jerusalem Prize; recipients have included Simone de Beauvoir, Eugène Ionesco and Jorge Luis Borges.

Israelis are addicted to dailies and periodicals—local ones and imports—so newsstands and bookshops obligingly pack reading matter in most tongues. Of Israel's 23 daily local newspapers, 11 are published in Hebrew and the rest in Arabic to Russian, French, Bulgarian, you-name-it. The English-language daily, *The Jerusalem Post*, is a great source for local happenings—especially its weekend edition's pull-out page, "The Poster." Look also for free small weeklies in hotels and tourist spots, listing accommodations, tours, restaurants, shopping, sights, sites and special events.

Art

A picture doesn't have to be on film to grab an Israeli's attention— he'll look and actively comment if it's a photograph or painting, and he's equally vocal about sculpture. There's at least one gallery (or community center doubling as one) in every town or settlement, and studios and workshops are all over the land. Israelis habitually browse through exhibitions, critiquing and even buying. With good art in demand, sellers offer choices at prices everyone can afford, and practically every Israeli home has original works of art. Recently it's become a vogue for wealthier ladies to sponsor one-man shows in their own homes, inviting friends and helping new artists become better established.

Tourists seeking local art buys often flock to easily spotted mainstreet galleries; to Artists' Houses in Tel Aviv, Jerusalem and Haifa; and to art colonies of Old Jaffa, Ein Hod and Safad. There they find works of well-known Israeli artists (Reuven Rubin, Nachum Gutman, Jacob Steinhardt, Absalom Okashi, Yehezkel Streichman, Avigdor Stematzky, Marcel Janco, Igal Tomarkin, Yaakov Agam, Menashe Kadishman, etc.), as well as works of younger Israelis (Michael Kovner, David Sharir, etc.). Many of these artists have been or are affiliated with Israel's two noted art schools: Bezalel Academy, founded in 1906 by artist Boris Schatz, and the Avi Institute, founded in 1936.

For museum viewing of local and international art, the Israel Museum in Jerusalem and the Tel Aviv Museum have the largest collections plus interesting traveling exhibitions.

Don't miss—Music: a performance by Mikhail Maisky, cellist; a concert conducted by Moshe Atzman, Uri Segal. Theater: any performance in the theater of your choice. Festivals: Israel Festival of Music and Drama, any production, especially at Caesarea's Roman amphitheater. Film: Uri Zohar's work—run! Dan Wolan's—go. TV: ask your hotel clerk if and when a local comedy or satirical show, like *Nikui Rosh* is on—even without understanding Hebrew, you'll enjoy it. Local musical productions also are well worth your time. (Both TV and radio programs are listed in the English-language *Jerusalem Post*.) Radio: Voice of Peace. Museums: Shrine of the Book and the rest of Israel Museum. Jerusalem; Hatzor Museum; Kibbutz Ayelet Hashachar. Crafts: craft fairs held all over Israel, spring and summer. Artisans bring handiwork ranging from macramé and enameling on copper to ancient skills in jewelry, pottery, unique items (ask government tourist offices or municipal information offices for dates and locations).

Note: tickets for all events, even films, can frequently be purchased in advance from ticket agencies. Don't count on being able to buy seats at box offices immediately before a show. Some special-event tickets are available through hotels or tourist offices.

EATING YOUR WAY ROUND
ISRAEL

Melting-Pot Cookery

by
JERILYN ROGIN and ROGER COSTER JR.

Ms. Rogin has edited Hello Israel, *an Israeli weekly in English for tourists, and has been on the editorial staff of* Israel Magazine. *The Chicago-born ex-New Yorker's work has appeared in assorted international publications. Roger Coster Jr., one of Israel's best-known food experts, is one of the youngest members of* Chaine de Rôtisseurs *international gourmet society. Son of a famous hotelier, and formerly from Haiti, Coster is also a hotelier with flair.*

In Israel, you can take a virtual gastronomic tour of the world by venturing out of your hotel. Israel's melting-pot—of people, that is, not food—blends an assortment of immigrants from more than seventy different countries and offers the greatest variety of authentic ethnic cuisines found anywhere in the world. At least that's what the international gourmet societies claim when they convene here just for this reason.

In recent years, Israel has earned its place in the world of food—indicated by the fact that the Israeli chapter of the *Chaine de Rôtisseurs* boasts six hundred members. Newspapers' gastronomy columns are widely read and followed, and prominent chefs have been known to tear their hair following unflattering reviews by one of the well-known food critics. However, as a country still in formation, Israel cannot yet present an unique national cuisine. Instead, you'll find a diverse array of dishes including Hungarian goulash, Italian pasta, Moroccan couscous, Chinese eggroll, Indian curry, Mexican tacos, Indonesian rijsttafel, French pâtés, and even American fried chicken or apple pie. Restaurants with such specialized cookery abound, as well as eating places offering the Jewish-style fare imported by each ethnic community.

The picture of the Israeli happily munching a felafel on the corner has become as obsolete as the *kova tembel* (the kibbutznik's dunce cap) which can be seen only on the heads of enthusiastic visitors or the local village nut. Today's Israeli travels overseas a great deal and has developed a definite feel for the finer things in life. Food has become not only a necessity, but an integral part of Israeli entertainment. Just take a stroll down major streets in any city—the restaurants are packed. Among the eateries favored by Israelis, it's difficult to find a bad one. The Israeli public has discriminating tastes and a poor restaurant simply will not survive, while good ones are highly successful commercial ventures.

Kosher-izing and Food for the Masses

Israel as the gourmet's delight may be an astounding notion to certain visitors, since some critics have labeled this land a gastronomic desert. This undeserved reputation may stem from common misconceptions concerning *kashrut* (often called *kosher*)—the biblical dietary laws. The Hebrew term simply means "fit and proper," though it's difficult to imagine why non-cud-chewing, smooth-hoofed beasties are so cruelly excluded from legitimacy.

While total separation of meat and dairy products and the taboo on eating the flesh of the pig may horrify some gourmets, others see certain advantages to kosher practices. Look at it this way: you'll never find a sadist kosher butcher, since animals are killed swiftly to cause minimum suffering; vampires disdain kosher meats since all traces of blood must vanish; and who wants to eat scavenger animals, grasshoppers, frogs or camels anyway? Remember that kosher is *not* a particular way of cooking or spicing, nor necessarily a limitation on taste, and you'll be ready to confront its existence with a minimum of apprehension and prejudice.

Critics may also be judging Israel's food by the fare the national airline or the hotels offer. Some even go so far as to say that this food isn't mouth-wateringly scrumptious simply because it's kosher. It's true that the Israeli airlines and all accredited local hotels are kosher, but we've already learned that this is no taste inhibitor. What *is* limiting is catering to the masses. Airline and hotel food is more or less standard the world over, and can never provide the treat to your tastebuds that small establishments can. El Al Israel Airlines, known as the world's safest carrier, will provide you with plenty of food. The cuisine is varied and tries to reflect what's often labeled "Jewish," but it is hardly a true introduction to local eating delights. If you fly from the USA you may be treated to your last bite of bagels and lox until you return home—Israel is almost totally void of this traditional American Jewish delicacy.

Israel's hotel dining rooms are sometimes not up to international standard because of inadequate food training among executives and general budget squeezes. However, many have succeeded in creating a distinctive cuisine. If your hotel has a specialty or grill room, by all means try it.

Wherever you stay, we hope your first meal will be breakfast. A veritable festival of colors and tastes awaits you: different cheeses—some spiced with paprika or vegetables; pimentoes, olives, fresh tomatoes and cucumbers, a grand assortment of fishes and some of the best herring you'll taste anywhere. Enjoy the marvellous sour milk called *leben* and the tempting yoghurts that are plain or fruity and always free of commercial preservatives. Add citrus fruits and juices, eggs, fresh bread and rolls and you're ready to start the day. Visitors are often stupefied by this Israeli eating orgy which has its origins in the kibbutz, where members wake early and work in the fields five or six hours before resting and eating again. On a hot summer day, our advice is to skip lunch after filling up on this earthy Israeli breakfast.

Anywhere in Israel

It's said that eating habits are the most representative national characteristic. Just a glance at the cuisine diversity in Israel reflects the international population. The gargantuan hotel breakfast is a throwback to the country's agricultural origins—but it's not totally misleading, because the farmers and kibbutzniks still eat this way, though modern city dwellers have generally opted for a quick morning cup of coffee or tea, accompanied by a buttered or jam-smeared slice of bread. British (Mandate) traditions have also left their mark since many Israelis' main meal of the day falls somewhere between America's midday lunch hour and England's 4–5 P.M. tea time. Most Israelis, unless they decide to spend the evening in a favorite restaurant, prefer a light dairy meal for dinner, similar to the hotel breakfasts though considerably less ceremonious.

Israelis *are* inveterate street munchers, and the streets are lined with stalls selling snacks and fast foods. Aside from the all-time popularity of roasted nuts and seeds, the "favorite" snack continually changes—proving Israelis' adventurous attitude toward eating. Traditional best-loved treats are *felafel* and *shwarma*. Felafel is like a sandwich made from balls of deep-fried ground chick peas plus chopped salad and pickles, with a dollop of *tchina* sauce (ground sesame seeds with oil and parsley) and an optional dollop of super-hot sauce, all inside a round and hollow Arab bread called *pitta*. Shwarma is very similar, if you substitute the ground chick peas with grilled lamb and/or turkey slices. Both are available in every town and city, but many mourn the fact that such traditional fare is slowly being replaced by the more continental pizza slices. There's even a small Jerusalem chain offering pizza without cheese and with sliced apples, onions, potatoes or other fruits and vegetables. Potato pancakes and French pancakes are easy to find in small street eateries; bourekas, sweet rolls and donuts; hotdogs in dinner rolls, hamburgers in buns or pittas, roasted chestnuts in bags, corn-on-the-cob, pop-corn, ice cream, candies and coconut bits, Middle-Eastern gooey pastries, breads and pretzels, steak in pitta, watermelon slices, sabras (the cactus fruit that gave the Israeli-born his name—sweet insides and a tough, prickly covering) and . . . and . . . and almost anything else you can imagine!

This grab-a-quick-bite eating is convenient for those who fancy spending a busy day touring on foot, with no time for relaxing in restaurants.

By the way, you'll come across *Oriental* eating places all over the country. Banish from your mind all associations with the Far East, and prepare for Middle-Eastern and Arabic fare—which includes Moroccan, Iraqi, Yemenite, North African and (believe it!) even Bulgarian, Greek and Turkish.

We have compiled an *Eating Your Way Around Israel* tour which appears later in this chapter. We hope that it will give you some pointers as to where the more interesting places for exploration are.

The Picnic

Maybe your tour schedule keeps you away from cities and towns for a day or more . . . perhaps you yearn for mountain-top solitude . . . possibly you're renting a boat for a day of Mediterranean sailing, or a car for ambling around on your own—grab any excuse, but picnic while you're here!

What you pack reveals your character, as well as your pocket-book. The splurging outdoor eater who wants elegance and sophistication will select a fine wine for starters—being sure to pack wine glasses, not plastic cups. Next, a series of pâtés and salads with bread sticks. The main course will perhaps be bite-size slivers of meat in a savoury sauce, a roast leg of lamb, or a baked fish, and dessert will include fruits and cheeses, chocolates and nuts. For this type of practical meal, merely order from a restaurant. Be prepared to buy and bring your own containers, plates, cutlery and the likes (though some fine restaurants have containers for sending orders to homes), and bring along a basket. Finesse is achieved by remembering the cloth, napkins, loaf bread, bottle opener, condiments and pre-moisturized towels.

Less luxury-minded picnickers may buy a ready-roasted whole or half chicken, a loaf of bread, raw vegetables such as carrots, peppers, cucumbers and tomatoes, with fruit and bottled lemonade, and pack all into a tote with plastic cups and eating equipment, and a large towel for spreading on the grass or sand.

Budget (and hurried) picnickers will pick up items from kiosks or streetside shops: a cheese sandwich, pita with meat or felafel, fried chicken or a hamburger. You might add a piece or two of fruit, a pastry or candy, and borrow enough napkins from the shop to wrap everything before stuffing the lot into a knapsack or shopping bag. You can always rely on water fountains or refreshment stands for drinks, and the special scenery selected for your picnic will always bring an enriched savor to the foodstuff.

Armed with an empty basket, you may want to try shopping around seeking out delicacies like *pâté de foie* and *quiche Lorraine* which are prepared in aluminum foil containers and guaranteed to stay fresh for six hours. All over Tel Aviv you'll find small delicatessens where delicious pastrami sandwiches can be packed up ready to travel.

Dieting picnic buffs will happily find fresh fruits all year in Israel, as well as a large selection of diet-conscious dairy products and flat breads or matzo thins. Add sliced carrots or a small portion of slaw from a store, and drink the water—it's safe as well as free, easy on the pocket-book and the waistline.

A trip through Israel's supermarkets, outdoor markets and specialty food or beverage shops will give you many ideas of your own for packed meals to be eaten under the sun or stars. Most large food stores—including those in department stores like Shalom Tower, Tel Aviv—have everything for wrapping or carrying any type of food or drink, even real plates, glassware and such for the finicky. And hotels, like Beersheba's Desert Inn, will pack a lunch for you, too; the staff will even direct you to archeological sites not far away, where you can munch, perhaps, in the ruins of an ancient state dining hall.

Israel's Basic Foods

Surprising as it may seem, mostly-desert Israel has gone a long way in providing its own food requirements plus large quantities for export. Remarkably delicious and tasty, the country's *fresh fruits* and *vegetables* delight the Israeli as well as most Europeans, all year round. "A land of wheat and barley and wines and fig-trees and pomegranates, a land of olive-oil and honey," says the Bible. Well, there's more. From the sub-tropical papayas and mangoes to peaches, apples, grapes and citrus, Israel's present-day agricultural produce is as varied as its geography. Bananas, avocadoes, guavas, tomatoes, onions, green peppers, groundnuts, sugarbeets—the mind-dazzling list goes on and on. Export of fruits and vegetables has become such a successful money-maker for Israel that the government has decided to create a special air-freight company solely for this purpose.

Fish lovers visiting the country can feast on the numerous species gathered from three of Israel's bordering seas, the Galilee, Mediterranean and Red. (No, Virginia, there are no fish in the Dead Sea!)

Though St. Peter's Fish is available throughout the country, Tiberias is the traditional site for eating this member of the perch family, as it is unique to Lake Kinneret (Sea of Galilee). Supposedly, it is the very fish Peter was gathering when Jesus summoned him away from his nets to become a "fisher of men." Tasting it is an experience not to be missed.

Visitors often ask why Israeli restaurants offer so little *shell-fish* like crab, shrimp and lobster. Although the kosher question comes into play here since such sea delights are forbidden by Jewish law, the main consideration seems to be pragmatic. Tnuva, the country's major food marketing agency, finds being Israel's principal shrimp exporter more financially worthwhile than selling shrimp locally. But don't despair. You'll be able to enjoy delicious scampi, lobster and other sea foods that are supplied to excellent restaurants all over the country by the other fishing outfits, including Arab fishermen of Gaza.

"White" Steak and the Noble Duck

Meat is, unfortunately, not one of Israel's strong points. It is mostly imported as a government monopoly according to the standards of kashrut. Local-slaughter beef is extremely limited, and, while fairly good steaks can be found here, the visitor shouldn't expect too much. But the local mutton is excellent and is best sampled in Oriental restaurants. Pork, contrary to many Jewish tourists' expectations, is openly sold in most restaurants around the country and has become a very popular substitute for good beef (just ask for "white" steak to get pork).

Local *poultry* is plentiful and tasty. Though the chicken may lack the special flavour of the little home-grown variety of southern France, it tastes very much like its brothers in America and England. When ordering Viennese schnitzel, be forewarned—turkey is most often used as a substitute for veal. One of Jerusalem's finest restaurants, *Alla Gondola,* has been serving Italian scallops made with turkey meat for years, and almost no one has been able to tell the difference. Most of France's *foie gras* originates with the Israeli goose. And duck has earned the respect due this noble bird in the country's fine French restaurants. Dove is mostly found in the Arab restaurants, and keep an eye out for menus offering partridge—both are rare treats.

Bagele and Baklava

Bread in Israel is an experience unto itself. You may begin with our special favorites, the *bagele* and *pitta*. The bagele is a big "O"-shaped seeded bread—distant cousin to American bagel, but lighter and yeastier. Sold on the street as well as in stores, it's best sampled in Arab sections, where you'll be offered an accompanying mysterious greenish spice, wrapped in a scrap of newspaper. Sprinkle the spice on top or inside, or merely dunk the bread into it, and take a delectable bite.

The round, hollow and flat Arab pitta bread is omnipresent in this country and is used to sop up Oriental salads and provide a delicious chewy home for sandwich fillings. The most scrumptious version of pitta is sold in Old Jaffa near the clock. Open bakeries with huge ancient ovens produce a special spiced, seeded and olive-oiled round. Warm and taste-teasing, it's a delight (find it in Jaffa, Jerusalem, etc.).

A visit to any supermarket bread section reveals all sizes and shapes of white, whole wheat, black, and traditional Jewish *challah* breads. Though Israel isn't the land of the white sliced-and-packaged loaf, you can find this here, too—provided especially for deprived foreigners who don't know any better. Take your pick. A visitor to Israel who doesn't buy a loaf of bread is truly cheating himself!

Nothing can describe the Israeli selection of *cakes* and *pastries* available in the numerous bakeries, cafés and conditoria. Try favorite international goodies at places like *La Javanaise* in Tel Aviv and Jerusalem, or savor exotic Oriental gooeys like *baklava* and *katayiff,* that usually crunch with nuts and sesame seeds and drip with honey. It all makes Israel a calorie-counter's nightmare.

Cheese and Pickles

Israelis are great dairy product consumers, and *cheeses* here run the gamut from hard to creamy. You'll want to sample the Israeli-style cheddar, Swiss, blue, camembert, parmesan, and a yellow cheese erroneously named "American taste." Try the tasty spreadables, spiced or with vegetable bits—great for crackers or tea sandwiches. Especially popular is the local creamed cottage cheese and a semi-soft white cheese made of cow's or goat's milk—very similar to Greek feta. Imported European types like edam and roquefort are available, though you'll have to squelch that craving for real cheddar until you return home to your own shores.

Pickles are an Israeli specialty. A trip to the market will reveal a dazzling array. Floating in those big spice vats, you'll discover eggplants, carrots, tomatoes, and onions along with the conventional cucumber. You'll also find here a delicious choice of green and black *olives* with Oriental tastes, very different from the American varieties. Pickles and olives dress the tables of most restaurants in Israel, especially the Middle-Eastern ones.

Thirst-Quenchers

If you've planned your visit for the summer months, you'll be seeking out the local *thirst-quenchers.* Bottled fruit juices and carbonated *Tempo* are popular soft drinks, though American *Coca-Cola* and British *Schweppes* have all but captured the Israeli market. Also popular is soda and fruit squash. Water is drinkable all over, though purists who favor it bottled can find that, too. We recommend dropping by one of the many juice stands where you can revel in fresh-squeezed orange, grapefruit, apple, and especially carrot juices in season.

If you're yearning for a taste of the *spirits,* you won't be disappointed if you choose one of the many excellent export-quality brands available in the country.

Israeli wines range from the very sweet types favored abroad, to the dry table wines that have recently attracted popular interest. Outstanding in the dry red class are *Adom Atik* and *Cabernet Sauvignon,* both produced by the Carmel Oriental winery. A distinctive dry white wine is *Hamarteff Winecellar's Semillon,* and the most pleasing rosé is the *Rosé Grenache* manufactured by Askelon Wines. New on the market is a sweet red, called *Masada,* bottled in an earthenware jug.

The distinction between kosher and non-kosher also exists among wines, since only wine that has been grown in accord with the biblical precepts for agriculture and has been prepared by the hands of an observant Jew is considered "fit and proper." Two non-kosher wine-cellars thrive in the country, Latrun and Cremisan, operated by the Trappist monks outside Jerusalem and the monks of Bethlehem.

Among the Israeli liqueurs, unusual and distinctive is *Hard Nut,* a walnut concoction of Eliaz winery—one of the few producers of this kind of liqueur in the world. You may have tasted the well-known chocolate and orange *Sabra,* produced by International Distillers of Israel. Yekev Hagalil wine-cellars specialize in the local aniseed-flavored aperitif, *Arak*—close relative of both French pernod and Greek ouzo.

The best brandy is *Stock's Brandy '84,* made by the same company that produces *Keglevich,* an excellent vodka. Good local vermouth and gin are also available, though imported liquors and liqueurs are readily accessible here.

On a hot day, when a refreshing glass of cold beer would just hit the spot, try the Israeli *Maccabee, O.K.,* or *Gold Star.*

Israeli *coffee* has many faces—choose between the thick and sweet Turkish coffee served in tiny demitasse cups (with *hehl*—cardamom—an Arabic treat!), espresso, or a close approximation of *café au lait.* The local instant coffee is very good, though some tourists prefer to tote along their familiar back-home brands in individual packets. By the way, there's nothing like sipping a cup of tea laced with mint leaves in an Oriental restaurant.

Bon appetit and cheers! Or, as it's said in Israel: *B'tay-ah-von* and *l'chayeem!*

EATING YOUR WAY ROUND ISRAEL

JERUSALEM, the once-quiet little capital city, has become a bustling center reuniting East and West sectors whose blended cuisines now give Jerusalem, apart from its unique historical character, a very special variety of foods and restaurants. Israelis poured into the Old City after the 1967 reunification—especially on Sabbaths and holidays when Jewish places shut tight—but Arab shops, restaurants and nightclubs hopped with life.

A number of joint business ventures between Jews and Arabs have come about in the last decade, and one of the most successful is **Dolphin**—often labeled Israel's "best fish restaurant." Don't try to reserve a table in advance, but do come early; it's worth the wait. Tourists may object to the chef's intricate cooking preparations and prefer fish *au naturel, meunière,* or with lemon. However, if you're ready to wait and experiment, try fish with orange sauce and fruits, in unctuous cream of mushroom, pungent curry sauce, or *à la bordelaise* with red (yes, red) wine. Start your meal with assorted Middle Eastern salads, or cold squid salad in tomato sauce. You must try the Dolphin!

Down the road from Dolphin, in Ali Baba and the Forty Thieves decor, is **Hassan Effendi**, an Arab/Oriental restaurant where meals are served on large copper trays and include abundant if not always consistent fare. Try the *maskin* —a quarter of a chicken roasted with baby onions, placed on a large Arab pitta bread and re-covered with onions. Also try chicken roasted with pine nuts, and this is *the* place to ask for dove dishes.

At the Jaffa Gate entrance to the Old City is the **Citadel,** a popular and cheap restaurant with excellent Oriental entrées and very good grilled meals like the skewer-broiled *kebab*—chopped and spiced lamb, and *shishlik*—pieces of lamb or beef flavoured with onions and tomatoes. (No, Virginia, there is *not* a food called "shish-kebab"!)

There's little doubt that Jerusalem's most noted restaurants are **Mishkenot Sha'ananim** and **Gruzia.** International critics have said that Mishkenot Sha'ananim has "the world's best" French food (despite its being strictly kosher). The atmosphere itself is unique, for this restaurant takes its name from its location in Mishkenot Sha'ananim, the renovated 19th-century Yemin Moshe quarter now housing guest artists and celebrities. The same kind of clientele favours the Gruzia, which specializes in the cuisine of Russian Georgia. We won't describe the intricacies of this cookery, but add it to the "must try" list.

An institution on Hillel St. of West Jerusalem, called **Taami** ("my taste"), is a six-table eatery with a most autocratic and dictatorial owner. You can't enjoy a relaxed meal here, but you can eat "the best *houmos* in the country." Sit down and it's promptly rushed to you. Eat as fast as you can, pay, and beat it. The culinary experience will have you dazed, as will the subtlety and fresh taste of hoummous. Some addicts have been known to order three or four plates of the stuff just for the privilege of sitting and enjoying their meal slowly and quietly. Hoummous, for the uninitiated, is a delicious ever-popular mixture of ground chick peas, spices, lemon juice and olive oil, which you scoop into your mouth via pieces of Arab pitta bread. It's generally served with olives, pickles and peppers. And watch out for those innocent-looking green peppers—they're fiery hot!

A note on the "Chinese Revolution" that has occurred in Israel: this land may not have diplomatic relations with China, but their food—if not their thinking—is rapidly conquering local palates. The trend began in Jerusalem many years ago and now Israelis will drive in from all over to eat Chinese food.

Jerusalem has always had character restaurants. **Fink's** is not only good, but fun, too—with superb goulash. **My Bar** is an old favorite (though not what it used to be) of diplomats and UN personnel, and just the place for late, late snacks like egg and bacon at 1 A.M.

On the outskirts of Jerusalem, in **EIN KEREM,** you'll find the Hungarian restaurant, **Goulash Inn**—an outrageous and marvelous experience in food. The owner will dictate the menu, and God help the poor client who can't finish his huge paprika-and-fresh-cream-covered portion!

JERICHO, one of the oldest cities in the world, used to be a vacation resort for the sheiks of Kuwait. The restaurants banking the highway, just out of the town's center, were created originally for these potentates. There're no English-language menus, but the food is simple and delicious Arabic, the service hospitable, the decor charming. Lunch in an open garden in Jericho after a visit to the Dead Sea is not to be missed. But beware! The huge, black, desert wasp thrives in this area; his sting is potently poisonous, and he covets these outdoor meals. However, weep not—you can always eat *inside* the restaurant.

BEERSHEBA, capital of the Negev, has yet to create much of a food tradition; eating places here are usually simple affairs. However, special mention goes to **Santos,** run by a Spanish family, where you can have the unusual mid-desert pleasure of eating fresh fish, shrimps, and large sardines grilled in olive oil with lemon. Also worth visiting is **Papa Michel.** Many folk from other cities go out of their way just for grilled mutton and other meat specialties.

Only a few years ago, **EILAT** offered nothing special to do or to eat. It was a beautiful wilderness with three hotels and only one of these, the **Neptune,** had any culinary reputation. Today, Eilat is a booming resort area swarming with nightclubs, restaurants and more than twenty hotels. The opening of Eilat to charter flights, and the fast-growing number of Israeli vacationers flocking there, has created an unprecedented tourist boom, which is reflected in the growing number of excellent restaurants in town. French, Chinese, Haitian, South American, Yemenite, and Arabic cuisine—just name it and it exists in Eilat. More than anything else, Eilat offers flair and atmosphere. Prices are outrageously high but quality is really good. Sea food restaurants, like **La Coquille** near the Old Port, serve fare straight from the gulf waters. Our favorite fish restaurant is **Yoske's,** operated by an old-time Eilati of the same name. **Mandy's,** of the Mandy Rice-Davis Chinese restaurant chain, also has a branch here.

For informal food, don't miss **Rafi Nelson's Village** serving entrées concocted by Mustafa, the Bedouin cook. Kebab, fresh vegetables, fruit, and a bottle of wine; all for less than $5. A meal at the Village, combined with sun, sea, and Rafi—bon vivant, world traveler, friend of film stars and celebrities, authentic Israeli "character"—as your host, is a total escape.

Cuisine competition among Eilat hotels is intense and constant efforts are underway to improve the fare. Two of Eilat's leading hotels are vacation villages: **Red Rock Hotel Club** and **Club Méditerranée.** Both offer non-kosher continental and Israeli-style food via large buffets.

Another resort city, **ASHKELON,** also has a vacation village: **Club Ashkelon.** The same familiar large buffets, unlimited wine with meals, and total informality provide distinctive vacation dining atmosphere so different from the standard hotels. And don't forget to sample fine European-style home cooking at the **Dagon Hotel,** one of Israel's oldest resorts.

The metropolis of **TEL AVIV** is Israel's commercial and tourist center. Tel Aviv and Old Jaffa together probably provide more restaurants per head of population than anywhere in the world.

Since the 1948 establishment of the State, the Old City of Jaffa—forebear of modern Tel Aviv—has become a major tourist attraction with the emphasis on atmosphere and eating places. Among its ancient stones have emerged a series of restaurants with architectural beauty and exotic-sounding names, which have become trademarks of gastronomy in Israel. From Rumanian restaurants serving succulent meat grills, to the little Oriental eateries crowding the area of the old clock, Jaffa is a pot-pourri of tastes and moods, and a delight for even the most demanding palate. It's difficult to choose favorites in Jaffa so we'll only mention a few places and apologize to the others for omitting them.

When Benny Andurski, famous Israeli singer and entertainer, created **The Patio** restaurant in an old Arab house for his fellow artists, he had no idea how popular it would become. The fare is a mixture of ethnic offerings that range from excellent Russian stroganoff to fish in Oriental tomato sauce and French onion soup. And Benny welcomes each guest with a glass of hot, canella-spiced wine straight from the fireplace. (His prices are so cheap it's a wonder he breaks even!)

Also well-known is **Yunis,** named after the biblical hero, Jonah, who first made Jaffa world famous. The restaurant is operated by a tribe of Arabs and has the best collection of Arab salads and entrées in the Tel Aviv area. If you still have room after the first course, order lamb chops or fresh fish caught every day by the owner's own fleet of fishermen. The setting is an open-air patio, and has the noisy mood of a huge festival.

Away from *vox populis,* enter the world of swanky restaurants in the reconstructed section of Jaffa. **Toutonne** and **Alhambra** are both very good French eating places. And special mention goes to **Taj Mahal,** owned by an El Al crew member of Indian origin. In a surrounding of Kharma Sutra sculptures, it offers excellent Bombay-style tandoori curry, where meat, fish and poultry are impregnated with various spices and oven baked in the only authentic tandoori oven in Israel. Taj Mahal is rated by the *International Herald Tribune* as one of the world's best Indian restaurants.

In Jaffa, authentic Polish food is found in tiny **M. & K. Lipski** (6 tables), but be sure to make advance reservations. Also in Jaffa, **Baiuca** boasts "Israel's sole Brazilian kitchen".

Hidden in a corner of central Tel Aviv, the Yemenite quarter—**Keren Hateimanim**—is famous for its Peduim Street eateries. On Saturday nights you'll see long lines of local Oriental food buffs waiting to enter their favorite places. An excellent restaurant in the quarter is **Zion.** It began in the late fifties as one small room and has expanded to house serving capacity for three hundred! In recent years, a "luxury Zion" was opened upstairs, catering to the tourist trade. If you're willing to forgo its elegance and would like to mix with the natives, you can enjoy basically the same fare for half the price. A meal here

**17th-century Torah Ark doors
from Cracow (Israel Museum,
Jerusalem)**

Israel old and new. The beach front of
Tel Aviv, lined with luxury hotels
and the Jaffa Gate entrance to Jerusalem's
Old City, with David's Tower

The Via Dolorosa is not only
the traditional "Way of the Cross",
but a vital thoroughfare through
Old Jerusalem

**The tranquil Mosque of
Al-Jazzar in Acre**

should start with one of three soups: ox feet, ox tail, or bean. Meat is served from the grill and is typical of what the best Oriental restaurants can offer.

Mandy's Singing Bamboo on Hayarkon St. is first a social institution and then a restaurant. This in place offers a piano bar, and a restaurant serving good Chinese food. Try the excellent shark-fin soup, spareribs, and sweet and sour pork. And drop in across the street at **Mandy's Candy Store,** where local beautiful people (and gapers) meet.

On the city's main drag, Dizengoff St., is a very good continental restaurant called **Tandu,** a favorite of interesting local folk. Also, among the exclusive Tel Aviv restaurants, **Casba** should not be overlooked. **Mandy's Drugstore** is a very popular spot across the street, with a USA-style menu.

Tel Aviv can pride itself on its excellent French restaurants. **Le Versailles,** on Geulah St., has gaudy decor but still serves the best French food in Israel. For the best meat in town, go to 3-table **Izafon,** and order steak or cheese-smothered fillet. But fast for 2 days first, and make reservations.

On the road to Ben-Gurion Airport, you can enjoy a luxurious Moroccan meal and excellent horseback riding facilities at **Casa del Sol.** Across from the *Avia Hotel* you'll find **Kahn ha Dekel** (the Palm Inn)—where the Oriental food is delicious, and the goose, turkey and chicken are fresh from the backyard. Another somewhat out of the way but very special Tel Aviv restaurant is the **Balkan Corner,** owned and run with great élan by the "King of the Eggplants," Arnold Benyesh—who offers limousine service to customers.

The best Chinese restaurant in Israel is **Pagoda** in HAIFA, with authentic, hot-spiced Cantonese fare. Owned and run by a Chinese family, all members do their part, from grandmother to grandchild. The food is served with an air of total indifference to the guest, as if the realization that the food is good is sufficient.

An outstanding gourmet restaurant on Haifa's Habankim St. is **Banker's Tavern.** The clientele is impressive, the menu is enormous in size and variety, and the food is terrific. You might start with the specialty—goose liver pâté that even Frenchmen vow is superior—or try stuffed artichokes or artichoke hearts in orange sauce; then move on to a choice of soups and salads, but leave plenty of room for superb steaks, chops, stroganoff or other main courses, and don't leave without sampling the desert selections.

Now for some out-of-the-cities suggestions. On busy days, the huge restaurant of **Kibbutz Ein Gev** looks like a Charlie Chaplin film factory with automated machines dipping St. Peter's fish in oil, popping it out, and serving it on waiting plates of french fries and salad. The fish is fresh, the view of Lake Tiberias great, and while a lot could be improved, Kibbutz Ein Gev is a unique site and worth the trip. Traveling there via the kibbutz-operated ferry from Tiberias adds an extra dimension.

Not far away, on the Tiberias-Safad road, is **Vered Hagalil** (see Towns listing)—a "dude-ranch" where USA apple pie, lemon pie, fried chicken, and other American favorites are dished up. You can rent a horse or take a picnic-toting horseback tour.

THE
FACE
OF
ISRAEL

TEL AVIV

With Jaffa and the Suburbs

It's perfectly possible to visit Israel without going to Tel Aviv, but this idea hasn't been known to occur to any tourist. The mere idea of a city of some 1,200,000 souls built on the sand in a handful of years is enough to arouse anyone's curiosity. The phenomenon exerts an even more understandable pull on immigrants. The dream of the Promised Land, the ideal that has lured them, should logically propel them to other parts of the country. Not so: sooner or later, most of them end up settling in Tel Aviv. However unprepossessing the setting, this is where Israel's pulse beats, where its strength is shown off to advantage, where the spirit of enterprise thrives, and where culture flourishes.

Not without a trace of envy, non-residents are wont to accuse the city of a vulgarity, of a thousand commercial excesses. Many non-residents insist they would never live there. Tel Aviv dwellers shrug: "That's all right, we're already bursting at the seams."

Industrial Hub

For many years there was good reason to wonder what Tel Aviv's bursting population was living on. More cynical observers claimed that Tel Aviv residents lived by selling the same bottle of fruit juice to one another over and over again. The number of bottles seems to have increased, because in Ramat Gan, the Assis plant alone exports millions of dollars' worth annually. Tel Aviv is the undisputed industrial and commercial center of the country and at the same time, because of its geographical location, it is the turntable for air and overland traffic. And it keeps on growing.

The city is laid out around several main arteries—Allenby, Rothschild, Dizengoff, Ben Yehuda—sometimes in perfectly orderly arrangements, other times a bit haphazardly. The map shows these roughly parallel arteries running vertically in a north-south direction and curving in toward the bottom in an easterly direction, except for Rothschild Boulevard, which veers off to the west. Allenby is a prolongation of Ben Yehuda.

One's tendency is always to scan a map from top to bottom. Actually, it is from the south, coming from Jaffa, that Tel Aviv springs out irresistibly toward the north and east. A second inspection of the map will give a clearer idea of the upward surge: the northern parts are laid out geometrically. An east-west thoroughfare, Arlosoroff, marks the boundary between what could, for the sake of convenience, be called order and disorder. It hooks onto the eastern edge—the Petah Tikva road—leading to the satellite settlements of Ramat Gan, Givatayim, and Bnei-Brak. Between them and Tel Aviv lies Haifa railway station. The Jerusalem station is now near Mikve Yisrael. The administrative complex of Ha-Kirya lies along the eastern limit of the city. Tel Aviv is bounded to the north by the Yarkon River. The latter, however, is only a temporary frontier, since the Lamed project already provides a zone of urbanization beyond the river—facing Ramat Aviv, inland. Further down beyond Jaffa, Bat Yam municipality fights to hold its own and not be absorbed. Sayvon, near the airport, and other nearby communities, do likewise.

Travelers arriving by plane cannot begin to distinguish among the various municipalities as the city sprawls out so. A night landing at the David Ben Gurion Airport, about nine miles away, is a fairyland enchantment, with millions of lights dancing against the sparkle of the sea.

Born in the Dunes

It wasn't always like this. At the dawn of the century, the area was a mass of lumpy sand-dunes, here and there a sparse thatch of dry vegetation. Jaffa—the ancient gate to Jerusalem—was the land's key port and this region's sole city. Today, Jaffa and Tel Aviv are joined under the same Municipality: something that would have been inconceivable to Jewish settlers in the late 1800s.

Back then, the first waves of immigrants strove to do the best they could with conditions as they found them in the old Arab port of Jaffa. In those days, ships had to load and unload cargo and passengers out in the roadstead. Everybody waited until the waves hoisted the launch up to deck height when—plop!—luggage, bundles, and people were poured from one to the other with as little splashing as possible. Picturesque but precarious.

Living conditions then were equally fraught with vicissitudes. The traditional hospitality of the Arab expresses itself better under a nomad tent than in a town. After all, the newcomers were accustomed to European ways and felt understandably nostalgic about plumbing, well-paved streets, good schools, and comfortable homes. But where could they turn?

Beyond Jaffa, everything was a desert with billowing sand-dunes. Aided by the Jewish National Fund, a starting nucleus of some sixty families, with Meir Dizengoff as their guiding-light, bought the sand-dunes. Everybody set to work. It was 1906.

Dizengoff himself was a true visionary, with his feet firmly planted in sand and a transcendent gleam in his eyes. On one occasion he was sufficiently carried away by his own surge of eloquence to predict that Tel Aviv would some day have 25,000 inhabitants.

How the city got its name is frequently discussed. City officials swear it's a literal Hebrew translation by Nahum Sokolow of Herzl's "Alt-neuland" (Oldnewland), with "Tel" being a hill of ancient settlement, and "Aviv" being spring, and symbolizing newness. Others argue it stems from a fact in time—for it was spring when the first handful of houses were built and to the first settlers, recently returned to their ancestral homeland, this was a daring, presumptuous act.

The naming of the first two streets—Rothschild Boulevard (named after the financier) and Herzl Street (so-called for the advocate of modern Zionism, Theodor Herzl)—was a stirring ceremony. Today, both are major arteries.

Little by little, progressively overcoming hesitancy, other families began building alongside the houses of the pioneers. But everything was done largely on a hit-or-miss basis, and actual city planning wasn't introduced until years later.

World War I took some of the wind out of the sails of the budding settlement. Worse yet, the Turkish government expelled its inhabitants in 1917. But they were able to return that very year, in the wake of General Allenby's British forces. It promptly became obvious that there were too many inhabitants, and the only solution was to expand the city limits and continue building farther out.

Again, dunes disappeared under concrete. All the while, the village was just a Jaffa suburb. In 1921 it was finally granted municipal status.

A Jewish City

A completely Jewish city? Unheard of, unthinkable! Immigration doubled. New land was constantly being snapped up, and sand was worth its weight in gold (still is).

The bas-relief on the monument commemorating Tel Aviv's founders, at the intersection of Nahlat Benjamin and Rothschild Boulevard, retraces the epic in three phases.

The bottom part shows the pioneers wielding shovels and trowels. In the background stand the tents in which they were living. The center strip depicts the impressive gymnasium, or secondary school, the very first Hebrew high school, which was Tel Aviv's pride and joy. The tents have yielded to solid structures, and there is even a water-tower.

The top part represents the last period, the complete achievement, the city of dreams. Skyscrapers and a fountain form the background; there's a museum to one side, and a theater on the other; there are trees; and, above all, there is the port. It appears on the right, represented by a double circular arc. The port construction project was launched in the 1930s and marked Tel Aviv's tenth anniversary. In 1936 an Arab strike paralyzed both Jaffa and Tel Aviv. After infinite difficulties, Tel Aviv got permission to build a jetty out to sea. Elder residents still recall feelingly the wild cheering that hailed the docking of the first ship. (Today, the Tel Aviv-Jaffa port has fallen largely into disuse, with Haifa's port and the new port of Ashdod taking over the job.)

Perpetual Motion

Since 1909 Tel Aviv has been one vast and continuous worksite, although the rebuilding of the earliest areas has necessarily had to be postponed. Construction work hasn't let up once in all that time. Where does all this amazing vitality come from? Everything hereabouts conveys the feeling that men labor without ceasing, scarcely pausing

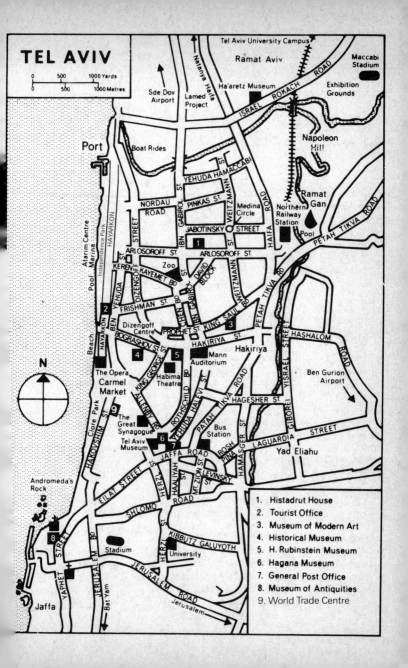

TEL AVIV

| 0 | 500 | 1000 Yards |
| 0 | 500 | 1000 Metres |

Tel Aviv University Campus
Ramat Aviv
Maccabi Stadium

Sde Dov Airport
Lamed Project
Ha'aretz Museum
Exhibition Grounds

ISRAEL ROKACH

Port
Boat Rides
Napoleon Hill

Atarim Centre
Pool · Marina
Independence Park
HAYARKON STREET

YEHUDA HAMACCABI ST.
NORDAU ROAD
PINKAS ST.
BEN GABIROL ST.
WEITZMANN ST.
Medina Circle

Ramat Gan
Northern Railway Station
Pool

PETAH TIKVA ROAD

JABOTINSKY STREET

ARLOSOROFF ST.
ARLOSOROFF ST.

KEREN
KAYEMET BD.
DIZENGOFF ST.
Zoo
DAVID BLOCK

FRISHMAN ST.

BEN YEHUDA
Beach

HAIFA ROAD

CHEN BD.
BEN GABIROL BD.
KING SAUL
WEITZMANN BD.
PETAH TIKVA RD.

Dizengoff Centre
BOGRASHOV ST.
PROPHETS
HAKIRIYA ST.

3

HASHALOM ROAD

Hakiriya

4
KING GEORGE ST.
5
Mann Auditorium

Ben Gurion Airport

The Opera
Carmel Market
ALLENBY RD.
Habima Theatre
ROTHSCHILD
YEHUDA HALEVI ST.

HAGESHER ST.

9
The Great Synagogue
HERZL ST.
PATAH TIKVA
Bus Station

YISRAEL
GIBOREI
STREET

HAKOVSHIM ST.
Clore Park

Tel Aviv Museum
6
7
JAFFA ROAD
HAALIYAH ST.
ROSH PINA ST.
HAMASGER ST.
LAGUARDIA STREET
Yad Eliahu

Andromeda's Rock

EILAT STREET
MT. ZION ST.
LEVINSKY ST.
SHLOMO ROAD

8
YAPHET STREET
JERUSALEM RD.
Stadium
HERZL
University
KIBBUTZ GALUYOTH

Jaffa
JERUSALEM ROAD
Bat Yam
Jerusalem

1. Histadrut House
2. Tourist Office
3. Museum of Modern Art
4. Historical Museum
5. H. Rubinstein Museum
6. Hagana Museum
7. General Post Office
8. Museum of Antiquities
9. World Trade Centre

N

for breath, going about their tasks with the same sheer joy they would show if on vacation.

It's a port of perpetual motion, the reverse of staying put or running on a treadmill. Once the bulldozers have started, a vacant lot that used to be a garbage-dump is apparently transformed overnight into a lively kindergarten or an imposing administrative building, whichever suits the needs of the moment. The school that was built back in the early, heroic times—the once-proud gymnasium—has now been replaced by the Shalom skyscraper, home of Shalom Department Store.

Pedestrians occasionally find themselves trudging over sand or dirt, sandwiched in between two impeccably paved sidewalks. An old cobbler's grubby den hugs up to an ultra-modern cleaning-shop, and Helena Rubinstein's neon sign rubs shoulders with a haberdashery that looks like something fresh out of Gogol.

"Sectionalized" City

As the city continues growing, it changes. In 1906 it had to cater to 600 people; today it must meet the needs of a greater-metropolitan population of some 1,220,000—plus hordes of tourists.

Feeding all these folk requires not only many supermarkets and such, but lots of restaurants, cafés, sidewalk snack bars and kiosks. Every type of menu imaginable is available here today. And, interestingly, the eateries and entertainment places have helped "sectionalize" the city. By the sea, Hayarkon and off-shoot streets—from the Dan northwards—incorporate an area full of places to eat and be entertained, including the marina area with its discos and summer-evening outdoor bands. Further south along the shoreline, more public beaches are faced by outdoor cafes, restaurants and amusement areas that extend south toward the new Dolphinarium and shopping complex at Charles Clore Park, just across the street from Laromme hotel and the towering buildings of Israel's World Trade Center and local business and industry offices. Jaffa is just moments away, with exotic nightlife and color.

Dizengoff Street, from the new Square northwards to about Arlosoroff, could be called two sections: the first is full of fast-food bars, cafés, ice cream parlors, Wimpy stands; then, the last two or three blocks have Café Stern and two Mandy eateries, plus a more quiet and stable atmosphere. Near the Yarkon River another "section" thrives— the largest and most versatile. It emerges along Yehuda Halevi, encompasses the northern ends of both Dizengoff and Hayarkon, as well as several small streets winding about the area. A relatively new area for Tel Aviv, it has fine restaurants, soup shops, bars—everything.

Each of these areas is great for strolling and look-it-ing. When Tel Aviv "natives" do it, they can hardly help recalling how the city "used to be." To them, each town lot has a history, and they're not shy about sharing it with you. Looking back they'll tell you, it seems as if the plush Dan Hotel on Hayarkon Street had just barely begun welcoming its first guests, and the nearby US Embassy was scarcely completed, when deluxe hotels at the other end of Hayarkon were full already, and foundations were being laid for more and more to march down the street and create, finally, the long beach-front chain of fine—usually crowded—tourist meccas.

The Birth of Israel's Hotel Industry

In 1947, however, the Kaete Dan was a small 21-room edifice, abandoned after World War II, when it had been requisitioned by the British. That's when young Dan Silberstein looked at it and went to talk with Yekutiel and Shmuel Federmann, brothers from a professional hotel family in Germany. The three envisioned restoring the tiny hotel and making it Tel Aviv's "finest," then welcoming international celebrities. They did their best and soon the Kaete Dan became swamped with personalities like Ben Gurion and Golda Meyerson (Meir, later); Eleanor Roosevelt, Ralph Bunche, Leon Uris and scores of newsmen. But it remained small—its expansion came about via hardship and chance.

The last illegal immigrant ship approached Tel Aviv shores on November 29, 1947, but the captain demanded $5,000 ship's claims before he would let the "human cargo" ashore. None of the locals had that kind of cash available in the middle of the night, but Yekutiel Federmann decided to request a loan from new guests at the hotel: Max Orovitz, Rabbi Irving Lehrman, and Jewish-American Study Mission. Orovitz agreed, but wanted to "see where it's going." With townsfolk and the Rabbi, Orovitz waded into the dark, chill Mediterranean and helped transfer shivering babies and youngsters into boats, then to the sea-front apartment of Golda Meir, where warm food and clothing were waiting. The impact on the Americans was tremendous.

Over coffee the next morning, Federmann had proposals that Orovitz—coming from a hotel city like Miami Beach—was quick to adopt. They agreed that developing luxury hotels would give newcomers job opportunities, plus make it easier for Americans and others to visit Israel. The Israel-Miami Group resulted from this meeting and, together with the Federmanns, provided the financial base for the assorted enterprises. The Dan Chain now employs 1,500 and has five properties: Tel Aviv Dan, Caesarea Country Club, Herzlya's Accadia, Dan Haifa, and Israel's most legendary hotel: Jerusalem's King David—where

Egyptian President Anwar Sadat stayed during his historic 1977 visit to Israel.

Israel now boasts several international-chain hotels that all came years after two brothers' dream was realized. In 1953, when the new Dan Tel Aviv opened with facilities then unknown in Israel (air-conditioning, wall-to-wall carpeting, colored bathrooms and so forth), it fathered a new era of tourism here. The newest Israeli-chain luxury hotel in town is the 17-story Laromme Tel Aviv-Jaffa.

Take Any Bus

Transport, of course, must also be good to accommodate the thousands who live in Tel Aviv or pass through. Of course there are taxis and sheruts, but the bus system—which happens to be excellent—is something uniquely Israeli and quite worth experiencing. So . . . take a bus, any bus. The big show lies straight ahead, right before your eyes. The driver has a transistor radio at his side and is listening to music as he rolls through traffic. The passengers are listening too.

When the news broadcast comes on, the driver turns up the volume and everybody stops talking. Apparently without lifting his hands from the wheel, and answering only to God, taking both curves and tickets in his stride, he also makes change, sorts coins, drops them into slots, punches tickets, honks the horn, dodges pedestrians, frightens small cars off to a respectful distance, shells and eats melon seeds and sunflower seeds; and even finds time to flirt with an occasional pretty passenger . . . all this without stopping the bus.

From one of the main arteries, Ben Yehuda, you turn off into Trumpeldor Street. A moment ago you were staring at the revolutionary convolutions of the El-Al building's spiraling fire-escape. A bare 300 feet further on and you're gazing at a poignant small provincial cemetery, preserved intact right in the heart of town.

Somewhere along the route your attention may be drawn by the presence of barrel-reservoirs on the housetops. Are they catching rainwater? Not at all. They are an Israeli invention for domestic comfort: hot running water heated by the sun's rays. Some 250,000 Israeli homes depend on solar energy.

Gradually the streets change in character. A business thoroughfare becomes a residential area and vice-versa: a handsome tree-lined avenue with rows of private houses imperceptibly transforms itself into an industrial center. The sightseer finds his center of interest shifting as he moves forward.

Ben Yehuda Street, which was designed to attract an élite, yields to its parallel rival, Dizengoff Street, and the public accordingly moves over, taking with it the concomitant fabulous increase in the price per square foot of land, the smart cafés, and the fashionable shops.

What to See

It's a city of constant surprise. Overlooking one of Tel Aviv's beaches is a flat, yellowish structure—an opera house, home of many a fine evening's entertainment. In the same vein, Tel Aviv has its Mann Auditorium, featuring the last word in acoustics. There is the sleek Dizengoff Center; the comprehensive Atarim Center, sprawling along the shore, with every possible tourist need, even boating at the marina; the Laromme Hotel/World Trade Center complex spanning almost to Jaffa.

There are two universities, including the Bar-Ilan which specializes in Judaism; three concert halls; six theatrical companies, one of them the famous Habimah (which emigrated from Russia, is dedicated to the great Stanislavsky traditions, and in 1958 became Israel's National Theater), the Israel National Opera House, the Cameri, and the satirical humor troupes; several night-clubs, 18 motion-picture houses, and 56 travel agencies.

By far the greatest attraction continues to be the Israeli Philharmonic Orchestra, which was founded by the violinist Bronislaw Huberman. It ranks among the world's top orchestras. The 3,000-plus seats in the Mann Auditorium don't begin to satisfy the demand for tickets and concerts usually have to be repeated several times. Outstanding solo performers invited to play in Tel Aviv find that their invitation is both a consecration and a responsibility.

There are several museums, interesting and worthwhile. The first was created in 1930 by the indefatigable Meir Dizengoff, who placed his fortune, his home, and his private collections at the disposal of the organizers of Beit Dizengoff Museum. This home was distinguished by an historical event: in the small salon in which chamber music is now performed, Israel's independence was proclaimed in 1948. Some of his collections are now at the Ha'aretz Museum Complex in Ramat Aviv, made up of nine museums: the Tel Qasile Excavation Museum, the Ethnology and Folklore Museum, the Lasky Planetarium, the Glass (ancient) Museum, the Kadman Numismatic Museum, the Alphabet Museum and the Ceramic (ancient) Museum. The Tel Aviv Museum, 39 King Saul Boulevard, has a rich collection of works by Jewish, Israeli and international masters. A center of cultural activity, it hosts concerts, lectures, films. The latest, most impressive exhibition is at the Museum of the Jewish Diaspora, on Tel Aviv University's campus—don't miss it! Helena Rubinstein Pavilion, beside Mann Auditorium, has fine one-man shows and temporary exhibits. There is also a military museum—the Haganah—which recalls some of the most dramatic episodes in Israel's recent history, as does Ben Gurion House, home of the late prime minister, 17 Ben Gurion Boulevard.

Don't miss the Great Synagogue, Israel's biggest, on Allenby Road just off Rothschild Boulevard. It's an impressive sight to see the faithful on their way to services on a Sabbath eve or a holiday. Tel Aviv's heavy traffic is detoured for such occasions. At the celebration of the Sukkoth, the neighborhood is filled with green branches for sale, to decorate tabernacles.

The Italian *corso* and the Spanish *rambla* have their local equivalent in Tel Aviv's Dizengoff Street and on the circular square of the same name. At the end of the day and far into the night people converge here to see and be seen, to meet friends, to talk, drink, dine, stroll and show off new clothes, especially some startling new style!

Tel Aviv's stadium at Ramat Gan accommodates 30,000 spectators. Every four years, on the pattern of the Olympic Games, the Maccabiades are held here, bringing together Jewish athletes from all over the world. 1981 is one of those years!

At the Shalom Diamond factory, 24 Achad Ha'am Street, tourists may watch the precious stones being cut and polished. You can even purchase stones at factory prices—one of Israel's best buys.

Steimatzky's Bookstore, with its main Tel Aviv shop at 107 Allenby Street, is Israel's largest bookshop. See its paperback basement, with a big range of American and English titles. Tel Aviv Zoo, at the end of Keren Kayamet Boulevard, is a good place for the children; elephants, lions, mountain goats, monkeys, tropical birds; the Dolphinarium, with its shopping complex and eateries, is another favorite place for kids and adults. An interesting way to see the city is from the deck of a coast-cruising catamaran: tickets at travel agencies, or 98 Hayarkon. Boating on the Yarkon River is a relaxing, cooling idea for a hot Tel Aviv afternoon. Boat Stations are at the end of Ibn Gvriol and Dizengoff Streets, between the bridge and the beach, an area with kiosks for snacks and playgrounds for youngsters. A big motored excursion boat leaves every 20 minutes for an hour's ride every Saturday. (Also see FAYF chapter for Tel Aviv Marina boating and yachting.)

While near the bridge, look for Tel Qasile, an ancient mound on the north bank, the site of a busy 12th-century Philistine settlement destroyed in 732 B.C. but rebuilt during the 6th century B.C. Theory says the "cedars of Lebanon," for building the two Temples, arrived here—not at Jaffa.

Further out in this direction is the Tel Aviv Country Club, where tourists may present their passports, pay a fee, and enjoy the 35 different sports facilities including swimming. There's a nursery for small children, cafés, sauna, and shops where you can buy t-shirts and other items with the CC motif. Not far from here is the Tel Aviv Tennis Center, with every possible facility for playing and tournaments. In Ramat Aviv is the home of Tel Aviv University—nearby lies Bar-Ilan University. Campus tours are available for both, and you also can visit modern city hall, Tel Aviv Municipality (Kikar Malchei Israel).

The Carmel Market

Perhaps by now you think you've seen all of Tel Aviv. Well, there's more. Amid the modern confusion and bustle of the city, there's a sort of sensory flood-gate, initiating the unwary visitor to the Eastern world. It's the Carmel market (the *souk*) one block from Allenby Road's Magen David Square.

There are three crossed rows of "regular" stores, temporary stalls, and the wares of itinerant vendors with hopes of making a sale. If you're coming in off Allenby you find yourself suddenly transported into a kind of Eastern world that has managed to keep a certain lingering Occidental flavor. Here a boy with an eye for design has artfully stacked a heap of artichokes while a one-armed vendor bawls the merits of his varicolored slips in Hebrew, Arabic, Yiddish, and Ladino, an offshoot of classical Spanish.

The grocery stores, fish markets and butcher shops are the "regular" places. They too have barkers who yell lustily and drown out the itinerant peddlars. On both sides, straddling the sidewalk and street, open-air carts spill over with fresh and dried vegetables, fruits and shoes. There are also little heaps of merchandise spread out on the bare ground right at the passer-by's feet.

Narrow passageways have been thoughtfully left clear between the heaps so that potential customers can shop around a bit. And there are flowers everywhere, hanging overhead, spread underfoot (you can hardly avoid stepping on them), in the market-basket of the prosperous housewife who has a car and in the sack of the poor soul who has to count every *agorot*. In Israel, life without flowers is unthinkable.

All the languages of the world are flung at you; the hapless visitor is helpless to make head or tail of what's Hebrew and what's Arabic amid the clamor of all these hoarse throats and husky voices. Often they shout at you just for the fun of it, if the camera dangling round your neck singles you out as a foreigner—who ever saw a tourist buying fillets of mackerel? But it's all in the day's work, and if they accost you in French, English, Turkish, Hungarian, German, remember they enjoy vying with one another.

You're wallowing through a morass of discarded peelings and trampled flowers, you're reeling from the redolence of food spoiling in the sun, and your head is aching from all this commotion that has long since exceeded the sound-barrier, but you yourself haven't even begun.

So pluck up your courage and head down one of the shopping lanes on your right for a look at the equally plucked chickens. It's easy to find the stalls—just steer towards that swirl of flying feathers. And cast more than a mere gaze at the maze of special food counters: inhale the roasting coffee, the pickled cucumbers, peppers (be a Peter Piper!), and onions.

Your good sense and better sentiments will propel you gently in the direction of the outdoor restaurants, for coffee with (or without) flavorful *hehl*. Get a grip on yourself, but at the same time be prepared to relax and enjoy it, and have a go at the thousand and one sausages that are sold probably by the yard. Only after all this can you honestly tell your friends that you "saw the Carmel *souk*." And you will have earned a medal for market-manship.

For a different type of market, head over to the main post office, two blocks behind Allenby, at Rehov Picciato and Yehuda Halvey: the Polish Market. Here, all manner of new and used goods are sold openly and loudly—watches, radios, clothing, luggage, umbrellas, you name it—all at bargain prices.

While you stroll here and along other streets, remember that it's now mandatory for Tel Aviv shopkeepers to sweep their front sidewalks every morning, noon and afternoon—or pay stiff fines.

Before leaving the downtown area, you might want to visit the Shalom Tower, Israel's tallest building—where shopping's great and there's a kiddie amusement area plus a Wax Museum. The view from atop the building is a must-see, letting you gaze at the city and environs, the Mediterranean and nearby Jaffa.

Jaffa, Ancient and Modern

Jaffa is the *Joppa* of the ancients. *Yafo* in Hebrew, its name probably derived from *yafé*, "beautiful." Some claim that the name came from that of Japhet, Noah's third son—the one everybody usually forgets to remember. It's one of the oldest ports in the world, Jerusalem's natural outlet to the sea, and in ancient times was strongly fortified. The reign of the Hasmoneans was marred by a tragic catastrophe here: the Greek settlers perfidiously sank some ships, aboard which they had lured their Jewish competitors. The Jews were more than once victims of ordeal by water: while some were fleeing the Romans after the destruction of the Temple, a violent storm drowned the survivors of the massacre.

Jaffa's Jewish community, although decimated, managed to survive amid dire hardships, continuously the butt of persecution by whoever happened to be the current occupier. There were periods of obscurity and of invasion, under Arabs, Turks and Crusaders, in a sort of perpetual motion of bloodshed. By the opening of the 19th century not one single Jew remained in a population of 4,000 Moslems. The pilgrims to the Promised Land chose that moment to begin their hesitant voyage home and the influx breathed new life into the sleepy old port.

Jaffa's history is also revealed extensively by archeological finds near the Artists' Quarter. Parts of a 20-foot-thick wall of a 13th-century-B.C. Hyksos citadel are there, and part of the city gate, bearing the name of Rameses II (also 13th century). Remains include a Canaanite city, a Jewish city built at the time of Ezra and Nehemiah, a 3rd-century-B.C. wall, a statue of Aphrodite, Hasmonean ruins, a batch of coins from Alexander Jannaeus' reign, and traces of Roman occupation.

The big Hassan Beq mosque, the advanced bastion that guarded the entrance of the old Arab city, served Moslem sharp-shooters as an ideal vantage-point in 1948. They aimed from the minaret to shoot up the Jewish streets straight down to Hayarkon Street. The entire area between Allenby Road and St. Peter's Monastery became a battleground; Jaffa had to be taken by storm. Except for a strip along the seashore, what had previously been the connecting stretch between the two cities became a jumble of rubble. Traveling the mile from Tel Aviv to Jaffa, it looked as though the war had been fought there last week, with ruins and dust everywhere. Today, the old buildings and the beach alike are wearing new faces and are full of activity. Any division between Jaffa and Tel Aviv is almost filled by Charles Clore Park, with its Dolphinarium, and the towering, futuristic buildings of Laromme hotel and Israel's branch of the World Trade Center.

Old Jaffa, tourist night-life center, traces its origins back to biblical times. Joshua gave over the region to Dan (JOSHUA XXIX, 46); it was a port under King David and King Solomon, and was later a landing point for the Crusaders. Still later Jaffa was occupied by the Turks, and was subsequently destroyed by Napoleon in 1799, to be rebuilt at the beginning of the 19th century.

The Flea Market

Jaffa welcomes you with open arms in the Flea Market. The little stalls are to the right and left of Aleytsion Street. Everything except food is on sale. In this market you see many out-of-the-way objects, sometimes rare "finds." Housewives coming here are usually after old or new household furnishings, and mix with tourists in streets of shops and through a couple of narrow, covered passageways going from one street to another. At night, iron curtains seal them off, thus locking up all the shops at once. This is the kingdom of junk, of old stuff, where scrap-iron and discarded furniture hold sway. It's also the lair of zealous artisans who work in full view of the public, naîvely letting the passers-by watch them conscientiously at work reproducing some antique object that will be hawked as having been "discovered at the site of an excavation and spirited away at incalculable risk from the long arm of the museums." Right across the street, in the window of an antique shop, you will undoubtedly find another finished replica of the same object, properly worm-eaten and with an impeccable patina showing under the careful coating of dried mud.

Legends and Rebuilding

As usual in Israel, legend and history rub elbows here. Jaffa supposedly was the scene of Jonah's departure for the famous junket that landed him in the belly of a whale. This mammal presumably coughed him up somewhere farther down the coast near Ashkelon. We are told that the timber from the cedars of Lebanon for building the temple of Solomon was loaded off the ships at Jaffa. And someone is bound to point out to you which of the various projecting rocks in the port is the one to which the beauteous Andromeda was shackled to await the sea monster. Not only did Perseus rescue her, but he also miraculously preserved the shattered chains, so that antique dealers can now sell them by the ton. There are at least two other places on the Mediterranean which claim the same legend. It was also on the shores of Jaffa that King Solomon found his famous treasure, after the waves had carefully dislodged it from the sunken ships and washed it ashore as an offering to Heaven.

Everybody seems to have left his mark at the entrance to Jaffa There is a so-called Crusaders' Tower, with rather disastrous stained-glass windows added later. The Turks contributed a prison, which was used by the British a bit more than strictly necessary. The Arabs built a lovely hammam (bath house), and the Jews have put up a monument for heroes of the Liberation.

Atop the hill the crumbling old stone quarter has been restored to its appearance of 100 years ago. Already a thriving Artists' Quarter, this is the Jaffa Development Project. A leisurely walk through the modernized, well-lit maze of alleys and courtyards reveals artists' studios, galleries, "new" antique shops, cafés, restaurants, soft or loud night life, you-name-it. A pleasing, harmonious effect has been achieved with old houses, stairways, figured windows, and iron-trimmed doors. Artists coming here have found both refuge and inspiration.

Ride the No. 7 bus on Keren Kayemet Boulevard or the No. 10 on Hakovshim Street. Starting from the Town Clock Square, visit the Mahmoudiya Mosque and St. Peter's Catholic Church.

At Abu Kabir, the Russian Monastery includes a cave tomb that tradition says belongs to Taib Tabitha (Dorcas), raised from the dead by St. Peter. Also here is part of an ancient Jewish cemetery dating from the 1st and 4th centuries A.D. The Franciscan Monastery of St. Peter, atop a hill, is also astride foundations of a 13-century Crusader citadel, a medieval fortress with well-preserved chambers entered via steps in the courtyard; the reputed house of Simon the Tanner is nearby—now occupied by a mosque built in 1730—on a winding lane to the old lighthouse overlooking the port. A fine panoramic view can be had from both spots.

The Environs of Jaffa

Two relatively new towns are located south of Jaffa: Bat Yam, founded in 1925, whose name means "the daughter of the sea" and which is the proud proprietor of the Rock of Adam, and Holon, founded in 1935, a center for fabric-weaving and other industries and one of the two last remaining centers of the descendants of the Samaritans (the other being Nablus, in Samaria).

Eastward from Tel Aviv lies suburban Bnei Brak, ancient home of Rabbi Akiba, famed as an ardent supporter of the rebel Bar Kochba. This is the domain of orthodox Jews and the seat of the orthodox Bar-Ilan University.

Six miles (ten km.) farther on is Petah Tikva, the "gateway of hope," earliest of the Jewish colonies, founded in 1878. In order to survive, its settlers were obliged to dry up the marshes and thus eradicate malaria. Just to the southeast you will find Mikveh-Israel, the country's first agricultural school, founded by French Jews in 1870.

Located farther to the south is Rishon Le-Zion (7 miles from Tel Aviv), which deserves special mention for its vineyards, wine-cellars, and wine tastings (the cellars are open to the public). While amassing his fortune, Baron Rothschild began acquiring vinestock from France. For three generations now Rishon Le-Zion has been providing Jews all over the world with Israeli wine from French grapes, indeed an ideal accompaniment to the Passover and other celebrations. Rishon Le-Zion is one of the first villages in modern Israel (founded in 1882), which is why the name translates to "First in Zion." *Hatikvah,* Israel's national anthem, was composed by Naftali Imber in Rishon Le-Zion.

In the same general direction, but 14 miles from Tel Aviv, the town of Rehovot tucked among orange groves since 1890, and now enjoys the prestige of being home to the Weismann Institute of Science. Israel's first president, world-renowned scientist Chaim Weizmann, lived and is buried here. One story is that, during World War I, Weizmann, who was already famous both as a chemist and for his ardent Zionism, turned over to Lord Balfour a discovery (acetone) that proved vital to the British war effort, in exchange for the promise to set up a Jewish National Homeland. Weizmann died in 1952.

You can tour Weizmann's home and the institute; pay your respects to his grave, and meditate in the beautiful grounds of the Institute that perpetuates his name. This is a beautiful compound of green lawns and well-tended gardens. Note the kidney-shaped lily pond in front of the physics building, and the novel design of the library building. The Institute provides its scientists with handsome housing (tourist accommodations nearby). In the classrooms and laboratories, scientists are freely pursuing studies and research in various fields, including mathematics, nuclear physics, electronics, experimental biology, organic chemistry—in other words, practically all the scientific disciplines. A revolutionary new method for heavy water was developed in the Rehovot laboratories, Israel's first atomic cyclotron is located at nearby Yavneh.

Vespasian was approached by one of the city's elders, Rabbi Yohanan, who asked permission to set up an academy at Yavneh. The request was granted, and a school was eventually founded there. So in a certain sense it is thanks to Vespasian that the biblical canon was established in the first century and that the compiling of the *Mishna* (the first part of the *Talmud*) was undertaken, to be completed a century later in Tiberias. After the destruction of the second temple in A.D. 70, Yavneh was renowned as a center of learning and wisdom; a popular adage of the day was, "Go north for riches, but go south for knowledge." Present-day Yavneh is 5 miles north of Ashdod.

From Tel Aviv to Jerusalem

If you make the trip by road, the first town of any consequence is Lod (formerly Lydda). Today, though mostly Jewish, it still bears indelible traces of its mixed history. The Greek Orthodox Church of St. George perpetuates the glory of England's patron saint, supposedly born here, and believed to have power to heal madmen.

Holy places founded here by the Byzantines were usually razed by Moslems, reconstructed by Crusaders; then destroyed again, to be rebuilt by Christians over the past three centuries. If legend is correct, Lod once ranked second only to Jerusalem as a center of learning.

Lod is great for Arab food and also has an interesting market. Each Tuesday, from 5 A.M. till about noon, you can wander through pitched stalls and haggle over baubles and beads.

A comparable sight is at nearby Ramle, where trading goes on all week long, on Market Street, naturally. If you decide to shop, maybe try a bite later at one of the market area restaurants, keeping an eye open for those selling kebab.

Though historically similar to its neighbor, Lod, in that it was built and sacked again and again, Ramle also is the only Palestinian town founded by Arabs, back in 716 when Suliman made it his capital. Today, its 35,000 population rises greatly in number on Friday nights, and simultaneously drops in average age, as young people from surrounding areas flock here for the shows and conviviality.

While here, look for the main attraction: the Tower of the Forty. Sometimes called the Tower of Richard the Lion-Heart, it was built in 1268 by Babar, designed as a minaret for the old "white" mosque (Jami-el-Abiad) that dated from 716. The ruins of its Roman arch and aqueduct make an impressive historical marker. The Great Mosque (Jami-el-Kebir) stands on the former site of the Cathedral of St. John of the Crusaders. There is also St. Helena's cistern, built in 879 for Haroun-el-Rashid, a familiar figure to devotees of the *Arabian Nights*. Under the imposing Gothic arches, you can have a precarious boat ride.

A short distance northeast of Ramle lies the War Cemetery, where the fallen of both World Wars are buried. The total number is 1,595, covering some 22 nationalities. This is the largest of the War Cemeteries in Israel though there are 12 others, the second largest being the one at Khayat Beach near Haifa.

From Ramle, two roads climb to Jerusalem. The shorter, faster one passes the Latrun Monastery, which rests above road-level, in high greenery. Stop and sample the home-made wines here; you can buy these, and other products made by the monks.

Some 45 minutes' longer driving, but rewarding in beauty, is the older Jerusalem road that winds upwards through Shaar Hagai, famed in song and story. On your right is the Forest of Martyrs: 6,000,000 trees planted here commemorate victims of Nazi fury. A magnificent monument 20 feet high, the Scroll of Fire, was dedicated in 1971 on this spot.

On the left is the Arab village of Abu Ghosh, the scene of the first Judeo-Arab fraternization and home of the Ark of the Covenant. The Philistines stole the Ark and bore it off, but hastened to restore it when they became convinced the Jewish God was punishing them for the deed. Later on, David, dancing the whole way, carried it the eight miles between here and Jerusalem. The two Jerusalem roads meet after Abu Ghosh, then branch apart again, with the left route leading on to the Golden City.

Perched on a hill to the right is the *Castel,* ruins of the ancient *Castellum Romanum.* This was the scene of one of the first victories in Israel's War of Independence. Now from the road, you can catch glimpses of the western outskirts of Jerusalem. We go up, down, and up again. To the right, notice the curious old Jewish cemetery on a hillside. Without really noticing too much, we've just climbed 2,400 feet and traveled 42 miles from Tel Aviv to Jerusalem's gates.

PRACTICAL INFORMATION FOR TEL AVIV AND AREA

 HOTELS. Greater Tel Aviv has more than 50 hotels, ranging from plush, swimming-pooled palaces to the simplest sort of pension—highest rates in Israel's biggest city are in the peak Mar.–Oct. period; rates at hotels drop about 15% in the winter. Food prices vary greatly, and seldom are included in room rates, especially in the better hotels. Most hotel food is strictly kosher.

Deluxe (5-star)

High season is March through October, and double rates range from $24.50 to $49, per person daily, usually including breakfast.

The newest full-luxury hotel in town is **Laromme Tel Aviv,** rising 18 floors above the beach at Charles Clore Park, with 474 double rooms and 30 suites, all modern, comfortable, with balconies. There's room TV, a health club, heated pool with snack bar and exotic drinks nearby, a shopping arcade, laundry/ cleaner, MD, baby sitters, even an interpreter. Caribbean steel bands play afternoons; live nightly entertainment and dancing; many special events. As official host for Israel's branch of the *World Trade Center* (those 3 tall buildings next door), it also has superb and unique *Laromme 11 Executive Services* that are impressive and important enough to be investigated by any business person who has or wants links with Israel. The *Dolphinarium* arcade is across the street; Jaffa is in sight down the road; other Tel Aviv hotels are in sight up the road, lining Hayarkon.

Dan Tel Aviv, 99 Hayarkon St., 310 rooms on 7 floors. Totally, luxuriously refurbished (1977), with great $500,000 pool overlooking beach. Shops, ticket office, bank, etc.

Sheraton Tel Aviv stands out on Hayarkon, the hotel strip, 365 well-equipped and well-managed rooms, and heated pool; great restaurant, grill room, and superb coffee lounge; with health club and nightclub. Room TV.

Tel Aviv Hilton, on Upper Hayarkon St., has 620 rooms with TV on 17 floors, and each room has a balcony with a view of the sea. Two hard tennis courts; good café and bar; heated pool, health club.

Ramada Continental, in same area, has 340 rooms, penthouse suite; children under 18 stay free if in parents' room. Bright American decor; heated pool, health club; TV in rooms; *Asia Grill* and *Europa Bar,* plus *America Club* nightclub with live entertainment.

Plaza, 155 Hayarkon St., fronts the beach by the Atarim Center. Total luxury, its 350 rooms have TV. There's the *Marina Lounge,* and *Paradise Bar,* with night music; pool, shops.

First Class (4-star)

Tel Aviv has several good 4-star hotels, where double rates usually range from $17 to $35 per person daily, including breakfast.

Most expensive of this category ($20–$35 double but worth it!) is the 138-room **Country Club**, on Haifa Road, POB 21077. Opt for a single room, or a suite with bedroom, bath, living room, dining area; total kitchen, balcony. Fine for families, too, who rent entire cottage—including extra single room. Part of the complex grounds of the posh Tel Aviv Country Club, and guests enjoy pools, sauna, tennis—a total of 35 different sports facilities and activities—with Israeli CC members. There's even child care, shops, cafés, shuttle service.

Facing the sea is the **Concorde,** 1 Trumpeldor Street. Woodpaneled lobby with black and white marble floor; 92 rooms green carpeted with warm color decor.

In the same price range is the new **Marina**—ultra-sharp, with 178 rooms, all facilities, and a night club in the new Atarim Center on the beach.

Park, 75 Hayarkon St., offers 99 rooms, tasteful decor and friendly staff; also coffee shop, bar.

Nearby, at 105 Hayarkon St., the 68-room **Astor** is popular for family-style, first-class atmosphere. Higher prices for rooms facing the sea.

Basel, at 156 Hayarkon St., has 138 rooms with sea views; also bank, pool, coffee shop.

Tal, 287 Hayarkon, offers 126 sea-side rooms.

Sinai is in the heart of town, 11 Trumpeldor St., with 250 air-conditioned rooms, TV, bar, bank, pool.

The 122-room **Avia,** with pool, tennis courts and a nightclub, is near David Ben Gurion Airport.

Ramat Aviv Garden Hotel, 122 rooms about 15 mins. from downtown **Tel Aviv,** has pool, tennis, nightclub.

Moderate (3-star)

The 3-star hotels range from $13.50 to $17.50 per person for double occupancy, with breakfast.

Recommended are the **Ambassador,** 2 Allenby St.; **Adiv,** 5 Mendele St., **Ora,** 35 Ben Yehuda St.; **Star,** 9 Trumpeldor St.; the **Shalom,** 216 Hayarkon St., across from the Hilton; the **Ami,** 4 Am Israel Chai; the **Florida,** 164 Hayarkon St.; **Maxim,** 86 Hayarkon St.; and the **Wishnitz,** in Bnei Brak. The **Commodore,** on Dizengoff Square, also has good restaurant.

Newer in the same price range are the **City,** 9 Mapu St., and the **Moss,** 6 Nes Ziona. The 18-suite **Habakook,** 7 Habakkuk St., charges $38–$51 per person for its hotel-apartments with kitchenettes.

Kfar Hamaccabiah is an unusually posh motel in nearby Ramat Chen; Holiday Village—where Maccabee Games ("Jewish Olympics") are played—in nearby Ramat Chen. It has great facilities for its 103 rooms, including tennis, pool and heated pool. (See Holiday Villages, *Facts At Your Fingertips.)*

Other Accommodation

Popular 2-star hotels, at $12 to $15.80, include the **Eilat,** 58 Hayarkon St.; the **Excelsior,** 88A Hayarkon St.; the **Imperial,** 66 Hayarkon, and the **Wagshal,** in Bnei Brak.

One-star hotels run $6.50 to $12. Most have only showers and only about half are air-conditioned: **Europa,** 42 Allenby; **Migdal David,** 8 Allenby; **Hagalil,** 54 Allenby; **Monopol,** 4 Allenby; **Riviera,** 52 Hayarkon; **Nes Ziona,** 10 Nes Ziona; **Nordau,** 27 Nachlat Benjamim, and the **Tamar,** 8 Gnesin St. Note: Some are in areas of questionable repute.

Tel Aviv has a unique service for those wishing to stay a while and live in an apartment. A 2-bedroom apartment, for a couple with 2 children, generally runs about $35 daily; a studio for one, with maid and linen service, is about the same. Contact Mrs. Lili Don Yechiya at Green Tours, 57 Ben Yehuda St., 10–1 daily.

KIBBUTZ GUEST HOUSES in the area are rated 3-star: **Hafetz Hayim** offers 57 rooms plus pool, beach, bar, coffee shop; south of Gedera; **Beit Yesha,** at Givat Brenner (also south), has 60 air-conditioned rooms, a pool and good tourist facilities.

YOUTH HOSTELS. Two here are: **Tel Aviv,** 32 Bne Dan St., POB 20078, in town with 250 beds, kitchen, air-conditioning, good facilities; and **Petah Tiqva,** Arlosoroff St., POB 786 in Petah Tiqva, between Tel Aviv and Lod (airport), 200 beds, kitchen, etc.

REHOVOT ACCOMMODATIONS. Home of the famous Weizmann Institute of Science, this town is quite near Tel Aviv, and visitors can find one-star facilities at **Margoa Hotel,** which has 17 rooms with bath or shower.

 RESTAURANTS. Tel Aviv has plenty of restaurants of all classes and kinds where you can find French cuisine (with certain reservations . . . .), and Italian, Central European, and traditional Jewish cooking. The list below indicates approximate lunch and dinner prices (drink excluded) as follows: L, *luxury* ($15–$20 and up, per person); E, *expensive* ($10–$15); M, *moderate* ($5–$10). Few of these serve kosher food.

Be not misled by a name: the **Casba** (L), 32 Yirmiyahu, features French dishes, including snails, *fondue bourguignonne* (which most French people disclaim as un-French in origin) and grilled meats; piano music from 8:30 P.M.

Steak House Bernhardt (E), 193 Dizengoff, has fixed-price steak-potato-salad meals or à la carte choices.

Café Stern (M), 189 Dizengoff St., opens for breakfast, and stays open till wee hours, as a favored hangout for TV folk, actors, artists and writers. Well known for goulash, Spanish steak and cassatas—ice cream cakes.

Galei Gondola (L), 57 Pinsker Street, serves peninsular dishes and the cooking is good. **Ron** (E-L), 86 Herbert Samuel Esp., has delicate Italian and French foods, sea fare.

America House (L), 33 Shderot Shaul Hamelekh, located on the 13th floor; magnificent view, elegant decor, cocktail bar, European cuisine and dancing to piano music.

Olympia (E), 41 Carlebach, caters to lunch-only fans, with regulars including ministers, parliament members, top journalists and executives. Famous local favorites like spinach with cheese mussaka, baked lamb, veal. Also shrimp.

Mandy's Candy Store (E), 300 Hayarkon, is a big favorite for good food, variety, "camp" decor, fun people day or night.

The Happy Casserole (M), on Dizengoff's northern tip, serves continental fare and happy atmosphere. Usually packed. Good bar.

Le Versailles (L), 37 Geulah St., is romantic and sometimes called Israel's best restaurant. Family-owned and run, the chef's a member of four major gastronomic societies and produces pure French haute cuisine.

Balkan Corner (E), Rokach Blvd. by Maccabi tennis courts, serves ten kinds of eggplant plus excellent Balkan fare. Dinner only. Call 444301 and be whisked there via vintage Citroën.

Out near David Ben Gurion Airport, **Casa del Sol's** Moroccan decor fakes tenting, but food includes genuine North African treats like couscous (L).

Dinner-dancing is at the **Dolphin** (L), 30 Ben Yehuda. Continental menu at the Viennese **Rishon Cellar** (E), 11 Allenby.

Hotels also offer fine food—particularly try Laromme's **Alei Esh** grill room (elegant), **Mama's Delicatessen** (central European plus Israeli treats), **Galei Yaffo Terrace** (dairy and scenery lovers' haven) and **Canaan Room** (live shows with dinner); Sheraton's **Kum Kum** or **Grill Room,** Hilton's **Milk and Honey** or the **Dan Grill Room,** with nightly pianist and gourmet prize-winning fare.

Kahn ha Dekel ("The Palm Inn") is almost opposite the Avia Hotel on the Tel Aviv-Lod road, and worth the trip (E).

Paprika hallmarks kosher food at **Nes Ziona** (M), 8 Nes Ziona St. For seafood, try **Shaldag Inn** (E), 256 Ben Yehuda; or **El Mar,** 49 Ibn Gvirol.

Tea & Sympathy offers light meals with music at 52 Yermiahu. **L'entrecot** (E), 195 Ben Yehuda, has superb French fare. **La Creperie** serves special dinner and desert crepes at 26 Yermiahu St, and **Banana** offers "natural" foods at 334 Dizengoff. **Pundag** (L) specializes in fresh local seafood, at 8 Frishman; **Goulash Corner** (M) treats you to fine meals at 108 Hayarkon; **Burger Ranch** (the U.S. chain) has about six locations around Tel Aviv, offering fries, a shake and Ranchburger for about $4.

Check the Italian food, particularly pizzas, at **Me & Me,** 293 Dizengoff St., or **Har El,** 6 Yordei Hasira St., or **Rimini** (M), 22 Ibn Gvirol. A good meal is always found at **Gamliel's** (also called **Pninat Hamizrah),** 38 Hakovshim St. And **The Derby,** 326 Dizengoff St., specializes in fine Italian cuisine.

Greek cooking at **Olympus** (M), 12 Hakishon St., and at **Acropolis,** 46 Hamazgher. At 11 Hakishon St., **Beit Hanan** offers Bulgarian treats. These three places close at 5 P.M. **Assa** Balkan restaurant, 49 Bograshov, also serves dinner.

For Chinese food and a piano bar, try **The Singing Bamboo** (E), 317 Hayarkon St., or the **Jackie Onassis** (M)—not "the"—at 52 Chen Blvd., or **Hong**

Kong House (E), 6 Mendele St., **Indonesia** (E), 4 Keren Hayesod, Herzlia Petuach, is Israel's home of the "rijsttafel."

Duck and draught beer are specialties at strictly kosher **Martef Habira** (M), 46 Allenby, while oriental specialties are nearby in Carmel Market's area, where many small, superb restaurants are moderately priced. Moderate to expensive tabs, inside Carmel Market area, are charged by well-known **Shaul's Inn**, 11 Elyahiv St.; **Zion's**, 28 Peduim; **Hirbe's**, 2 Nagara St. All three serve fine Mid-Eastern fare; the first two are luxurious in every way; the last is moderate.

Approximately at the corner of Frishman Street and Hayarkon are two (M) choices: **Fisherman's Inn** and **Goulash** (their menus are obvious!).

Crepe Suzette (M), 313 Hayarkon, offers 12 different tastes of Israeli blintzes, and **Pilintzi** (M), 17 Yermiyahu, one-ups by offering 26 types.

For quick meals, Dizengoff Street, near the fountain-square, has dozens of counter-seat places featuring grilled meats, steaks and burgers, stuffed into round pitta breads with spicy salad, and tasty lamb called shwarma. Self-service **Milk and Honey** is at 11 Frishman St., cafeteria **Frack** is at 131 Dizengoff. **Pizza Domino** is a favorite with locals—it's at Ibn Gvirol corner of Hameasfim St.; also has take-away service. All (M). The "big orange" **Drugstore**, towering over Atarim center, is cool with great view and souvenir/gift shopping below. Other eateries stud the seashore complex, nice for snacks, light meals.

JAFFA

RESTAURANTS. Taj Mahal (E) takes honors for elegant Indian atmosphere, and exciting Indian food. Everything but price is luxurious, even the sea view. The small bar faces the main square of reconstructed Old Jaffa—Tel Aviv's "Montmartre"—where shops and galleries, cafés and restaurants and night spots crop up in delightfully ancient buildings. **Toutoune** lies across the square. **Jeanette's** (E) at sea-level, specializes in fish, and **Ariana** serves Greek dishes.

Yunis, hidden deep in the old town, offers an exotic atmosphere, excellent Arab dishes—on Sheeshim Street, which some call Kedem.

Poiseidon, 14 Kikar Kedumen, Old Jaffa, serves great seafood (L) nightly, along with piano music. **The Patio** specializes in fine French home cooking, at 48 Sha'arei Nicanor St., and **Acropolis** (L), opposite the Museum of Antiquities, offers Greek and seafood specialties.

Near the port entrance is **M. & K. Lipski**, a six-table place serving finest Polish fare at first-class prices, and attracting many local diplomats. Reservations needed. (Old place; new management.)

Baiuca (M), 103 Yehuda Hayamit St., boasts of being Israel's sole Brazilian kitchen.

Alhambra (L), on Jerusalem Street opposite Alhambra Theater, cuts no corners in preparing fine French dishes, so don't expect a rush meal, but do look for its small, candlelit intimacy. Least expensive eating, and quite good, is in outdoor cafés lining the reconstructed area.

On the Jaffa-Lod road, right near Jaffa, look for **Abu Cabir** ("The Palms Inn") for tasty Balkan and Oriental foods, particularly stuffed items. Attractive atmosphere.

Newer restaurants are **Yamit,** 16 Kikar Kedumin, with Mediterranean food served on terrace overlooking same sea, and **Afandi** (Andromeda), 16 Hazorfin, serving Oriental and Israeli kosher dishes. Both (M).

Cafés

The natives reportedly suffer from constant thirst. Visitors will also appreciate the cold fruit juice and ice creams that are for sale at every street corner. The boulevard cafés have terraces and operate as combined snack-bars, pastry-shops, and tea-rooms; *habitués* meet their friends and carry on business there.

Among the interesting ones: **Stern's,** 189 Dizengoff, is always crowded, serves full meals, too—see details under restaurants. You can get a light meal at **Nitsa,** 40 Allenby.

Tel Aviv's literary hang-out is the **Pinati café** on Dizengoff Street, the unofficial "club" of the intellectuals. And writers, journalists, politicians and such can be found at **Stern's, Mandy's Drugstore** or **Mandy's Cherry** (health snacks), and **Tel Aviv HaKitana**—all on Dizengoff's north end. Great sweets are also at **La Javanaise,** 74 Ibn Gvirol. **El Sombrero,** 50 Dizengoff, has authentic Mexican food served at Dizengoff Center.

Note coupon/booklets of *Tel Aviv Tourist Gift Vouchers* are now available for individual tourists through your home-town travel agent or Tel Aviv IGTA. Worth getting.

 NIGHTLIFE. All along the beachside hotel strip, the top hotels have interesting nightlife. All feature special evening entertainment that varies with the season, and most have very live regular happenings, too. There's nightly dancing, dinner and super live shows at **Laromme's Canaan Room** ($20 each); Sheraton has **Joshua's Trumpet** for casual, good music, plus **Dancecoteque,** a campy disco for all ages of tourists and local private members; Hilton's **The Terrace** has happy hour most nights from 5–7 P.M., plus weekly, popular party evenings (IS150 each) such as Tea-n-Symphony, Beer-B-Q and Bar-B-Q; **The Roof** has dancing, drinks and food most nights, and Splash-n-Dance summer parties, atop **Moriah hotel.** Also look for piano bars in most hotels.

Another piano bar to try is **Rafi's** (E) at 1 Yordai Hasira St., with food and dancing nightly.

Peacock's Disco is very popular in Atarim complex on Hayarkon; nearby **Kraus'** is another favorite, and new **Club November** looks promising.

Pubs are becoming big in this town, and royalty of the lot happens to be **Prince of Wales,** near City Hall. Other favorites with tourists and locals are **Shmulik's Corner,** Ben Yehuda at Jabitinsky, and the **BBC,** at the north end of Ben Yehuda. **My Bar,** 10 Frishman, also serves English and U.S. breakfasts. **City Pub,** 267 Dizengoff, serves drinks and snacks and stays cozy till 2 A.M.

Just outside of town, the **Jet Club,** at the Avia Hotel, is popular with air hostesses, pilots and Tel Aviv's beautiful-young-people set. In the same hotel is the **Pub,** a copy of old English pubs in decor, food and drinks; darts, too.

NIGHTCLUBS. Though many night spots in this revitalized ancient town have a way of appearing and disappearing, the **Omar Khayyam** has already enjoyed a long, continuously successful life, and is still going strong. It's in a 500-year old Arab stone mansion; cave-like atmosphere, vaulted ceilings, fish nets draped everywhere. The accent is on Israeli entertainment. Rates are steep. **The Cave** features an Israeli folklore program and, like Omar Khayyam, caters more to a tourist crowd. To be entertained along with Israelis, try the **Khalif,** the **Caravan** and **Zorba** or the newer **Peacock.** All these have live entertainment and lively audiences, and all charge about the same entrance fee.

Another evening treat in Jaffa is the **Sound and Light** show. Every evening except Fridays and eves of holidays; English-language at 9 P.M. Tickets at agencies, hotels and Box Office.

 ENTERTAINMENT. Plays are performed in Hebrew at the *Habima, Cameri, Soldier's House* and Weizman Street theaters. The *Alhambra,* on Jerushalayim Boulevard in Jaffa has **Hebrew musicals. Road shows** are played at the *Dekel Hall, Mifa al Ha'pais Hall, Ohel Shem,* and *Nahmani* theaters.

The *National Opera,* on Allenby Street, is Israel's biggest **opera** house, and the ultra-modern *Mann Auditorium* on Huberman Street (open to visitors mornings at 9:30) is the home of the world-famous Israel Philharmonic. In winter, **chamber music** performances are given at *Dizengoff House* on Rothschild Boulevard and at the *Z.O.A. Club* on Daniel Frisch Street. Big centers along the beach feature frequent **live music and entertainment;** watch local publications for details. Some **moviehouses** have continuous performances, but most of them are open only at set hours.

The Annual **Israel Festival**—all sorts of performing arts, local and international—plays Tel Aviv and Caesarea in July and August; check with IGTA for dates. And in Rehovot, there's a new English-language theater group: see ticket agencies.

 MUSEUMS. The fine **Tel Aviv Municipal Museum** opened on 39 Sderot Shaul Hamelech in 1971. Set in three acres of ground, this complex includes four large exhibition halls, several smaller rooms, the Leon Recanati auditorium seating 450 people, a large lecture hall and a cafeteria. Representative paintings from the Flemish, Italian, and English schools, a few interesting Chagall works, and a collection of English watercolours, several French Impressionist canvases, plus 20th-century works by Israeli and other artists (Max Ernst, Juan Gris, etc.). The old museum on Rothschild Boulevard is due to reopen as the Museum of the Birth of the State of Israel.

Beth Hatefutsoth—Museum of the Jewish Diaspora opened in 1978 at Tel Aviv University Campus. Drawing crowds and raves, it incorporates assorted methods to present story of Jewish survival around the world over 2500 years (from the Second Temple's destruction to 1948 statehood of Israel). Extremely well done, it's a must.

Haaretz Museum complex in Ramat-Aviv (10–5), was recently transferred outside the city limits to Tel Qasile on the Haifa Road beyond the bridge. Its separate museums include Glassware, Ceramics, Numismatics, Ethnography and Folklore, Alphabets, Science and Technology, and Archeology. Most of the objects displayed in these museums are of keen interest to history students, and everyone will enjoy the glass collection, one of the world's finest.

Hagana Museum, 29 Rothschild Blvd., is the former home of Eilahu Golomb, one of the founders and commanders of Hagana, the Jewish underground army that later formed the core of the Israel Defense Forces. Open 10 to 5.

Museum of Antiquities of Tel Aviv-Yafo, 10 Rehov Mifratz Shlomo, near the old port, has fascinating archeological finds relating to Jaffa's rich ancient past. Open 10 to 5; Wednesday to 8 P.M.

Jabotinsky Institute Museum, 38 King George Street, documents the underground movements that grew out of the politics and philosophy of Ze've Jabotinsky, one of the most controversial figures in modern Israeli history.

Museum of the History of Tel Aviv, 27 Bialik Street, displays fascinating photographs and documents relating to the city's foundation and early history. Open 9 to 2, 4 to 7.

Helena Rubinstein Pavilion, 6 Rehov Tarsat, has regularly changing modern art exhibits. Open 10 to 1 and 4 to 7.

Note: It's always a good idea to double check on museum hours; they have a way of changing abruptly, and they do charge.

TOURS. (coach and taxi) **Eggea Tours,** 59 Ben Yehuda, 242–271; **United Tours,** 3 Allenby, 50–131; **ISTA** (student tours), 2 Rehov Pinsker, 59–613; **Gat Touring,** 288 Ben Yehuda, 442297 or 56101; **Hemed Tours,** 118 Hayarkon, 243077; plus nearly 100 independent travel agencies. Check at the Marina and with tour agents for frequent boat cruises.

SHOPPING. Ready-to-wear knit dresses, suits, jerseys, *Bat Adam,* 144 Dizengoff Street; *Iwanir,* 129 Dizengoff Street, 31 Allenby Street, and in the Dan and Hilton hotels. Jersey specialty shops: *Sisters Englander,* 66 Allenby Street, *Boutique Fanchette,* 121 Dizengoff Street, *Schneidman & Sons,* 128 Dizengoff Street.

There are several exciting shops at *Dizengoff Center,* including *Hamishbir Lazarhan,* which also is at 115 Allenby St.—a big department store with plenty of bargains. Several interesting shops are in the Laromme Hotel, and many more are slated to open before the beginning of 1981 across the street at the Charles Clore Park shopping center. Not far inland, at 9 Achad Ha'am St., is

Israel's first department store, *Shalom Stores,* a Mid-Eastern Macy's. Occupying the first three floors of the Shalom Tower (Tel Aviv's Empire State Building). There's even a bargain basement here. Local and foreign-made items are on sale throughout the store—everything from women's fashions to rugs, linens, musical instruments, books and cosmetics. The store has a coffee shop and restaurant. At the top of the 30-story building is an observatory, open 10 A.M. to 10 P.M.; on a clear day, the view's terrific.

Leather and suede (suits, etc.): *Snia,* 133 Dizengoff Street. Men's clothing: *Adam,* 40a Allenby Street; *Victor's Fashions,* 6 Ben Yehuda; *Leon Style,* 33 Allenby Street; *Begged Or,* Old Jaffa; *Danaya,* 7 Bograsov Street; *Schneidman,* 25 Zamenhoff.

At *Shalmon Diamons Ltd.,* 24 Achad Ha'am St., you can choose from a wide display of jewelry.

Arts and crafts, gifts, souvenirs: 119 *Arts and Crafts Gallery,* 119 Rothschild Blvd.; *Domus,* 94 Ben Yehuda; *Batsheva,* 9 Frug Street; *Judean Gallery,* 123 Ben Yehuda; *Masakit* crafts centers. EL-AL Building, Sharon Hotel in Herzliya; *Wizo,* 87 Allenby St.; *Godny,* the Pal Hotel; *Rachel,* 45 Ben Yehuda; *Menora,* 40 Allenby. Jewelry and diamonds: *Padani,* the Pal Hotel; *Topaz,* 121 Dizengoff St.; *H. Stern* has jewelry shops at Pal and the Hilton Hotel and Lod Airport, as well as around the country.

Records: *Schreiber,* 63 Allenby Street. Photography: *Photo Reflex,* 68 Allenby; *Leophot,* 19 Allenby; *Rapid,* 68 Ben Yehuda. Stamps and coins: *Stanek,* at the Pal and Hilton Hotels; *Official Government Shop,* 3 Mendele Street.

SPORTS. Swimming: There are pools in all the big hotels in Tel Aviv and Herzliya and they are open to the public for a fee (Egged bus from the Mendele Street terminus) during the May-through-September season. The two pools in Ramat Gan are good and less expensive: Maccabi Club (No. 35 bus from terminus) and Galei Gil (Nos. 61 and 62 from Ben Yehuda Street). The Egged bus from Mendele Street goes to the Hotel Avia and its pool at Savyon, and the Egged Nos. 85, 86, or Dan Nos. 18, 25 from the terminus go to the Bat Yam Beaches. Other beaches include Tel Aviv's *Gordon Hilton, Sheraton,* and Herzliya's *Sharon* and *Zevulun. Tel Baruch* offers special buses in July and August. Pools also include *Galit,* at Yad Eliahu (buses 33, 36), *Tel Aviv Municipal,* near beach (buses 4, 5). *Ramat Aviv* Hotel (buses 25, 26), Herzliya hotel pools, and the Tel Aviv *Country Club* (bring passport for entry).

Tennis courts at the big hotels and at the Tel Aviv *Country Club,* at *Hapoel Tennis Club* (Sderot Rokach) and *Maccabi Zafon,* also on Sderot Rokach. **Bowling** is on Ibn Gvirol, near Arlosoroff. **Horseback riding** at Gordon's "Sports Farm", near the Ramat Aviv Hotel, with two-hour small group excursions into the countryside. Reservations: phone 41–045. Winter season: **Soccer** games at Maccabi stadium and Ramat Gan stadium, also Bloomfield Stadium, Jaffa. The best basketball games are at the Yad Eliyahu stadium, 51 Gibborei Yisrael St., where Israel's *Sabras* play others of the new European professional basketball league.

Boating: At the Boat Stations, at the end of the Ibn Gvirol and Dizengoff street, rowboats and kayaks can be hired by the hour for 1–5 people. Boats also for rent at Kikar Namir (Afarim)—the marina. Or take a boat sight-seeing tour with the Catamaran—tickets at 98 Hayarkon St.

Tel Aviv's *Safari Land,* in the suburbs, offers closed-car rides through **wild-animal nature reserve** territory. See IGTA for details.

Note: *The Maccabee Games* ("Jewish International Olympics") are played every four years at the Maccabi Club—and 1981 is a games year!

RELIGIOUS SERVICES. Synagogues: *Great* (main) *Synagogue,* 110 Allenby; *Bilu,* 122 Rothschild Blvd.; *Ihud Shivath Zion,* 86 Ben Yehuda; *Ohel Moed* (Sephardic), 5 Rehov Shadel; *Kedem Synagogue* (Progressive), 20 Carlebach Street; *Great Synagogue* (North), 314 Rehov Dizengoff; *Bet El* (Ashkenazi), Rehov Frishman, *Emet V'Anava* (Progressive), Rama Hall, 57 Rehov Jabotinsky, Ramat Gan.

Churches (all of them in Jaffa: take the No. 41 bus): *St. Anthony* (Franciscan), 51 Rehov Yefet; *St. Peter* (R.C.), Mifratz Shlomo; *Maronite Church,* 22 Hadolphin Street; *Immanuel* (Lutheran and Anglican), 15 Rehov Beer Hoffman.

 USEFUL ADDRESSES. Tourist Information. *Israel Ministry of Industry, Trade and Tourism Office,* 7 Mendele Street, tel. (03)223266/7. *Tel Aviv Municipal Tourist Information Offices:* Town Hall, 42 Frishman Street, 223692; Central Bus Station, 31101; Jerusalem Boulevard (Jaffa), 821133; 19 Brodetzky Street (Ramat Aviv), 415176.

Embassies. *US,* Hayarkon Street, 56171; *Great Britain,* 192 Hayarkon Street, 249171; *Canada,* 218 Hayarkon Street, 267121; *Australia,* 145 Hayarkon Street, 221263.

Post-office. 132 Allenby; Telegrams: 7 Mikveh Israel; Stamps for philately, post-office, 2 Pinsker St., and 5 Mendele St.

Car hire. *Hertz, Avis* and many local firms vie to rent cars from offices in hotels, at airports and around town. Travel agents also can help you find cars and guides for hire. Excellent miscellaneous data about driving in Israel is yours at the *Automobile Touring Club of Israel,* 19 Derekh Petah Tikva, 622961.

Sherut taxis to Beersheba-Eilat, 622555; to Jerusalem and Haifa, 622888; to Nazareth, 611055; to Safad and Haifa-Nahariya, 615011.

USEFUL PHONE NUMBERS. Police 100; **Ambulances** (Magen David Adom) 101; **Fire Dept.** 102.

JERUSALEM

Crossroads of Religion

Jerusalem is a holy city for the three great monotheistic religions that embrace half of the world's population. It is also Israel's capital, the residence of its president, the center of government, the seat of the High Rabbinate (the supreme Jewish religious body), of the *Knesset* (parliament), of the Jewish Agency, and of the World Zionist Organization. Perched 2,400 feet up amid the Judaean hills, the city is home to 376,000 persons of all races and creeds.

Despite the fact that Jerusalem is one of the world's most ancient cities of continuous habitation, it manages to look unfinished in many areas. This is because it is constantly growing. Jerusalem's longterm project is to double its present size. In its center, which used to be the outskirts, the *kirya,* or administrative complex, is taking shape. In addition to the government buildings, it also is the site of the Hebrew

University and the Israel Museum. Much new housing is under construction, so, on all sides scaffolding and cranes tower above the old, low buildings, and silhouettes of practically completed or half-finished buildings pierce the skyline. Even so, the city is beautiful, and Jerusalem's famed pinkish-golden stone is displayed to peak advantage here, combining inate strength with durability.

There is still empty space—open stretches, rises, slopes and valleys—between the various housing complexes. Much of this will remain open as green parks and squares, flowered terraces and public monuments. Some of it, however, is allocated to become sites for low-rent apartments (*shikun,* or *shikunim,* in the plural).

In this chapter, we deal with the newer, or Western, Jerusalem, and then go into the Eastern, or older, Jerusalem. But first, some history.

A Glance at History

Barely a century ago, an English Jew bearing the flowery Italian name of Sir Moses Montefiore started to build housing developments outside old Jerusalem's walls. This venture was further underwritten by a wealthy American, Judah Touro. The Turks who were then occupying the country didn't mind. As far as the Jews in Palestine were concerned, it was merely the fulfilment of one of Isaiah's prophecies. The very first house built here with American dollars can be seen today outside the enclosure in the Montefiore quarter named after its creator. The windmill, down the street from the King David Hotel, was also built with Montefiore funds. Refurbished and restored, these old buildings now house guest VIP artists.

When the British evicted the Turks in 1917, the city once more became Jewish, but under British Mandate. Thirty-two years were to pass before it became the capital. A long road had been traveled since biblical times, when Jerusalem was known simply as Salem. In the *Torah,* the book of holy writ, it is recorded the "Melchisedech, the King of Salem, a priest of the true God, came bearing bread and wine."

The occasion was the celebration of Abraham's victory over the king of Elam, whereby his nephew Lot was delivered from captivity. Six centuries later Pharaoh Akhenaton's special envoy was appointed governor of Urusalim: this fact is borne out in the envoy's letters to his ruler (c.1375 B.C.).

David wrested the city by force from the Jebusites. At that time, it was going under the designation of Jebus. Such were the etymological derivations of the name of Jerusalem. Only 3,000 years ago it was David's capital, hence the familiar title of the "City of David."

Amid grand pomp (II SAMUEL, VI) David caused the Ark of the Covenant to be borne here, where it remained in a somewhat precarious plight until the First Temple was erected by his son Solomon (975–935 B.C.). In those days Jerusalem was the real center of the country, its religious, spiritual, and political hub. In II Chronicles (CHAPTERS II TO V), we learn that 153,000 laborers worked for seven years to build the temple. The country was later divided into the two kingdoms of Israel and Judea, and Jerusalem remained the capital of the latter. In about 587 B.C. its last king, Zedekiah, was defeated by Nebuchadnezzar who, with his Babylonian army, destroyed Jerusalem and its temple and trapped the residents.

Host of Invaders

A "count-down" of the pre-Christian era shows that this destruction lasted until 538 B.C. but shortly after that, Cyrus, the Persian ruler, allowed the Jew Nehemiah to rebuild Jerusalem. The drawback was that this land of milk and honey continued to remain a temptation to conquerors. Two centuries later, Alexander the Great took Jerusalem; his successors, Hellenized Syrians, tried to enthrone Zeus in the reconstructed temple. That was pushing matters too far. The Maccabees armed for battle, and recaptured the city from the Greeks in 165 B.C. The ensuing reign of the Hasmoneans lasted barely 100 years.

In the wake of a new invasion—by the Romans this time—a usurper became king: he was the grandson of Antipater, a notorious fifth columnist, and his name was Herod the Great, and he ruled from 40 B.C. till his death in 4 B.C. His sons then ruled, but rebellion of Jewish Zealots led to general revolt of the hard-pressed Jews in A.D. 65. Vespasian harshly subdued it, then turned his command over to his son, Titus. Rebellion and fighting continued until, in A.D. 70, Titus stormed Jerusalem, destroyed the Temple, enslaved thousands of Jews. Masada fell to Rome via mass suicide. A.D. 133 saw Simon Bar Kochba's short-lived revolt, before Emperor Hadrian destroyed Jerusalem in A.D. 135, rebuilt it and decreed no Jew could enter the city again.

WEST JERUSALEM

What to see in West (New) Jerusalem? Count on seeing practically everything! You can concentrate on any or all of the three main fields of interest—religion, relics of antiquity, and monuments of the present and the future.

Let's take the religious tour first. The various shrines and holy places overlap. Some of them date from the pre-Islamic era. Still others go back to the time when most Christians were converted Jews and point up the direction the new faith was to follow. They have in common the shared legacy of the Old Testament. Most pilgrims are eager to see Mt. Zion first, the hill that is crowned by the Church of the Dormition and the Tomb of David.

The Church of the Dormition and its monastery were dedicated at the beginning of the 20th century. They stand on ground presented by the Turkish sultan to the German emperor. According to Christian tenets, this was where the Virgin Mary "fell into eternal sleep." The sanctuary is ringed by chapels; the walls are covered with medallions commemorating Jesus' forebears, the Kings of Judea; and the floor is adorned with symbols of the months, saints, and prophets. The crypt contains a stone sculpture representing Mary in her last sleep.

The inscription around the wall is from the Song of Solomon (II, 13): "Arise, my love, my beautiful one, and come." These were the words of Jesus calling his mother, as the decoration of the dome shows. The Roman Catholic Church has adopted the Assumption of the Virgin as dogma. The chapels surrounding the crypt were donated by different countries, the Austrian one being in memory of Dollfuss, the prime minister who fell a victim to Nazi persecution.

The Last Supper

The Cenacle, or Upper Chamber, is a Gothic room built on the site of Christ's Last Supper with the disciples, on which the Eucharist is based. Seven weeks after the Passion, the Holy Ghost appeared here to the assembled disciples. This was the origin of the Pentecost, as recorded in the Acts of the Apostles. The old part of the city is clearly discernible from the rooftops.

A medieval building leads to the Tomb of David. The cenotaph contains an impressive sarcophagus. Brocade hangings adorn the walls and the solid silver crowns of the Torah provide a decorative motif. Although this site was not discovered until the 12th century, during the preceding 200 years people had been claiming that the great king's remains lay buried here. David is believed to be entombed with the other kings of Judea on the Ophel, the southern slope of the hill on which the Temple stood.

To the left of Mt. Zion stretches the Montefiore district, Yemin Moshe, a fascinating artists' quarter. In its midst is a windmill that served as a lookout tower in the War of Independence. The Hinnom canyon (from Ge-Hinnom, the source of Gehenna) was the scene of the desecrations that caused Jeremiah's wrath: this was Tophet, where children were sacrificed to Moloch.

Down the street, taking a left turn at the railway station, is another observation-post, Abu-Tor, a name meaning father of the ox, after the nickname of one of Saladin's lieutenants who refused to ride any other animal. Formerly, the Jordanian frontier cut through here. Today, a new housing development is going up.

In the region ahead lies the complete setting of the original Passion: the Mount of Olives, the Garden of Gethsemane, site of the Holy Sepulcher and Golgotha. On top of all this, ensuing ages have been busy adding other accessories in the course of the last two millennia. The gleaming gold Dome of the Rock marks the spot on which Abraham was preparing to immolate his son Isaac.

Below the Israel Museum in Jerusalem lies a deep ravine. Formerly, this valley was forest land. On a certain Easter in that forest a tree was felled from which a heavy cross was fashioned. This event is commemorated by a medieval fortress-like structure called the Monastery and Church of the Holy Cross; a magnificent Gregorian-inspired building.

Three Excursions

For the purposeful pilgrim to Jerusalem, there are three important excursions that are a must.

First of all, there's Ramat Rahel, the Hill of Rachel (Bus 7). This is a *kibbutz* located at what was the southernmost point of the Israeli part of Jerusalem. Bitter fighting went on here during the War of Independence. The buildings have all been restored, except for a small patch on one façade that has been left with its scars intact as testimony to heroism. During the Six Day War, Ramat Rahel traded lead in a furious battle with Jordanian troops, who had a strongpoint at Mar Elias Monastery across the way.

Excavations here have brought to light vestiges of an ancient settlement, plus the casemates of a Jewish royal citadel. Together with various fragments, seals bearing Hebrew inscriptions have made it possible to assign a reasonably accurate date to the seven superimposed layers of these ruins—from the 7th century B.C. through the 7th century A.D.

From the terrace overlooking the excavations you can discern a few short miles away on the horizon, the town of Bethlehem, Jesus's birthplace. Visible are two landmarks: the Church of the Nativity and, closer in along the highway, the Monastery of St. Elijah (or Elias).

The main yard of the kibbutz contains a modern sculpture commemorating Rachel and her children. The inscription is a prophecy from Jeremiah (XXXI, 15 TO 17):

"A voice was heard in Ramah, lamentation, and bitter weeping,

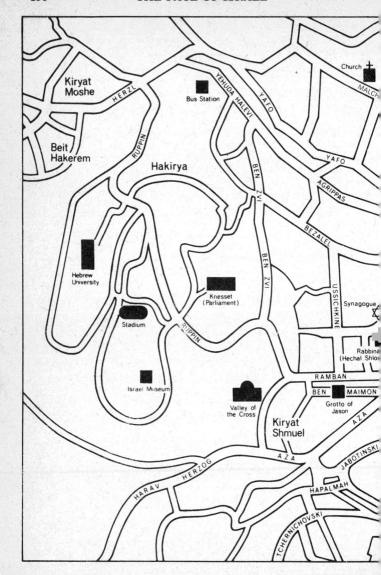

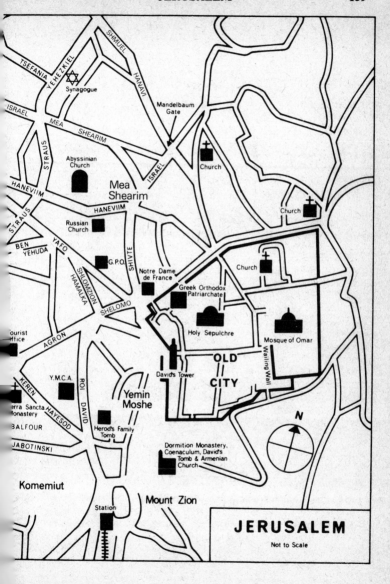

JERUSALEM

Not to Scale

Rachel weeping for her children; she refuses to be comforted for her
children for they are not . . . And there is hope for your future, says
the Lord; and your children shall return to their own border."

Ein Kerem

The second excursion is to Ein Kerem (Bus 27), whose name sig-
nifies the spring of the vineyards. The spring itself greets you at the
entrance to the charming small village. It was the birthplace of Za-
charias, the priest, struck dumb for disbelieving God's promise that he
would have a son, but who regained the power of speech when his son,
John the Baptist, was born. Elizabeth, his wife, received a visit from
one of her relatives, Mary, who was herself soon to become a mother.
The Church of the Visitation commemorates the meeting between
these two mothers-to-be, just as the Church of St. John commemorates
the grotto in which the great Baptist was born. In addition, the Russian
Church and the Franciscan Monastery are both dedicated to St. John.
The contributions that modern times have made here are lavish ones
indeed: a children's village established by the Labor Federation; a city
for 20,000 people now under construction; and the Hadassah Medical
Center, high up on the north side.
It is the largest hospital in the Middle East. The blueprints were
drawn in the United States, whence came also the necessary funds and
equipment. This fact may partially explain why the final result doesn't
quite fit in with its surroundings. From the medical and therapeutic
standpoint, it is a perfect achievement, and that is what really matters,
even if the building's ventilation system wasn't designed in terms of
Jerusalem's temperatures. The new Kennedy Information Center provides tour information and lunches.
The imposing complex also includes a modern-style synagogue. Its
stained-glass windows, designed by Marc Chagall, were exhibited in
Paris and New York before their installation. The subject is the twelve
tribes of Israel.
Where the road leading to the Hadassah Hospital forks, a left turn
will take you out into the hills past the Moshav Aminadav. On a high
mountaintop 20 minutes from Jerusalem stands the *Kennedy Memorial*
(Yad Kennedy), opened in 1966. Designed in the shape of a cut tree-
trunk, the dramatic memorial is built of bent struts, each column
bearing the seal of an American state. Inside, it is empty—save for the
eternal light in the middle of the floor and a bust of the late President.
The view from the parking lot and picnic grounds is magnificent: a
panorama of slopes and valleys that looks the same today, one feels,
as it did in biblical times.

Abu Ghosh

Abu Ghosh is the last on your list of excursions with a religious interest. At one time this was a hideout for highway bandits who robbed travelers going to Jerusalem. A few years ago Jewish fighters received aid and protection from its Arab inhabitants, a few of whom even joined the underground terrorist movement.

This is the original site of Kiryat Yearim. The Ark of the Covenant was kept here until David transferred it to Jerusalem (I CHRONICLES, XIII, 6). The Crusaders mistakenly identified this village with the city of Emmaus that is mentioned in the Gospels. The Church of the Crusaders, at the entrance to the village, is one of the best-preserved relics of the Crusades. It was built around 1142, and spared destruction by Moslems because of the spring on which it stands. Destruction of the church would have meant loss of the indispensable water source. Some seventy years ago, the French government acquired title to the church and turned it over to the Benedictine Order. It has since been transferred to the Lazarist Fathers, or mission priests.

On the top of a nearby hill is a gigantic statue of the Virgin and Child. It is guarded by the Sisters of St. Joseph, who call it Our Lady of the Ark of the Covenant. They claim that the building, which dates from 1924, was constructed over the remains of one occupied by Abinadab in biblical times. One thing does appear certain, that the present building was constructed on the foundations of a 5th-century Byzantine church. There are mosaics to prove this, plus the fact that stones and columns belonging to the previous building were incorporated into the new one. Underneath it lies evidence of even earlier constructions, probably Hasmonean (second century).

The devout religious pilgrim in Jerusalem will also want to see the many other holy sites representing a variety of faiths and beliefs.

Archeological Itinerary

It is as ticklish to disassociate archeology from history as it is to distinguish clearly between History with a capital H, and the mass of recorded events that make up the annals of time. Most visitors are interested in seeing the Tomb of Herod, a series of burial vaults hewn right out of the rock and sealed with a great rounded stone. Scholars are well acquainted with Herod; the average person, however, has a vague notion that Herod was somehow connected with the story of Jesus, but the exact connection escapes him.

Wasn't it Herod who had John the Baptist beheaded and served up the head on a silver platter to his daughter-in-law Salome after the famous dance of the seven veils? Various well-known composers, including Richard Strauss, are responsible for perpetuating this legend, as are certain artists, and, of course, the movies.

We'll take the opportunity here to summarize a few of the facts concerning Herod. First, there was Herod the Great, the usurper enthroned by Rome in about the year 40 B.C. It was he who ordered the Massacre of the Innocents, hoping in that way to get rid of the Infant Jesus. It was this Herod who founded the city of Caesarea. It was another Herod, Antipas, who yielded to the arguments of Herodias, his wife, as well as to Salome's ravishing good looks, and cut off John the Baptist's head. And when Pontius Pilate, after washing his hands, deferred the final decision about Jesus' fate to Herod, it was Herod Antipas. But when we say "as old as Herod," we mean still a third king by that name, Herod Agrippa II, king of Judea from A.D. 52 to 68, who lived to be 100 years old, dying in Rome in the year 100. Let us add, too, that the true Tomb of Herod is in the Herodion—a fortress built by Herod on a hill to the south-east of Bethlehem. The distinctive conical hill on which the Herodion stands is visible on a clear day from Ramat Rahel.

Another set of tombs, a short walk north of Mea Shearim, is the Sanhedriya, also known as the Tomb of the Judges or the Catacombs. Three separate levels of alcoves hewn out of solid rock serve as burial-places. The name derives from the tradition according to which, in Jesus' time, the prophet Samuel and the members of the Sanhedrin were interred here. (The latter was the supreme political and ecclesiastical council of 71 Wise Men, which also functioned as a high court.)

There's also the Alfasi grotto, in the Rehavia residential district, discovered by accident in 1956. The workers who were excavating for foundations suddenly struck thin air. Experts took over and carefully cleared around the diggings. To the boundless delight of archeologists (and the dismay of the property owner) they uncovered a necropolis presumed to date from the Maccabean era. The walls bore odd motifs, such as a couched stag and ships waging a naval battle. The grotto was officially named after an inscription carved in the stone: the Tomb of Jason (or Yason).

Memorial to Six Million

Although the preceding pretty well covers the visits of archeological interest, there are still other places considered sacred by many people. Whatever their basic motivations, all pilgrimages stem from the underlying desire to pay homage to an important person or a significant event. The trip to Har-Hazikaron, the Memorial Hill, meets this definition with its imposing and deeply stirring monument to the six million

Jewish victims of Nazi persecution: Yad Vashem. An eternal flame burns here. Rarely has a monument designed by men blended in such perfect communion with the occurrences of facts that it commemorates.

The building itself is simple, low structure, with walls that look as if they were composed of random fallen boulders. The low, ponderous ceiling adds to your overwhelming feeling of oppression, of being closed in and crushed the instant you cross the threshold into the main enclosure, where names of concentration camps are inscribed on the floor. Other areas illustrate the persecution of six million Jews, leaving nothing to the imagination, including the story of the rise and fall of Hitler's regime, and library files with details of Holocaust victims. You easily could spend half-a-day here, going from place to place and reflecting.

Other Jerusalem Sites

Many visitors will want to make the trip to Mt. Herzl, the last resting-place of Theodor Herzl, the Austro-Hungarian journalist who "invented" Zionism. Devoted hands have carefully constructed a replica of the Viennese study in which Herzl worked.

When Jerusalem had to defend itself against the attacking Arab forces in 1948, its entire artillery consisted of a single improvised mortar more like a toy, called a *Davidka*, after the name of its inventor. This contraption is displayed in a monument on Jaffa Road. Along these same general lines, you might also be interested in seeing the former British prison in the Russian compound, containing the cell in which two Jewish prisoners, sentenced to death by the British, committed suicide with a hand-grenade rather than be hanged by the mandatory authorities. How had the Resistance managed to slip grenades to these prisoners right under John Bull's nose and despite the extraordinary security precautions? The history of the new Jewish State is written on many a blood-soaked page.

The Romema Memorial commemorating General Allenby's entrance into Jerusalem in December, 1917; the Roman Catholic Ratisbonne Monastery of the Zionist Fathers; the YMCA building (a fine view from the top of its tower); and, just across the way, the King David Hotel, the British headquarters. When an anonymous phonecall one day informed them that a bomb had been planted in the hotel and would explode at a certain hour, they didn't budge. With traditional British phlegm, they decided that this was just another practical joke. They simply couldn't believe that anyone could have slipped a bomb into their citadel. The bomb went off from its vantage point in a milk can in the basement of the hotel.

In addition there are the Franciscan College of the Terra Sancta, and the Yeshurun Central Synagogue, Jerusalem's finest, containing an impressive Hebrew library. The Mandelbaum Gate, once the only means of access between the two parts of the city, is now just another thoroughfare. Now we come to the edge of an amazing quarter, Mea Shearim.

Mea Shearim

Two different origins are assigned to the name of Mea Shearim, which is generally translated as the "hundred gates." The only sure thing about it is the figure 100. One of the meanings of Mea Shearim is "hundredfold." However, it could also refer to one hundred gates, for according to one story this neighborhood was originally surrounded by a wall containing many gates, possibly as many as a hundred. Whichever, the attractions here are right in the streets, especially on Fridays when everybody is out shopping for the Sabbath.

Open-air stalls line the tiny streets on both sides. Wherever you look there are swarms of all kinds of picturesque characters, some clamoring loudly, others going quietly about their business, bearded men with long hair, clean-shaven men, faces smiling or serious, everybody thronging the narrow lanes, entering and leaving shops, buying, selling, haggling over merchandise, pretending to disdain an offer and then suddenly resuming the bargaining, people off in a corner discussing politics, religion, ritual, arguing over the meaning of an isolated word in the Torah, or meditating in solitude, impervious to the bustle and racket.

Similar scenes, minus the merchandise, can be found in the quarter's many synagogues of all sizes, in the Talmudic schools, called *yeshivot,* or sometimes designated simply by the German word *Schul.*

The inhabitants here are the most extreme and pious of Israel. So much so, that some don't even recognize the existence of any modern State. Their reasoning is elementary: "Man cannot take his fate into his own hands, he must merely wait for the Messiah— *then* there can be a Jewish State." Others see today's Israel as the beginning of the redemption. The women keep their heads shaven, and wear kerchiefs over wigs: once safely married, they have no more use for the extraneous adornment of crowning glory. (Actually, it might take the husband's mind from scripture study.) In contrast, most of the men fairly exude hairiness, their beards and fringes untouched by any barber's shears. They usually wear short French culotte-type breeches, tight-fitting around the knee, the familiar long cloaks, and the fur-edged velvet hats reminiscent of the early Eastern ghetto scene. Their facial pallor is the result of long hours of poring over the sacred writings of the Torah, and their faces are framed in long ringlets frequently falling to their shoulders. These ringlets are the only unshaven part of their heads, for the Bible forbids them to be cut. The rest is shaven so as not to interfere with direct thinking towards heaven: despite the skull cap worn between head and heaven at all times.

These people live in strict observance of Jewish precepts. When, as it sometimes happens, different interpretations of Jewish Law find themselves at variance, a new sect is born. Schisms occur over details that would strike an outsider as utterly trivial. The ritual procedure adopted is scrupulously adhered to down to the dot of the "i." People here have a fixed, intent gaze in their eyes.

For them life is meaningless unless sanctified by the Word of the Lord as they choose to interpret it, only they never consider "choose" as having anything to do with their interpretations. Although they are aware of the outside world and recognize scientific progress, the centuries mean nothing to them. It's impossible to tell whether they are living in the past, the future, or quite simply in eternity. A five-year-old child playing in the street has already begun to resemble an elderly wise man. One familiar story concerns a schoolmaster in a literature class who admonished one of his young pupils by saying: "If you make one mistake in reading, I'll put out one of your eyes. If you make two mistakes. I'll put out your other eye. At the third mistake . . . ." Here he was gleefully interrupted by the child's exclamation: "When both my eyes are gone, there can't *be* any third mistake!" This flash of precociously enlightened mischief must surely have filled the teacher's own eyes with that special gleam of malice and childlike delight that strikes you in the gaze of these hirsute worthies and their parchment-like skin.

Be sure you are on your best sartorial behavior, for right in the market-place is a warning sign written in English, Hebrew, and Yiddish; "Jewish Daughter—The Torah obligates you to dress with modesty. We do not tolerate people passing through our streets immodestly dressed—Committee for Guarding Modesty." It's a fact that girls in bermudas have occasionally been spat at, insulted, shoved and chased when they've wandered in here. The Committee for Guarding Modesty means what it says.

For the 24-hour beginning with Friday evening, the entire quarter relapses into a kind of lethargy. The Israeli Sabbath is observed with thanksgiving and prayer, and in Mea Shearim this statement can be multiplied a hundred-fold (again the mystical number) without exaggeration. Precepts and prohibitions are enforced here more relentlessly and in a more straitlaced manner than anywhere else.

The hapless driver of a car whose exhaust-pipe pops and bangs its way through this fortress of faith may find a few samples of local stone flung at him and his offending vehicle for violating the Sabbath. This is the doughty citadel of Jewish orthodoxy, the private preserve of the Orthodox, the pious ones.

Not everyone in Israel wholeheartedly approves of this radical attitude. When the tension mounts in Mea Shearim, serious clashes occasionally break out between the more progressive citizens and the partisans of rigid tradition. Yet, the sturdy defenders of the old faith won't budge an inch. When all is said and done, such steadfastness of purpose commands respect. Every Jew realizes that the very fact that his people have been able to survive 2,000 years of persecution is due to such strength and perseverance. There is no question that their stubbornness can be exasperating, but the real question that arises is whether or not Judaism itself would be in existence today without that very stubbornness.

The Israel Museum

Admirers of antiquity, lovers of old parchments and inscriptions, of ancient and modern art, of history, of archeology—in a word, of pure beauty—will find ample satisfaction in the four parts of Jerusalem's fine museum.

This vast complex includes the Samuel Bronfman Biblical and Archeological Museum, the Bezalel National Museum of Art (both housed in the main building designed by two Israeli architects, A. Mansfeld and Dora Gad), the Shrine of the Book (which is the work of two Americans, Frederick J. Kiesler and Armand P. Bartos), and the Billy Rose Sculpture Garden, created by the famed Japanese sculptor and architect Isamu Noguchi. The overall achievement, set amid lovely gardens, is a tribute to its founders and in glorious keeping with Jerusalem's venerable past. (Buses 5, 16.)

The art treasures from the Bezalel Museum, consisting mainly of hand-crafted artisan objects, have been transferred to the main building and are arranged and displayed in conformity with the latest techniques of lighting and didactic impact. In addition to its sumptuous examples of Jewish and Middle-Eastern religious art—including jewelry, ritual objects, wrought gold, pearls and other precious and semi-precious stones—paintings by Picasso, Dufy, Chagall, Braque, Léger, Marchand, Gleizes, Masson, Soutine, de Kooning, Stuart Davis, and Lynn Chadwick, among others; engravings and drawings by Rembrandt, Van Ostade, Miró, Pascin, Zaritzky; as well as ancient frescos and mosaics, are displayed.

An entire room has been given over to the faithful reconstitution of the Vittorio Veneto synagogue, which was transported here and put together again with all the careful attention due its position as a treasure of 17th-century Venetian art. All of the above is in Museum No. 1.

Museum No. 2, in the same building, offers a chronological record of history in an archeological context, from the prehistoric era through the 17th century. The collection includes stones, steles, inscriptions and ceramics. You can cover from six to eight millennia in ten hours or ten minutes, depending on your interest in mankind's past. Descriptive notices in Hebrew, French and English provide information on the various successive stages in the evolution of men and their civilizations.

Museum No. 3 is the Shrine of the Book. Architects Kiesler and Bartos derived inspiration for this building from the Mycenaean *tholos* (beehive tombs similar to the famous tomb of Clytemnestra and Atreus), considering it ideally suited to receive the Dead Sea Scrolls. Its peculiar shape is styled after the top of a jug in which part of the Dead Sea Scrolls were discovered.

The members of the Essene community regarded themselves as the Sons of Light, believing that the rest of the world was inhabited only by the Sons of Darkness. This intellectual contrast is strikingly conveyed through the interplay of lighting effects and an unusually low entranceway: you stoop down to cross the threshold, exactly as if you were entering the cave in which the scrolls were discovered. In addition to the Dead Sea Scrolls, the shrine also contains the letters of Bar Kochba—which include the Isaiah parchments—and cooking vessels and clothes from the same finds. Recent finds at Masada have greatly enriched this collection. The scrolls found in this latter locality bear authentic pre-A.D. 70 dates. (The subject of Masada is treated in the chapter on the Negev.)

It would be understandable for lovers of old books and manuscripts, admirers of the recorded word, to fear that a museum devoted exclusively to ancient parchments might quickly begin to pall on the beholder. We hasten to reassure you. The impeccable taste that is reflected everywhere here, in the construction, the decoration, and the exhibits themselves, makes a visit more than worthwhile. There is no question as to the outstanding intrinsic interest of these records.

Museum No. 4 is a private bequest. Throughout his career, New York's great showman Billy Rose was an ardent and enlightened collector of classic and modern sculpture. In his will he left his entire collection to Israel. Through his generosity, works by Henry Moore, Daumier, Rodin, Maillol, Germaine Richier, and the other eminent sculptors are ensconced in an ideal setting amid the enchantments of one of Noguchi's gardens.

The Israel Museum underwent renovations and revisions in 1978, adding a new Youth Wing and expanding exhibitions.

What other sights and things should you see and do in Jerusalem? Just look around. Breathe the air. Stroll in any direction. The eternal past surrounds you.

EAST JERUSALEM

The 1948 Arab-Israel war left Jerusalem a divided city. A winding armistice line—twisting like a thread idly dropped on the ground—cleft Jerusalem into two parts: West Jerusalem (also called New Jerusalem, or Jewish Jerusalem) in the Israeli sector, and East Jerusalem (also known as Old Jerusalem or Arab Jerusalem) in the Jordanian sector, and a barbed-wire strip cut between the two like a livid scar.

Within the confines of East Jerusalem lay almost all of the Holy City's religious sites (Mt. Zion being the only exception) sacred to Christians, Jews and Moslems—the Church of the Holy Sepulcher, the Wailing Wall and the Dome of the Rock being chief amongst them.

For 19 years, the only link between the two parts of the city was the Mandelbaum Gate, where non-Jewish tourists could make a one-time crossing (Jordanian authorities did not permit re-entry into Israel, nor re-entry into Jordan, if the tourists made the crossing from there).

Ironically, the Jordanians themselves triggered the city's reunification when they started bombarding West Jerusalem, June 5, 1967. Two days later, East Jerusalem was in Israeli hands after some of the bitterest fighting of the Six-Day War.

After the war, bulldozers began tearing down the wires and makeshift rubble dividing the city and on June 29, 1967, Jerusalem was united again, with 200,000 Jews and 66,000 Arabs milling together like Sunday strollers looking in wonder at the Jerusalem they had not seen for two decades. Today, there's no trace of that war, unless it lies in the area's prosperity.

Almost every turning in East Jerusalem reveals some significant site of religious or historical interest and one could spend weeks, months . . . even years combing every street and alleyway without exhausting its treasures. Many visitors feel East Jerusalem holds more enchantment per square foot than any other place in the world.

Almost all who come to East Jerusalem for the first time—whether as pilgrims or vacationers—make a bee-line for the old City. Within its walls, built by Suleiman the Magnificent four centuries ago, lie three great shrines of the monotheistic religions: the Church of the Holy Sepulcher, the Western (Wailing) Wall, and the Dome of the Rock.

These precincts, venerated by Christians, Jews and Moslems, have a special aura about them, one not found anywhere else in the world. Few moments are as inspiring as to stand by the remnant of the Second Temple, hearing the murmur of prayer rebounding from the ancient Wall and rising to join the call of a muezzin from a nearby minaret . . . both sounds mingling with tolling of church bells.

The Way of the Cross

The Damascus and Jaffa Gates are the principal entries to the Old City, but the Christian visitor may seek out St. Stephen's Gate on the eastern perimeter to make his entry. This way he will follow in the footsteps of Jesus, for this is the entrance to the Way of the Cross—the Via Dolorosa. This too, incidentally, is the way Israeli troops entered the city on June 6, 1967. The gate is known in Hebrew as Lion's Gate.

Immediately to the right after the gate is the Church of St. Anne, a gem of Crusader architecture. This church, according to legend, is built over the spot where Joachim and Anne, the parents of Mary, had their home. A crypt shows the spot where Mary was born. This too is supposed to be the site of the Pool of Bethesda mentioned in the Gospel of St. John. Outside the walls at this point is the Pool of Mary.

On the left side is the Gate of the Tribes, which leads to the Temple Mount.

Further down the street, to the left, in the yard of an Arab school, formerly the site of a fortress—is the first of the 14 Stations of the Cross. It was here that Pontius Pilate questioned Jesus, washed his hands of the affair and condemned him. Across the narrow street, the Chapel of the Flagellation stands on the spot, also formerly within the fortress, where Jesus was stripped of his clothes, whipped, and forced to wear the Crown of Thorns and the robe of royal purple.

Then Pilate declared to the crowd, *Ecce Homo*—"Behold the Man" —and Jesus started his final journey up the Via Dolorosa. This, the Second Station, is marked by the "Ecce Homo" arch which spans the narrow street, but was not built until A.D. 135—about 100 years after Jesus's death—by the Emperor Hadrian.

As you pass up the narrow street, following in Jesus's footsteps, your guide will point out the other stations. All are marked:

3rd: Jesus falls for the first time. A small chapel commemorates the event; 4th: Jesus meets Mary; 5th: According to all but one Gospel (John), at this spot Simon of Cyrene takes the cross from Jesus and carries it the rest of the way. In contradiction, John contends that Simon merely tried to help him with the burden; 6th: Jesus' face is wiped by Veronica. Her veil, which still carries the imprint of his face, is in St. Peter's in Rome; 7th: Jesus falls for the second time; 8th: A small cross set into the wall marks the spot where Jesus spoke to the women of Jerusalem, "Weep not for me but for yourselves, and for your children;" 9th: Jesus falls for the third time. A column at the entrance of a Coptic Church marks the spot; 10th: Jesus's robe is taken away; 11th: Jesus is mounted on the cross; 12th: He dies; 13th: His body is laid on a slab of stone; 14th: Jesus is buried and from here resurrected. (Stations 10 through 14 are within the Church of the Holy Sepulcher.)

The Holy Sepulcher

Some visitors to the Church of the Holy Sepulcher may be disappointed. It is dark and gloomy, and since the church is shared by several sects—Greek Orthodox, Roman Catholics, Armenian, Syrian, Coptic and Abyssinians—the building is cluttered with their various chapels and hanging lights. And while Protestants are barred from holding services in the church, this is the holiest of holy sites to all Christians. The repairs to the church, begun several years ago, are being continued and visitors may find scaffolding, ladders and piles of tools in their path.

The church is set on the Hill of Golgotha, literally Skull Hill, as it derives from the Hebrew word for a skull, *gulgolet.* It is called Calvary from the Latin translation of the word. Legend has it that Adam's skull was buried here. The hill itself is today indistinguishable under the church but is exposed here and there in the nether reaches of the ancient structure.

Just inside the entrance is the Stone of Unction, where Jesus was anointed after being taken down from the Cross. In the high-domed Rotunda is the Holy Sepulcher. There are two chapels on the spot. One, called the Angel's Chapel, shows the stone covering the tomb, which the angel rolled away. The other contains the tomb or sepulcher, lined with marble.

There are numerous tombs and chapels throughout the church among them the Tomb of Joseph of Arimathea; the tombs of two Crusader kings, Baldwin and Godfroy; the Chapel of Adam and the Chapel of St. Helena, dedicated to the mother of the Emperor Constantine. It is said that Helena, in the year 326, was divinely guided to this place, where she discovered the True Cross.

Every Friday afternoon, there is a procession along the Via Dolorosa to the Church of the Holy Sepulcher.

During the Holy Week, the rites, ceremonies and processionals of the various Christian sects sharing the church are particularly colourful and impressive.

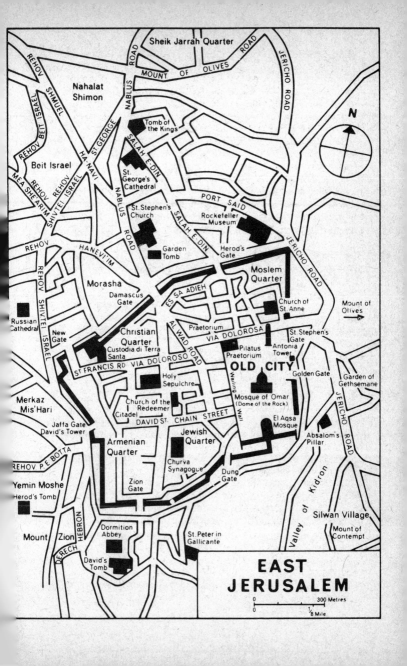

The Western (Wailing) Wall

Signs through the Old City will guide you "To The Wall." The closest gate to the Wall is the Dung Gate, so called because the city's garbage was taken out through there in olden times, to be dumped down the slopes of the Valley of Kidron.

Jews call the Wall the *Kotel Ha'maaravi*—the Western Wall, its stones deeply embedded in Jewish consciousness. In physical fact, the Wall is a section of the retaining and supporting wall of Herod's temple extension, as far as the lower layers are concerned, while the upper layers were contributed by Sir Moses Montefiore in the middle of the 19th century. The delightful legend that the huge lower blocks were from Solomon's temple has no foundation, sadly. One would like to imagine his tame djinns whisking the amazingly vast stones through the air.

The name "Wailing Wall" was applied to it as Jews came here to pray and bewail the destruction of the Temple, the Exile and the hard fate of the Jewish people. In the chinks between the stones, there are little rolled-up papers—notes scrawled with prayers or names of loved ones. The stones themselves are worn smooth by the loving caress of millons of hands over the centuries.

Men and women pray at different sections of the Wall in accordance with Orthodox Jewish custom. As it is a synagogue, *men are not to go to the Wall bare-headed*. If you don't have a hat, an attendant will give you a skullcap.

When Israeli troops took the Old City in the 1967 War, they found the Wall one side of a narrow alleyway, with crumbling houses and public conveniences facing it. These have been cleared away and a broad plaza now stands before it. On the three Jewish pilgrimage festivals—Passover, Succoth (the Feast of Tabernacles), and Shavuot (the Feast of Weeks), as many as 250,000 Jews come to pray here.

Teams of Israeli archeologists have been digging down along the base of the Wall since late 1967, and have come up with numerous important finds, including vessels used in Temple offerings and coins millenia old. The longterm dig continues and tourists benefit by now being able to visit the excavations. At ground level, a tunnel has been opened that leads to Rehov Hagai (a ten-minute walk from the Damascus Gate). Its roof is a series of arches dating from Herodian and Crusader periods. The dig is well worth a visit, and you can traipse through the tunnel day or night.

The area facing the Wall is the recently reconstructed old Jewish Quarter. The scores of ancient and venerable synagogues and houses of Jewish study—the *yeshivot*—were torn down by the Jordanians after

1948. The Yohanan Ben Zakkai, four Shepardi synagogues, dating from the 16th century, have now been reconstructed and are open for prayer and visits, as are other nearby places.

The Dome of the Rock

The Temple Mount, or Mt. Moriah, forms the southeast corner of the Old Walled City. This was the site of the First and Second Temples. Now, the broad, flat area is surmounted by the Dome of the Rock, with its glittering golden cupola, and the El-Aqsa Mosque, with its smaller silver dome. Moslems know the 30-acre rectangle as *Haram es-Sharif,* the Noble Enclosure.

It is deduced from the Book of Genesis that this was the mount where Abraham prepared to sacrifice his son, Isaac, on the Rock. Islam holds that the Prophet Mohammed ascended to heaven from the rock enshrined by the Dome of the Rock.

Since the time of the Temples, the places of worship on Mt. Moriah have undergone several metamorphoses. The Romans built a temple to Jupiter on the site; in the seventh century, a mosque—the precursor of the Dome of the Rock—went up here; the Crusaders in the 12th century turned it into a church. It was a mosque again after the Moslem reconquest of Jerusalem, and has been reconstructed and embellished since then.

The Dome of the Rock (sometimes called the Mosque of Omar) is an exquisite octagonal structure; a symphony of glazed tile, mosaic and marble. Note the calligraphic skill of the quotations from the Koran decorating the inside and outside of the mosque. Stepping inside(*leave your shoes outside*), you'll marvel at the opulence of decoration as you pad along on the floors decked with oriental carpets.

The focal point of the mosque is, of course, the Rock, from which Mohammed is said to have ascended to heaven. You can discern the spot from the railing around the Rock and, indeed, it looks like the imprint of a human foot. A small box near the footprint holds a few hairs of the Prophet. The cave dug into the Rock is called "The Well of Souls."

On the east side of the Dome of the Rock is the miniature Dome of the Chain, which is said to have been the model for the larger mosque.

South of the Dome, going through arched portals and past a large, ornamental fountain called *El-Kas* (The Cup), we see El-Aqsa Mosque. This is only slightly less revered than the Dome of the Rock. It's over one thousand years old, though it too has been rebuilt and modified through the ages. From its shape, it looks somewhat more like a church than a mosque, and it is believed that it may have been constructed over a basilica dedicated to St. Mary, which was built by Justinian in the sixth century. King Abdullah of Jordan was assassinated in 1951 just inside and to the left of the entrance of the mosque.

A curious legend attends two pillars standing cheek-by-jowl near the front of the mosque—those of the faithful who can squeeze through the space will also be able to pass through the gates of heaven. It's a pretty tight squeeze.

Next to El-Aqsa, on the southeast corner of the Temple Mount, are the subterranean Stables of King Solomon. These were used later by the Romans and Crusaders.

One of the eight gates of the Old City is in the Noble Enclosure. This is the Golden Gate, through which—according to Jewish tradition—the Messiah will enter Jerusalem, ushering in the Redemption. The gate was sealed up about nine centuries ago.

On the northwest corner of the Temple Mount is a tall tower. This was the site of Herod's Antonia Fortress and the place where Pontius Pilate condemned Jesus to a sentence of death.

Jaffa Gate and Damascus Gate

The Jaffa Gate marks the beginning of the road to Jaffa, the city on the Mediterranean, which was for thousands of years the port of Jerusalem. The walls of the Old City are high here and the portal large; it was opened to its present size in 1898 so that the Kaiser Wilhelm II of Germany could pass through in his carriage (with his entourage on horseback).

To the right of Jaffa Gate as you enter is the Citadel, surmounted by the Tower of David, which has become symbolic of Jerusalem. King David built a tower here, supposedly, but the present structure probably dates to medieval times. The Citadel, built on the remains of a Herodian fortress, is primarily a Crusader site, yet it was used as a bastion by succeeding generations, and by the Jordanian Army. Now it is a museum, with audio-visual programs plus exhibitions, Sound and Light shows, and special events. Though excavations and restorations here sometimes stop the shows, they also have made it possible for tourists to walk part of the wall's ramparts. Other types of walks start here, too—regular, free "Jerusalem Through the Ages" tours.

Just past the Jaffa Gate, on the left, is the Government Tourist Office. The large square inside the walls then branches off in two directions; to the right, Armenian Street, leading through the quiet Armenian Quarter; the one going straight, to David Street, one of the principal shopping streets of the Old City. A bus drives from Jaffa Gate past the Armenian Quarter to the Western Wall.

The Damascus Gate, the largest and most impressive of the entrances to the Old City, is so called because it leads to the time-worn road to the Syrian capital. The road stemming out from it, however, is not so ambitious and is merely called the Nablus Road—Nablus being the principal way-station in Samaria, on the road to Damascus.

The Damascus Gate bustles with activity inside and out. In front of the gate is the bus terminus of East Jerusalem. From here, buses depart for all parts of the West Bank and Amman in Jordan (this last one is not for tourists). Most of the city's nine buslines start here, too.

Within the great gate itself there are stalls and shops, a harbinger of the fantastic *souks* of the Old City, which begin about 100 feet past the gate. On the way to the Street of Spices, there are money-changers' shops (now turning more to souvenirs) and coffee houses, where men in half-Western, half-Oriental garb watch the eddying flow, sipping Turkish coffee, smoking *narghilas* or noisily playing at *shesh besh* (backgammon).

Around the Walls of the Old City

Just a short walk up Nablus Road from the Damascus Gate there's a small path on the right-hand side leading to the Garden Tomb. This is thought by some to be the actual tomb of Christ. The place is sometimes called "Gordon's Calvary" for General Gordon, the hero of Khartoum, who tried to prove its authenticity. The two-part rock cave is built on a skull-shaped hillock. (You will recall that Golgotha is from the Hebrew *gulgolet,* skull.)

Farther up the road, where Nablus Road intersects with Saladin Street, is the Tomb of Kings. This is a misnomer, as it is actually the tomb of a queen and her family—Queen Adiabene, who came to Jerusalem in the first century A.D. and was converted to Judaism.

Going back towards the walls, you'll see St. George's Cathedral, the largest Anglican edifice in the country and the Anglican Commission's center for the Holy Land.

Before reaching Herod's Gate (also called the Flower Gate), there's a small iron-grill door leading down to King Solomon's Quarries, not far from the Damascus Gate. Also called Zedekiah's Cave, the area is open daily from 8:30 A.M. through 4:30 P.M., and you can tour it for less than one shekel. From these labyrinthine caves, the stones for Solomon's Temple are believed to have been cut. The Masons consider this the birthplace of their order. With numerous galleries covering thousands of feet, the quarry penetrates more than 700 feet in a direct line into the Old City. Some people are convinced it stretches even further. Legend has Zedekiah, last King of Judah, fleeing here to escape Babylonian enemies. He emerged miles from Jerusalem—in the Plain of Jericho—only to be caught, anyway.

Opposite King Solomon's Quarries, down a narrow street, is Jeremiah's Grotto. It is supposedly the dungeon into which the prophet was cast and whence he was rescued by Ebed Melech, the Ethiopian.

To the left, beyond Herod's Gate, where the road slopes down to the Jericho Road, is the Rockefeller Archeological Museum. Built in the '30s from a $2-million grant given by John D. Rockefeller, the museum is a treasure house of antiques discovered in the Holy Land. Much of its pottery and tool collections came from the area around Acre and the Galilee. Architecturally, it's influenced by Oriental and Moorish trends, particularly its interior and the handsome colonnaded court.

The Slopes of the Mount of Olives

Returning to the Jericho Road, we see the northeast corner of the Old City walls. The parapet here is called the Storks Tower. Walking southward now, the descent begins into the Valley of Kidron (which also comprises the Valley of Jehosophat). Past the road leading up to St. Stephen's Gate, on the left-hand side of the road, at the base of the Mount of Olives, is the Tomb of the Virgin (St. Mary's Tomb). On the way down to the subterranean church, there are chapels on either side. To the right are the tombs of Mary's parents, Joachim and Anne; on the left, the tomb of Joseph, Mary's husband. Almost 40 feet under street level is the church itself, and the Tomb of the Virgin, where, according to tradition, she was laid to rest by the Apostles. Several sects are represented in the church and there is even a Moslem prayer niche.

On exiting, before reaching the street, note the passage to the left, leading to the Cave of the Agony (LUKE XXII, 41).

Continuing down Jericho Road, you will see the Basilica of the Agony, also called the Church of All Nations, looming up in splendor. Built on the site of the Garden of Gethsemane, where Jesus was betrayed by Judas, it seems older than it is (less than 50 years). The mosaics on the façade depict God the Father over Jesus and the peoples of the world. The church was built from donations of people from more than a dozen countries. Inside, by the altar, is the rock where Jesus is supposed to have rested with His disciples. It is known as the Rock of Agony. Near the church, you can stand in a grove of ancient gnarled olive trees which reputedly date back to the time of Jesus, but it is more likely that they are descendants, albeit very, very old, of the original trees. The olive press, or *gat shemen,* that stood in this garden, is now in a cave called the Grotto of the Gethsemane.

Farther up the slope is the Russian Church of St. Mary Magdalene, with its seven distinctive onion-shaped domes. This too is a fairly new church, having been built by Czar Alexander III around 1888. The hearts of some members of the Russian royal family repose in the church.

Still higher up the Mt. of Olives is Dominus Flevit, the place where Jesus wept over Jerusalem. The spot is marked by a small Franciscan church.

Just before the summit of the Mount is the Tomb of the Prophets, where the prophets Zachariah, Haggai and Malachi are said to lie at rest. Their underground rock tombs are in a corner of the ancient Jewish cemetery on the summit of the Mount of Olives, described later.

Back on the Jericho Road, the path forks after the Basilica of the Agony. The main road continues to Jericho, about 30 miles away: the right fork goes along the Valley of Kidron. Following the valley road, we can see three large tombs on the left-hand side. The first, Absalom's Tomb, seems to be carved out of the mountainside. The edifice does not date to the time of King David's son, though an earlier tomb was probably on the same spot. Known also as Absalom's Pillar, it most likely dates from the Second Temple. Medieval Jews were wont to throw stones at the pillar as they passed and bring their children here when they got unruly to remind them of what happened to King David's rebellious son. Next are the tombs of Hezir (or the Grotto of St. James) and the prophet Zachariah, both dating from the Greco-Roman period.

Further down the valley road, on the right, is the Virgin's Fountain. Here, it is said, the Virgin Mary took water to wash the clothes of Jesus. The fountain is fed by the Spring of Gihon.

To the right, Mt. Ophel slopes up. This was the area of the City of David. On its side is the Pool of Siloam. King Hezekiah built a tunnel almost 2,000 feet long from the Spring of Gihon to the Pool to ensure a water supply were Jerusalem attacked. It was, and the city held out because of it. This was about 700 B.C. and you can still go through the winding tunnel today.

On your left is the Arab village of Silwan. Above it is the Mount of Contempt, surmounted by a Benedictine monastery.

Retracing our steps back to the Jericho Road, between the Tomb of the Virgin and St. Stephen's Gate, we see another road veering off the the left. This follows the eastern and southern sections of the Old City walls. Going by the sealed Golden Gate, observe the old Moslem cemetery. Moslems believe that the resurrection of souls will begin here. The road goes by the Dung Gate, the closest to the Western Wall, and continues on to the Zion Gate. This gate, which faces Mt. Zion, was the principal thoroughfare to the old Jewish Quarter. The evidence of stiff fighting around this portal during the 1948 Arab-Israel War is still inscribed in the stones.

The road twists to the right after the Zion Gate, following the corner of the wall, taking us again to the Jaffa Gate.

Mount Scopus

Two mountains dominate Jerusalem from the east: Mt. Scopus in the northeast, and the Mount of Olives, due east of the Old City.

The ascent of Mt. Scopus can be made by following the Mount of Olives Road (which turns out of the Nablus Road) or heading north from the Rockefeller Museum and continuing on Nureddine Street through Wadi El-Josos.

Mt. Scopus is the Greek translation for the Hebrew *Har Hatzofim,* "Hill of the Lookout" (scouts)—which literally looks over the city and has been a strategic military point for thousands of years—even for Alexander the Great, the Emperor Titus, the Crusaders and the British.

Mt. Scopus was an Israeli enclave in Jordan from 1948 to 1967. A small caretaker force of police stood guard on the mount, where the buildings of the old Hadassah Hospital and Hebrew University stood. A relief and supply convoy, supervised by UN observers, went up to Mt. Scopus from West Jerusalem every fortnight. The small garrison, though surrounded on all sides by Arab forces, held out during the Six-Day War till Israeli Army reinforcements came.

Fighting was very heavy there. Just ahead as the road curves to the right is the British World War I Cemetery, where those who fell in the 1917 fighting in the Palestine campaign are buried. There is a Jewish section on the left side of the cemetery.

Farther up the road are the old Hadassah Hospital and the original campus of the Hebrew University. The cornerstone for the university was laid in 1918. The 50th anniversary of the event was commemorated here in festive ceremonies in July, 1968, yet the true 50th birthday was held in 1975—for the university was only opened in 1925, in the presence of such dignitaries as Lord Balfour (of Balfour Declaration fame) and Dr. Chaim Weizmann, who was to become the first president of the State of Israel. Also here, until 1948, was the National Library building, now in Giv'at Ram; but it will be transferred back to Mt. Scopus in the near future.

After the Six-Day War, hundreds of volunteers from all over the world pitched in to clean out the rubble on the Mt. Scopus campus and put the old buildings into shape. They are back in use again and new buildings have been constructed beyond and around the old campus in order to make room for the constantly growing numbers of students. On the summit of the mount, there is a breathtaking view of Jerusalem to the west and of the Wilderness of Judah and the Dead Sea to the east. On a clear day, you can see the Mountains of Moab across the Jordan.

The amphitheater facing east was where the inauguration ceremony took place in 1925. It has been reconstructed. Going up right next to it is the Harry S. Truman Peace Center, a large research center and Library dedicated to the former US president.

From here, the road descends, and a few hundred yards further on, the large Augusta Victoria Hospital comes into view.

The road rises again up the slope of the Mount of Olives. To the left is the Arab village of Et-Tur. Soaring above the whole panorama is the tall Gothis spire of the Russian Monastery.

The Summit of the Mount of Olives

The Mount of Olives is known by the same name in Hebrew (*Har Hazeytim*) but in earlier times was known as *Har Hameshiha*, the Mount of Anointing. It was a place of worship in the time of King David and, during the Second Temple, sacrifices were offered up here. Some Jewish lore holds that the Messiah will make his appearance coming down from the Mount of Olives. In the Christian faith, it is believed that Christ ascended to heaven from here.

Here also Jesus often preached to His disciples and here He first taught them the words of *Pater Noster*, the Lord's Prayer.

At certain times of the day, the view of Old Jerusalem from the top of the Mount of Olives has a mystical, timeless quality that makes it easy to understand why three great religions have gravitated to this small corner of the world. From the Mount of Olives, looking to the east you can catch a glimpse of the Dead Sea. The walls leading down to the Dead Sea turn many shades of rose and purple in the late afternoon just before dusk. From this vantage point, Bethany, the Good Samaritan Inn, the Jericho Road and the Mountains of Moab are also visible.

The Church of the Ascension is a small circular building within the grounds of a mosque. (Jesus, you may recall, is considered a prophet in the eyes of Islam.) Votive candles burn in niches on either side of the chapel. As you go back through the small compound, you see Roman pillars and pedestals strewn about. To the left is the small mosque. Inside, there's a flight of stairs going to the roof, from which there is an excellent view of Jerusalem.

Next door to the mosque is the purported tomb of the prophetess Hulda. A small Arab boy with a large key will offer to open it for you for a small compensation; alternatively, he'll offer you a ride on his donkey.

A few steps further is the Church of the Pater Noster, the Carmelite Convent and the Basilica of the Sacred Heart. At the Pater Noster Church, the Lord's Prayer is set into the tiled walls in 62 different languages. There's a beautiful colonnaded courtyard, reminiscent of some medieval churches and monasteries in France and Spain.

The road rist to a crest here and stops in front of the Jerusalem Intercontinental Hotel. This looks out on one of the world's most exquisite views: the slopes of the Mt. of Olives, the Valley of Kidron, the walls of the Old City, the Temple Mount and the domes and minarets of timeless Jerusalem.

The road, built by the Jordanians, once went beyond this point . . . over the graves in the cemetery on the Mount of Olives, which is one of the largest (and perhaps the oldest) Jewish cemeteries in the world. Graves were uprooted by bulldozers and tombstones taken away wholesale to be used for diverse purposes. Some of them became pavements for sidewalks, others were used in buildings, still others were used for latrines. The Rabbinate is still in the process of collecting the gravestones and re-interring the bones of those cast out of their resting place.

New East Jerusalem

In vivid contrast to the Old City is the modern part of East Jerusalem, north of the city walls. This takes in the area roughly bounded by the Nablus Road, and Saladin and Aztahra Streets. Here the bustle of the city takes on a different character. There are smart shops, clean, attractive restaurants, tea rooms, travel agencies, airline offices, movie theaters, and even nightclubs and discos. It is a metropolis in miniature. Long after the Old City is asleep, the New East Jerusalem is still alive.

PRACTICAL INFORMATION FOR JERUSALEM

 WEST JERUSALEM HOTELS. The peak season, with rates to match, is from March to October, while most hotels charge 15% less November to March. Winters here can be quite chilly, and any Jerusalemite will tell you that a blanket is welcome at night even in summer months. Most hotels feature central heating as well as air-conditioning.

Deluxe (5-star)

The city's venerable 5-star hotel is the **King David,** a national institution. Opened in 1930, this hotel has innate character. It is at once regal, Victorian and Oriental. Take a room facing the ramparts and mosques of the Old City. Cocktails on the terrace overlooking the Oriental gardens is a must. The Regency Grill bar specializes in mixed grills and beef stroganoff. Pool, health club, bar, banks, shops, tennis; 258 rooms; a Dan Hotel.

Another 5-star hotel is the 500-room **Diplomat,** in Talpiot. Great views, good Taiwan-Chinese restaurant, shops, shuttle service into city. Fully air-conditioned, all rooms with bath. TV; health club, pool, and nightclub.

Jerusalem Hilton, atop Givat Ram hill, with magnificent view, has 420 rooms with TV, tennis, heated pool, health club, shops, free house movies and shuttle service. Next to the Binyanei Ha'ooma convention halls. (Ask for Hilton's excellent "Self-Guided Walking Tour Map.")

Jerusalem Plaza, 47 King George St., 414 rooms, has heated pool and health club, plus rather frigid atmosphere. $40–50 daily, double.

First Class (4-star)

On a quiet side street (Achad Ha'am), a 15-minute walk from the center of town, is the **President Hotel,** with pool and tennis courts; a comfortable place, it has 54 rooms, most with bath.

Closer to town is the **Kings Hotel,** 60 King George St. 214 rooms with bath, on a big four-corner intersection.

Central Hotel is named for its location, on 6 Pines Street just off Davidka Square; strictly Orthodox: two restaurants, all of its 77 rooms have private bath, air-conditioning.

Holyland, out in Bayit Vegan section, has 120 rooms with bath or shower; groves of cypress frame its hillside pool, 10,000-book library for the use of guests, a museum with reproductions of Persian, Egyptian and Arabic items, a mineral spring in a pretty garden, and the fantastic model of biblical Jerusalem, Second Temple period. Outdoor terrace is ideal for lunches and snacks; also, tennis courts and nightclub.

Jerusalem Moriah, 39 Keren Hayesod, now entirely rebuilt, has 170 rooms with bath or shower; fully air-conditioned. It has a reputation among Jerusalemites for fine European cuisine.

At 42 King George, **Tirat Batsheva** has 70 rooms, with bath or shower. The 51-room **Jerusalem Tadmor** in Beth Hakerem has an attached hotel school, good service, varied cuisine.

The 4-star **Ramada-Shalom,** in Bayit Vegan, with 288 rooms, TV, health club, sauna, pool, and terrific club on top with good views, fine dance music, open till wee hours.

Newest 4-star is the **Ariel,** 31 Hebron Rd., with TV, piano bar, coffee shop and 140 rooms (or beds).

Moderate (3-star)

The 3-star **Jerusalem Tower,** in heart of business center, has 120 rooms with bath, TV, and self-service cafeteria. **Neve Shoshana,** 5 Beth Hakerem, offers 27 rooms with bath,

Among other 3-star hotels are the **YMCA** (locally called "Yimka"), 26 King David St., whose tower is one of the city's most impressive landmarks, 68 rooms, most with showers, heated pool, cypress gardens, tennis courts, and a regular cultural program; **Eyal,** on Shamai, 71 rooms; **Rama Gidron,** 19 rooms, in Talpioth. **Ram,** at 234 Jaffa, is a new 156-room hotel with coffee shop and bar.

Not yet graded, the **Dor,** at 3 Mendele St., promises comfort in 133 rooms, and also in its coffee shop and bar.

Other Accommodation

Two-star hotels include the **Or Gil,** 58 rooms on Hillel St., and the 23-room **Palatin** (showers only) at 4 Agrippas St., **Har Aviv,** in Beth Hakerem, 12 rooms; **Ron,** 42a Jaffa Rd., 21 rooms; **Zion,** 4 Luntz St., has 23 rooms (showers only). Not yet graded, **Vardi-Rosenbaum** has 20 rooms, most with showers, at 21 Mekor Haim St.

KIBBUTZ GUEST HOUSES. There are three just outside of town in the Judean hills. **Ma'ale Hachamisha** offers 146 rooms and **Kiryat Anavim** has 93. All are rather luxurious, 3-star. There is also the holiday village of **Shoresh.** All three feature swimming pools. Tranquility, inspiring views of mountains and valleys and the first and third also have tennis courts.

In the Jerusalem Forest, the **Judean Hills Recreation Center** boasts 38 rooms with bath or shower; facilities on the pine-filled mountain slopes include tennis and swimming.

YOUTH HOSTELS. There are several in and near Jerusalem—**Beit Atid** is in the center of town; **Louise Waterman-Wise** near Mt. Herzl (added new social/cultural activities wing in 1978); **Ramat Rahel** lies south of town; west of town are **Haezrachi, Ein Karem** and **Jerusalem Forest;** in the Judean Hills are **Ramat Shapira** and **Bar Giora.** Ranging in size from 90 to 250 beds, most serve 3 meals daily. All are on bus lines, many have kitchens, but only the last has family accommodation. **Ein Hamed** at Bet Neqofa is the regional camp site, with very good facilities.

Mevo Betar Camping offers exclusive European-type holiday homes, or elaborate 2-bedroom mobile homes, or 2–6-bed bungalows; also has pool, tennis, basketball, volleyball, snack bar, mini market. Very nice, great for families. Located in Jerusalem hills, 25 miles from town, ten minutes from Bethlehem. (See *Border Area* chapter for Bethlehem information.)

CHRISTIAN HOSPICES abound here. In West Jerusalem they are: **Jerusalem YMCA,** Rehov David Hamelech (3-star hotel, with rates to match), Protestant; **St. Charles Hospice,** German Colony, Roman Catholic, German; **Notre Dame de Sion,** Ein Kerem, Roman Catholic, French; **Sisters of the Rosary,** 14 Rehov Agron, Roman Catholic, Arab; **Dom Poslki,** Hakhoma Hashlishit No. 8, Rehov Shivtei Israel, Roman Catholic, Polish; **St. Andrew's Hospice,** Rehov Harakevet (near railway station), Church of Scotland; **Romanian Hospice,** 46 Shivtei Israel; **Foyer St. Joseph,** Haneviim St., POB 771 (students only).

EAST JERUSALEM HOTELS. Ranging from 5-star to modest, the hotels in this older part of Jerusalem number almost twice those in the newer part and, category for category, sometimes offer more for the money. But remember, during Christmas or Easter weeks, you'll be charged an additional 20–25% here.

Deluxe (5-star)

On the Mt. of Olives, the **Jerusalem Intercontinental** is undoubtedly among the best-situated hotels in the world. Its sweeping view of the Valley of Kidron and the Old City of Jerusalem is unforgettable. Elegant luxury and service in the old tradition, it blends Oriental and modern, and all 200 rooms have TV and are beautiful. There are tennis courts, too. Of the 3 restaurants and snack bars, the most sumptuous is the **Seven Arches**—overlooking the Old City—where lunch and dinner always include Continental, Oriental and Jewish specialties. The Saturday buffet luncheon is deservedly famous. There's also a beauty parlor here, and room TV.

St. George International, on Salah Eddine St., has 150 rooms, modern, with pool. Convenient for sightseeing, shopping.

Mt. Scopus. In the Sheik Jarrach section north of the city center. A well-run hotel with 65 rooms, all with balcony, TV, air-conditioning. Attractive dining room opens on terrace garden. Shops and garage on premises.

First Class (4-star)

The 102-room **American Colony,** on Nablus Road, should really be in a category by itself. The main building was once a pasha's palace and still remains its old-time glory. Huge rooms make you feel like a visiting potentate; some have ornate, beamed ceilings with Oriental traceries. Rooms in the two annexes cost slightly more than in the main building. The hotel is a favorite with writers, diplomats and UN personnel. It has a great Saturday buffet, and happens to be—unbelievably — Israel's most economical 4-star hotel, complete with TV, bar, pool, beauty parlor.

Panorama, aptly-named, has 74 rooms (with TV) in five floors on the Hill of Gethsemane. Superb vistas from here include the Old City, the Mount of

Olives and the Judean Hills—all three are visible from the top-floor dining room.

National Palace, with 108 rooms, is in the heart of shopping and entertainment districts on Az-Zahara St. It offers room TV, bar, some kitchenettes.

The four-story **Capital,** off Saladin Street, has 54 rooms with bath. Also good is the **Ritz,** 8 Ibn Khaldoun St., 103 rooms. Both have room TV.

Ambassador, 56 Sheikh Jarrach St., has 118 rooms, fully air-conditioned; also beauty parlor, bar, room TV, coffee shop.

Moderate (3-star)

Palace, with 69 rooms, is set by itself in the vale between Mt. Scopus and the Mount of Olives. Popular, quiet, with fine views.

Holyland East, reached through a court on Rashid St., has 99 rooms and a roof garden, close to the Walled City (Herod's Gate) and the Rockefeller Museum.

YMCA Aelia Capitolina, 29 Nablus Road, is a medley of Middle East and modern architecture: heated pool, squash and tennis courts and a snack bar, 57 rooms with bath. Another **YMCA,** on Wadi Jose, has 30 rooms with bath; also room TV, bar.

Back in the center of town, on Saladin St., is the small **Christmas,** 21 rooms, bar, bank, and is well known for its delightful garden restaurant (but open to residents only).

Just past Damascus Gate facing the walls of the Old City is **Pilgrim's Palace,** on King Suliman St., with 95 rooms, partly air-conditioned; also room TV, bar; all clean, and modestly priced, room TV and partial air-conditioning, 95 rooms.

Gloria is within the walls of the Old City, just past the Jaffa Gate. Despite a rather grim exterior, it's surprisingly pleasant inside. The top-floor restaurant looks out on the Old City, 64 rooms, partly air-conditioned.

Shepherd, on Mt. Scopus, is another good hotel; 52 rooms with bath. Newer 3-star hotels include the 55-roomed **Strand,** at Ibn Jubeir St. (Sheikh Jarrach area), with some kitchenettes, bar, coffee shop, room TV; the **New Metropole,** 8 Salah-A-Din St., with 25 rooms, and the **Alcazar** with 38 rooms, coffee shop, bar, TV.

Jordan House, Nur El-Din St., (near the Rockefeller Museum), has 25 rooms, most with bath; the **Commodore** offers 45 rooms on the Mt. of Olives, partly air-conditioned.

Other Accommodation

Vienna East, in the Sheikh Jarrach section, is a recommended 2-star hotel, 39 rooms. The 22-room **City** is on Mt. Scopus, as is the 20-room **Parklane.** Not yet graded, new **Victoria** is on Mt. Scopus, with 50 partly air-conditioned rooms, bar and coffee shop.

Others include the **Lawrence,** Salah-A-Din St., 30 rooms; and its neighbor, the **Metropole,** 30 rooms; in the same area, **Pilgrims Inn,** on Rashidia St., has 15 rooms (showers only); and the **Rivoli,** 3 Salah Eddine St., 31 rooms. In the American Colony is the **New Orient House,** 22 rooms. **Mt. of Olives,** 63 rooms, is on the road of the same name, as is the **Astoria,** 23 rooms; **New Regent,** 20 Az-Zahra St., 25 rooms. **Az-Zahra,** 13 Az-Zahra St., 24 rooms.

The 1-star hotels are generally clean and well-run. Try the **Knights Palace** at New Gate, 42 rooms (showers only); **New Imperial** at Jaffa Gate, 52 rooms; and the nearby **Savoy,** 17 rooms with showers.

See West Jerusalem listings of **KIBBUTZ GUEST HOUSES, YOUTH HOSTELS** and **CAMPING** in the vicinity.

CHRISTIAN HOSPICES. Aside from those listed in West Jerusalem, the city's East side has its own: **Casa Nova,** PP. Franciscans POB 1321, Roman Catholic; **Christ Church Hostel,** Jaffa Gate, POB 14037, Anglican, British; **Ecce Homo Convent** (Notre Dame de Sion), Via Dolorosa, Roman Catholic; **Filles de la Charité,** Bethany Shiya, POB 19080, Roman Catholic, French; **Franciscaines de Marie** (White Sisters), 9 Nabius Rd., Roman Catholic, French; **St. George's Hostel,** Nablus Rd. and Saladin St., Anglican/Episcopal; **Evang, Lutheran Hostel,** St. Mark's St., Lutheran, German; **Maison d' Abraham** (for poor pilgrims only: apply to Abbé J. Gelin, Director), Mount of Offence, POB 19689; **Sisters of Nigrizia,** Bethany Shiya, POB 19504, Roman Catholic, Italian; **Armenian Catholic Patriarchate,** 3rd Station of the Cross, Via Dolorosa; **Fraternite Bethesda,** Maronite monastery, 25 Dier El Mawarneh, Roman Catholic, French; **Foyer Des Pelerins—Greek Catholic Patriarchate,** POB 14130; **Centre Notre Dame,** opposite New Gate, POB 20531, Catholic-Ecumenique; **YMCA,** Nablus Rd.; **YMCA,** Khaled Ibn El Walid St.

 WEST JERUSALEM RESTAURANTS vary in price according to cuisine and pomp. Luxury fare will run $20 and up each, minus drinks. Your own selection of dishes can double that tab. Expensive range here goes from $10–$20, with moderate running $5–$10. The restaurants listed here have (L), (E), or (M) as price indicators.

Top places include **Mishkenot Sha'ananim** (L), fine French food in the Yemin Moshe Artists' Quarter. Also Moroccan foods; all uniquely kosher. Reservations needed.

Georgian food—Russian Georgian—is yours at **Georgia** (L), 24 King David St., where the decor vies with great food; two dining rooms. Pianist.

Chez Simon (E), 15 Shamai St., is a friendly spot with fine cocktails and service, good continental foods.

Gondola (L), gourmet Italian restaurant, at 14 King George St., entrance through an apartment building. Besides traditional dishes, they also serve steaks.

Across the street, **Fink's** (E) is one of Jerusalem's smallest, oldest and best restaurants as well as foreign correspondents' hang-out.

Kathy (L), is elegant and intimate, fine for lunch and dinner; **Kathy's Bar** for snacks, drinks; 16 Rivlin, opposite Government Press Office (Beit Agron). **Bistro,** 37 Hillel, has international menu, in Beit Agron. **Lev Jerusalem** (E) offers fast self-service, good international foods, at 31 Hillel. **Hesse** is really 2 restaurants: (M) upstairs, (L) French downstairs; at 5 Ben Shetah. Nearby is **Venezia** (L), open daily for fine meals; great continental foods, pastas.

Mandi Tachi is the latest posh Chinese place, usually full of beautiful people, on Horkenos St. There's also the **Formosa** Chinese restaurant and tea house, 36 Ben Yehuda, with Szechewan fare.

Cohen's (E), Yeshayahu (corner Yellin Street), is minuscule, has good Oriental fare.

In Ein Kerem, the **Goulash Inn** (L), offers an intimate atmosphere and Hungarian food. International dinners are held frequently at the **Jerusalem Tadmore Hotel Training School,** Bet HaKerem, for IS35—good buy; great food.

Fish fans can head for **Dagim Beni** (E), at 1 Mesliat Yesharim St., where the slogan is: "We fish our own fish!"

Sova, a two-floor cafeteria on Histadruth St. seating 400 people, offers wide variety; separate self-service dairy and meat cafeterias, as well as a regular dining room.

Stark (M), 21 King George St. (walk through the passage) dishes up fine Hungarian cuisine.

Opposite the old Knesset Building (Beit Froumine) on King George Street, is the **Alpin,** which attracts Jerusalemites with its large bill-of-fare featuring fresh vegetarian and fish dishes.

Two big restaurants at the top of Jaffa Road are the **Jerusalem** and **Fefferberg's,** both (M), 52 and 53 Jaffa Road, respectively. They specialize in a wide range of meat, Oriental and dairy dishes, at various price ranges; the latter is known for its "very good Jewish kitchen."

The dairy vegetarian **Liber Vegetarian** (M), at 10 Ben Yehuda St., features fish specialities, omelets, and many delights for health food faddists.

Palmachi (E), 13 Rehov Shamai and **Rimon,** 4 Lunz Street, are long-time favorites of the local student population, which means the food is good, plentiful. Also, **Rehavia** (M), 15 Kerem Kayemet St., has good Hungarian food.

For "quick" type lunches, Jerusalem has a whole crop of places that feature either grilled specialties or counter service; the **Shemesh,** 31 Ben Yehuda, outside is (M); inside, in back, is an expensive good restaurant. The **Deshen,** 3 Lunz and the **Sinai,** 6 Ben Yehuda, are others. Nearby **Rimini** (M) has pizza and Italian foods. **Heppners,** at 4 Lunz, is a U.S.-style (M) deli. **Uncle Sam,** 7 King George, vends hot dogs and burgers.

Beit HaOmanim (Artists' House), at 12 Shmuel Hanagid, is a popular place to fill up and see/buy local art.

Abu Tor Observation Tower also has a self-service and waited-table restaurant, plus gift shop, art gallery and fantastic view of old city.

IN THE ENVIRONS: Samson's Inn, at Eshtaol, on the Jerusalem-Tel Aviv highway; **Caravan,** at Abu Ghosh, open daily, 10–10, all year, all days, small, inexpensive, fine view. **Motza Inn** (E), stands outside Jerusalem, open 9 A.M. to midnight all year and specializes in North African food. If you watch the road's turn outside, you're almost guaranteed to see at least one accident while you eat, so there's also a towing service here, and a regularly stationed police car. Whenever they make the entrance to the Holy City more safe for drivers, this place may disappear.

CAFÉS AND SNACK-BARS: Alno, 15 Ben Yehuda, Viennese atmosphere; **Atara,** practically next door; **Habourekis,** 40 Yafo St. (student favorite); and **Nova,** 44 Yafo Street. **Taamon Coffee House,** corner of Hillel, and **Tur Taam,** corner of Ben Hillel and King George Streets is a favorite student spot. Best houmus in town, Jerusalemites say, is at simple, inexpensive **Taami,** 3 Hillel St. And they also dig into low-cost Oriental fare at **Hanizahon,** on Jaffa St. near PO.

A popular "student" bar-coffee house is **John Sebastian Bar** in Ein Kerem, where you'll also find **Yan's Tea House.** Then there's the **Little Gallery** back in town. For pastries, cakes, candies, and great coffee, try **La Javanaise,** 1 Rehov King George, **Mishkenot Haroim**—Shepherds' tents Bedouin encampment in East Talpiot—is a great atmospheric place. Sit on colorful, hand-woven cushions, drink bitter coffee and sweet tea, listen to Bedouin and modern music (9–5 P.M.). Breathtaking panorama of all Jerusalem from this hill that's 750 meters above sea-level.

EAST JERUSALEM RESTAURANTS. There are a handful of good restaurants in East Jerusalem and their numbers should increase under the pressure of the tourist boom. Two old standbys are the **Jerusalem Oriental** and the **Hassan Effendi,** which stand practically opposite each other on Rashid Street (not far from Herod's Gate). Both are opulently Oriental in their furnishings and mood. Most Arab and European favorites are on the menu, including minuscule roast pigeons. Dinner runs about $10 and up, each.

Sea Dolphin, on Rashid St., is the most expensive, but considered the best by many Jerusalemites.

Arches, 38 David's Street, has European cuisine at moderate prices. Mostly a lunch crowd. Also (M) is Rami's for ribs and chops, near Arches. Best buffet brunch on Saturday—East or West—is at **American Colony Hotel:** super favorite treat. For great fish, try exclusive **Leviathan,** (E) 11 El Rashida St. **Philadelphia** is another favorite, for good, expensive Oriental food, Rehov Ha Perachim. **The Citadel,** 14 Jerusalem Brigade Rd., opposite David's Tower and below Jerusalem Arts and Crafts Center, serves fine (E) Szechewan Chinese fare. The **Hametzuda** complex here has art galleries, café, restaurant and bar. An interesting experience.

Diplomats' favorite is **Patisserie Suisse,** Saladin St. Great for refreshments while touring or shopping, and after theater. It offers fine confections, sandwiches, pastries, ice cream—all top quality, including service.

On Az-Zahra Street, there are a few tea-rooms and snack bars, among them the **Café Europa.**

As for restaurants within the walls of the Old City, cleanliness is not their chief virtue. There are a few welcome exceptions around Jaffa Gate and David Street, the bazaar leading down from the Gate. Some serve only snacks, others also meals.

SOME LOCAL FOOD HINTS. You'll find kebab and shishlik the staples of every Oriental restaurant throughout Israel and Jerusalem. For variety of true Middle Eastern cooking, we suggest you try some of these delicious specialties:

Mansaf, broiled lamb with a yoghurt sauce on a bed of rice seasoned with pine nuts (pigniolas) and onions.

Moussakhan, chicken split lengthwise, covered with sumac herb and oil and served on a large circle of Arab bread.

Farrouj Mishwi, charcoal-grilled chicken, served with garlic sauce.

Mahshi, finely minced meat and rice wrapped in grape or cabbage leaves, or stuffed in tiny marrow squash.

Ful, a favorite breakfast dish, is made of long-simmered dried kidney beans, oil, tomatoes, garlic and other seasonings. Heavy but tasty.

Maza, not a single dish but a variety of *hors d'oeuvres* usually served with arak or other strong beverages. *Maza* with a glass of arak usually brings forth three or four small plates with houmus, techina, pickled string beans and soft, spreadable *lebeneh* cheese along with a *pita* or two. Some times as many as 23 diamond-shaped maza dishes may be put before you, so if you indulge in *maza,* think twice before you order a big main course.

WEST JERUSALEM NIGHTLIFE is on the upswing, with a few well-established places plus new ones springing up every year. This is a selection of the city's best. The **Khan,** in a reconverted caravan inn, is packed with atmosphere, plus bar auditorium, art gallery, nightclub cave and super floorshow with Israeli folklore and international entertainment. $20 each for a rare evening. Seven nights a week, show starts at 10.

Brothers Club (L), 24 Rav Hagan, has nightly dinner shows (reservations, please) with belly dancers, local folk singers, and dancers; also serves lunch. **Jerusalem of Gold,** at Abu Tor, has nightly shows, singing, dancing; **Assaf's Cave,** on Mt. Zion, specializes in Hassidic music, folklore and dance. **Tavern,** 14 Rivlin St., has a pub atmosphere and features folk groups often on Thursday nights.

Goliath Bar (E) was so named because it's but "a stone's throw" from King David—the hotel, that is. American cocktails, snacks and sandwiches by day, plus good piano at night, makes it very popular especially with newspaper folk, writers and such. Great holiday parties welcome everyone. Another nice bar, on Ben Shetach St., mid-town, is **Hesse.**

Club 32, at Betzalel 32, is a students' piano bar—for the jeans crowd.

The younger set also hangs out at **Bacchus,** a cellar place on Rehov Yavets; quite local, rather than international standard.

Dining and dancing nightly (except Fri.) at the **King David** and **President** hotels, Sat. at the **Holyland** and **Hilton.**

EAST JERUSALEM NIGHTLIFE can be plain or fancy. Plain, it can take the form of walking by the Old City walls, which are illuminated at night. The lights focused on the centuries-old walls, towers and battlements create the illusion of going back in time; one almost expects Turkish horsemen on Arab steeds to come prancing out of the Damascus Gate. It's not what most people would call entertainment, but try a stroll to the Wailing Wall late at night. There are always small knots of people praying there, whatever the hour. The Wall looming up into the darkness is at once an eerie, spiritual and awesome sight. For more fancy fare:

Taverna, on Nuzzeha Street, is a lively nightclub with bar and restaurant. The nightly floorshow features belly dancing, conjurors, and cabaret artists from abroad.

Cave du Roi on Az-Zahra Street, a two-level eatery-nitery, is decorated in existentialist style and has fairly moderate prices.

For drinks only, try friendly **Key Bar,** on Az-Zahra Street.

Along the main streets, especially around Derech Nablus, you'll find several night-type places that never stay in business very long. Mostly, these are discothèques with canned music and less than pristine atmospheres. Appealing to youngish crowds, the best of today's lot seems to be **Dalia.**

Night—and day—year-round, but especially in summer, tourists and locals rub shoulders at **Chutzot Hyotzer** art and craft fair, outside Jaffa Gate and the **Jerusalem House of Quality,** with exhibition hall, shop, restaurant, 15 workshops—all in 1882 buildings at 12 Hebron Rd.

 JERUSALEM ENTERTAINMENT. Season subscription **concerts** in winter. *Israeli Philharmonic* at Binyanei Haoma Hall, Yafo St., *Kol Israel Radio Symphony,* YMCA auditorium, Tues, in winter. Once a week: **chamber music** at the Jerusalem Khan (opp. rail station), and the Wise Auditorium on the Hebrew University campus. **Folk music** and **dancing** at Beit Ha'am Hall, Rehov Bezadel. Part of the **Israeli Festival** program is held in Jerusalem during July and August. Also check with *Cahana Ticket Agency,* tel. 222831, for tickets to Monday **chamber music** at *Targ Music Center,* and to performances of the *Jerusalem Symphony Orchestra* and *Israel Chamber Ensemble.*

Annually, **Sacred Music Week** takes place between Dec. and Jan., sponsored by the *JSO* and the Israel Broadcasting Authority.

All year, fine **films** are viewed at *Jerusalem Theater,* in Rahavia District—especially at 2 P.M. Fridays. *Cinemateque,* at mid-town Beit Agron, screens art films and selected films daily.

WHAT TO SEE IN WEST JERUSALEM. It's possible to visit West Jerusalem in a single day, but that would be a mistake. You can visit inside centuries-old sheltering walls the Coenaculum, or *Upper Room,* where Jesus partook of the Last Supper with His disciples. Also on **Mt. Zion:** the Dormition Abbey containing *Mary's Crypt;* the nearby *Tomb of David,* to which pilgrims flock during the Jewish holidays; *Yemin Moshe,* a quaint artists' quarters, with memorabilia of Sir Moses Montefiore in the windmill house. The *Terra Sancta,* a handsome Franciscan Monastery complete with school, is on Keren Hayesod Street. The *Biblical Pontifical Institute* on Paul-Emile Botta Street welcomes visitors to its archeological museum and Jesuit bookshop stocked with works on the Bible and the Eastern World (buses 6, 13, 15).

The *Monastery of the Cross,* near **Rehavia** residential quarter, rises over the site on which the tree that supplied the wood for the cross was supposedly felled; originally 6th-cent., restored by the Crusaders, now Greek Orthodox (buses 5, 16). Nearby in Rehavia is the Alfasi Grotto called *Jason's Tomb* (Hasmonean period, 2nd century B.C.), which displays curious graffiti. In the Russian Compound, in town, the *Russian Orthodox Cathedral* holds up its green dome, just off Yafo Street. Next to it is the former location of the Palestine Mandate Police Headquarters—a bitter reminder. In nearby Abyssinians' Street stands the Abyssinian church, with its statue of the *Lion of Judah.* Other Christian points of interest in **West Jerusalem** are the *Convent of St. Peter of Ratisbon* (near the Yeshurum synagogue); *St. Claire; St. Andrew's Presbyterian Church* at Abu Tor; *St. Paul's* near *Notre Dame Hospice;* and *St. Simon's,* the Greek monastery in the southern part of the city.

Ein Kerem. The 27 bus takes you to the outskirts of Jerusalem, to the village suburb of Ein Kerem, John the Baptist's birthplace. The *Franciscan Church* and *Monastery of St. John* mark the site on which he was born. Close by lies the Franciscan *Church of the Visitation,* dedicated to St. Elizabeth, John the Baptist's mother, and the charmingly quaint *Russian Convent of St. John.* On a hill near Ein Kerem, those ubiquitous Franciscans have still another monastery, right by the cave in which John the Baptist lived out the last span of his life. The *Hadassah Medical Center,* one of the world's most modern hospitals, is located in Ein Kerem, near the sites devoted to St. John the Baptist. The Center's synagogue is embellished with Chagall's famous stained-glass windows depicting the Twelve Tribes of Israel. Guided tours (buses 19 and 27).

Along the highway from Jerusalem to Tel Aviv you come to the picturesque Arab village of **Abu Ghosh:** near the *Church of Our Lady of the Ark of the Covenant,* the famous statue of the Virgin holding the Infant Jesus is visible for miles around. Also in Abu Ghosh: remnants of a 12th-century Crusader church built over Roman foundations.

Among the various distinctively Jewish buildings and institutions, those devoted to religious worship must be differentiated from those of a more national character. Jerusalem's largest synagogue is the *Yeshurun Central Synagogue* (Rehov Hamelekh George, buses 4, 5, 13, 19, 30). In the same street, note the impressive modern façade of the *Hechal Shlomo,* the headquarters of the

Chief Rabbinate, featuring among other things a museum of religious objects and an Italian-style synagogue.

For a glimpse of the ultra-orthodox Jews, visit the **Mea Shearim** quarter, where you will see men dressed in the traditional kaftans of the Eastern European Jews. The quarter is also noted for its many small synagogues of the Eastern Communities and Talmudic schools, and for its colorful markets, particularly animated on Friday mornings when all the housewives are doing their Sabbath shopping.

A short distance away lie the *Tombs of the Sanhedrin Judges* who were the members of the Supreme Court during the Second Temple period. The young trees that serve as a setting here were planted by tourists as remembrances of their visits.

National sentiment is expressed in various different monuments. The *Yad Vashem* commemorates the 6 million Jews who perished at the hands of the Nazis and contains a permanent exhibition, a synagogue, library, and perpetual flame: this memorial is located on the western slope of **Mount Herzl** (bus 12 direct). Nearby is the spot where lies the tomb of Theodor Herzl, the visionary of the Jewish State (buses 12, 18, 20, 23). A military cemetery occupies Mt. Herzl's northern slope. Back in town on Haherut Square, notice the makeshift *"Davidka" mortar* contrivance, named after its inventor; this is a reminder of the pitifully few artillery pieces that defended Jerusalem in 1948. Now branch off on King George Street and soon you'll come to the *Ministry of Tourism building,* with the information office. Continuing on, you make a transition to *National Institutions,* including the buildings of the Jewish Agency, the Jewish National Fund, and the Keren Hayesod (or United Israel Appeal), next door to the Chief Rabbinate: head office of the World Zionist Organization, Zionist archives, Golden Books commemorating those who contributed funds (buses 4, 7, 13).

On Giv'at Ram is *Hakirya,* the *government buildings,* dominated by the *Knesset,* where you can see the famed *Chagall tapestries* and floor. A short distance away, the modern buildings and landscaping of the *Hebrew University:* its campus contains the National Library and University Library, a large sports stadium, the William Planetarium, the Wise Auditorium, a synagogue, in addition to the classroom buildings and student residence halls set amid spacious grounds. Open to the public, daily guided tours, English-speaking guides.

Opposite the university campus stand the futuristic buildings of the *Israel Museum* (free guided tours, in English); the *Bezalel National Museum,* the *Biblical and Archeological Museum* and the *Shrine of the Book* (where the Dead Sea Scrolls are displayed) plus the outdoor *Billy Rose Art Garden* with its sculptures (Sunday, Monday, Wednesday and Thursday, 10 A.M.–6 P.M., Tuesdays 4–10 P.M., Friday and Saturday 10 A.M.–2 P.M. Tickets for Saturday visits may be bought the day before at the museum or ticket agencies). Also a new *Youth Wing* here. And a *Numismatic Gallery*—courtesy Bank Leumi Le'Israel on its 75th anniversary—with coins from 37 B.C. through today, plus several important collections.

At **Ramat Rahel,** formerly a border outpost, you can see archeological digs and enjoy a view of **Bethlehem** (bus 7). The 60-foot high *Kennedy Memorial* is five miles from *Hadassah Hospital,* near Aminadav Moshav.

The *Biblical Zoo* (Romena quarter, bus 15, tickets for Saturday on sale at the Barak Photo Shop opposite the main post-office); here you can view specimens of almost all the animal life mentioned in the Old Testament. The *Mamilah Cemetery* on Agron Street contains the tombs of both Crusaders and Saracen warriors, plus a natural reservoir that might well be the one mentioned in the Bible . . . On King David Street, visit the burial chamber hewn out of sheer rock, the *Tomb of Herod's family.* Also the imposing *YMCA building,* with a tower providing a sweeping view over the Old City and housing a fine set of 35 musical bells which provide carillon concerts four times weekly, playing classical music and Israeli songs. The building also features sport facilities, a collection of ancient artifacts, and a concert hall.

At the *Holyland Hotel,* there is an amazing display of a scale model of ancient Jerusalem (scale 1:50), showing how the city looked during the Second Temple period. Teams of specialists worked on this project; therefore, in addition to being a marvel to behold, it is also painstakingly accurate. The entire model is made from Jerusalem's famed orange-pink stone. Open 10 A.M.–5 P.M. (3 P.M. on Fridays).

The *L.A. Mayer Memorial Institute for Islamic Art* is well worth visiting. It is in the **Talbieh** district, near the residence of the President of Israel. There are guided visits to the *Presidential Residence* on Thurs. and Sun., between 8.30 and 10.30 A.M.

WHAT TO SEE IN EAST JERUSALEM. All holy and religious sites, encompassing Jewish, Christian and Moslem faiths, are open to the public and you can get a long, long list of them from the Israel Government Tourist Administration offices on King George St., or at any IGTA branch.

The Citadel—Jerusalem City Museum, is at Jaffa Gate. An archeological site, mainly Crusader, it has an interesting museum, a 30-minute multi-visual-and-audio presentation of the city's history since King David's time; a fine summer Sound and Light Show: *A Stone in David's Tower,* and various other events and activities. For details, check here or at the new *Municipality P.R. Office*—set up near the Jaffa Gate (17 Jaffa Rd.) just to help tourists. IGTA is also right here, with information on often strenuous $3 *Walking Tours,* and summer *Night Tours* of the city.

WEST JERUSALEM TOURS. Aside from nearly 100 travel and tour agencies in this Holy City, there are several tour operators offering tours you may book directly or via agents. Both coach touring buses and chauffeured taxi service is ready all days, to offer a wide variety of tours for half-days, full days, and several days out of Jerusalem, plus tours within the city and its many special areas. For details, contact **IGTO** or any of these: **Egged Tours,** Central Bus Station and 42A Rehov Yafo; **Nesher,** 21 Rehov Hamelech

George; **United Tours,** King David Hotel Annex; **Eshcolot Tours,** 36 Rehov Keren Hayesod; **Travex,** 8 Rehov Shamay; **Yehuda Tours,** Hotel President; **Neot Hakikar Desert Tours,** 9 Shlomozion Hamalka St.

One of the more unusual and fascinating treks is the full-day tour of the Judean Wilderness. Heading across the wild terrain, around the Dead Sea edge, to and past Jericho, it features Mar Saba monastery, King Herod's mountain fortress (Herodion), Canyon of the Steps, Ein Freshkha springs, Mt. of Temptation, St. George's monastery across a rocky gorge, Wadi Kelt, and back. **Neot Hakikar Desert Tours.**

Other interesting jaunts include Saturday morning walking tours with lectures, tour of Hebrew University, tour of synagogues and their various communities, tour to Masada (full day) and tour of Hadassah Medical Center. Further details from **IGTA.**

Call (02) 222357 for data on free guided hikes and motor/walking tours arranged through the **Society for the Protection of Nature.** To visit *Temple Excavations* near the Western Wall, call Prof. Mazar's office, (02) 284669.

EAST JERUSALEM TOURS. *Half-day tours* of the Old City: *Basic tour:* Western (Wailing) Wall, Dome of the Rock, Via Dolorosa, Holy Sepulcher; *Around the Old City:* Mt. Scopus, Mt. of Olives, Garden of Gethsemane, Kidron Valley; to *Bethlehem and Hebron;* to *Jericho and the Dead Sea;* Synagogues Tour (Fri. afternoon); Rockefeller Museum, Ammunition Hill, Mea Shearim. One-day tours to Nablus, Sebastia and Caesarea (incl. lunch). All moderately priced.

 WEST JERUSALEM SHOPPING. Haute couture, jerseys, ready-to-wear: *Anita Fischer,* 4 Lunz Street; *Iris,* 1 Dorot Rishonim Street; *Stock,* 2 Ben Yehuda, and *Rosenblum,* opposite *Kings Hotel.* For men: *David Co.,* 44 Jaffa Street; *Vigo,* 23 Ben Yehuda,

Souvenirs, gifts, arts and crafts; *Moshe, King David Hotel; Cabasso,* King David St. at Mamila St.; Hebrew name rings and other jewelry and gifts: *E. Ben David,* 4 Ben Yehuda and *Antique No. 10,* almost next door. *Zadok,* King David Hotel Annex; *Charlotte,* 4 Koresh Street (behind the post-office); *Idit,* 16 Ben Yehuda Street; *Esther Zeitz,* 14 Bezalel Street. Arts and crafts centers: *House of Quality* near railway station, workshops and sales room; *Maskit,* 33 Jaffa St., *Wizo,* 34 Jaffa St., and *Khutzot Hayotzer,* near Yemin Moshe area, where you can see craftsmen at work. *Book Nook,* at Ben Yehuda and King George Streets, stays open 8 A.M.–7 P.M., selling books, religious articles, and terrific do-it-yourself-stitchery-design sets of Israeli and Judaica motifs. *Yemin Moshe Quarter*—a residential/workshop area for artists, painters, sculptors, authors—offers interesting arts-crafts buys.

Antiques: *Philipps,* Shlomozion St.; Jewelry by *R. Moussaieff,* at King David Hotel Duty Free Shop. Most hotels have excellent, reliable shops—like Hilton's *The Collector.*

Records: *Radiophone,* 6 Ben Yehuda St. Photography: *Photo Eden,* 3 Ben Yehuda. *Photo Stern,* 7 King George Road.

EAST JERUSALEM SHOPPING. It's fun and fascinating to shop in the bazaar here, but a word to the wise. Don't buy "antiques" without official authenticity guarantees—they'll likely be fakes. If you want costly items, go to a store recommended by the Ministry of Tourism (sticker on door), where quality isn't in question. Comparison shopping is the rule in the bazaar, where there are no fixed prices, and quality fluctuates wildly. Haggling is accepted procedure here, so don't let the first price put you off.

Shopping in virtually any East Jerusalem store, you'll be treated to the famed Arab courtesy and hospitality. There are so many stores and they're so competitive, it's hard to single them out. Some representative examples in the Old City, however, are: *Nijmeh A. Kharoufeh Stores,* 18 David St. offers a large array of items, ranging from rosaries to rugs, antique lamps to headgear. Farther down the street at Number 32 is *Khaled Barakat,* with a tasteful assortment of Bedouin rugs, table covers, Arab costumes, and exquisite hand-embroidery in marvelous patterns. The *Barakat* clan is large and there are other *Barakat* stores along the street, all in friendly competition with one another. The one at No. 36 specializes in Arab dresses, at about $30 and up. The others carry copper items, Persian works, antiques, rugs and assorted souvenirs.

On the Dabbaga Road in the Souk Aftimous, a few steps away from the Church of the Holy Sepulcher, Zouhier Ali Hejazy has an interesting shop that's literally overflowing with leather goods and sheepskins. Particularly attractive are the camel-skin travel bags with side pockets, which sell for around IS45-IS60 and up.

In the Ritz Hotel building, visit *Jordan Products Exhibition* shop, where a stitched Nativity scene of 9 figures runs about IS70; stitched dresses start at IS25, and there's a large selection of other items. Near Herod's Gate, the *Baptist Book Store* offers beautiful, inexpensive gifts, especially carved wood and mother-of-pearl items, plus books.

Also, don't miss the *Jerusalem House of Quality,* a non-profit and non-commercial arts/crafts project at 12 Hebron Rd., where you can watch work, buy it, and have food and drinks.

 SPORTS. Swimming: *Beit Taylor,* Kiryat Hayovel (bus 18); *Holyland Hotel,* Bayit Vegan (taxi); *Ivy Judah Youth Center,* Jerusalem Forest (bus 33); *Diplomat Hotel,* Talpiot (bus 7); *Jerusalem Swimming Pool* (least expensive but most crowded), Rehov Emek Refaim (buses 4, 18); *King David Hotel,* Rehov David Hamelech (buses 6, 7, 15, 18) and next door is the year-round indoor *YMCA* pool; *President Hotel,* Rehov Ahad Ha'am (buses 4, 15); *YMHA,* Sderot Merzog (buses 17, 19). *Hilton Hotel* also has pool; *Shoresh Resort* pool is outside town toward Tel Aviv—as is *Maale Hachamisha* Kibbutz pool; both very nice.

Tennis: Many swimming areas also have tennis, including *Beit Taylor, Holyland Hotel, Ivy Yehuda Youth Center, Shoresh,* the *YMCA,* and *Mitzpeh Rachel* Tourist & Sports Center, Kibbutz Ramat Rachel. Courts are also at the *AACI* (Association of Americans and Canadians in Israel), 9 Rehov Alcalay (bus 15), and at the *Jerusalem Sports Club,* 30 Hatzefira, German Colony (buses 4, 18).

Try a **Turkish bath** at Hammam Yehezkel St. Bathhouse: Sun., Tues., Thurs. for men; Mon. and Wed. for women; open 10 A.M. to 11 P.M. You'll also find hairdressers, cosmeticians, cafeteria, and extras like half-hour massage.

RELIGIOUS SERVICES. Synagogues: The Western (Wailing) Wall. The IGTO have listings of the dozens of other synagogues and more up-to-the-minute details about them than we can carry.

Protestant Churches: *St. George Cathedral,* Nablus Road and Saladin Street; *Christ Church* (Anglican), Jaffa Gate; Church of the Redeemer (Lutheran); *Baptist Southern Worship,* Rashid Street; *First Baptist Bible Church,* Saladin Street; *Church of Christ,* Az-Zahra Street.

For details of the numerous **Catholic and Orthodox** churches and their services, the IGTO have excellent listings, with all the latest times and details.

TRANSPORTATION. See *Facts At Your Fingertips* for road, air, and train service to Jerusalem from David Ben Gurion International Airport and Tel Aviv. Local bus, sherut and taxi services in Jerusalem are excellent.

USEFUL ADDRESSES. Tourist Information: *Israeli Min. of Tourism Offices:* 24 King George St.; Jaffa Gate *Tourist Municipal Information Center:* tel. 228844.

Consulates, Embassies: *US:* 18 Rehov Argon, tel. 223491. *United Kingdom:* Rehov Harakayet, Tower House, tel. 37724.

USEFUL PHONE NUMBERS: Police, 100. **Ambulance,** 101.

עה"ק צפת תו

THE NEGEV—ISRAEL'S SOUTH

Including Beersheba, Eilat and The Dead Sea

Ask a dozen people to define what is or isn't part of Israel's Negev, and it's likely you'll receive a dozen varying answers. Many people think *negev* means "desert." Not so. The Hebrew word simply means "south." With the obvious exception of the Arctic Circle, any geographical location is necessarily south of some other place; there's no boundary limitation for this directional designation.

Israel's Negev actually encompasses nearly half the tiny nation. From a point at Eilat, on the Red Sea Gulf, it rises almost as a cone, shaped by the sloping angles of Jordan's borders and those of the Sinai Peninsula. Official literature makes no bones of the fact that Ashdod—the country's largest Mediterranean port not far from Tel Aviv—belongs to the Negev, as does the entire coastline south of Ashdod, including Ashkelon. East of Ashdod, the top of the cone-shaped Negev could be defined by an imaginary line marking off the Lachish Region and running through the Judaean Hills and the Wilderness of Judah to the Dead Sea. Almost directly south of the Lachish Region industrial hub is Beersheba, called the "capital" of the Negev. Somewhat further south lies the Wilderness of Zin, with the Wilderness of Paran even more southerly, marked on maps at a point about half-way between Beersheba and Eilat.

One reason why many people have reckoned *negev* and "desert" to be synonymous is that parts of this territory are arid wastelands, where oases contain all the greenery. But there are some patches of downy moss or short-lived desert plants that occasional rain manages to wring out of the parched and cracked soil. Otherwise, this barren land is a frantic tumble of sun-scorched rock, rugged craters, stark mountains, startling geographical formations and shapes that seem to wind endlessly beyond the horizon.

Here also are bleached ruins of civilizations long vanished. In these ruins lies a clue that all this land hasn't always been so barren: it has supported men, their crops and animals, and towns and cities that hosted caravans which trekked this region, since pre-historic days, from the African continent to Cathay and back.

Biblical Israelites lived 40 years in the wilderness; likewise, many modern-day people live in the Negev wildernesses—Jews, Arabs, Bedouin—where flocks can graze and the soil can be nurtured to yield grasses, grains and other crops and greenery. Though during Mandate years British engineering and agricultural experts termed everything south of Kiryat Gat as non-reclaimable desert and said it was impossible to develop the land beyond that point, each year the areas of cultivated land have eaten further and further into the wilderness. Just two decades ago, Beersheba and Eilat were sandy outposts and Dimona was just being founded. Today, Beersheba is a large, flourishing city, ringed with lush fields, Eilat is a resort paradise, and Dimona is the "old, established" town among dozens of newer, thriving settlements.

Each year, more and more newcomers migrate to the southlands, not merely adding to the growing population, but also helping to make the desert bloom—which pays off quite well in year-round fine export foods and flowers. Also, as Israeli military bases and airfields have moved back from Sinai into the Negev, they continually attract more permanent settlers plus all the additional infrastructure needed to support these technological posts and the ever-increasing non-nomadic, desert peoples.

Heading South

Several highways crisscross the Negev and connect its towns and cities to the rest of Israel. The road traveled from Tel Aviv to Jerusalem, which roughly follows the railroad, is intersected at several places by roads leading to different cities and settlements in the Negev. Of the many routes leading from the Holy City into the southlands, we select one which winds through hills that boast the Hadassah Medical Center complex at their crests. As we travel, community settlements, including both *kibbutzim* and *moshavim,* emerge along the road like sentinels of agriculture at strategic points in the countryside. Gradually the landscape changes, with chaotic jumbles of rocks interspersed with sown fields, neat rows of vineyards and scattered buildings here and there.

Although narrow, the highway is in perfect condition. The road passes through the valley of Elah, famed as the scene of history's most lopsided duel, the encounter between David and Goliath: a deep slash cleaves the hillcrest, marking the spot where the giant's head struck when he fell, causing the earth to quake and the mountains to split asunder. Nor are we far from Samson's neck of the woods, Beit Shemesh, a few miles north, where you can visit Stalagmite Cave and stop for lunch with members of Kibbutz Tzorah, nearby.

The rocky slopes on either side of the road become more barren and are gashed with deep clefts. Early Christians took refuge in these caves, which interconnect with one another by means of underground passages hewn out of the solid white limestone. You can find signs of the Cross cut into the stone here. And a readily identifiable pagan altar is still standing in the vicinity of Netiv-Halamed-Heh, at the top of a flight of steps carved in the rock.

The first town of any size is Beit Guvrin, 32 miles from Jerusalem. This was once a settlement of importance, according to historical annals. The ruins of the Roman city and of a church are still visible—the Crusaders were here, too. Through the centuries its name has undergone several successive deformations. The Arabs called it Beit Gibrïl (Gabriel), nonchalantly turned into Gibelin by the Crusaders. In one of their more Hellenic moods, the Romans had previously called it Eleutheropolis. Emperor Septimus Severus went to the trouble of paying a visit here. The French Archeological School of the Dominican Fathers, in Jerusalem, carried out exhaustive examination of Roman and Byzantine mosaics here. Maresha, fortress of King Rehoboam of Judea is nearby, as is Lachish.

The Lachish Region

The hub of the region, Kiryat Gat, was founded in 1955 as pilot village for a new rural development technique. In addition to its residential dwellings, it contains primarily stores, warehouses, and office-buildings, as its main function is to serve settlements in the outlying periphery.

The town acts as the supplier of raw materials, equipment, machinery and tools, and as the central collector for produce and manufactured items. The various industries set up in these places are geared to supporting and complementing the agricultural program, including sugar refining, cotton milling, peanut processing, diamond cutting, and electronics.

From here, it's 25 miles south to Beersheba, capital of the Negev.

Discovering Beersheba

"And Abraham took sheep and oxen, and gave them unto Abimelech; and both of them made a covenant . . . Wherefore he called that place Beer Sheba, because there they sware both of them" (GENESIS XXI:27, 31). Isaac and Jacob lived here during those days when Abraham and King Abimelech pledged, before the well Abraham dug some 4,000 years ago, not to harm each other. The site's been Beersheba ever since, though archeologists have dug up remains of a civilization, dating about 1,500 years earlier, of clever farmers, traders and craftsmen living about 3 miles outside of today's town: Nabateans. The whole Negev area once held many such towns and their ruins, plus those of Rome and Byzantine, are impressive for sightseeing ventures.

Despite its ancient past of heavy population and commerce, the area of Beersheba was merely a few wells for nomadic flocks around the turn of the century, when the Ottoman Turks decided to forge it into an administrative center. More precisely, they built a jail here. Then came World War I and Germans constructed railway links with Sinai, only to be ousted (with the Turks) by British General Allenby in 1917—which is how Beersheba became the first British-captured town of Palestine in that war. The British Mandate years created little change. When those forces moved out on the eve of the implementation of the United Nations Charter for the State of Israel, in May, 1948, Beersheba was in for more fighting as Egyptian troops swarmed up and fortified the town heavily. They held on until October 22, when Israeli Defense Forces recaptured the town.

In 1948, Beersheba was still only a main road and cluster of buildings and dwellings, with no resemblance to today's town which covers over

54,000 dunams and comprises the Old Town and sprawling new areas built according to a Master Plan for integrating building into the environment. There are many parks and a belt of greenery is being completed to circle the town. Empty spaces are also part of the Plan, "to ensure urban continuity." The Old Town displays traces of all the century's inhabitants, but new areas show experimental architecture geared to this dry, desert climate: 30°-12°C summer-winter average temperatures, with 200 mm rain per year.

Jumping wildly from 2,000 in 1948 to 101,000 today, the city's population is forecast at 250,000 by the year 2,000. In recent years, thousands of Soviet immigrants have poured into Beersheba, to join the thousands from Arab lands and some from Western countries. Education is the key for welding all into one, and Beersheba is justly proud of its educational facilities, though it keeps increasing them. David Ben Gurion University has faculties for Humanities, Social Science, Engineering Sciences, Medicine; it gives academic support to the local College of Technology, the Research and Development Authority, and (in the past) to the Negev Research Institute. The Municipal Conservatory of Music gives lessons in all instruments, has bands, orchestras, concerts and choirs. There is a Seminary of Physical Education for Teachers, a Nurses' Training College, a Teachers' Training College, plus several supplementary education courses and schools for learning Hebrew, the unifying language.

The Changing Bedouin

Important industries are here, and more are en route or underway at the new industrial center southeast of town. As Beersheba really is the administrative center of the Negev now, many people here work in local or government administrative agencies, building and public works, and the large factories. While all this goes on, the town remains a trading center for the 19,000 Negev Bedouins. These once-wholly-nomadic people have begun to settle down in Tel Sheva, four miles out, where six permanent settlements are underway. Tents still can be seen, sometimes pitched alongside shacks or the good, sturdy houses most Bedouin build. When we visited one home, we found it filled with hospitality, cleanliness, handembroidered pieces, coffee and soda and lots of laughing children and modest adults. A bookcase held tomes in Arabic, Hebrew and English: Pearl Buck was there, and Lawrence's "The Fox"; atlases were near "Theoretical Linguistics." Some members of the family were in Europe; others had nice cars parked outside, ready to drive to their homes or visit friends, or perhaps check some of their crops—for since they have enough water to cease roaming around, Bedouins have become farmers as well as herdsmen.

Romantically, it's perhaps sad to see the dashing, fierce nomads disappearing into the 20th century, but it's simultaneously good to realize their lives are longer (thanks to doctors, the nearby Bedouin Clinic, etc.) and less painful; they are educated and able to move in many directions, no longer bound to thirst-quenching wells in the wilderness. They sit in government, including Knesset, and though some are apolitical and only pro-Bedouin, and some are political and pro-Arab, most seem happy with the fusion achieved between them and the Jewish state.

Completely citified Bedouins do occupy new apartment houses, and the souk passageways swarm with Jews speaking fluent Arabic. Nomads still abound—look for the many patched tents outside town— but in many cases they are merely economizing on rent, or being "professional Bedouins." Lots of them punch time-clocks every morning.

Sometimes, the Bedouin tribes adopt Beersheba folk, and two such "tribal family" members are Susan Egar and her son, Miki. Aside from the friendship involved in the adoption, Mrs. Egar found it terribly helpful to "belong" when she needed to buy a baby camel—her "family" could bargain for her! If you're wondering what a nice widow-lady wanted with a baby camel, the answer's simple: as manager of the Desert Inn Hotel, she decided to create a biblical zoo, and the camel was the first of several animals to arrive. By the way, this is a good person to ask about the local art events and artists who have settled in Beersheba where, they say, desert light gives colors unexpected tints and brilliance.

You can tour the environs of Beersheba by bus, car and air. Check your map and transportation schedules and start early, as you may find it so interesting you'll be glad of the extra daylight hours.

The Wilderness—Poles and Pipelines

Having seen the marvels of civilization already carved out of what was, until recently, desert wilderness, tourists traveling south of Beersheba may now believe all things possible. Assured that these progressive settlers are capable of taming wastelands, it can come as somewhat of a shock when tourists encounter the boundless region of barren terrain, broken only here and there by small settlement towns and villages. "Why haven't Israelis planted gardens out here yet?" some may wonder. The answer is, they're working on it.

Wherever possible, trees have been planted along the roadside to hold the sand and soil in place. Otherwise, the roads resemble tiny asphalt ribbons, gingerly pasted onto arid land, a thin carpet that might be nonchalantly pushed aside by seasonal torrents, or by the road-building apparatus of man, in continuous attempts at improvement. In spite of the overall impression of sand, stones, rock masses, dizzy depths and sheer walls, what stands out here more than anything else is something wrought by the hand of man: a telegraph system. The means of human communication have never seemed more immediate than right here, with this endless array of poles and wires. And beneath the surface, with incredible patience and obstinacy, man has sunk the pipes that transport his most vital possession—water.

At intervals you see pipes emerging from under the ground, climbing up hills, going down slopes, stretching out horizontally, dipping, reappearing. The pipeline is a dual one. Water is piped from north to south, and oil from south to north. And then?

Israel's magnificent obsession, the salvaging of the desert, began clandestinely as early as 1946. Literally overnight, the occupying forces found themselves confronted with a *fait accompli.* In one single night, eleven villages had mushroomed in the desert! Others followed, totalling 27 by the time independence was achieved.

Water was channeled to them via a makeshift arrangement, which was actually 120 miles of firehose that had survived the London blitz. In 1948 the Egyptians destroyed these lengths of hose when they attacked the fledgling state and besieged the 27 villages in the Negev. But only one village fell into their hands. After the victory and armistice, it was necessary to dig new wells and build a new pipeline, more durable this time.

Since King Solomon's day, subsoil had not been exploited here, but a 1949-50 survey revealed Israel to be one of the rare countries in the world with all of the three raw materials used in making chemical artificial fertilizers: phosphate, nitrate, and potassium. By 1965, 200,000 tons of phosphates alone were mined, half of which was exported.

Half of the 200,000 tons of phosphates mined in 1965 were exported. Near Solomon's mines, at Timna, the copper and manganese output was some 23 million tons before economics of mining copper forced the mines shut in the mid-1970's. Recent mineral prices have caused them to reopen, however. Oil was struck in the Heletz region, southeast of Ashkelon, and 28 wells were drilled, the output from which already meets one-tenth of domestic needs.

There are natural gas deposits, feldspar, mica, sand for glass-making, kaolin, clay, sulphur, bitumen, fluorite, and gypsum. (A full description of the mineral resources of the Dead Sea area is contained in the related section of this chapter.)

Traveling on, you see a water-tower, silhouetted against the blue sky. That's Yeroham, 20 miles from Beersheba. Its 5,300 residents live on the site of the first *ma'abara,* or immigrants' transit camp, established south of Beersheba. A small, man-made lake lies on the other side of the highway, unseen from the road. Marshy ground edges much of the lake, but trees and greenery are thick. Folk come to walk, picnic or fish—for the lake was stocked with young fish, with the mental reservation that little fish may some day grow big if God grants them life.

Yeroham has a service station, a strange looking hotel for workers, and a café that matches. It also has neatly intersecting streets, traffic lights, and road signs. It is predominantly an industrial and mining center. Its quarries produce kaolin for procelain and sand for glass. Fill up the gas-tank while you're in town—gas stations don't grow on trees around here, and even if they did, there wouldn't be too many of them.

A road juts out to the left toward Dimona, 7 miles to the northeast. A third highway shoots out to the southeast, going via Machtesh Gadol (the Great Crater) to reach Oron, 10 miles distant.

Right now we're heading due south and the next bit of green you'll see will be Sde Boker, 11 miles away. This kibbutz was founded in 1952 by a group including the late Prime Minister Ben Gurion, who lived here until his death. A little further south is the Sde Boker College, named after Pola Gurion, Ben Gurion's wife. Visitors are welcome to see his library, and the homes and graves of the couple.

In the Hebrew and Yiddish languages there's a word *chutspah,* that means something midway between nerve and gall, between optimism and blithe unawareness. It took plenty of chutspah to create these pastures and tilled fields out of nothingness, in a place without water, roads, or electricity in the midst of nowhere. Yet, countless eons ago, this area had already been inhabited by man, as proven by the prehistoric paintings that have been discovered in the caves and shallow rock recesses around Sde Boker.

Avdat and Ein Avdat

A few miles south, on your left, is a road leading to Ein Avdat where you'll find water—a thin trickle bubbling up out of rock. You'll probably enjoy a dip in the technicolor-green natural swimming pool at the base of a canyon. Then back to the main road, heading south. In the Wilderness of Zin, atop an imposing mountain, the awesome ruins of Nabatean civilization's peak lie. Nabath was the son of Ismael, the hapless offspring of the patriarch Abraham and his maidservant Agar. For a long time, Arabs were known as Ismaelians (not to be confused with the Moslem sect of Ishmaelites), although the real Arabs were overthrown by barbarian tribes centuries after the Nabateans were presumed to have come from the Arabian desert. They had many cities and towns in the desert—including the area of Beersheba—and the city of Petra, in nearby Jordan, was their capital. Avdat was a fortress stronghold and a compulsory toll-house stop for the legalized robbery of caravans traveling the Spice Route.

Sharp traders, clever politicians and formidable warriors, Nabateans allied themselves with the Hasmoneans (or Maccabeans) in the latter's fight against the Greeks. Then they managed to hold out against the Romans, and not until Trajan's time was their resistance finally overcome. Through the centuries, through Roman occupations and Byzantine invasions, Avdat remained faithful to its vocation, to which no stigma was attached in those days, of gently relieving travelers of their cash.

The Nabateans were excellent ceramicists, and also devised a highly successful and ingenious system for trapping and storing water, and for irrigating their fields.

Farmers of Note

Since Avdat was situated at the crossroads of two vital caravan routes—from Petra and from Eilat—it developed into the most important city in the central Negev. But such a crossroads station would have been useless if it couldn't supply water to man and camel. The Nabateans developed an expertise with water, digging cisterns, dams and channeling networks to capture and store water.

They controlled the central Negev during the third and second centuries B.C. and when the Romans took over the crossroads franchise, the Nabateans were able to use their water-storage genius for agricultural purposes. On and off for the next seven centuries, under Roman and Byzantine rule, the Nabateans remained on their desert farms. In A.D. 416 a furious assault by the Persians wreaked havoc on their settlements, and their culture never recovered from the shock.

The desert winds had the next thirteen centuries in which to cover their traces. When archeologists discovered the ruins in this century, they were amazed at the sophistication of the farming methods. Some of them, in fact, are still a mystery, but agronomists have been hard at work for years trying to duplicate the Nabatean farming feats: apparently these desert farmers of 2,000 years ago knew a few tricks about arid-zone farming that present-day specialists still haven't figured out.

The city looked down on the valley from its perch high above, with an unobstructed view and invulnerable fortifications. People in those days knew how to combine business with pleasure. The traces left by the original Nabateans consist of the remains of an altar, a necropolis, and the water cisterns. The Romans bequeathed us baths, which really date from their Byzantine successors, located at the base of the hill, along with the rectangular outlines of a military campsite.

The Byzantines themselves were more generous. On the top of the hill they built St. Theodore's Church, one of the first in the land, now perfectly preserved except for its lack of a roof. Marble slabs graven with Greek inscriptions cover the tombs. One of them assigns an approximate date for all this—the 4th century. A monastery stood next to the church, and you pass through its ruins to enter what were once the castle and watchtower beyond.

On the walls of the caves underneath there are signs of the Cross cut into the stone. On the way down, you can notice in certain places the original steps that were hewn out of the living rock. But the overall effect is somehow overwhelming with the hill surmounted by great dismantled walls, set out in the immeasurable solitude of the desert. Should we rejoice or lament at the sight of what more recent times have provided? Parked sightseeing buses, a gasoline-pump, and a brand-new dwelling, which is both the home and the laboratory of a botany professor, who moved out here to pursue on-the-spot research into plants that live without water, greet the eye.

Shivta

Another Nabatean-Byzantine town, circa 2nd century B.C., lies slightly northwest of Avdat and is well worth a visit for anyone interested in archeology. As in Pompeii, you can stroll through streets and terraces 2,000 years old—this is one of the best preserved ancient towns of the Middle East. Three Byzantine churches of the 5th and 6th centuries are here as well as Nabatean houses with the second stories still intact. Shivta is most easily reached via the road leading through the heavily settled area just east of the Gaza Strip, which offers another interesting stop at Revivim—settled in 1943 and flourishing as one of the Negev's first settlements.

Mitzpeh Ramon

Just 13 miles from the ruins of Avdat, 50 miles from Beersheba, you suddenly can't believe your eyes! If you were at the movies, you'd know this was just another fake backdrop, some sort of optical illusion. When you see it before your eyes you can't believe it's real. Here lies a small town nonchalantly teetering on the brim of a gigantic crater, overlooking the vertiginous depths of the Machtesh Ramon, as if it were the most natural thing in the world for a city to do!

The Book of Numbers tells us that when they reached the Wilderness of Zin, the children of Israel rebelled against the authority of Moses and his brother Aaron, the high priest, reproaching them thus: "Why have you made us come up out of Egypt and have brought us into this wretched place, which cannot be sowed; nor bringeth forth figs, nor vines, nor pomegranates neither is there any water to drink?" (NUMBERS xx:5). It took the Jews 3,300 years to disprove this complaint and bring in what was necessary. And what did they proceed to do next? They dreamed up an international sculpture show. The pieces of modern, abstract sculpture are displayed in the open air, right along the highway.

On the opposite side of the road, the sand plunges straight down in a sheer wall to form a huge arena of majestic beauty and untamed grandeur, looking as if it had been created solely to remind human builders that the desert isn't to be outdone by mere man. In reply, man has made his road run right along the edge of the precipice, brutally exposing the crater and winding down clear to the bottom before calmly proceeding due south. Once you're at the bottom, your backward glance reveals an awesome spectacle. The side of the cliff looms like an amphitheater, blocking off half the horizon. In the distance two *mezas* stand guard, dark, sawed-off sentries.

Mitzpeh Ramon to Eilat

Although some people may find Mother Nature inhospitable in this region, scholars find her rewarding. She has thoughtfully laid in provisions of fossilized remains that yield information about the area as it was 200 million years ago, give or take a few millennia. Zoologists rave notably over the remains of the *tanistropheus,* the giant lizard whose neck was shaped like a giraffe's.

From the Wilderness of Zin, stretching across the first third of the road from Beersheba to Eilat, we've moved into the Wilderness of Paran. Over to the left are the Hills of Moab, a mountain range in Jordan that seems the same deep brown color as on your geography maps. About 90 miles from Beersheba, the road swerves and heads for the Arava, the "arid valley," before continuing along the frontier. A fork shoots up to the north: that's the second Negev highway, which follows the valley all the way to the Dead Sea, the road that we'll be taking on our way back.

A cluster of buildings at a crossroads and a reservoir announces the Nahal settlement of Ktora. A mile and a half further on is the Grofit kibbutz. There's a real surprise further on: a pasteurized milk vending machine called the Milk Bar! The sign strikes you as quite funny—way out here. Now only 24 miles from the Red Sea Gulf town of Eilat, you find orchards and cultivated fields.

Yotvata and King Solomon's Mines

The Yotvata Kibbutz is remarkable in that it was founded by young-sters from Haifa and Tel Aviv who were probably tired of hearing their parents boast of pioneer accomplishments.

Most of these self-made farmers would be qualified today to hold good-paying city jobs but they prefer agriculture and stock breeding. Their trucks supply Eilat with dates, milk, yoghurt, eggs, and fresh green produce. Some of them drive daily to the northern markets, occasionally beating farmers from Ein Gedi.

The early melons that are seen in many English shops each year are flown in from Yotvata, which also exports other fruits, as well as flowers. Yotvata has its own water supply, and its springs provide water for Eilat also. The Books of Numbers and Deuteronomy mention a stop at Yotvata during the journey across the desert from Egypt to Canaan. Today the village is a classic garden spot in the desert, and is well worth a visit.

In former times, during the centuries in which the people gradually progressed from a nomadic to a sedentary existence, this was a bustling region; the current aim is to recover some of the area's earlier anima-tion. A small road turning off to the right 10 miles farther on passes King Solomon's fabulous mines and leads on to modern Timna mines, where copper and manganese were mined and processed until the mid-1970's. The landscape has changed color, with reds and purples predominating. When tourist buses grind to a halt, passengers pile out, eager to discover some of the green-blue semi-precious stones streaked with black, brown and white—"gems of Eilat"—despite the strict regu-lations against carrying any of them off. In Deuteronomy (VIII, 9), there's a verse describing a land "where the stones are iron, and out of whose hills are dug mines of brass"—the reference must be to Timna, not far from Jordan's border, and 15 miles from Eilat.

Nearby, a natural monument, Solomon's Pillars, thrusts up its mon-strous shapes that have become familiar to everyone through photo-graphic illustrations. These pillars are indeed a true red color, huge and overwhelming. The crucibles into which Solomon's men poured their molten metals were discovered a short distance up on the hillside. They are still there for all to see.

In this same neighborhood, you may run across uniformed Israeli youngsters. Young *Gadna* scouts, high-school seniors, are given agricultural instruction along with para-military training and learn to improve the land they'll soon defend, as part of IDF, after graduation. They have a camp at Be'er Ora, an oasis where they carve the names of their heroes on the mountainside. Mother Nature has more than outdone herself by planting the Pillars of Amram (Moses's father) at the entrance to Eilat.

Not to be missed in this area is the Hai Bar Nature Reserve, finally open to the public after 17 years initial work, where wild animals mentioned in the Bible have been gathered together in their natural habitat, many thus saved from extinction. Here they roam free, protected from passing motor vehicles by fences. Just riding past the reserve offers a chance to glimpse many of these wild creatures, some nodding in the shade of sparse desert trees and bushes, others grazing or racing from the noise of your car.

As you continue toward Eilat, you'll note that white fledgling eaglets, perched on the telegraph poles, have reappeared and don't condescend to move even when cars drive by. You now catch a first glimpse of the next settlements. Jordanian Aqaba lies to the east, its international airport heralds your approach to the Red Sea Gulf where the cities of Aqaba and Eilat—often called the Gulf's twin cities—stand almost side by side.

Hot Tourist Town

Eilat has variously been dubbed an "emergency exit," a "service entrance," "the gateway to Asia and Africa," "the end of the world," and the "gateway to Sinai." A better appellation today would be "tourist city." Local tourism industry projections are geared to transform this town into the "Caribbean of the Red Sea." And you already can see it happening.

A huge lagoon has been built as part of a multi-million-dollar project to make Eilat the most unusual and best-equipped seaside resort in the Middle East. The marina bristles with yacht masts; small boats and wind-surfing and scuba gear are easily rentable; a resort center around the main lagoon has floating restaurants, all sizes of elegant hotels, an amphitheater and tourist center, several bars, pubs and fine restaurants, plus many special amusements. These facilities spill over into town, where several commercial and tourist centers beckon visitors. And then there's Coral Beach, past the refinery piers, where an oasis of tourist delights is called Laromme Eilat, a hotel with everything. More hotels are slated to open soon, including well-known international names like Sheraton, Hilton, Americana, Hyatt and Canadian-Pacific, and new tourism enterprises already are springing up to meet the annually increasing demand that peaks in October.

Eilat's busy airport is newly expanded and refurbished, and constantly growing. From here, Arkia Airlines offers 13 flights each day to and from other parts of Israel. Further north, a military airfield has been adapted to handle all types of civilian and commercial aircraft, and is outfitted with passport and customs controls, lounges and snack bars—the better to serve those European charters.

The big bus station crackles with activity, too, as crowds mass to ride air-conditioned vehicles from here to both northern and southern destinations. Nearby are offices for *sherut* service to the entire country—jitney-like special taxis that race between towns. The railway is slated to run right to Eilat but, as railroads are so vulnerable, that probably won't happen until the growing peace in the Middle East becomes more widespread.

Ties between Israel and Egypt, however, make it possible to jump from Eilat to Egyptian areas of Sinai, via the same Israeli-operated tours that covered the peninsula when it was under Israeli administration. You can ride down the east coast of the Sinai Peninsula to Sharm-el-Sheikh, where swimming and diving are ranked tops by international professionals and the desert air is fanned by breezes from Ethiopia. You can head for the Sinai Peninsula tip, Ras Muhamed, for more skin diving and even enjoy two-country tourism from Israel to Egypt.

Much closer to Eilat is Coral Island—a storybook isle a few miles south of the city, with the remains of a fortress that first was a stronghold of Pharaohs, then Mamelukes, and finally, Crusaders, with most of its ruins dating from the 12th century. From the nearby Fjord, all the way back to Eilat, the Red Sea Gulf offers a paradise to underwater enthusiasts who flock here year-round to dive. Glass-bottom boats, large or small, operate here, too, plus boats thoroughly equipped for all sorts of underwater filming and exploration. One "must see" for underwater buffs is the glass-sheathed underwater observatory (one of four in all the world), where you descend to watch the "world of silence" and the approximately 300 species of marine life along the reefs. Back on the shore, there is also a live museum displaying flora and fauna from the briny Red Sea.

Excursions from Eilat are regularly scheduled or can be tailored to suit your convenience. They include visits to the town's "children's forest" (where a new tree is planted for every child born here), Hai Bar Nature Reserve, the Gadna farm at Be'er Ora, the Pillars of Solomon and of Amram, Timna mines, Coral Island, the Fjord, Sinai and its Santa Katerina Monastery at the foot of Mt. Sinai. They also include jaunts to Taba—the fascinating, zany retreat created by Rafi Nelson, one of Eilat's many colorful characters—where sunning, diving and good-natured fun are enhanced by thatch huts and the Bedouin and their animals that live with Rafi.

From Solomon to Now

Local residents vigorously boast Eilat's place in history; it was here that King Solomon in all his splendor came to welcome the Queen of Sheba. Furthermore, he had a big fleet built for him here by his ally, the Phoenician King Hiram, and the timber used for the ships was fir and cedars of Lebanon. His copper and metal mines were all right around here, too, and their sites have been located. Now, all the above rings true, except for one little detail: it all happened at Ezion-Gever. It's quite possible that in ancient times the industrial port extended as far as today's Aqaba, in Jordan. The most generally accepted hypothesis is that Eilat and Aqaba were once a single city, but archeological explorations here have been disrupted by war and territorial divisions, so proof hasn't yet substantiated this.

Though this was part of the U.N.-mapped Charter for Israel, Israeli forces took possession of Eilat on March 10, 1949. When they went to hoist the blue and white Israeli flag with its Star of David emblem, the eager troops discovered that in their haste they had forgotten to bring one with them. A piece of bed-sheet was made to serve. In those days Eilat was still the old police outpost of Um Rashrash. Foundations for the new town were dug all around it, and work began in earnest. Although an armistice had been signed with the Arab countries, and despite the stipulations of the big powers who undersigned it, Egyptian guns kept Israeli ships from entering the gulf. Not until the lightning campaign of Sinai in 1956 were the guns silenced.

Before May, 1967, few people could pinpoint Eilat on the map. Then at the end of that month, when Nasser blocked the Strait of Tiran and cut off shipping, the city became the focus of world-wide attention. In fact, it was the cutting off of Eilat that precipitated the Six-Day War.

The U.N. garrison at Sharm-el-Sheikh, guarding the Strait of Tiran, which had been set up there in 1956 to ensure freedom of shipping through these waters, was dislodged by Egypt. The southern entrance to the Red Sea was sealed off again (as it was by Egypt before 1956), Israel's vital lifeline to Asia and Africa was severed and this was taken as an act of war.

Ironically enough, that war did not touch Eilat. The neighboring Jordanian city of Aqaba made no hostile moves and Egyptian forces to the west of Eilat made a U-turn back toward Egypt once the war started. When Israeli paratroops and amphibian craft (from Eilat) reached Sharm-el-Sheikh on the third day of the war, they found it deserted. The Egyptians had fled.

Although Eilat was hardest touched by 1973's war, its tourist trade has mushroomed—thanks largely to charter flights landing here from

Europe. Then, having port facilities makes it possible for Eilat to trade with Asia and Africa, two natural outlets and suppliers, without resorting to the detour from Haifa clear around the African continent. And now, Israel cargoes have gone via the Suez Canel—cleared after the 1973 war and opened to international shipping.

The annual freight handled by the port of Eilat currently amounts to some two million tons, exclusive of the oil brought in here to be piped into the interior. To find a sound basis for its future development, in addition to trucking goods across the desert, the three development goals that Eilat has set for itself are tourism, industry, and expansion of port facilities. But the city and the port must follow a parallel development. Between 1949 and 1956, Eilat's population rose from 200 to 800. Since then it increased greatly and today there are almost 18,000 residents. Every sort of official encouragement is offered to settlers here, special allotments plus tax exemptions.

The question of water remains an issue. The sea furnishes a theoretically inexhaustible supply, but it has to be desalinated for most purposes of domestic consumption. However, the matter of running economic desalinization is fraught with problems. Present processing procedures are five times as expensive as artesian wells would be. By 1967 Eilat had two desalinization plants, using two different processes. But things move so fast here that after only a year, one of the plants was "retired," and now there's a third one—plant and process!

Even with such worries, Eilat is a paradise. The sun nearly always shines, and though temperatures occasionally soar over 100°F in the summer, the constant breeze assures comfort even then. The climate is dry, and during winter months of January and February the mercury seldom drops below 70°F. Claims that the sky is infallibly blue are exaggerated. Scattered clouds appear at least once a month. However, the clouds don't linger long, and the barometer cheerfully returns to its usual "fine weather" reading.

Eight Hours on "Another Planet"

There is one attraction you mustn't miss at any cost, one that you can't recommend too enthusiastically: this is the excursion called "A Day in the Eilat Mountains." Although perhaps not exactly advisable for the elderly, or mothers-to-be, it's by no means an exclusive monopoly of the young. You do this trip in all-purpose jeeps along trails that normally serve as roads for military maneuvers in the desert, rather than along the fine highway.

You slip into a 12-seat jeep—or choose an air-conditioned GMC—and you go. You won't even notice if you're a bit shaken up, because your enchantment begins just the other side of Coral Bay, on the way to Wadi Shlomo. You feel as if you personally were helping to hew out a road after the debris had been cleared away from a landslide in the wake of a glacier.

This road is famous as the trail followed a thousand years ago by caravans bearing the perfumes of Araby between the Red Sea and the Mediterranean. Not too long ago, the British patched it up as a sort of emergency exit against a possible catastrophe in North Africa. It was part of the Darb-el-Hadj, the Pilgrims' Route, which the Moslems took on their way to Mecca. There are fascination, anguish, and exaltation in the seemingly endless array of scenery—the sea plus the mountains, with their crevasses and unexpected flat stretches amid strange black granite shapes silhouetted sharply against the sky.

The bold display of colours is even more fantastic in Ein Nefatim, once a border point with Egypt. The stingiest rainfall a week ago will have decked this otherwise barren soil with a blanket of flowers whose blooms are completely unknown elsewhere. If an uninterrupted spell of dry weather has prevailed, the interplay of dull and bright, shiny surfaces is all the more striking—they vie with one another in retaining or reflecting the dazzling light. The rock has been gaudily streaked from mineral oxidation, and the stones are like so many outsized precious gems casually strewn about by the hand of a desert god.

The dusty brown surfaces bear crazy streaks of deep green, shading off now and then to the palest yellow. This arrangement is occasionally disrupted by a bright red or purple patch or line. Your gaze embraces a sweeping view of a wild terrain. Through the clefts between the peaks behind you stretches the sparkling mirror of the Red Sea.

A short way ahead, Nature has apparently thought better of the situation, and has repented by returning to the pale greens and pinks of school maps.

Below, water that swirled around for several millennia without finding an outlet has hollowed out a gigantic flat trough, once used by the U.N. as a landing field. Elsewhere, streams and torrents born out of the latest rainfall, only to die after a single hour, have impetuously raced right through the rock. For generations, annual flash floods carved all the roads hereabouts. Caravans and armies flowed in the paths left by the waters. Wide swaths that weave and dwindle, they sometimes changed greatly in each flooding. But always, as soon as the tumultuous flood has subsided, tiny orphan flowers thrust their petals into the sunlight. They breathe a moment and then sweetly expire.

The Desert Conquers

What about human life in this desert? Though it exists strongly along the coasts of the Mediterranean and Red-Sea Eilat Gulf, where water refreshes the sand and rocks, human life's scarce when you hit the desert. This part of the world's more for crossing, than for dwelling in.

A few hardy volunteers did once attempt to set up a kibbutz out in the midst of this sheer nothingness. Their experiment was short-lived. So say the pleasant and congenial young men who guide this fascinating trip, and particularly enjoy doing so. They love the desert. Their eyes reveal the gleam of the true adventurer. Local regulations require them to cart a rifle with them, by which the passengers are regularly impressed, but not they themselves. Neither are they impressed with any brand of weather. When it's hot, they wear shorts and a hat out here. When it's freezing cold, in the middle of the desert winter, they keep driving the open jeep bare-footed and usually with no jacket—or an open one—and the same shorts. Seems like the desert is really a part of them, or they're one with it.

The vehicle now starts climbing, heaving and straining up the more than half-mile of rough ribbon that passes as a road, and reaches another frontier marker, followed by still a third marker half a mile farther on. You can feel the full force of the wind by now, and you're glad to have that tour-provided wind-breaker in spite of the heat.

Now everybody out for the Red Canyon, which is the feature attraction of this trip. The climb down is easy, even though you may have the illusion that you are performing feats of acrobatic mountain climbing skill in getting through a 15-foot rock funnel.

The guide scrutinizes the face of each of his charges in turn, eager to see the enthusiastic reactions and exclamations. It's as if all this were his own private property, and in a sense it does belong to him, because he was born in Israel and considers it part of his birthright.

Ensconcing yourself as comfortably as you can, you dig into the picnic lunch provided by the tour—sandwiches, pickles, fruit and coffee. The air at this altitude is incredibly light and pure. "Fill up," admonishes the guide. "It's going to get colder." He's not kidding. The vehicle heads east toward the road that follows the other frontier.

Instead of riding through the dried-up bottom of the *wadis*, you're now going up and down their steep sides, crossing and recrossing, back and forth. In a few spots where there are extra-sharp angles, wire gratings have been set up to prevent skidding. It can sometimes take several tries to maneuver certain hair-pin turns that would make ordinary mountain roads look tame. You're in for your shares of thrills.

There are other excursions that combine the ordinary road with certain other roads that are hard on private vehicles. You spend two nights or more, and explore the two gigantic craters, Machtesh Gadol (Great Crater) and Machtesh Katan (Lesser Crater), and you visit Masada and Ein Gedi on the western shores of the Dead Sea. It's also possible to make this trip on horseback. You return with a feeling of elation, as if you yourself had elucidated the mystery of the desert. But however you go—don't miss desert tours of the Negev, and Sinai!

Heading North Again

There's something to be said in favor of making at least one part of this trip by plane, which will reveal a different aspect of the desert. When you see this topsy-turvy land from the air, with all its streaks, scratches, and gouged-out space, what strikes you is how clearly the traces of man's settlements stand out, even though time has done its best to obliterate them through the centuries. Aerial reconnaissance has been responsible for locating most of the *tels,* or protuberances caused by the sand and silt that cover ancient settlements.

When you begin your return journey, you will, for a short distance, retrace your steps along the road you came in on. It branches off to the east at Grofit some 30 miles from Eilat. The distance between the two forks increases and the western one forms virtually a direct route between Eilat and Beersheba.

The eastern fork follows the Jordanian frontier towards the north, crosses the now relatively fertile Arava (or Aravi) valley at the foot of Mt. Edom and Mt. Moab (both in Arab territory). All along the way, Israeli settlements flourish. The road gradually slips down to below sea level in the Ghor, the lowland that prolongs the Dead Sea, which finally reaches its lowest point 1,295 feet below sea level.

If you have a car that can handle the steep climb, you'll be glad that you took the extra time to turn off left from Hatzeva towards the Machtesh Katan (Lesser Crater) just for the view from the top of the Scorpion Rise, Ma'aleh Akrabim. In the Old Testament, this pass marked the southern boundary of the Promised Land. The consensus is that this may well be the most unforgettable sight in all Israel, certainly the most indescribable.

The pass climbs to 2,000 feet and the gradual shift in level is distributed along a distance of well over half a mile. You have a sweeping view from the south shore of the Dead Sea, the deep gash of the Ghor, and the Wadi Arava at the foot of the proud range of the Moab Mountains, over to a *meza* on the south, Hor Hahar, where the high priest Aaron died and was buried. It looks strangely like a lunar landscape and, seen by twilight, it gradually tones down to become infused with a livid violet mist, with the spiky peaks twisting and writhing in the sunset flames.

You are already 425 feet below sea level when you come to the two branches of the Beersheba road. Both these roads go through Dimona to the south, and Arad to the north. You are now entering the "Valley of the Moon."

Another World

The setting looks like something Goya might have dashed off in his blackest mood. As you drop lower and lower below sea level, you are apt to feel as if the sky were closing in on you instead of getting higher above you. This impression of stifling other-worldliness is enhanced by the sight of what man has wrought here, as if in a desperate last-ditch effort to placate Nature—the incongruous shapes of industrial plants looming in the haze and smoke stacks groping up out of the sand with smoke streaming out and causing the background scenery to waver. The sun seems so far away that its beams dwindle down to a tiny twinkling glare. The earth has been caught and immobilized for eternity. Modern science has furnished plausible explanations for the cataclysm that blew up this section of the earth.

But man is more apt to ascribe this tragic atmosphere to the effects of divine wrath than to rational causes analyzed by scientists. Plowing into this fossilized awesomeness, man has cut roads that wind precariously among the shapes and masses. He has also planted signs that read: "Attention! You are now entering the world's deepest depression!"

What you are now approaching looks like the ghastly realm of some fearful sorcerer who had sworn to blast open the world. But it's only a potassium processing plant. Trucks clatter back and forth loading and unloading ore, and titanic shovels disembowel the tortured earth. The keen eyes of the plant manager focus only on the work load and he thinks in terms of the thousands of tons necessary to fill domestic needs and orders from abroad, which bring in foreign exchange.

Across the way, other crews are extracting bromine. The Dead Sea is why Israel has no shortage of fertilizers, the reason that the chemical and pharmaceutical industries have been able to expand. Graduate engineers with advanced degrees return here and pore over the Bible to learn where they should do their next prospecting. The chapters on Sodom and Gomorrah are full of handy hints about this area. The water in this vast lake is so mineral-heavy that no form of life can either live or drown in it—it contains one half-pound of salt per quart, eight times the concentration found in ordinary sea water. Salt marshes surround the Dead Sea right up to its domesticated edges, separated from it by dikes. After the water evaporates from the marshes, a heavy crystalline salt layer remains, flashing and sparkling in the sunlight.

The glazed, motionless liquid gives off iridescent reflections. Not a single minuscular fish—not even a salted herring—swims beneath this glassy surface, which can be rumpled only by a storm. Opposite, on the eastern shore, the somber Jordanian range towers like a stark challenge against the changing blue, green, and silver of this mirror that reflects nothingness. For a stunt photograph, a man in a bathing-suit ambles out into the water and proceeds to read a newspaper, calmly seated on what amounts to a soft mass of matter. To the north, golden sand glints in the sun.

The Dead Sea Region

Nothing remains of ancient Sodom and Gomorrah but a heap of salt. Let loose among these tortuous stone shapes, man will never cease searching for the outlines of Lot's wife. The guides all have their personal preferences, but everyone is free to dote on his own.

All around is desolation, hardly affected by a few man-made structures—Newe Zohar, the administrative center of the area, a renovated guest house, a camp site and a youth hostel, as well as a museum on the Dead Sea area. Ein Bokek also has pure drinking water, as well as lawns—the Israeli craving for greenness is nowhere more noticeable than here. And here Israelis have created a posh resort area where people come from around the world, year-round, for the healing mineral-rich waters.

Cape Molineux is a slender prong of land advancing some distance toward the Israel shore from Jordan. In the good old days, camel caravans waded across here under the protection of a formidable fortress—Masada. You can tour or overnight here now in relative comfort, or wander further to the lush fields and palms of Ein Gedi, where David's Springs flank a prosperous kibbutz and tourist mecca.

Citadel Stronghold

An isolated mass stands out majestically amid the mountains and *mezas*. You have come to Masada.

At its base is a youth hostel whose front wall bears the inscription "Masada shall not fall again." You can see openings and crevices that stud the mountainside above, each marking an entrance to the inner galleries in which Masada's defenders lived.

It was in the second century B.C. that Judas Meccabeus first transformed this rock into a stronghold. Later, Herod built a palace-fortress here. The name itself is derived from *metzuda,* "citadel."

Archeological diggings were carried on at Masada for eleven months under the direction of Professor Yigael Yadin. The sum of one million pounds sterling was contributed to this work by the Wolfson Foundation, sponsored by the London weekly, *The Observer.* Volunteers from thirty different countries poured in to join forces with Israeli youth in this enterprise. The stronghold was so inaccessible that helicopters were necessary for a while. In his *Wars of the Jews,* the Romanized Jewish historian Josephus Flavius describes the pathway as accessible only to the most venturesome. It leads clear to the top, and was called "the snake" because of its narrowness, its many twisting curves and its myriad dangers. At the very top lies an open space 1,000 feet wide and 2,000 feet long.

The name of Masada had never completely fallen into oblivion. The Israelis had been going to look at it for a long time, but even those who managed the climb didn't find much to look at once they had reached the top. They knew only that at one time, amid this mass of ruins and rubble, stupendous events had taken place. Herod had built a sumptuous palace holding a whole garrison and during the Great Uprising, the Zealots had entrenched themselves in Masada and held out against the Roman Legions for three years.

In 1965, the history of Masada was at last revealed to the world by Professor Yadin's team. The world has seldom witnessed a more abundant factual harvest. The scientific contribution yielded by these excavations is incalculable. More intriguing still is the dramatic interest of these historic facts which, combined with the rest of the desert, has made Masada one of Israel's chief tourist attractions. Today it is more popular and more accessible than ever since a new road to the foot of Masada was completed in 1970, coming from the western side of the fort to the site of the Roman camp.

One-third of the palace fortress has been reconstructed. The debris has been cleared away from another third, and the rest has remained in the state in which it was found. King Herod's "hanging" palace crowns a tangle of defense installations and living areas, some of them more comfortable than others, a few of them even luxurious. The usurper whom Rome had designated as the King of Judea was afraid of the Jewish patriots. Moreover, he suspected Cleopatra, the Queen of Egypt, of coveting his kingdom. Masada was designed to serve him as a refuge against his numerous enemies. However, his apprehension proved vain, and he really came there only for brief holiday spells before finally dying peacefully in bed.

The Fight of the Zealots

Later in A.D. 70, Jerusalem was razed, the temple destroyed, and Titus believed that the rebellion had been crushed. But a little band of Zealots occupied the Masada fortress in order to continue their resistance. They lived there with their wives and children, 967 souls altogether, under the command of Eliezer Ben Yair. The Roman warrior Silva, anxious to have done with this battle once and for all, laid siege to this Gibraltar of the Dead Sea. The camp sites of the besiegers, the Tenth

MASADA

PARTIAL PLAN OF THE FORTIFIED PLATEAU

(after Prof. Y. Yadin)

0 —————— 100 Metres
(327 ft)

HEROD'S HANGING PALACE

N

1
2
3
4
5
6
7
8
9
10
11
12
13
14

Roman assault ramp

Casemate in which first scrolls were found

Jars with silver shekels found here

Casemate wall built by Herod (151 yds, 110 rooms)

Mosaics
Throne Room (presumed)

Casemate with utensils and coins

Towards pool ↓

1. Lower terrace—double columned room decorated with frescos
2. Middle terrace—round pavilion
3. Higher terrace—living quarters
4. Inclined separating wall
5. Roman-style baths
6. Synagogue
7. Probable quarter of the Zealots
8. Shops and warehouses
9. Villa
10. Buildings and court in Byzantine style
11. Byzantine chapel
12. Herod's Palace of State
13. Villas
14. Byzantine structure

Legion (Fretensis), are still clearly recognizable. The fortress remained impregnable for three years, and its defenders exchanged blow for blow with their assailants. Finally Silva built a gigantic ramp so as to reach the walls at the top and set fire to them. That was the end.

Watching the flames on that day in the year 73, the Zealots knew their time had come. A council was held, and Eliezer ordered his men to destroy all their possessions except the provisions of food, "so that the enemy will see that we voluntarily chose to die rather than submit to slavery."

Families kissed for the last time, "and everyone lay down in close embrace" according to Josephus. Ten men chosen by lot then set about their grim task of putting to death these voluntary martyrs "who bared their necks to the blades of their charitable executioners." When this had been done, one man of the ten was again selected by lot to end the lives of his nine companions. "And the last one of all, the last of the living, gently examined the bodies in order to make sure that none needed his coup de grâce. When he had satisfied himself that all were dead, he set fire to the palace and impaled himself on his own sword."

But not everyone was dead. Two women and five children, who had hidden away in a cistern, survived. The Romans duly attacked and took the fortress, meeting no resistance. When they reached the scene of desolation, they were so stricken that they spared the lives of the survivors. One of the women recounted the story to Josephus Flavius, who faithfully transcribed it for posterity.

The remains of about twenty of the Zealots have so far been found. The others are probably still in galleries that have not been cleared away. Although the public is now being admitted, excavations are continuing. Professor Yadin is convinced that some of the heroic defenders of Masada must have left written messages. A few parchment scrolls have been discovered—the only ones not to have been found in caves—and the Shrine of the Book in Jerusalem has given them a place of honor.

The archeological finds here include polychrome mosaics from the pre-Christian era, columns, mural frescos, primitive water-heaters, ceramics, cosmetics, weapons, ammunition, hoards of projectiles of all kinds, and coins. The fortress's living quarters can be visited, as can the meeting-rooms, public and private Roman baths, rooms for men's and women's ritual bathing, defense installations, cisterns, and Herod's storerooms.

And above all, there are the scrolls, which have already kindled the flame of polemics among the experts, with the dispute stemming from the prior discovery of the Dead Sea Scrolls. The fact appears to have been established that the entire Jewish population, not the Zealots alone, participated in the uprising of the year 66. Professor Yadin asserts that there is reason to believe that a contingent of Essenes was among the defenders of Masada.

But even if you didn't know this background, your gaze would still be riveted on the great mass that rises up from the desert floor. Around it the wild Judean desert flings out its harsh shapes and bottomless ravines, while Masada holds itself proudly erect, its majesty intact.

Those making the climb should know that there are two paths; one from the west, from Arad, and another from the Dead Sea. The western ascent is the easier and takes 20 minutes on foot. You can, of course, take a cable-car from the snack-café-shop area—but be warned: you'll still have 80 steps to climb, plus much walking around the top. A visit to the Masada Museum is worthwhile: it is located in the Youth Hostel and displays finds from the excavations.

Ein Gedi, Oasis of David

The Jordanian frontier was once but a short distance to the north. What appear to be cultivated fields on either side of the road are actually stretches covered with mounds of weathered stones and pebbles deposited by wandering streams.

Wayside parks and picnic-swim areas, plus a huge and shiny gas station, declare you've reached the kibbutz of Ein Gedi, "the Fountain of the Kid," an oasis 11 miles from Masada, where you can pause for a meal, spa baths or overnight stays. There are indications of David's having passed through here. In fact, the story goes that, after incurring King Saul's wrath, David fled to the desert of Ein Gedi (or Engaddi). The king followed in hot pursuit and entered the cave in which David had taken refuge, but the complete obscurity prevented him from finding either the fugitive or his companions.

In the darkness, David tore off a piece of hem of Saul's mantle before the angry, frustrated monarch finally went on his way. David ran to overtake him and proved that he had spared the king by showing him the scrap of cloth.

Thus, the fresh spring bubbling out of these rocks 600 feet above sea level was named for the young David. Unquestionably Israel's most beautiful natural swimming hole, it tumbles down over the rocks and waters the surrounding countryside. In 1949, a kibbutz was founded here, where settlers could keep watch on the frontier and raise vegetables, grapes, cotton and flowers. Their produce reaches the markets ahead of everyone else's.

Since the Six-Day War it has been possible to travel beyond David's Fountain and to poke around in the many caves of the region. They too, had served as a refuge for a still later rebel, Bar Kochba, who fomented an uprising against Rome in A.D. 132. In 1947, the famed

Dead Sea Scrolls were discovered in the ruins of a Qumram Monastery, linked with the Essene sect that flourished around Christ's time. By now, everyone knows the familiar tale of how a young shepherd, searching for a lost lamb, wandered into a cave and discovered there the first of the now famous Dead Sea Scrolls.

The Essenes, one of the most important of the Jewish sects, lived near the Dead Sea. A peaceful people, known for their deep piety and their asceticism, they organized their lives around a community existence and lived in strict observance of Moses' Law. These facts have all been confirmed by the archeologists who discovered this "monastery" barely a mile south of the cave into which the shepherd boy wandered.

The Essenes were also renowned for their study of astrology and medicine. Various references in the manuscripts confirm these aspects of their knowledge. In addition, Josephus Flavius mentions their having established an agricultural center at Ein Gedi.

In 1960 a joint expedition organized by the Israeli government and the Hebrew University explored the region, literally inch by inch, in the hope of discovering other documents.

A team led by Professor Yadin found a number of papyri wrapped in a goatskin, all of them remarkably well-preserved because of the dryness of the air. These papyri contain orders written by Bar Kochba, the leader of the uprising against Rome, and are now on display in the Shrine of the Book in Jerusalem.

The Return Trip

Now, turning back, we can choose one of two possibilities: return to Beersheba, or proceed northwards through Jericho, to Jerusalem. Via Arad the climb is steep, and we slowly ascend back to sea level where we shall at least have the illusion of breathing more freely. Progress is halting, because we pause at every turn in the road to gaze back upon and fix in our memories this unique spectacle of a motionless sea 1,295 feet below sea level, with its tenacious industry, fancy spa hotels, chauvinistic settlers, and salty landscape.

Under the bluish grey skies and amid the blackened rocks, the Dead Sea shimmers in a quivering, silvery mist. The rare showers that find their way here transform the most insignificant gully into a raging torrent.

At another turn in the road, 2,150 feet high (and 3,300 feet above the Dead Sea), Arad rises out of the sand. Arad, begun in 1961, was planned as an industrial city, and already sets sights on bidding for Dead Sea tourism overflows, plus health tourism. The employees of the various Dead Sea plants live here, commuting back and forth to their jobs—the distance isn't great, only 16 miles.

You'll find references to Arad in the Bible: the Jews coming out from Egypt met armed resistance from the local ruler, and Divine intervention was necessary in order for them to capture the city. This was the promised land's southern sentry-post. Today, with natural gas discovered in its subsoil, Arad has joined the ranks of desert boom towns, while its 6,000 citizens look to tourist enterprise for healthy future revenues. Healthy in more than one sense, for this is the place to stay, especially if you happen to suffer from respiratory ailments, for the air and climate here are proven effective fighters against such diseases, and clinics have been set up which have shown excellent results in their treatments. It is, after all, 3,000 feet above the Dead Sea.

Many tourists and spa addicts stay here, too, while taking the waters of the Dead Sea, or just while visiting there. Buses do the trip regularly.

The remaining forty miles of road leading to Beersheba are relatively uneventful. Three rows of eucalyptus trees have been planted along the edges of the highway, baby trees that will some day be giants and shade the road. (You'll notice eucalyptus trees along many of Israel's highways. They're a sturdy species, with roots going deep into the ground, thereby helping to prevent soil erosion.)

You see fields of hemp growing in the sand, and tiny purple flowers surrounding them, sort of rear-guard of vegetation for protection against the rigors of a harsh environment. The earth's surface gradually flattens, and here and there grass has hesitantly begun to sprout, with optimistic flocks of sheep already grazing on it. You pass a succession of Bedouin nomad tents, small townships, assorted buildings and low-rent housing-units, and soon are in the outskirts of Beersheba.

The second road, farther to the south, joins the Eilat-Sodom highway in the middle of the Ghor, and when you pause for the traditional backward glance (no risk of being turned into a pillar of anything), you catch sight of a panorama that is probably unique in the world. It embraces two separate archeological sites between Sodom and Dimona: Tamra with its ruined Roman fortress, and Mamshit (Mampsis, also Kurnub), where recently several large groups of Nabatean buildings, a Roman military cemetery, mosaic floors and other remains have been excavated. Mamshit was later a Byzantine city. There is even a legacy from the British Mandate, built with the ancient stones found here: a jail.

Twentieth-Century Joke

Dimona (pop. 8,000), on the Sodom-Beersheba road, is a boom-town of industry and absorption. Built in 1955 and located 30 miles from Sodom and 23 miles from Beersheba, it serves as a clearing-house for the vast Negev.

The workers from the Dead Sea factories lived here, before moving on to Arad, which is closer to where they work. Dimona was none the worse for this desertion, since it has plenty to tend to all by itself. Its citizens are employed in potassium plants, textile factories, flour-mills, and glassworks. And there's something else. See those weird-looking buildings along the highway on your left?

Ask any Israeli what they are, and he'll smile slyly and tell you it's a textile factory. That was for a long time, and it still is, the traditional joke, because of the secrecy that surrounded the beginnings of this enterprise: this is the nuclear center near Oron, 12 miles away, on the precipitous lips of the Great Crater (Machtesh Gadol). Oron also has processing plants for its inexhaustible reserves of phosphates.

There's little to see between Dimona and Beersheba except a small archeological site, Aroer, some 3,000 years old, and a much more recent village, Nevatim, settled in 1946 by Jews from Cochin, India.

Even if you're only a few hours in Beersheba, try to make an excursion through the southwest. Your destination is Shivta (Subeita), 22 miles away. Here you will see marvelously well-preserved Byzantine ruins from the fifth and sixth centuries. The Greeks had merely built on top of Nabatean foundations. You will notice again the haunting preoccupation with water.

The streets and flat-roofed buildings slope gently to allow the rain water to drain into cisterns. An ingenious network of dikes and trenches extending for miles around also helped to channel the water. The ruins have been restored and you feel as if you were in a sort of miniature Pompeii. The place had three churches (north, south, and central), a mosque built by Arab conquerors, wine-presses, bake-ovens, potters' wheels, and many residential dwellings. Don't fail to see the cross-shaped baptismal font in the south church, and the *mihrab* in the mosque, that points in the direction of Mecca.

If you're interested in recent history, then push on to Nitzana, five miles west of Shivta and flush against the Gaza border. It was captured from the Egyptians in 1948, the victory opening the way to the Suez Canal for the fledgling Israeli army. In the 1967 War, Israeli armor darted out from Nitzana to rout the Arab forces massed at Abu Ageila. Thanks to the buffer zone of Israeli-administered Sinai, no heavy fighting erupted here in 1973's October War. See the old Byzantine church while you're here.

From Beersheba, set out north again, this time turning left at Tifrah, 7 miles away, surrounded by its fields of sisal, the fibrous hemp plant that is used in the textile industry and thrives in hot climates and sandy soil. Now you're headed towards the coast along the Gaza Strip, which was captured from the Egyptians in 1956, during the Sinai campaign, then given back; only to be taken again in the Six-Day War. In this area every available square inch has been plowed and planted. You turn off again at Sa'ad, a kibbutz of Orthodox Jews that withstood repeated Egyptian attacks in 1948. Studded with kibbutzim and new townships, this region is only 18 miles from Ashkelon. At Heletz, nearby, oil derricks dot the horizon. Although Ashkelon and Ashdod theoretically belong to the "south" you have, for all practical purposes, come out of the Negev.

Other Roads

There is a shorter route from Jerusalem to Beersheba via the Hebron Road. It leads through Bethany, Hebron, several small villages and settlements until, finally, it arrives in Beersheba via Tel Sheva. Very scenic and interesting, it's also much shorter—*sheruts* take this road (see *Border Areas* chapter for more details), and it is favored by most public and private transportation.

The highway that runs along the Jordanian border, from Sodom to Eilat, is the fastest road from the middle of Israel to the southern tip, and also peppered with settlements and wayside rest stations and eateries.

If you're rushed on your return trip from the south, and want to bypass Beersheba, a new road carries traffic from the Shoket Junction, N.E. of town, to the Be'er Sheva-Bet Kama road leading north towards Kiryat Gat.

PRACTICAL INFORMATION FOR THE NEGEV

A WORD TO THE WISE. Bear in mind that the Negev is swelteringly hot from mid-May to mid-October. Plan your trip accordingly, and stick to these precautions during the hot season:

Get off to an early start; avoid having to hurry
Never go bare-headed; keep in the shade between noon and 3 P.M.
Drink lots of liquids; eat light foods and in small amounts
Go easy on sun-bathing: sun-stroke is the most common tourist affliction in Israel.

BEERSHEBA

The capital of the Negev offers accommodations, eateries, shopping, tours, an airport, cultural events, a Bedouin market and every facility for overnights of one or several days.

HOTELS. The city's 4-star hotel is the 110-room **Desert Inn** on the edge of town, a spread-out, four-wing oasis with garden, tennis, Olympic pool, heated pool, great grill restaurant, room TV, gift shop, coffee shop, piano bar and nightclub; fine atmosphere.

A big, comfortable 3-star hotel, the **Zohar**, 64 rooms, in the new part of town across the street from the municipal pool, and also has room TV, bar.

Two-star hotels include the **Arava**, 27 rooms; **Aviv**, 22 rooms; **Hanegev**, 22 rooms. Only the first two offer a few rooms with bath; other rooms are with showers only. All are fully air-conditioned and pleasant.

Beit Yatziv Hostel is modern and popular for all ages, 300 beds, including family accommodations; three meals served daily, plus cooking facilities.

RESTAURANTS. El Patio de Santos, 41 Hadassah St. has fine fish and meats cooked in European and Oriental style. Legendary **Papa Michael,** Hahistadrut corner of Rahov Rambam, dishes up tasty meats and meals. Both range (M) to (E). Authentic is the word for the **Chinese Restaurant,** 79 Hahistadrut (E), which stays open even on Friday nights.

The young crowd, and soldiers based nearby, hang out at **Witmann's Ice Cream Parlor**-cum-disco. Aside from these, the town has many good places for snacks, light eating, etc. At the Negev Brigade Monument, **Andarta Milk Bar** is most welcome to hot, thirsty tourists.

ENTERTAINMENT. An Artists' Quarter recently opened on Rehov Smilansky in the Old Town. Several galleries exhibit Israeli artists' work from 10-2 and 6-midnight. The gallery-coffee-house has emerged here as a favorite local eatery. Open till the wee hours, two interesting ones are **Liraz Club** (No. 25) and **Sheva** (No. 29). **Beit Ha'am Center** and **Keren and Gilat Halls** are the places to find frequent performances of the local and highly-rated orchestra as well as visiting groups. **The Conservatorium** is Beersheba's newest music hall, where you can hear one of Israel's best chamber orchestras. Theater includes performances in English of a group formed by newcomer Americans. And, of course, there's cinema.

Swim at the *Desert Inn* pools or municipal pool. **Tennis** also at *Desert Inn*.

Sights are headed by *Abraham's Well* since this is what really made Beersheba famous. A *Bedouin Market* is held on Hebron Road on Thursdays, dawn till 9 or 11—worth watching even if you don't buy. The *British War Cemetery* is not far from the *Municipal Museum,* housed in a former mosque that offers a great panoramic view. The Old Town section has narrow streets, Arab houses with courtyards, etc. Outside town is the striking *Memorial of the Negev Palmach Brigade.*

Between Jerusalem and Beersheba is **Bet Shemesh,** a historical and biblical site near today's *Avshalom Nature Reserve,* where interesting *Stalagmite Cave* now may be visited without advance reservations (IS5). Many tours stop here. Nearby (12 kms. from the Sha'ar Hagai junction of the Tel Aviv-Jerusalem Road Hwy.), *Kibbutz Tzorah* offers tourists luncheon and a tour of the kibbutz, plus discussions of its lifestyle and a chance to visit its factory and buy fashions and crafts at discounts; all for $7.

TOURS. Cover the entire country from Beersheba, via leading operators such as *Egged Tours, Arkia Airlines* and *Zakai Tours,* which features visits to local Bedouin camps plus dinner with sheikhs.

USEFUL NUMBERS. IGTA, (057) 36001; **Hospital,** 77111; **Magen David Adom** (emergency first aid), 78333; **Police,** 100; **taxis:** 77525, 75555.

MITZPEH RAMON

In the heart of the wilderness, modern tourists can find shelter and good food. There is even a new **Art Museum** to visit. Two new tourist facilities are due to open soon: a 60-room top-quality motel and a restaurant said to cost $200,000. Meanwhile, the **Beit Noam Hostel** offers 160 beds, caters mostly to families, serves three meals daily and offers cooking facilities, too. Picnic supplies are yours from the town shops and stores.

EILAT

Israel's southern resort mecca has its peak season from October to May, when hotel rates are highest and tourism booms with air charters landing directly from overseas—full of sun-worshipping vacationers ready for free-wheeling good times.

HOTELS. In the 4-star category, **Laromme Eilat** is like a luxury oasis at Coral Beach. Posh in every detail, it has 300 rooms with TV; health club and sauna; huge pool with a bar right in the water; exciting nightclub; piano bar/ lounge; plus cruise boats, mini-golf, well-serviced private beach with shady huts and a zoo, beside a scuba-diving center. It also has regular transport service into town, excellent shops, several good restaurants and a tour service right in the lobby.

Toward the center of town is North Beach, where most hotels are located in a tourist area with lagoons, bridges, restaurants, bars and entertainment and information offices. Here, the **Neptune** offers a futuristic facade and 100 rooms looking down the length of the Gulf of Eilat; pool, bar, nightclub, gift and beauty shops, and now taking over the finally-finished mass of hotel rooms next door.

Moriah Eilat is the oldest 4-star hotel. Excellent beach facilities: the sea is 20 yards away from the lobby doors. Every room faces the Red Sea. Distinctive brick-walled bar with hammered copper base; 103 rooms, all with bath or shower, great piano bar, pool, Lucky Divers Scuba Center; bank and beauty parlor.

Shulamit Gardens is huge and elegant: 224 rooms and apartment facilities, plus lounge bar, room TV, pool, beauty parlor, nightclub.

Queen of Sheba, 92 rooms, is to the left of the public beach. Public rooms decorated with a running stream and cave-like carpeted ceilings. All rooms face the sea. Room prices slightly higher in the 9 duplex cottages; pool, tennis, piano bar.

Caesar boasts 230 rooms, 8 suites, all with modern facilities, tennis courts and pool. Its fish restaurant seems to sit on the water, thanks to its three glass walls. There's also a nightclub, water sports and great bar with terrific view of Aqaba.

The 3-star **Americana Inn** offers 104 rooms, pool, sports facilities, bar, night-club. **Eyal** has 90 3-star rooms, some with kitchenettes, plus pool, piano bar, nightclub. Also 3-star, the **Center** has 31 rooms, some kitchenettes, dining room, coffee shop; in town, **Etzion** has 97 rooms, pool, sauna, piano bar.

Two-star hotels include the **Adi,** 31 rooms with TV; the **Red Sea,** 41 rooms with TV; **Melony Club Aparthotel,** with 36 apartments, bar, nightclub and heated pool; and **Melony Tower,** with 42 apartments, coffee shop, bar.

Out on Coral Beach, the 2-star **Caravan Sun Club** is like a U.S. motel; 108 rooms, plus skin-diving and wind-surfing center, yachting, biking, pools, piano bar, fun nightclub, barbecue, grill room, tennis, private beach and kids' play-ground. **Red Sea Flotilla,** 6 houseboats linked and plying the Gulf, is an interesting accommodation offered by Caravan Sun Club owners.

Back in town, **Dalia** offers 52 rooms; **Bel** has 84, and 1-star **Hadekel** has 17.

Next door, but on Lagoon Beach, is the **Sun Bay,** 63 rooms, a bungalow motel, with private facilities and desert coolers, fishing, diving, and a camp site, plus horse ranch and riding lessons. Right on the beach, close to Aqaba and inexpensive. Nearby is **Blue Sky Caravan** holiday village, with 74 rooms and self-service restaurant.

Another camping site is at Coral Beach, south of hotels.

The **Red Sea Hotel,** with 41 balconied double rooms, was not recommended by IGTA for several years; now it is.

Eilat **Youth Hostel** is a 5-minute walk from the center of town, in the direction of Coral Beach, with 160 rooms, breakfast and supper served plus cooking, and great view.

Eilat is the site of another **Club Méditerranée**—Hotel de Coraux—skirting North Beach, with 128 rooms, swank disco and interesting crowds on its private beach (members only). See *Facts At Your Fingertips* for addresses.

RESTAURANTS. Prices often are higher here than elsewhere in Israel, yet fees are still quite good, with Inexpensive (I) at $5 and up per person; Moderate (M) at $10-$20; Expensive (E) from $15 and up, up, up.

Yosky's (M), long unchallenged as Eilat's best seafood house, serves daytime snacks and meals with great Red Sea views from its outside terrace at the New Tourist Center; or elect to eat inside near the mini-aquariums.

La Coquille host Robert serves shrimp specialty, French cuisine, delicacies prepared by your table. Super place; reservations a must. Dinner is *very* expensive, but well worth it in the taste of the food and the intimate decor in its new home near North Beach hotels.

Rimini (I), Israelis' favorite Italian food chain, tops the New Tourist Center tower, offering full meals to pizza. While here, climb to the Watch Tower on top and gaze through mounted binoculars at Jordan's Aqaba and Red Sea traffic.

Mandy's Paradise (E) is sleek, hip, expensive: Chinese plus Thailand menu. Two-or-more menu. (Try Peking Duck, but order it 24 hours earlier.)

Au Bistrot is family-run, specializing in French and North African cuisine, with cous-cous being a local favorite here. Both range from (M) to (E).

Sea Rose, at the glass bottom boat complex, is in the (M) range, with fine meals. **The Caesar Restaurant** is, naturally, at Hotel Caesar, serving popular seafoods and mixed cuisine, at (M-E) prices, as does its neighbor: **Shulamit Fish Restaurant.**

Beer Inn offers (M) tabs for homecooked Hungarian meals. **Taverna Pub,** at New Tourist Center, has beer, drinks, light inexpensive meals—locals love it. And along the beach, toward the marina, you'll see several small cafés and spots for refreshments, meals. If the new **Red Sea Tower** is finished, by the marina, you'll find a good Chinese restaurant, shops, even showers.

La Baracuda (M), at Coral Beach, performs real wonders with seafood; has friendly, intimate atmosphere. In town, **Shrimp House** (I-M) also specializes in sea fare, as does **London's Fish'n'Chips** at Eilat Tourist Center (I-M). **Little Italy** (I-M) is quite "Americanized," on Hatmarim St.

More good food is yours at **Chick Chock Steak** (I), New Tourist Center. The owner also operates **The Golden Fish,** next door, one of the better fish restaurants, which also serves other types of foods. Downstairs, **Pundak Arava** has good grills and burgers. **Safari** is nearby, with more burgers; **Milk Bar Capricio** has great pasteries; **Palatini** dishes out homemade Italian ice cream; **Fried Chicken** has tasty, elegant deli fare at (I) prices.

NIGHTLIFE. Eilat is a simple tourist town in summer, but in winter it becomes a super resort, full of top entertainment, live shows, lively tourists. Yet, all year, it has a flavor of fun in places like New Tourist Center, where outdoor cafes and eateries compete with **Picadilly Pub** and **Pub Tavern**, or **The Factory**, which draws a young set.

The **Oasis** disco, in Laromme, is easily the town's finest night spot; beautiful decor and people; IS20 cover includes a drink. Discos also flourish at **Caravan Sun Club (Magic Carpet); Americana** (UN and young crowd); **Caesar; Etzion, Snapir** and **Red Rock** hotels, and many hotels do great business in their piano bars *(see hotel lists).* The most romantic night spot probably is **The Boat,** a restaurant/club floating in the lagoon or cruising (Ya'Alat Tours).

Nophit was the local Soldier's House, for entertaining young army personnel, and it still caters to a younger crowd, presenting interesting evening programs.

Watch for instant, big beach parties where everyone's welcome; for outdoor concerts and street dances, and great nights at Nelson's Village—a good day spot, too.

Also watch for hotels' special event evenings, parties, films. **Texas Ranch** is a wild western town near Coral Beach, offering tons of fun plus horse riding.

Guests and locals alike head for **Philip Murray Center** for 6:30 P.M. **Friday Folk Dancing** (kids 6-15 especially love this), and go again at 9 P.M. for special entertainment live from this country and others.

WHAT TO SEE. *Modern Art Museum. Children's Forest.* Don't miss the *Coral World Underwater Observatory & Aquarium,* at Coral Beach: from a long pier, descend to watch submarine life above "Japanese Gardens" natural reef, one of four such places in the world. Also the *Maritime Museum* in this complex; restaurant. Bus 5 from Eilat Center.

TOURS. *Ya'Alat Tourist Service Co., Ltd.,* at the New Tourist Center, is the expert address for seeing the town and its surroundings, and booking you on its own or other tour programs. Ask for *The Red Sea Booklet* of coupons that give you 5%-20% discount on tours, meals, film and rented cameras, jewelry, fashions, souvenirs, rental cars, pottery and art buys, diving lessons and gear, boat rides, etc. Ask about special Bible Study tours, "Eilati Christmas Party" on Coral Island's Crusader ruins, Passover Special "Song of the Sea" Event. *Rent A Bike* touring, etc. And be sure to ask about *Rent-A-Camel*—by the half-day, hour, or for organized 7-day desert tours. You can even charter a special camel tour! *Dolphin* and *Baracuda,* Ya'Alat's cruise (motor) ships for morning and afternoon 3-hour trips to Coral Island, evening romantic/fun cruises. *Kopel Tours* offers a wide range of service for all Israel. In Eilat, the office is located in the New Tourist Center. *Rotem Travel Agency* handles overseas tourism bookings.

Pleasure Boats—including romantic historical models—tour the Red Sea Gulf from 3-8 hours along the Sinai coast stopping at main sightseeing spots. You can charter the luxury racing yachts *Nirvana* or *La Gabon du Jour* —both docked at marina. Or try small boats, wind-surfing, all water sports. The *Laromme Cruise Yacht* offers elegant buffet with wine, plus all day sailing, stops at the Fjord and Coral Island and to fish, for $40. *Caravan Sun Club* and several private firms have similar services. *Kopel Tours* provides a diver's charter boat with all diving gear, guides, even a lab for developing underwater films. And don't forget *Ya'Alat's* floating disco-dance-restaurant that operates nightly.

Glass-bottom Boats, from Coral Beach, tour the coast regularly, letting you see fabulous underwater life plus awesome land scenery and sites. Go with a group or rent a small glass-bottom boat at Laromme.

For a day trip, try *Nelson's Village,* Taba Beach, for sun-water sports, food, diving, animals, Bedouin, relaxing. Desert tours into the Sinai hinterland are among the most exciting in Israel—try *Neot Hakikar* and *Johnny's Desert Tours* offering a wide range of tours from half-day to a week or more. Fantastic adventure.

Bird Watching Tours are especially good in this region, particularly between March and May. For details on both these tours, see *FAYF* chapter. And don't miss seeing *Hai Bar Nature Reserve* and its biblical wild animals. *Israel Government Tourist Administration* (IGTA) has maps and schedules of all events and programs—which change frequently. Located in New Commercial Center.

Note: Though parts of Sinai are Administered by Israel and parts governed by Egypt, all Sinai can be visited by Israeli tourists via Israeli tour firms, and most tours operate out of Eilat. For more details, see *Border Areas* chapter. And don't miss Santa Katerina!

SHOPPING. *Aladdin,* opposite the Philip Murray Center; *Kadurit,* Arava Road, Industrial Zone, has artists' works in pottery, stone, glass, wood, silver, iron, jewelry; *Maskit* and *Begged Or,* Israel's top fashion and crafts shops, both are at Laromme Hotel, for crafts and fashions; *Hadar Boutique,* Shopping Center, Etzion Hotel, for men and women. All at New Tourist Center: *Octopus,* beachwear; *Boutique Marcelle,* ladies fashions; plus many other fine shops. The *Music Box,* Hatamariim St., carries hordes of local and international records, nice souvenirs, gifts.

SPORTS. Swimming: The smooth blue waters of the Gulf provide year-round swimming. There are two beaches: North Beach and Coral Beach, open to the public all year, with lifeguard; with another being prepared near Sun Bay. **Skin Diving** centers flourish here, and necessary equipment and gear can be rented on the spot for this and other water sports (see pp. 19, 29). From *Adomite,* you can rent small boats and **water-ski** by the hour. You can also rent desert vehicles and various automobiles, from *Hertz* or local firms. Or rent a bicycle. All in New Commercial Center.

USEFUL NUMBERS. IGTA, (059) 72268; **Police,** 72444; **Ambulance** and **First Aid,** 72222; **Taxi,** 74141.

DEAD SEA REGION

Luxury hotels, hostels, camping areas and terrific modern spas of international standards and fame—all cluster in this sun-drenched region where biblical towns disappeared and archeological sites abound. Sodom is south; Ein Bokek is followed by Masada; Ein Feshcha and Qumram round the bend; Kalia is next. In the mountains above the Dead Sea is Arad.

SODOM. Mt. Sodom features caves formed by the dissolution of salt plus flowing water; the **Dead Sea Works** are here, and **Massad Tamar**—an ancient fort restored and reconstructed, plus archeological diggings. The nearest accommodations are at Newe Zohar.

NEWE ZOHAR. The regional center for the Dead Sea area, just a skip away from Sodom. **Beth Hayotzer** museum here specializes in exhibits linked to Dead Sea research. Hotels are further along the shore, but here there is the **Beth Hayotzer Youth Hostel** and **camping site,** with bungalows, cafes, tents, all facilities; open year-round.

EIN BOKEK. Big luxury hotel-resorts are here, all air-conditioned, all benefiting from 1980 area improvements.

HOTELS. The 5-star, 220-room **Moriah-Dead Sea** is an oasis with everything: bank, shops, eateries, pool and beach, health club, spa center, beauty farm, room TV, tennis, nightclub, bar and synagogue; all catering to the very Orthodox.

Shulamit Gardens (4-star, 184 rooms) offers health club, beauty parlor, pool, shops, restaurants, piano bar, nightclub. **Galei Zohar** (160 rooms, 4-star) has beach, pool, bar, nightclub, and medically-supervised posh Dermatologic and Rheumatic Clinic. **Ein Bokek** (96 rooms, 4-star) has tennis, pool, eateries, bar and nightclub.

Here, too, are the **Hamai Zohar New Clinic** and **Ein Bokek Bathing Beach.** The New Clinic offers all the works: examinations, pools, electro-agitated galvanic bath, air bubble or vibration bath, mud bath, sulphur bath, massages and treatments. Both places have mud and waters that Cleopatra sent slaves trekking for days to lug back for her secret beauty rites. (It will cost *you* a pittance!)

MASADA. Don't miss this central historical and archeological site! Modest museum with area artifacts. Climb to the ancient fortress year-round, via the hair-pin curves of Snake Path, or opt to ride up on the cable car that runs daily (one-way or round-trip; youth/students pay half).

HOTELS. New **Masada Motel** offers limited accommodations; contact in advance. The **Y. H. Taylor Hostel** is directly below Masada fortress, with 200 dorm rooms, air-conditioning, eateries and recent improvements.

RESTAURANTS. Masada Restaurant, the **3.5 Restaurant,** and the hostel eateries.

EIN GEDI. The area of biblical **David's Springs** is revived and thriving. The Society for the Protection of Nature and the Tamar Regional Council sponsor the **Ein Gedi Field School** here, with its small, interesting museum and regular, excellent guided tours of the area, focusing on its nature *(see FAYF chapter).*

HOTELS. The new, 90-room kibbutz-run **Ein Gedi Guest House** offers plusses like room TVs, pool and private beach—but its best treats are thermal baths, spa services. Reserve in advance; weekly basis only. Recent 200-bed, air-conditioned **Beit Sara** hostel, with all modern facilities and good bus service. There is also camping here and the **Ein Gedi Pension.**

RESTAURANTS. Ein Gedi Restaurant, at the kibbutz, serves more than fine food; $5 buys bathing in the Dead Sea and sulphur mineral pool, beach facilities (showers, awnings, deck chairs), plus a 4-course meal. There's also **Ein Gedi Beach Inn,** for cafeteria fare.

EIN FESHCHA. Nature reserve on Dead Sea. Mineral and sweet-water pools, nice tourist facilities, beach restaurant.

QUMRAM CAVES. Not far from Ein Feshcha, the ruins of an ancient Essene settlement are near caves where the Dead Sea Scrolls were found. Fascinating, despite somewhat rough tourist facilities at this National Park site.

KALIA. Following the same road past Qumram, you'll find sea-bathing, showers, cafeteria and patio foods, plus a gift shop, at **Lido Kalia,** just as the road heads inland to branch towards Jericho or Jerusalem.

ARAD. A town known for clean air, healthy climate, and year-round tourism. Frequent transportation from the hotels to the Dead Sea (25 minutes) for baths at **Hamai Zohar** hot springs, then back. Also, the nearby route for climbing Masada is much easier than the Dead Sea paths.

HOTELS. Massada is 4-star with 104 rooms, pool, nightclub, bar, coffee shop. **Margoa,** with 107 rooms, has a nightclub, piano bar, pool and tennis, and is 3-star as is **Nof Arad,** which has 101 rooms, pool, nightclub, grill room and coffee shop. Two-star **Arad** is new, with 51 air-conditioned rooms (showers only), tennis, bar, coffee shop.

An excellent hostel, the **Beit Blau-Weiss,** is handy for climbing Masada from its western slope; it has bungalows, and family accommodations, 250 beds plus 3 served meals or do-it-yourself cooking.

Horseback riding at Abir Riding School, industrial area; a **municipal pool;** shopping and **restaurants,** several synagogues. Don't miss Moab Observation Point for panoramic view of wilderness and Dead Sea.

USEFUL NUMBERS: IGTA, Commercial Center, P.O.B. 222, 057-98144. **Emergency,** 97222; **Police,** 100.

THE COAST

Sun, Sand and Gardens

In both the Old and the New Testaments, references to the coastal regions are few and far between. It was mainly the Philistines and the Phoenicians who occupied the coast, whereas the events and dramas of Jewish lives and history took place in the interior of the country. Even Jaffa, from whose port the timber hewn from the cedars of Lebanon for the building of Jerusalem's temple was loaded, comes in for only a bare mention. It was also the home town of Simon the Tanner, in whose house Peter heard the celestial voice. The book of Isaiah (xxxv:2) extols the "glory of Lebanon" and the magnificence of the Carmel and of Sharon. The Book of I Samuel (v: 9) proffers lamentations for the disappearance of the Ark of the Covenant, which had been captured by the Philistines and taken to Ashdod. From Old Testament evidence, the coast was pretty much in the hands of Israel's enemies.

Today, most of Israel's population is concentrated along the shores of the Mediterranean. Tel Aviv and Haifa alone account for about one-sixth of the total. Many additional towns and cities have been built or rebuilt, on sites both new and ancient. Some of them, like Caesarea and Acre, stand out in our minds and evoke definite associations. Others, like Natanya, Nahariya, and Binyamina, sound unfamiliar and fail to strike a responsive chord.

Israel's Mediterranean shore stretches in practically a straight line over some 100 miles, punctuated at one point by the shallow indentation of Haifa Bay. At the two far ends of the coast there are two resort villages run by French companies: the *Club Méditerranée* holds forth at Achziv, near Nahariya, and *Tourisme Intercontinental* (Paris) promotes the Histadrut-owned vacation village at Ashkelon, to the south. Both are popular with tourists as well as with Israelis.

We set out on our journey from the south and meander up the coastal plain, but exclude Tel Aviv and Haifa (for which see separate chapters).

Ashkelon

Ashkelon is a garden spot. We're not forgetting that the original Biblical terrestrial paradise was also a garden, the Garden of Eden, *Gan-Eden.* But remember also that the reason Israel is blessed with its particular Edens, paradises, and vacation dreamlands is thanks to the stubbornness of men determined to change the face of a barren land so long uncared for. The hand of man has conscientiously recreated here all sorts of green-growing oases for the traveler who, wearied by the sight of so much rock and sand, joyfully welcomes the relaxing shade of trees and flowering hedges and the refreshing cool proximity of water. Much of Ashkelon is trees and gardens. No doubt about it, this is the ideal spot in which to soothe jaded nerves after the hustle and bustle of a hard year's work.

Like all properly civilized countries, Israel has its own official agency responsible for historical and archeological sites and for ancient and modern monuments. Israel's National Parks Authority has performed miracles everywhere by preserving and beautifying, and also by planting, near excavation sites, lovely gardens, often vast parks complete with piped-in water, sometimes even with swimming-pools. The National Park at Ashkelon is only one of its many outstanding achievements. Splendid tamarisk trees cast protective shade over ancient stone figures rescued from the very bowels of the earth. People like to come here for picnics, one of Israel's favorite pastimes, and convenient wood and stone tables and benches have been thoughtfully provided. Outings are enhanced by the unequaled opportunity for effortless acquisition of culture afforded by the many statues of the goddess of victory *(nike)* that have been dug up here. There is one particularly memorable figure perched on a globe of the world, which in turn is precariously supported by a reluctant Atlas who looks somewhat the worse for wear—and for the weight of the lady. The profusion of green, blooming plant life is a fitting embellishment for the mellow old walls.

Afridar, the newest district in the Ashkelon township, was conceived and designed entirely as a garden city. Its beach is one endless expanse of shining fine sand, and even the Mediterranean cooperates by being gentler here than elsewhere. The most amateur snapshot with Ashkelon as its background would make an alluring travel poster.

Is it merely because we've so recently emerged from the Negev desert that we feel this way? Not entirely. In this singularly well-favored retreat, nature shows herself to be truly hospitable. The hot winds streaming over from the desert meet and mingle here with a temperate sea wind; it's a fine marriage of the elements. Summer humidity is unheard of, and the winter climate is mild, warmer than that of Tel Aviv. Plenty of pure, cool drinking water is on tap. You're just far enough removed from the big city to be able to forget all about it, but close enough, 35 miles, to get there in a jiffy if you have to. Ashkelon's inhabitants have provided everything possible to ensure both their guests and themselves maximum relaxation, restfulness, quiet, and comfort.

A Bit of History

Long before Moses had led his people out of Egypt, the Pharaohs were busy making tracks to Ashkelon, which, like Acre and Jaffa, is one of the world's most ancient known cities. A minimum of 4,000 years old, the site was strategically placed on the *Via Maris* . . . the sea road route of caravans. Although the Canaanites who lived here naturally fought tooth and nail to defend themselves, they weren't always so successful. In the historical documents known as the Tel-el-Amarna letters, Ashkelon is described as a center of rebellion as early as the fourteenth century B.C. A century later the port was captured by Rameses II, who subsequently immortalized this significant exploit in the bas-reliefs at Carnac. When the Philistines found themselves repulsed by the Egyptians, they withdrew to Ashkelon, which became their main port. And, of course, once they were entrenched there, they lost no time in picking a fight with their new neighbor, the Jews.

At this point, history and legend have become inextricably intermingled. If wars were being waged as ceaselessly as the records would have us believe, how then was it possible for the great Jewish hero Samson to be standing on an enemy beach gazing at Delilah, the lady who was to spell his doom? And remember David's grieving exhortation after learning of Saul's death: "Publish it not in the streets of Ashkelon, lest the daughters of the Philistines rejoice, lest the daughters of the uncircumcised triumph!" That's all part of history.

In any case, Egypt exerted pressure from the south on the Philistines, who duly transferred it by pressing on their Jewish neighbors to the north and east. Jehovah wasn't always to be counted on when the Chosen People needed help. The Jews suffered a serious setback at Shiloh, where the Philistines went a little too far by making off with the Ark of the Covenant. True, they soon decided that their outlandish deed was the source of their own misfortunes; the presence of the Ark destroyed their god Dagon. The Philistines hastened to restore their booty to its rightful owners amidst great pomp and ceremony.

Many Conquerors

Ashkelon was successively destroyed, rebuilt, and subjugated by the Assyrians, the Babylonians, and the Persians, and finally got off to a new start under the Greeks. Then came the Roman conquest. History records that Herod the Great was born in Ashkelon. The Arabs next took it over, and then the Crusaders. But hardly had the deadly strife ended between Christians and Moslems than the Turks put in their appearance. But by then Ashkelon had practically ceased to exist, having never fully recovered from its despoliation by the Arabs in 1270. Under ground water springs, blithely indifferent to mere man's comings and goings, continued to pour forth their life-giving waters, gradually transforming the ruins into a virgin forest of lush vegetation.

The Turks began their occupation in 1517 and ignored the ruins of Ashkelon. It wasn't until the nineteenth century that Ibrahim Pasha, casting about for ways to earn himself a bit of extra pocket money, hit upon the idea of setting up Egyptian weavers in nearby Migdal-Gad. At the same time, and at the taxpayers' expense, he built himself a fortress on the seacoast. Invading armies through the centuries had already done a pretty thorough job of stripping Palestine of its timber and trees, so that, to find building materials, architects had to use whatever they could close by—stone, marble, columns, statuary, stairways—from every possible source, including Greek, Roman, and medieval. Like Caesarea, whose scattered remnants are found incorporated everywhere in Turkish buildings, Ashkelon was doomed to become an official supplier of materials for the public works program.

Although professional and amateur archeologists had for years been engrossed with the stupendous discoveries unearthed from the layers of silt and centuries at Ashkelon, really serious digging didn't get under way until 1920. The garden district of Afridar today features an archeological museum of local finds mostly from the times of the Greeks,

Romans and Second Temple. Around town you can see a Roman tomb, excellent mosaics, a Byzantine church, and Crusader remains, but the two 3rd-century Roman sarcophagi are what have caused some problems. You see, both the Tourist and Cultural Events Center of Afridar and Bet Eli Public and Pedagogic Libraries (also a cultural center, in fact) want to exhibit the really splendid pieces. While the rivalry goes on, tourists become confused: the sarcophagi sit on the lawns of Bet Eli, but the map for tourists clearly and artistically shows them at the Afridar Center.

Dagon's New Home

In addition to the usual swank places and less expensive but comfortable hotels, Ashkelon also boasts one rather special hostelry, the Dagon, special in its friendly atmosphere, and also because it's named for Dagon, the Philistines' Neptune. It was Dagon's temple that Samson destroyed when he pulled those pillars down around his head in Gaza. Nearby lies a Roman tomb embellished with exquisite frescos, preserved only by extensive precautions to protect them from sunlight. The tomb is locked, but you can request the custodian to let you in. And let's not overlook Ashkelon's claim concerning yet another Biblical personage, Jonah, gulped down by an obliging whale. Although the Bible doesn't say so, legend has it as Ashkelon's shores where the great fish coughed up its passenger.

Housewives often evoke the name of Ashkelon without realizing it. The etymological truth is that, in ancient times around these parts, a particular species of onion flourished, called by the Romans *caepa ascalonia,* later shortened to just *ascalonia.* Passing time, plus inevitable linguistic corruptions, found the onion known as *escalotte*—our scallion or shallot, whose pungent aroma graces some of the best salads. You'll find such salads, along with assorted naturalist health foods, at Ashkelon's Beit Frumer, where food and exercise regimens promise to cure certain ills and overweight woes.

Ashkelon is the starting point for a number of excursions, including one to a kibbutz, Yad Mordechai, which before the 1967 War had the distinction of being the last Jewish settlement before the border with the Gaza Strip. The highway runs parallel to the railroad that once connected the Israeli coast with the Suez Canal. Sycamore trees dot the landscape.

Your visit to Ashdod, 22 miles away, will be an extremely rewarding one. Ashdod is Israel's largest port, docking world-famous liners as well as giant freighters. The township itself was carved out of the sand in 1957, and already it has some 41,000 inhabitants—part of the 106,100 who live from Ashdod to Ashkelon and southwards. Once the operations were under way for digging the deep-water port (in anticipation of some 4,000,000 tons of freight annually), several industrial firms set up branches in Ashdod, impressed by the prospects and encouraged by the proximity of Tel Aviv. Ashdod's name is a hangover from biblical times. The Ashdod mentioned in II Chronicles (XXVI, (6)) became *Azotis* under the Greeks and *Isdud* under the Arabs. Together with Gaza, Ashkelon, Gat, and Ekron, it was one of the Philistines' main strongholds, which brought down upon it the maledictions of the prophet Zephaniah.

North from Ashkelon

Rehovot lies 27 miles north of Ashkelon on the Tel Aviv highway, 14 miles from Tel Aviv. Tucked in among orange groves, Rehovot has been in existence since 1890, and now enjoys the prestige of having the Weizmann Institute in its midst. Israel's first president, Chaim Weizmann, a world renowned scientist, is buried there. One story is that, during World War I, Weizmann, who was already famous both as a chemist and for his ardent Zionism, turned over to Lord Balfour a discovery (acetone) that proved vital to the British war effort, in exchange for the promise to set up a Jewish National Homeland. Weizmann died in 1952. In accordance with his last wishes, his remains were interred right here. You can pay your respects to his grave, and meditate in the beautiful grounds of the Institute that perpetuates his name. This is a beautiful compound of green lawns and well-tended gardens. Note the kidney-shaped lily pond in front of the physics building, and the novel design of the library building. The Institute provides its scientists with handsome housing quarters right on the grounds. In the classrooms and laboratories, scientists are freely pursuing their studies and research in various fields, including mathematics, nuclear physics, electronics, experimental biology, organic chemistry—in other words, practically all the scientific disciplines. A revolutionary new method for heavy water was developed in the Rehovot laboratories, Israel's first atomic cyclotron is located at nearby Yavneh.

Vespasian was approached by one of the city's elders, Rabbi Yohanan, who asked permission to set up an academy at Yavneh. The request was granted, and a school was eventually founded there. So in a certain sense it is thanks to Vespasian that the biblical canon was established in the first century and that the compiling of the *Mishna* (the first part of the *Talmud)* was undertaken, to be completed a century later in Tiberias. After the destruction of the second temple in A.D. 70, Yavneh was renowned as a center of learning and wisdom; a popular adage of the day was, "Go north for riches, but go south for knowledge." Present-day Yavneh is 5 miles north of Ashdod.

Next, there are Rishon Le-Zion to the north, and Ramle to the northeast. Both are described in the Tel Aviv chapter, as are nearby inland towns of Petah Tikva and Lod. Bat Yam lies just south of Tel Aviv-Jaffa and, if you keep to the major Tel Aviv-Haifa road that parallels the coastline, after passing Tel Aviv you'll see suburban communities of Technot Lamed, to your left, and Ramat Aviv—home of Tel Aviv University—to the right. The Tel Aviv Country Club lies just a bit further, on the left.

Some 16 kilometers north of Tel Aviv where the land gradually rises, on the right, a crossroad leads up to the town of Herzliya, or left to the industrial and resort areas of Herzliya-by-the-Sea—where seaside tourist extravaganzas vie with costly residential villas of interesting design. Sometimes called Israel's Riviera (and a great exaggeration at that), this actually is a quiet, spread-out community, built in sands that once boasted fortresses for Crusaders and those who came before and after them. *Sidni Ali* towers above the beautiful, sandy beaches of the Mediterranean here. Formerly a way station for caravans, this huge graceful structure has been restored as a recreation site primarily used by Arab youth. In the sands below these cliffs, you'll find small fragments of glass, burnished smooth by the sea, in all shades of aqua and green. Though some say these are relatively new shards, others vow they are the remains of three different glass works, built in ancient times atop the cliffs that erosion caused to topple into the sea. Obviously, ruins have fallen beneath the waves here, and more crest the hills— perhaps, as some believe, parts of a fort that sheltered Richard the Lion-Heart.

Whatever the story of these beaches may be, it is true that Herzliya is home to Israel's fledgling movie industry, and the local TV satelite link is here, too. Many diplomats serving in Israel favor this area, some living here and others found in the beautiful residential areas of Kfar Shmaryahu, across the highway, where the American School enrolls their offspring. Further north, and inland, Ra'anana, dating from 1921, and Kfar Saba together occupy the major part of the corridor which once connected the north and south of Israel.

A short distance further north is the nation's most important physical education teachers' training-school. This school is dedicated to General Wingate, the British officer famous for having trained Haganah troops in 1939, and Burmese commandos in World War II. As a captain in the British army from 1936 through 1939, he organized, in the very heart of the Haganah, special assault groups for night operations, which eventually became the Palmach, the commandos of the pre-independence Jewish army.

Netanya, just north of Herzliya, looks like the inexpensive little vacation spot that it is. The town is a succession of rooming houses, small hotels, cafés, restaurants, parks, and signs pointing the way to the beach, one of Israel's finest. It was founded in 1928, and became a major pre-State landing point for "illegal" Jewish immigration into Palestine. About 70,700 people live in Netanya, "Pearl of the Sharon." Netanya is famous for its diamond-cutting industry, introduced here by Belgian refugees. Today, diamond exports rank next to citrus fruits as Israel's biggest income-earner. (Tourism holds first place.) Of interest in Netanya are the diamond factories on Rehov Herzl, Sderot Binyamin, Pinsker Street, and Rehov Hayahalom Street (open 8 A.M. to 4 P.M.); the Jewish Legion Museum (concerning the Jewish units in the British army during World War I), and the Braille Library, 73 Rabbi Kook Street. In case there's any confusion, Netanya can be spelled in the following manner: Nathanya, Nathania, Netania, Netanya, and Natanya: so you can make your choice.

Through 1926 the region north of Netanya was ridden with marshes. Now that the swamps have been dried up and malaria eradicated, this region has become one of the most fertile in Israel. You will realize just how fertile when you see the Kfar Yedidia, the name of which is derived from that of the famed philosopher Philon of Alexandria. There is also the Hefer valley, which is listed in I Kings (IV, 10) as one of the 12 tributaries responsible for supplying Solomon's table each month. Mishmar-Ha-Sharon (the Guardian of Sharon) is noted for the gladioli it exports, great clusters of which find their way into the living rooms of English homes.

The main occupation of Moshav Michmoret, right on the sea, is fishing. The Israeli Government has established a Fisheries Institute here as part of its overall plan to develop the fishing industry. Some of Israel's leading citizens also live here.

The Sharon Valley

Inland the heady, sweetish fragrance of orange groves assails your nostrils, and Hadera isn't far away. This is the Sharon Valley. In the early days of Zionism, pioneers settled here in 1891 despite the fearful living conditions. They somehow managed to hold out until the marshes had been finally dried up, and fortune then began to smile on them at last. Since that time, Hadera has been one of Israel's main citrus fruit centers. Its first residents had lived in makeshift fashion in an old and decrepit Arab caravanserai open to the elements, which had been included in the land purchase. The remnants of this building are carefully preserved in the shade of the synagogue.

The name you will undoubtedly encounter everywhere in this area is that of the Rothschilds. With the vast means at its disposal, this family contributed heavily to land purchases, the only possible means of founding a Jewish National Homeland in Palestine. The township of Binyamina bears the Hebrew first name of the Rothschilds, and Ramat-Hanadiv, the "Hill of the Benefactor," contains the Rothschild grave. It is set amid strikingly lovely grounds. On certain days the mausoleum is open to the public, and grateful Jews pay their respects to the memory of the baron and baroness. Zichron-Ya'akov is one of the first villages founded by the Rothschilds, and its benefactors also gave it French vineyards. There is also the Aaronson Museum, recalling the pre-Mandate exploits of a local family.

To the east of Binyamina, Zichron-Ya'akov and Pardess Hana are the Valley of Iron and the Hills of Ephraim, which merge some distance farther on with the even more famous and fertile valley of Yezre'el. It was a favorite battlefield in ancient times. The two great ancient powers, Egypt and Assyria, controlled the two far ends of the valley, and their ambition was to continue to dominate the connecting route between Africa and Asia that passed through the Middle East. King Solomon eventually meddled in the affair and his might prevailed. Starting with Pharaoh Tutmose III in 1478 B.C. and continuing through to Allenby's defeat of the Turks in 1917 and the fierce Israeli-Jordanian strife in 1948, warfare has been waged almost unceasingly here.

Caesarea

Compared with Ashkelon, whose earliest known history extends back some five millennia, Caesarea, midway between Tel Aviv and Haifa, is a relative upstart—barely 2,200 years old. This "new maritime colony" of the Philistines, then called by its original name, the Tower of Strato, is referred to in a report sent by the merchant Zenon to his customer, the Egyptian intendant, in the second century B.C. (He had just bought some wheat there.) Its true grandeur began with Herod, who incorporated the coastal strip into his vassalized kingdom and transformed the Tower of Strato into a great metropolis, which he duly proceeded to dub Caesarea in honor of his overlord, Caesar Augustus. The writings of Josephus Flavius give us his solemn assurance of the veracity of these events. The author adds that Herod built a harbor "larger than Piraeus" to serve as a port of call between Dor and Jaffa. This harbor was an outstanding achievement for its pioneer builders, one that guaranteed survival to Caesarea. The city itself was a large-scale metropolis, with its white stone buildings and its regularly spaced streets that converged down to the waterfront. Wherever the Romans touched base, they concerned themselves with *panem* and *circenses*. Acting in the best of traditions, Herod built a splendid theater, a market-place, and a hippodrome. An athletic competition called "Caesar's Games" was held every five years.

Jesus was six years old by the time the procurators of Judea established their headquarters at Caesarea, after Herod's demise. The city was the focal point for the Jewish uprising in A.D. 66. When a riot broke out between Jews and Syrians, Rome supported the latter, and the matter ended with the massacre of some 20,000 Jews. Thus was the War of the Jews begun. In A.D. 70, Titus had remnants of the demolished temple brought to Caesarea for the celebration of his triumph. The main attraction of this celebration was the immolation of 2,500 Jews in the arena. At that very moment, Silva, another general, was laying siege to Masada. Later on Peter baptized Cornelius the centurion in Caesarea. And here, 60 years later, Rabbi Akiba, the wise man of Israel, was tortured and put to death by the Romans.

In case you're interested in more dates: 639, arrival of the Arabs; 1099, arrival of the Crusaders; 1187, return of the Arabs under Saladin; 1228, return of the Christians. Alas, poor Caesarea. But let us acknowledge a debt of thanks to France's St. Louis, who fortified the city and thereby preserved it for posterity despite the ravages wrought by Baibars shortly afterwards.

The Holy Grail

One item of priceless value escaped disaster: this was a glass vessel found by Baudouin I when he captured the city during the first Crusade. It is supposed to be the one used by Jesus at the Last Supper. The Genoese fleet, which had taken part in the fighting, laid claim to the relic, which is known as the *sacro catino,* and is on display today in the big Italian port city of San Lorenzo. It is wrongly or rightly identified by many scholars as the Holy Grail.

Today, the Roman theater and the Crusaders' City also have been retrieved from the sands of time. At a stone's throw from the golf-links there is the hippodrome, with an obelisk in its middle and a cross, still intact, behind the portal. The hippodrome seated 20,000. In it flowers now grow wild covering the arena and the stone steps with a blanket of blooms. At this juncture, the camera-minded visitor is urged to shoulder arms and prepare his spare rolls of film; he's going to need them, because there's so much to shoot. In the next few minutes he'll be going crazy, not knowing where to focus his lens next. He'll find himself torn between the fifth- and sixth-century Byzantine mosaics; the aqueduct with its proudly preserved arches (some of them are still partially buried); the remains of the fourth-century synagogue uncovered by the Hebrew University team; the Roman theater; the innumerable columns standing in the bay waters or springing up like cannons from the battlements, with the Crusaders' fortress looming large in the background.

A compiler of guidebooks today is reluctant to describe in detail things that are so intelligently arranged and displayed as to hit the spectator right in the eye. This remarkable archeological site lies right along the traveler's route. He needs no one to tell him to stop dead in front of the two great statues of white marble and red porphyry that embellish the ruins. They date from the second and third centuries, according to the National Parks Authority sign. (And maybe we should also add that there's an excellent little restaurant inside the Crusaders' City.) Unfortunately the manner in which the theater has been restored makes it a mite newish-looking.

Looters

It won't hurt you either to pause a minute and brood over the systematic pilfering of Caesarea's treasures that has gone on through the ages. Herod had rare and precious materials brought at considerable cost from Rome. Each succeeding civilization salvaged the remnants of its predecessor's buildings in order to rebuild over the ruins. One of the first things of which a traveler becomes aware is that, as far as archeology is concerned, history is written in stones, and chronology is rendered by the stacking up of superimposed cities. All along the seacoast you can find tacky Arab shacks with marble floors. The Crusaders paved their streets with carrara marble and used the columns that they found nearby to reinforce their walls. Lintels and friezes of priceless value have been indiscriminately intermingled in a hodgepodge of ordinary partition walls. The fortifications built by St. Louis are in fine shape: walls, moats, and ramparts have been cleared of their encumbrances. (And there's always the element of surprise: a minaret rears its spire smack in the middle of the Christian stronghold!) Things hit a new low when the Turks were in power: they pilfered Caesarea and carted off their booty to build with it elsewhere. Both Jaffa and Acre are full of stones brought from Caesarea. So is Ashkelon, for that matter. In fact, the more you think about it, the more it seems a miracle that there's anything at all left in Caesarea.

Before leaving the subject of archeology and history, just one word in passing about the inscription found on a stone during the excavation of the Roman theater. It includes the name of Pontius Pilate. Maybe this doesn't strike the layman as too important, but it was a considerable relief to scholars! Prior to this discovery, nothing had been known of the existence of Pontius Pilate, the Procurator of Judea, aside from references in the Gospel and in the works of Josephus Flavius. This inscription, therefore, was the irrefutable proof of his presence in Palestine at the time of Christ. Mr. Yaakov Yannai calls Caesarea a "paradise for archeologists and sportsmen." As far as the archeologists are concerned, the proof has been amply demonstrated. Among sports enthusiasts, and quite aside from the swimming and water sports in the former small Roman port, Caesarea has acquired a most enviable reputation because of its golf course, unique in Israel, and fenced in with barbed-wire like a military camp. On Saturdays it is invaded by golfing fans from all over the country armed with their clubs.

With the help of the golf links, Caesarea's promoters would like to make the place a sort of Palm Beach of Israel. Part of their planning has included a whole colony of luxurious villas built between the golf course and the sea; some can be rented to transients when not occupied by their regular owners.

From Caesarea to Haifa

Dor, about ten miles north, stands near the abandoned Arab village of Tantura; turn off the main road at the "Nahsholim" sign. It is an important archeological site, but for the moment is not being as extensively exploited as Caesarea. In Roman times this ancient biblical settlement was famous for producing a dye known as the purple of Tyre, derived by processing an extract from a locally abundant shellfish. As a matter of fact, Palestine for a long time remained a prime furnisher of coloring matter, including indigo blue, saffron yellow, and beet red. For some reason the world has tended to forget that up to the Middle Ages the Jews ranked among the most highly skilled dyers of the times.

Dor (the Romans' "Tantura") traces its glorious past as far back as ancient Egypt, King Solomon, and the splendor that was Canaan. To this day, you can still see the vestiges of its proud fortress rising from an eminence along the shore, the remains of a once bustling port, and the ruins of a Byzantine church in the outskirts of nearby Nahsholim. So far, the excavations that have been going on here have failed to attract many people, but they do come to enjoy the natural swimming pool formed by a group of lagoons and reefs. It is one of the finest and least crowded beaches in Israel.

We're now about 18 miles from Haifa, and on our right looms the unmistakable shape of the Carmel ridge, following roughly parallel to the coastline. The slopes are punctuated with grottos and caverns that were inhabited in the Stone Age, yielding artifacts and other precious indications of the existence of the troglodytes. As will be seen in the next chapter, the most famous of all is the grotto associated with the life of the prophet Elijah, whose native haunt was Mount Carmel. It was there that he prayed for rain, and there also he besought Jehovah to send him fire for his sacrifice. He is revered as a saint by the three great religions—Judaism, Christianity, and Islam. In I Kings we read of Elijah's confronting singlehanded the 450 prophets of Baal and the ensuing victory that Jehovah gave him. Amos likewise preached on the Carmel, and Isaiah extolled the "magnificence of Carmel and Sharon." (The subject of the Carmel will be dealt with more extensively in the next chapter.)

The Pilgrims' Castle

Midway between Caesarea and Haifa, the Templars built Atlit, the Pilgrims' Castle. The Knights Templars and the Knights Hospitallers, both religio-military orders, assumed in intense rivalry the responsibility of protecting all wayfarers. For nearly a century the Atlit Pilgrims' Castle was the most formidable of the Crusaders' strongholds in the Holy Land, and remained truly impregnable. Now the Israeli Navy rides in the roadstead of this port in which Phoenician galleys and ships bearing pilgrims once cast anchor. In olden times, Atlit lustily vied with Acre in luring the pilgrim trade. The Templars gave all merchants stiff competition, and the city prospered as a result. But with the fall of Acre it was clear that any further fighting would be of no avail for the Crusaders, and the Templars set sail toward Cyprus, abandoning their uncaptured fortress intact. The main reason that the Moslems dismantled it was to discourage the Christians from any eventual come-back. The walls of the Pilgrims' Castle were so mighty that even the great earthquake that occurred five centuries later, in 1837, failed to disturb them. After one more century had passed, Atlit was again called on to shelter a new type of pilgrim, the clandestine Jewish refugees who had eluded their Nazi captors and illegally entered their Jewish National Homeland. Despite the ravages of time, of the elements, and of man, the remains of Atlit Castle are still a monumental sight, with its more than 15-feet-thick walls, its octagonal church, and its wharf that is now under water.

Ein Hod—Artists' Village

On the opposite side of the highway facing Atlit lies the abandoned Arab village of Ein Hod, which is more than worth your climb up a gentle incline of a few hundred yards. Israeli artists took over this village, began living in it, and have now restored it. About one hundred painters, sculptors, and artisans of various crafts (mainly ceramists) are grouped here in a semi-collective community. Roughly 25 per cent of the proceeds realized from sales is paid into a mutual fund that is used for advertising, exhibits, and the purchase of equipment and materials. The village features a popular-priced restaurant, student rooms, art classes and seminars. Many concerts are held here in the amphitheater, and world-famous soloists consider it an honor to be invited to perform in Ein Hod. The local residents' dream is one day to establish a National Academy of Plastic Arts. Way back in 1953, when a small group of enthusiastic artists led by the Dadaist painter Marcel Janco rolled up their sleeves and got to work, they had no roads, no water, and no electricity. While the central Government more or less stood by and let them shift for themselves, the enterprising mayor of Haifa made an energetic contribution to the resurrection of this village. Today, many tours come here from Haifa, especially for the frequent Art Fairs and special events like theater performances or concerts.

Now the inland road has widened, and we're entering Haifa, which is covered in the following chapter, along with its neighbor, Acre. So we pick up the coastal trek again about a mile outside Acre, still traveling the highway parallel to the shore.

Fighters and Lovers

In this region of ancient aquaduct ruins and flowing, fertile fields, a kibbutz was built by survivors of the Polish ghettos, most of whom fought later in the ranks of the Jewish Resistance in Palestine. Aside from the kibbutz, they also built a large square structure—*Lohamei-Hagetaot* ("Fighters of the Ghetto")—that is a museum of Nazi barbarism, a monument erected so that no man should ever forget that Holocaust.

The next village along this route is Shavei Zion, a township founded in 1938 by German Jews from the Black Forest. Recently, interesting mosaics were discovered here. Nearby, in the resort town of Nahariya —often called "Honeymoon Headquarters" because it is a favorite place for newly-weds and lovers—the ruins that were found could hardly be more suitable.

Workers in Nahariya who were digging foundations for a building stumbled across the ruins of an ancient Phoenician temple. Only two known Phoenician shrines have so far been discovered in Israel, the other one being in Megiddo. The one at Nahariya was dedicated to Astarte, the goddess of fertility—and it likely was built here because of older traditions, not "by chance." Archeologists say springs gushed from the ground here about 2500 B.C. and women came from miles and miles away, just to bathe in the spring waters which, they believed, would make them fertile. The springs are under the sea today, but still flow along the beach, and local folk swear to an interesting story. It seems a childless couple, married ten years, visited Nahariya in 1977 and, of course, swam in the sea. In 1978 they returned—with their infant child—to thank the townsfolk. Locals also say the town has "plenty of babies—even twins."

Nowadays, the town also has plenty of U.N. folk—pouring into the warm resort town for R-and-R (Rest-&-Recuperation) leaves from U.N.I.F.I.F. border posts.

Decidely German

Dating back to 1934, Nahariya was, like many settlements at that time, founded by German Jews. Some of the oldtimers who were around in those days still relish and relate the tale of Nahariya's prompt reaction when it was slighted back in 1936 by the British High Commissioner, who had devised a partition plan for a future Jewish State in which he was reluctant to include Nahariya. The latter's staunch residents immediately telegraphed Chaim Weizmann: "Whatever happens, Nahariya will remain German!"

This settlement has been transformed with great care into a resort village combining the advantages of town life (30,000 population) with all the relaxing features of a resort atmosphere. A river runs through inexplicable concrete canal-banks right down the main street. On streets beside it, horse-drawn carts provide color and transportation. Where the river runs to the sea, a pool for children's boat rides attracts tourists and locals. Nahariya's beaches rank among the finest, and some of them are completely sheltered by breakwaters, thus providing safety for swimmers. A sailing center is due to open nearby by 1981, renting boats and providing lessons. In the same area—just across from the ancient temple ruins—you'll find a heated swimming pool and other tourist facilities. None of these achievements just happened all by itself; men have worked hard here. Almost a whole mile of beach was reclaimed from the sea, the rocks being carefully buried under sand dredged up from the ocean floor. A breakwater jetty was built with the future port and beaches in mind. A local agency organizes cruises to the frontier, five miles away.

The railroad crosses through town, as does the *nahar* (river), from which its name comes. There are plenty of shops and stores. This is a favourite summer vacation spot for families, and transportation is fast and efficient, including weekend trains for commuting husbands. Today, Nahariya has about 340 hotel rooms, and more hotels planned. Many private homes have rooms for rental. The only trouble is that on weekends about 25,000 people crowd onto its beaches. For this reason, a real effort is now being made to supplement the old German custom of renting out rooms in private homes by adding new hotel accommodations. Well, any new hotels in this town will undoubtedly soon be filled with tourists, but that may have very little effect on those Old World customs.

Achziv and Beyond

Achziv is about as far north as you can go along the coast. Don't look for any Achziv township; there is none. The largest local institution up this way is the Club Méditerranée, whose legions of thatch huts sprawl over a prime, lagoon-studded beachfront. Adjoining the club is a new public beach, built to satisfy the cries of the local citizens who protested at the Club's acquisition of such choice sea frontage. This frontage, by the way, no longer includes those lovely ancient ruins—the National Parks Department tends them and keeps them open to the public. Diagonally across the road is the Achziv Memorial, next to the bridge. It commemorates the 14 young men who in 1946 decided to blast the link between Palestine and Lebanon, a show of strength aimed at the British. A chance rifle bullet set off the explosive which blew up the bridge and the 14 men as well.

Further north, Rosh Hanikra is a big rock complete with a snack bar and a frontier barricade, with a marine grotto down underneath it all. Swimming in and around the Sulam Tzor grotto is most enjoyable and highly recommended, but it must be undertaken only with certain precautions. It is more easily reached by the cable railway, that takes you down in less than a minute. The grotto is as fascinating as the one on Capri, and has the advantage that you wander about inside on foot. It is accessible in almost any weather; in fact, the rougher the sea, the better the show. The frontier line dividing the water is rather ill-defined; so if you venture into the sea around Rosh Hanikra, watch out for the Lebanese border guards, who don't fool around with unauthorized immigrants.

The road comes to an abrupt end just beyond an inclined curve. That's the frontier. Terminus. If you cross over the line you'll be in Lebanon.

The distance from Rosh Hanikra to Eilat, the southernmost point of Israel, is officially 298 miles.

A bazaar nestles beneath one
of Nazareth's many churches

**An immemorially peaceful scene
on the Jordan at Degania**

The bells of Bethlehem proclaim
the coming of Christmas every year
to the whole world

**Crafts are booming in Israel.
There are lots of pots in
Galilee and masses of masterpieces
in Safad**

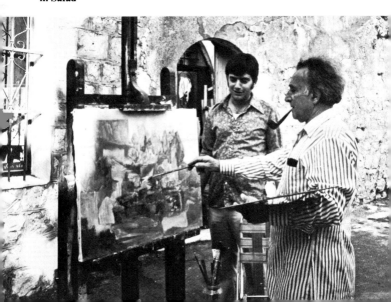

PRACTICAL INFORMATION FOR THE COAST

ASHKELON

A year-round popular resort that encompasses an old Arab town and a Jewish settlement—both of which grew until they overlapped. The Old Town is now a place to stroll and maybe buy curios, but the beachside is where the tourist action is. Peak rates prevail from July 15 to August 31, as well as over the Jewish holidays in the spring and the fall.

HOTELS. The old-established **Dagon** (4-star) has partial air-conditioning for its 52 rooms and 10 cottage suites in a garden setting, with mini-golf, pool, fine restaurant, health club and great bar. Also 4-star, **Shulamit Gardens's** 104 rooms are air-conditioned. The most expensive, modern and posh hotel in town, it has tennis courts, pool, health club and bar. **Frumer's Natural Health Resort** has taken over a complete floor of this hotel, where it offers diets for weight loss and chronic illnesses (heart and digestive troubles, high blood pressure, asthma, diabetes, rheumatism, etc.). Medical supervision plus exercise and cultural programs.

King Saul (3-star), 108 rooms, is recent. Air-conditioned. Nightclub, health club, pool and grill room.

In a class by itself, the **Ashkelon French Village** sprawls over a sandy knoll—well run, great food, lively. Partly air-conditioned, 196 rooms, tennis, riding, private beach, pool and nightclub.

One-star **Samson's Gardens** has 22 partly air-conditioned rooms with baths or showers. Other inexpensive accommodations are found through the Tourist Office, which will provide rooms rented out in local homes. Ashkelon camping colony, in park near beach, has bungalows, caravans, tents and superb facilities.

RESTAURANTS. In Afridar, **Ma'adan** is about the best moderate spot, open 9-8 in winter, to 11 P.M. or later on Fri. and Sat. and in summer. Also try some of the snack bars. Friendly, and Oriental is the **Apollo.** In Barnea, **Puerto de Sol** serves fish specialties, meats, spaghetti, etc. Also at Barnea Beach is **Mario Restaurant,** with popular Italian fare plus seafoods and meat grills. In the Old Town, try **Mifgash Golani,** and **Nitzahon** is a 20-year favorite for Oriental fare. South of town, **Hei Daroma** has nice moderate café-restaurant, plus shopping for picnic items. In town many markets and shops can supply picnickers—and you couldn't ask for a better place to spread lunch than in the National Park, amid antiquities and greenery. **Rico,** on the beach in the park, has good Oriental food, fun atmosphere, moderate prices.

ENTERTAINMENT. Cafés with dance floors: **Holiday Village; Café of the Antiquities** (National Park). Some hotels have disco dance bars that open and close with little warning, but are good when they're there.

SIGHTS. National Park including fragments of antique statuary and columns, the new section at Afridar, and, a stone's throw away, the ruins of a 6th-century Byzantine church, Roman sarcophagi, etc.

Hunting is excellent hereabouts, with a season running November through February.

Active **Municipal Tourist Organisation** and *IGTA,* in Afridar Commercial Center—(051) 27412; **Ashkelon Tours,** Municipal Center, many area tours to kibbutzim, etc., and also all over Israel. Police: 100. Ambulance: 2333.

HERZILYA

Yes, people flock to this "Riviera" every month of the year. But there is a Special H.I.T.—Herzliya Inclusive Tours—available from travel agents, a winter program combining facilities of all hotels here, even allowing you to eat and enjoy facilities in affiliated hotels in other cities. Shuttle service to Tel Aviv operates almost hourly via United Tours.

HOTELS. The original 140-room **Sharon** 5-star hotel has expanded considerably in the course of the last few years, and now counts a total of 230 rooms. It now has also a 14-storey apartment hotel— **Sharon Towers** —consisting of 132 double rooms or suites, built on the roof of one wing of the original hotel. The rooms are the last word in luxury. There are shops, piano bar, health club and massage, physiotherapy, turkish baths and kneipp treatments, even a bank, nightclub, heated pool (one of *the* places for swimming in Israel), tennis courts, and health club, TV in rooms, nightclub/bar, etc.

The **Dan Accadia Resort Hotel** on the southern part of the beach has 192 newly-refurbished luxury rooms built in the grand manner and outfitted with a super-sized pool surrounded by several acres of landscaped rock gardens. (Visitors welcomed at pool.) The dining room is distinctive, with stately Doric columns and three glass walls; on a brilliant, clear day, it's like dining on a ship. Health club plus Finnish sauna ritual; tennis courts. Famous for its Friday night dances. Heated pool, piano bar, cinematheque, gymnastics.

Newest of the 5-star hotels is the **Daniel Tower Sonestra Hotel,** 180 rooms with bath and shower, room TV; health club, heated pool, tennis court, private beach, duty-free shop, bank, everything.

The 3-star, 68-room **Tadmor** is Israel's hotel training school and the attention to service here is nothing short of scrupulous. Also, once-weekly, student chefs learn to whip up some special international cuisine, and people come for miles to try it.

Looking a little like an Austrian chalet by the sea, with Alps-style dining room and pools and pretty gardens, the 2-star **Cymberg** features European cuisine, a family-type atmosphere and moderate rates for its 11 rooms with bath or shower.

Not yet graded, the **Hod** offers 28 rooms with baths, at 89 Hanasi. The **Eshel,** across from the Sharon, boasts TV for all 49 neat rooms. Nearby is a 3-star, 96-room beachside kibbutz guest house, **Shefayim,** with private beach, air-conditioning, restaurant, swimming, tennis and many other sports, plus a new convention center.

Further north, **Kfar Vitkin Youth Hostel** has 270 beds, family accommodations, kitchen, 3 meals served daily, sports grounds, swimming, bus and RR stops.

RESTAURANTS. Local eateries usually are above average, and include **Henry VIII,** with great British cookery and atmosphere in Shalit Center. Also here are **Swiss Cottage Pub/Restaurant,** serving quiches, fondues, draft beer; **Osteria do Antonio,** with Italian and French fare (tasty!); **Le Bistro,** with fine salads, grills, Argentinian ice cream. **Taverna** Greek restaurant is at the Haifa Rd./Kfar Shmaryahu junction, not far from **Indonesia,** which offers rijst-tafel at Holland Friendship House, 4 Keren Hayesod St. **Taste of Sze-Chaun** is one of the popular Mandy's eateries, in Kfar Shmaryahu, and Col. Sander's "finger lickin' good" recipe is koshered at **Kentucky Fried Chicken** on Ben Gurion St. Back on the beach, between the Sharon and Daniel Tower hotels, a fine, romantic dining place is **Zevulun. Sea Gull,** nearby, serves French cuisine, dinner only.

NETANYA

This seaside resort town is quiet, sun-filled and blessed with one of Israel's finest stretches of beach.

HOTELS. There's one 5-star hotel, the high-rise **Four Seasons,** 90 rooms with bath and TV, tennis courts, health club and heated pool. Canadian management.

The following are 4-star hotels: the **Grand Yahalom,** the **Metropol Grand, King Solomon,** the **Goldar** and the **Park** —having 48, 61, 99, 146 and 90 rooms respectively; air-conditioned and well appointed, all have pools; **Goldar** has a sauna; **King Solomon** sports a health club. The **Galil** has 84 rooms with bath, a heated pool and a nightclub. **Beit Ami** has 85 rooms, heated pool, tennis. **Blue Bay** has 236 rooms, TV, private beach, pool, health club, beauty parlor and nightclub.

Not graded yet, but probably in the 3- or 4-star category, four new hotels are the 90-room **Maxim,** the 147-room **Princess,** the 36-room **Hof,** and the 256-room **Blue Bay**—which offers TV, tennis, private beach, pool, and health club.

Recommended 3-star hotels include: the **Palace,** 71 rooms and sea view; the **Topaz** with 64 rooms; and the 48-room **Yahalom** with bath (same management as the Grand Yahalom). The non-kosher **Hakibbutz** is air-conditioned, but its 86 rooms have only showers.

Highly rated is the **Gan Hamelech** ("Garden of the King"), with its pine-paneled lobby, Scandinavian furniture and nice design flairs in 49 Israeli-styled rooms, partly air-conditioned, with bath, radio, phone and nightclub.

Newer 3-star hotels are the 28-room **Feldman** at 9 Hasziva St.; the **Residence** at 18 Gad Makhnes, with 96 air-conditioned rooms, and the 54-room air-conditioned **Orly.**

Most 2-star hotels also are air-conditioned, and the list includes the 25-room **Ast;** 22-room **Gal Yam;** 37-room **Greenstein;** 20-room **Atzmauth;** 36-room **Margoa;** 27-room **Metropole;** 28-room **Mizpe Yam;** 10-room **Winklesberg.** The 35-room **Ginot Yam** offers showers only. New **Galel Ruth** has 18 rooms; **Reuven** has 29.

Both 24-room **Galei Hasharon** and 18-room **Galei Ruth** lack ratings this year, but probably rank 2-star. Also not yet graded are **Galei Zans,** with 83 partly air-conditioned rooms, and **King David Palace,** with 56 rooms.

In the 1-star category, most Netanya hotels have only showers, but the 90-room **Zuke Yam** is partly air-conditioned, as is the new 15-room **Dekel.** Others are the 7-room **Orit** and the 17-room **Daphne.**

The **Green Beach** seashore bungalow village is just north of the city; 150 rooms with bath or shower, partly air-conditioned. Private beach plus pool, tennis courts, nightclub, health club.

RESTAURANTS. The **Restaurant Renaissance** is on Haatzmaut Square, its street-side café has coffee, coke, ice cream, and light food, while the back restaurant is posh. But we have had some adverse reports. Nearby is the new **Taipei** (E), Chinese, with service indoors and outside. Try **Capris,** 27 Herzl Street, for cakes, toasts and light meals respectively.

ENTERTAINMENT. The **Aristo,** 3 Rehov Tel Chi, is a recent club, highly recommended. There are two discothèques, charging about IS15 including the first drink: the **Don Camillo,** at 2 Smilansky St. and the **To Hell,** 1 Smilansky St. A disco just for students and teenagers is the **Bar-Orion,** 31 Herzl St., for young adults; a nice place with no hard drinks, record music, minimum cover charge.

Gaily-bedecked horses pull carriages around town for an unusual form of sightseeing; sherut service is frequent and good as well as the local bus service. **National Brewery Ltd.,** located here, offers visitors free beer, guided tours, gift shop, etc., in its hospitality center at the brewery, east of Abir (Poleg) Junction.

USEFUL NUMBERS. Most tourist activities are staged in and about the hotels; check with **Tourist Administration Office,** Kikar Haatzmaut, tel. (053) 27286.

Police: 100. **First-aid:** 3333. **Taxis:** *Hasharon* 23838, *Ritz* 23383. *Hashahar* 24645, *Jerusalem Sherut* (also Hasharon) 23838.

NAHARIYA

Often called "Honeymoon Headquarters" as it's a favorite place for newly-weds and lovers, this is a resort town with 30,000 population (originally German). Today it's also a UN (UNIFIL) R & R town.

HOTELS. The 4-star hotel is the 99-room **Carlton,** right on the main street, with a posh nightclub, heated pool, and tennis. The 3-star **Eden** has 50 rooms and a piano bar, and the **Pallas Athene,** near the beach, has 53 rooms with TV, billiard room, health club, sauna, nightclub and bar. The **Astar** has 26 rooms; the **Frank** has 50 rooms, plus TV and fine kosher food. Local 2-star hotels are air-conditioned and have restaurants: the 35-room **Rosenblatt,** the 28-room **Karl Laufer** and the 20-room **Kalman.** New and not yet graded, but with 2-star prices, **Panorama** had room TV on request for all 25 rooms. **Beit Erna** is the sole 1-star hotel, 11 rooms, partly air-conditioned, showers.

In the vicinity is a camping site, **Cabri,** with bungalows, tents, restaurants, telephone, provisions for sale, hot showers, first-aid station, electricity, gas, fridges, swimming. Also nearby is **Beit Hava,** a kibbutz guest house, 3-star, with 92 rooms, a pool, bar, coffee shop and restaurant.

RESTAURANTS. The **Penguin,** Gaaton Bd., is a lively café-restaurant with orchestra for dancing. The **Frank Hotel,** 4 Rehov Aliyan, has good kosher cooking. Dancing weekends in the bar at the **Carlton.** Tea-dancing at the **Eden Hotel,** Jabotinsky Street.

ENTERTAINMENT. A kids' **Amusement Park** with special boat rides lies near the beach at the end of the river running through town. Near ancient Astarte Temple ruins, look for the heated swimming pool (entrance: IS10) at the well-tended, free **Galei Galil Beach.** A water sports center here rents sail boats and other equipment, daily, summer and winter.

Bacall Riding Academy, near the police station, supplies boots free. Horseback excursions to the Crusaders' castle, Montfort. Moonlight rides. Open Saturdays, **Bicycle Rental** from Rudi Stern, Gaaton Blvd.

GIFTS AND SOUVENIRS at *Maskit,* Municipality Way. Fast **photo service:** *Nahariya Photo,* Municipality Way, and *Waelder,* and also *Ron,* both on Gaaton Boulevard. **Foreign newspapers:** *Paul Palk,* 28 Gaaton Boulevard.

WHAT TO SEE: On the way to Nahariya: the **Roman-Turkish aqueduct** and the **Kabri springs** that flowed into it; the house and grounds of Baha-Ullah, Behai sect founder; the **Museum of Nazi Atrocities** in the *Lohamei Hagetaot kibbutz,* founded by the survivors of the Warsaw ghetto. In Evron (Nahariya), the ruins of one of Israel's earliest **Byzantine churches.** Near Nahariya beach, the ruins of **Astarte's Temple,** one link in the chain of Phoenician vestiges along the coast; in Achziv, the ruins, **Memorial Bridge.**

Mr. Sassoon Levy, *Municipality Tourist Office,* room 28 of the Municipality Bldg., arranges for tourists to visits concerts in nearby kibbutzim, and to meet friendly local townsfolk (about 400 tourists take advantage of this each month). For $8.50, you can lunch with kibbutzniks at **Kibbutz Beth Haemeg,** enjoy a tractor or trailer ride across their banana, orange and avocado plantations, then break to their lounge for coffee, tea and cakes, and talk.

TOURIST INFORMATION. In **Egged Bus Station,** tel. (04) 922126. **Taxi:** Arie, 922922.

OTHER COASTAL SPOTS

ASHDOD. This fast-growing port city is big on immigrants but somewhat short on tourist facilities, but it does have a great beach.

HOTELS. The handsome **Miami** (3-star) is right on beach, 38 rooms with bath or shower, partly air-conditioned, restaurant, nightclub, bar, coffee shop. The 33-room **Orly,** on Nordau St., also has a coffee shop and piano bar.

BAT YAM. A thriving large suburb of Tel Aviv, this beachside resort town and newcomer-absorption center offers quiet, relaxing vacations.

HOTELS. The 3-star **Panorama** has 44 rooms, and **Armon Yam** (3-star) has 66; both are air-conditioned and have bars. **Royal,** not yet graded, has 297 air-conditioned rooms with baths, plus health club, sauna, pool, tennis, coffee shop, etc.

In the 2-star grade are the 20-room **Bat Yam,** the 20-room **Bosforus,** the 23-room **Palm Beach** and the 27-room **Via Maris;** all are air-conditioned. Then there's the 2-star **Sarita,** with 10 rooms, showers or baths.

The **Municipal Tourist Information Office** here is at 43 Rehov Ben Gurion, (051) 889766. **Eldan Rent-A-Car** is nearby, (051) 22284.

CAESAREA. This modern resort town lies on an ancient site with important ruins and a fine summer festival.

HOTELS. Dan Caesarea Hotel, one of the most beautiful in Israel was, until 1967, the property of Baron de Rothschild. Now run by the Dan chain, it is still an experience to stay here. It is a 5-star 110-room hotel and boasts the only 18-hole golf course in the country, and has tennis, bicycles, horseback riding, pool, fishing, underwater sports center. One of Israel's most expensive and elegant hotels. Totally renovated in 1980, it also offers room TV, sauna, health club and bar.

In a different price category is the kibbutz-run Caesarea bungalow colony, **Kayit Veshait Short Resort,** 55 rooms, part air-conditioned; private beach, tennis courts; self-service restaurant.

Nearby camping at **Bitan Aharon.**

RESTAURANTS. The Caesarea Development Corporation recently took over operation of the concessions in the fortress port: including the **Straton** restaurant—good, but expensive. At night, watch the romantic floodlights play on the minaret, the fortress ruins and the onrushing breakers. The same sights are yours at **Chez Charly** restaurant, with 8-12 summer hours; 9-5 winter. More a milk bar and pizza spot, it draws big local crowds. The **Harbour Citadel Restaurant** *(Mitzudat)* sits high above an art gallery, has great views and wonderful self-service buffet, plus waitress service. **Herod's Palace** is a new restaurant/nightclub (live music).

ACHZIV. Fascinating ancient site, ruins, on beach.

HOTELS. The **Club Méditerranée** village stretches along a wide, lagoon-spotted beach. Only advance arrangements accepted for its 250 rooms.

Gesher Haziv kibbutz guesthouse has 60 air-conditioned rooms, plus pool, bar, beach, tennis, coffee shop and restaurant.

Nearby **Yad Layad Youth Hostel** has 300 beds, full family accommodations, hot showers, telephone, and three meals available daily.

Achziv Camping, 100 yards from the sea, rents bungalows, tents and caravans in the shade of tall eucalyptus trees. Camping at **Lehman** is run by the Lehman Moshav, offering the same facilities. Both camps are near the Grotto Sulam Tzor—see Rosh Hanikra.

ROSH HANIKRA. Hotels. Below this Lebanon frontier spot, try accommodations at the **Hanikra Kibbutz Guest House,** among mountain scenery, with pool, good food, and 57 rooms. The **Rosh Hanikra International Vacation Village** is nearby. Franco-Israeli, it is a members-only area, with 80 rooms; 270 beds, primarily for families. For prices and membership, write **Le Village** POB 350, Rosh Hanikra.

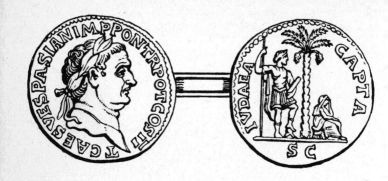

HAIFA AND ACRE

Modern Center, Ancient Fortress

Etched into the mountainside, overflowing in every direction, and finally spilling onto the flat coastline that's lined with fine sandy beaches, the city is most beautiful when viewed from the deep natural bay cupping between Haifa and Acre, or when seen from atop Mount Carmel.

To the east, the suburbs are tucked among the hills. Southwards, Mount Carmel thrusts forth peaks that eventually melt into fertile plains and valleys of the Galilee: the portions of land allotted to Issachat and Naphthali, while Zebulon and Asher established their tribes in the north—also Galilee region.

Officially, Haifa is on three levels: the port below, the main town area—Hadar-ha-Carmel—in the middle, and ha-Carmel at the top. Actually, there's more, including Ahuza, a sort of upper suburb, plus the Technion and University of Haifa complexes striding other peaks overlooking the bay—small cities in themselves. Altogether, these comprise one of Israel's most populous cities (228,000), today a far cry from the way-station it was at the turn of the century, when Jaffa was the land's main port and a sleepy Acre was the only important city this far north.

When the British arrived, they immediately took advantage of the fine natural harbor by starting to dredge right away. Now, for some 40 years, Haifa has been Israel's leading seaport. It's also an excellent jumping-off point for trips into the Galilee, and as such, caters to an ever-rising demand as an international congress and convention center. German colonists settled Haifa from the end of the 19th century, giving the city its distinctively solid, well-ordered appearance.

Today, Haifa's citizens are fiercely chauvinistic. They are convinced they live in Israel's most beautiful city. Though some listeners might shrug or start to discuss other beautiful places, almost nobody would argue about Haifa's cleanliness. In a land of inveterate litterers, the city owes its tidy look to a past and beloved mayor, Aba Khoushy, who waged a campaign against litter until his death. Since then some folk may mutter under their breath about it, but they still knock themselves out trying to keep things clean. What's all the more amazing about this cleanliness is that Haifa's often considered an industrial town—and it's true that factories, plants, blast furnaces and such crowd the northern sector and impose themselves on views of the bay and suburbs. Furthermore, the bay is the key port and has heavy traffic with constant bustle and commotion; cranes, noises and smells. All this activity, and the cleanliness and staunch, sturdy architecture, tend to give Haifa a quite solid-as-a-rock atmosphere, despite the beauty of the natural scenery.

A Glimpse of History

Nobody has ever pinned down the etymology of Haifa's name conclusively. If the word *yafé* occurs to you, meaning "fine" or "beautiful" in Hebrew, that's already been spoken for by Jaffa. One group claims that the city was founded by Caiphas, and for a long time the place was called Caifa.

The Bible doesn't mention Haifa by any name, though this area was certainly important during biblical times, and the Song of Songs notes its sheer beauty.

There's no reference to Haifa in the Talmud until the third century A.D. Haifa had barely gotten off to some sort of start under the Arabs when the Crusaders arrived. As always happened in such cases, Haifa got destroyed, even though it wasn't half as important then as St. John of Acre.

In the nineteenth century, under Turkish rule, the Haifa-Damascus railway was built and the city acquired its first real prominence. But it was mainly under the impetus of the Zionist influx that Haifa finally blossomed into an important city. Its real development began with the British. They took up where the Turks had left off, expanded and modernized the port, and built an oil refinery in Haifa, which is a pipeline terminus. Later, when the British had left and the Arab countries had altered the course of the flow of black gold, Eilat took over and supplied the refinery.

People still discuss with deep feeling Haifa's role beginning in 1939 with the publication of the British White Paper that restricted Jewish immigration. The shipwreck of the *Struma*, with only one survivor out of 764 passengers, the explosion of the *Patria* right in the harbor—with 250 dead out of 1,080 "illegal" immigrants who had been sentenced to deportation by the mandatory authority—the countless tragedies splotching the record of those who forced the human blockade—none of this has ever been forgotten. In those dark days, the little ships that managed to elude the long arm of the British law and its patrol boats stopped at secret landing spots along the coast to put ashore their clandestine cargoes of immigrants and refugees who had escaped the concentration camps. But the ships captured by the British remained under guard in Haifa's bay, under the hot sun. The outstretched arms of their brethren in distress, the pleading lamentations of these unfortunates who, so close to their cherished goal, were being ruthlessly turned back, all this deeply affected the people of Haifa. After 1948, their rejoicing knew no bounds when, finally, immigrants could disembark freely.

Boats from the Beginning

Starting a tour from the port, the bustle and commotion as you stroll along the embarcadero enhance the fascination of the shifting scene. You can tour the harbor by boat—for 30, 60 or 90 minutes, depending on whether you include only the port facilities, or also want to see the auxiliary port at the Kishon River mouth and the 10,000-ton floating dock. And in this region where wild wheat first appeared, you can take a fascinating trip to the "Museum of Grain" in Dagon silo at the harbor entrance. For a long time this tower was Israel's tallest structure.

And while you've still got your sea legs, pull off to one side, hoist yourself up three decks, and have a look at the Maritime Museum, now located at 198 Allenby Road. This rather unusual museum was conceived and pushed to completion against all sorts of obstacles by Ben Elie, an ex-Israel naval officer. The background story is interesting. Ben Elie's hobby was ship models, and he began by exhibiting his personal collection under the sponsorship of the municipality. The displays now trace the development of navigation in the Middle East from prehistoric times, and include tiny carved figures of members of crews manning the decks of miniature vessels. Some of the items are originals; others are copies of models from various periods of history. The models of Egyptian funeral barges from 4,000 years ago are particularly interesting. In the former premises, if he thought he was dealing with someone who genuinely appreciated the museum, the director would personally trouble himself to shift furniture around in order better to display certain objects that had been crowded into corners for lack of space. His hospitality might include an invitation to come into the den that he used as an office. Coffee was served along with an extraordinary flotsam and jetsam of old maps, globes, and ancient prints amid the indescribable jumble of anchors, chains, and sextants. The conversation touched on ship models, historical events, and scientific discoveries. His ambition was to move into surroundings more commensurate with his treasures, and the new Maritime Museum on Allenby Road provides a splendid setting for all those interested in the sea and ships to share his dream.

Hadar and Jaffa Road

One of Haifa's biggest bookshops is Steimatzky's on Haatzmaut Street, and nearby are a number of modern-style ice-cream parlors and quick-lunch places. A block farther into the city is Jaffa Road, where pottery, copper, and souvenirs sell for less than in the central Hadar section. By the way, the black market operates in the open around the port area, so don't be concerned about all those fellows trying to sell you everything from watches, transistors, fine toothpaste and razors to denims, lingerie and shirts. The Carmelit station (*Paris* stop) is three blocks north on Jaffa Road. In the opposite direction, past the central bus station and the railway station, you move out onto the beginnings of the main highway to Tel Aviv where a ship has been parked alongside the road. Named the *Af-al-pi* ("nevertheless" is a good translation), this ship ran the British blockade, loaded with immigrants. It now stands opposite Elijah's Cave, on the grounds of the Illegal Immigration and Naval Museum, on Rehov Yafo.

Walk across the street from City Hall and enjoy the extraordinary view from Independence Park. Go up Herzl Street, the main thoroughfare, past butchers' shops, cafés, and shoe stores. At Herzl and Balfour Streets you enter the old Technion campus, now used for Technion-sponsored seminars and meetings, special courses. It looks like a Sultan's Palace—and for good reason. It was originally built during the Ottoman reign (1912) by an organization of German philanthropists. The Germans, who were helping to build roads and buildings throughout the fast declining Ottoman Empire, hoped to train Jewish engineers here who would go on to work for the Turks. But the classes never got started: the Germans insisted on German as the language of instruction, but the Jewish students wouldn't hear of any other language but Hebrew. Both student and faculty went on strike—and then came the war. Best *felafels* and *shwarmas* in Haifa are sold at the stands on Haneviim Street, diagonally across from the Hadar post office.

The new Haifa Museum Center, 26 Rehov Shabtai Levi, houses the Museums of Ancient Art (collections through 7th century). Modern Art, and Ethnology (Jewish and Mid-Eastern)—worth a long visit. Then back to the funicular, the Carmelit, which runs partly underground.

No matter how hackneyed it may sound, the fact is that everything is marvelous on Mount Carmel. You'll see the Merkaz, the business district, all blooming with flowers, and Panorama Road, the upper ridge road lined with private homes and hotels. The Dan Hotel has a café-restaurant in a big circular room fittingly called "The Rondo." Go there in the early evening to watch the sunset and see the lights go on all over Haifa. You must wait while the millions of light bulbs, the signal lights and the garlands of deck-lights on the ships at anchor in the bay shine forth on the water, and the headlights of moving cars flash their zigzag patterns through the streets. Totally ethereal. Better still, order 7 A.M. breakfast to your private Dan balcony, then tan *au naturel* as you eat, while drinking in the fabulous view. Great sight from a boat, too: A.M. or P.M.

Halfway up the Carmel slope you'll see a big golden dome with a gleaming gilt cupola. This is the Bahai Temple. Haifa is the world center for the Bahai ("glory" in Persian) sect, which has several million followers. Persia, its founder's native country, prohibited the sect, and publicly executed Mirza Ali Mohammed in 1850. He had called himself "El-Bab," the portal, signifying the gateway of communication with the Supreme Being. His remains have been transferred here. Bahai's prophet, Baha-Ulla, is interred near Acre, where the Turks held him prisoner for 24 years.

Many non-Moslems in other lands have joined the Bahai faith. What do Bahais believe? Basically, they advocate unity and brotherhood, goals they believe are attainable through a common world language and religion. They view the prophets of the great religions—Moses, Jesus, Buddha, and Mohammed—as messengers of God, one and all, sent to different parts of the world at different times in history. To the Bahai, all the world's religions preach the same basic doctrine—brotherhood, love and charity. Religion, say the Bahais, should bring men together, not raise barriers between them. The herald of this faith, El-Bab, is buried in the domed temple; the Corinthian-styled building, across the Persian Gardens, houses the library and archives.

Don't overlook the public parks in the Merkaz, in the central part of the Carmel. The Gan-Ha'em, or Mothers' Garden, and the Zoological Garden are particularly renowned. Every year at Passover the city organizes a flower show which attracts visitors from all over Israel, and

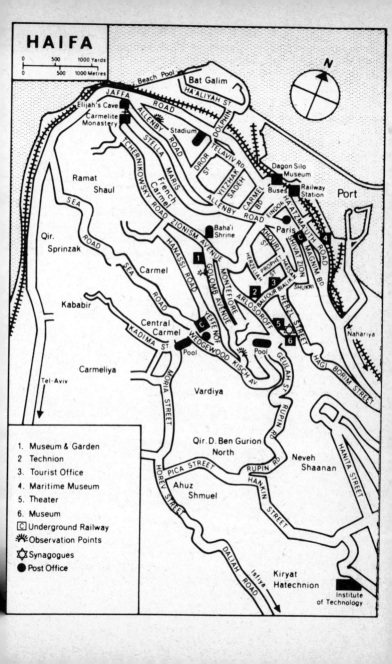

which travelers go out of their way to see. There's also a Museum of Japanese Art up here, 89 Sderot Hanassi Street.

A Sculpture Garden, in a natural setting overlooking the bay, has 17 bronzes by Ursula Malbin: opposite 135 Zionism Avenue. Near Panorama Observation Point is the Mané Katz Museum, in the late artist's home: 89 Yefe Nof Street.

The name Carmel may be a contraction of *Karem-El,* "The Vineyard of God." The prophet Elijah was no stranger to these haunts, specifically those of the French Carmel. Certain religious orders under French authority, mainly the Carmelites, became the proprietors of the place. Several monasteries and convents are dedicated to the fiery defender of the original monotheistic faith. Elijah is supposed to have challenged Baal at El-Muhraka, the southernmost point of the Carmel ridge. A good road now leads to El-Muhraka, which lies behind Haifa slightly north.

At the base of Mt Carmel is a grotto sacred to Jews, Christians, Moslems: Elijah's Cave—where the prophet supposedly fled from the wrath of Queen Jezebel and King Ahab. Christians regard it as the School of the Prophet where he taught; some also believe the Holy Family sheltered here when returning from Egypt.

As one more place of interest, we should list here the *Stella Maris* monastery, the buildings of which are now the headquarters of Israel's navy.

Taking advantage of your presence in Ahuza, explore this southern residential quarter of the city, along with Neveh Shaanan, a housing development set amid gardens. To go back to the beach, take the Tel Aviv road. The shore and pools aren't far from the mound on which the ancient Sycaminos of the Greeks stood, now called Shikmona. You're already somewhat acquainted with this neighborhood—it's near Elijah's Grotto.

The Environs

Excursions from the center of town include the Institute of Technology (Technion) and its grounds, a good 15 minutes' drive up into the mountains. The road is like a scenic railway, up hill and down dale. (Bus 19 from Hadar.) The Institute includes residence halls, administrative offices and, of course, facilities for teaching technical and scientific studies, law, medicine and many other subjects, plus 40 research institutes. Nearby, the University of Haifa sprawls, with living and study facilities for 25 departments.

One intriguing excursion is a visit to the Druse villages of Daliyat el Carmel and Isfiya. (Bus 92.) There you'll find several shops catering to local and tourist trade. Israelis go out of their way to shop here for furniture pieces, rugs, basketware, native fur throws and items, wall hangings hand-stitched and woven.

The Druse are a unique people, with a secret religion that supposedly incorporates parts of Islam, Judaism, Christianity and perhaps more. Fierce fighters, loyal members of Israel Defense Forces and Border Patrol units, they are anti-Arab in a very personal way—so even if you think they appear to be Arabs, it's best not to mention it. If you look at the men's headgear, you'll notice it's pure white, minus the black cord usually worn by Arabs and Moslems. There are many other subtle differences in clothing of both men and women—who seem to prefer white with bright colours like green, orange and purple and gracefully drape veils over their heads without covering their faces—and in their modes of life.

Walking around the villages, you'll see people working in agricultural chores, building new houses, engaged in activities that blend ancient and modern ways. Babies are carried straddling their mothers' stomachs and conveniently supported by crossed maternal hands. Druse houses are, traditionally, gaudy with many colors, blue predominating—it's equally effective against the evil eye, wicked spirits and flies. In these villages today, however, so many new and large modern homes have sprung up that one becomes hard-pressed to find all the old traditional native housing. Economic blessings have also brought in predominantly Western garb. And as the 20th century irrepressibly invades such villages, they all will disappear soon—absorbed into today's world, for better or worse. One medium for fast assimilation is television, and the flocks of antennae you'll see perched atop the houses here receive not only Kol Israel TV broadcasts, but also Arab programs from neighboring countries—just like most Israeli homes!

The landscape couldn't be wilder, and you find yourself held in its grip. At a stone's throw from Daliyat, Isfiya enjoys a superb view. You see a sweeping horizon, including Haifa bay, the coastline stretching beyond Acre, eastern Galilee nearly as far as Safad, and the tallest peak of the Carmel ridge, Rom Hacarmel.

At the end of Mount Carmel's Rehov Kadima is another village: Kababir. Its people are Moslems of the Ahmadiya sect, founded in India in 1889 by Achmed el Kadiania.

Back at the base of the steep Carmel, you'll find a site dating to biblical times: Shiqmona Tel, on the coast. Named for the "shiqma" (sycamore) tree which once grew hereabouts, this ancient township is still under excavation, but some of its "found" items can be seen at the Haifa Museum.

The Heritage of Zebulon

At the time the country was divided up among the twelve tribes, one of Jacob's sons, Zebulon, received the plain north of Haifa up to Acre—Akko—and his name has remained attached to his land. For the first eight miles on the way out of Haifa, heading north, you see nothing but factories and housing developments.

To your right flourishes a kibbutz, Kfar Masaryk, founded by Czechoslovakian immigrants. You cross the Naaman River, actually a stream, which the Greeks called Belos. According to a legend, when Hercules was suffering from a blood infection after his fight with the hydra, he came here to gather herbs with which he concocted an antidote called Aki—which became Ako, and later Akko. Pliny tells of the survivors of a shipwreck who were washed ashore on this stretch of beach. While cooking a frugal meal they accidentally stumbled on the process that led to glassmaking.

The Naaman-Belos river was once the frontier between Zebulon and Asher, and Acre began on the opposite shore. It had great fisheries, which were so renowned that a popular saying of the time was "It's like carrying fish to Akko," just as Englishmen speak of "coals to Newcastle."

Acre: Fortress to Many Empires

Even if they didn't do things the way everybody else did, the Greeks at least had a word for it: they called Acre "Ptolemais." In order to retrieve a semblance of its previous name, Acre had to wait for the Knights Hospitallers of St. John to get firmly ensconced with its walls, at which point it became known as St. John of Acre. Over the centuries the city withstood 17 sieges. Although it did finally fall to Asher (JUDGES I, 31), it held out against Simon Maccabeus 1,000 years later, and against Napoleon 20 centuries after *that*. During the First Crusade, Acre capitulated to the overwhelming force of an amphibious landing by the Genoese fleet. Saladin also captured Acre after inflicting a severe defeat on the Christians at the Horns of Hittin. However, Richard the Lion Heart and Phillip-Augustus of France managed to wrest it from the infidel, and hence it belonged to Christendom for fully 100 years before being relinquished definitively to the Moslems.

By something like historical coincidence, the last time Acre yielded to assault was, as in the First Crusade, under the brunt of a combined land and naval operation. However, there was one striking difference: this time the Jews were the besiegers, and they won the day. Acre today has a population of 35,000, including 5,000 Arabs, Christians, and

Moslems, plus a few Druse and Bahais. Many men have made names for themselves at Acre, some of whom are virtually unknown to the Western world, such as Daher el-Amar, a Bedouin sheik who in 1750 rescued the city from the total abandon in which the Turks had left it. Another personage, perhaps more infamous than famous, was Ahmed el-Jazzar, the eighteenth-century Turkish governor who bequeathed to posterity his dual heritage of brutality and imposing monuments.

Since those times, the port of Acre has gradually become sand-filled, and the city has declined as Haifa has progressed. People from Haifa come here on Saturdays, their Sabbath day of rest, to enjoy the swimming, visit the crusader excavations and to devour *humus, tehina, felafel,* and broiled fish in Abu-Cristo's picturesque seashore restaurant. Still others come from greater distances and are bent on more serious pilgrimages. Rare indeed are the families who didn't suffer from having a brother, a son, or a father imprisoned in the British citadel-prison in Acre. In fact, it was right here that the Jewish resistance organization staged the most spectacular escape of recent history, grippingly depicted in the motion picture made from the novel *Exodus.* In this somber building, which has now been converted into a mental hospital, a small museum recalls the times of those underground fighters.

Left largely to its own devices, the city of Acre has preserved its special personality and remained romantic and alluring, like a thriving captive held prisoner in its own ancient ramparts, steeped in the waters of the Mediterranean, in Arab dwellings, in its *souk,* and in its very traditions. It is a fortified peninsula so deeply entrenched as to be almost voluntarily shut off from the outer world's march of progress.

Of Streets and Shops

Meandering through Acre's streets is as enjoyable a pastime as visiting any of its monuments. Whether the city's prevailing mood is lively and boisterous or calm and quiet, the kaleidoscope of the passing scene fully grips your attention. On all sides, traces left by Crusaders and Moslems alike are natural attractions beyond the wildest dreams of any chamber of commerce. You're not likely to get the two mixed up, since the Christians doted on enormously thick walls and the Arabs stuck to their hermetically sealed dwellings. An Arab house is mostly a low-slung cube with a cunningly unobtrusive exterior as if specifically designed to foil the nefarious intentions of sorcerers, and its street door looks as if it's permanently shut tight, with nary a window, not even an opening with an iron grating over it. If you're lucky, you may just happen to pass by when a door is slightly ajar, revealing a fleeting tantalizing glimpse of the secluded inner maze of courtyards, gardens, and apartments. A refreshing wave of cool air drifts out from the green patio, and the murmuring babble of fountains reaches your ear.

As in any self-respecting Arab town, the streets in Acre converge onto the market, or *souk* (you'll hear some people pronounce it "shouk"). The dense throngs mill about wherever there's space.

It's quite likely that the shopkeepers have grown wise in the ways of tourists and are deliberately contriving to keep their neighborhood's Eastern flavor alive. Whatever the case, it's a huge success. There are flourishing oases in the form of small cafés, delicatessens with meat roasting under the customer's attentive gaze, pastryshops with baclavas swimming in cloying sweet syrup to tempt the passing palate.

At the entrance to the *souk,* the well-known name of "Woolworth" in front of a little hole-in-the-wall establishment hits you in the eye. The boss speaks eleven languages, his wife only eight. The shop next to it has about the same set-up, except for a difference in name. You stick one foot in the door and glance casually around at the usual sundry oddities and bric-à-brac, until the sight of the big samurai sword gives you a turn: what's *that* doing here? You stick your other foot in and find yourself exchanging pleasantries, being welcomed as a friend of the family, your hostess already busy brewing the inevitable cup of coffee. You protest, but your hosts will have none of it—they out-protest you! And so it goes. You inquire about a price, they wring their hands and roll their eyes in anguish—you're insulting them! At least have the decency to drink your coffee first, if you simply have to talk business.

When you've finally made your getaway, laden with purchases, there's a small boy waiting outside to tug your coat-tails and insist that you come with him because he has something important to show you. You wonder if he's merely herding you to his uncle's shop inside the walls, where there are *souks,* but once again your resistance is overcome, you're charmed by so much self-assurance in one so young, and besides, why shouldn't a sucker also be *reborn* every minute? Most likely, you'll find the boy will lead you over to a nearby column and solemnly swear that this is the very spot at which Napoleon threw down his hat. He will then add, drawing himself up with all the full dignity of a *mullah,* "You need guide. I find guide. Ten pound, okay?" And so you find yourself putty in the hands of the little boy's big brother, who is waiting to steer you through the hidden underground parts of the ramparts, the secret dungeon in which Ahmed the Butcher got his victims high on hashish before he slit their throats. Your self-appointed guide pauses in front of one part of the wall. "See? This is only six feet thick here—all other walls 90, 150 feet thick. If Napoleon knew, he attack here. Whole world different today!" You repress a querulous impulse to murmur, "So that's why he threw down his hat?"

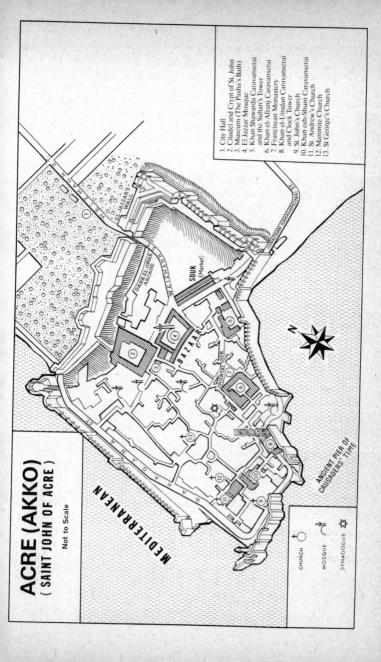

ACRE (AKKO)
(SAINT JOHN OF ACRE)

Not to Scale

MEDITERRANEAN

EL JAZZAR'S WALLS

DAIR EL-OMAR ARCADE

WA'IZMAYIN

SOUK (Market)

BAZAAR

ORIENTAL SOUK

HAGANA

EL-JAZZAR (HAMIFRATZ)

WEIZMANN (HA'ATZMAUT)

ANCIENT PIER OF CRUSADERS' TIME

N

1. City Hall
2. Citadel and Crypt of St. John
3. Museum (The Pasha's Bath)
4. El Jazzar Mosque
5. Khan Shawarda Caravanserai and the Sultan's Tower
6. Khan el-Afranj Caravanserai
7. Franciscan Monastery
8. Khan el-Umdan Caravanserai and Clock Tower
9. St. John's Church
10. Khan esh-Shuni Caravanserai
11. St. Andrew's Church
12. Maronite Church
13. St George's Church

CHURCH   MOSQUE   SYNAGOGUE

In the first place your guide isn't interested in comments, and besides, he's already off on another tack.

And now you've been playing truant long enough, time to pay up. Ah! A slight misunderstanding about the price? You agreed on ten pounds? Sure ten pounds— *sterling!*

The Mosque of the Butcher

The regular entrance charge to official monuments via conducted tours is a flat rate. Your tour will probably begin with a visit to *Jami-el-Jazzar,* the mosque of Ahmed the Butcher, recently restored by the government to its pristine state. Built in 1781–2 by Ahmed el-Jazzar, Pasha of Acre, it supposedly tops the site of Acre's Cathedral Church, St. Croce, and its courtyard definitely straddles vaulted Crusader structures. Before entering, don't worry about removing your shoes, but do be sure you are dressed modestly, and do not step on carpets, reed mats or wood planks. Inside, you find yourself in a lovely, palm-decorated quiet courtyard, its whitewashed walls graced with proud arches. A Koranic Institute runs the entire length of one wall. The mosque itself is all the way in the back, looking somehow dwarfed by the other buildings. Inside, you enter a vast, bare high-ceilinged chamber with rugs covering the floor. Oblivious of everything around him, a solitary Arab is absorbed in his prayers. There is a holy relic enshrined here, a single hair from the beard of the Prophet. Take a good look at the columns, which came from Caesarea, and maybe also from Ashkelon.

The *Municipal Museum* is now housed in what were once the pasha's Turkish baths, the Hammam-el-Basha, erected by our indefatigable builder friend, or fiend, Ahmed el-Jazzar. The museum's exhibits are devoted to the folklore and everyday objects of past and present inhabitants, including Crusaders. Its annex features ceramics, coins, and other articles of daily use, all of which were dug up in the course of excavations right here at Acre. Nearby is the *Knight's Stable,* recently restored to reveal soaring original Crusader arches—now a place to shop for art and souvenirs.

We have the Crusaders to thank for the *Crypt of St. John,* which is the room in which the kings of France and England held their war councils. It is located just opposite the Museum's exit. Some 25 feet of rubble separate this great hall from the exterior street level. Everything about it seemed to suggest that this was a likely place for digging—the size of the ogival arches, the ten-foot-thick walls. This expectation was more than confirmed by the discovery of a glazed vessel embellished with a time-eroded cross, possibly the oldest cross of the Knights of St. John. There was no longer any possible doubt that this room was the refectory of the Knights Hospitallers. You advance into a tremendous Gothic hall containing two naves, classified by archeologists as a low room. There are also two consoles, adorned with *fleurs-de-lys* in relief. This emblem of France's royalty dates from a decree issued by Louis VII, who participated in the Second Crusade (1147–1149). Saladin and his heirs struck their coins with *fleur-de-lys* emblems. The most Christian kings merely lifted their ideas from the art of Islam!

As you enter the Crypt (the name by which the room will undoubtedly continue to be known), you perhaps do not realize that this is one of the oldest examples of Gothic architecture in the world. The basilica of St. Denis (1144), near Paris, antedates it by only four years. So far, the excavations here have disclosed three superimposed cities: Roman, Crusaders', and Turkish. Although these excavations are far from complete, a goodly portion of the lower Crusader buildings are showing.

The Turks erected their citadel on top of thirteenth-century Christian foundations. The Citadel Museum in the mental hospital contains the cell that confined Ze'ev Jabotinsky, who is revered for having organized the Jewish Resistance Movement between the two World Wars, well in advance of the events of 1944 through 1948. In the nineteenth century, these great walls sheltered still another distinguished captive, Baha-Ulla, the Bahai cult leader, who now lies buried near here.

The so-called "Turkish Tower" marks the entrance to the Khan el-Umdan, a vast courtyard with many porticos built over the ruins of a Dominican monastery. The word *khan* means caravanserai—inn or hostelry—and *umdan* means columns. The latter, too, were originally part of Caesarea. Another courtyard announces the Kahn el-Afranj, the Inn of the Franks or Inn of the Foreigners. Like the preceding one, this hostelry was built over the site of an earlier monastery. There is a third caravanserai, Khan el-Shawarda, flanked by the square Borj el-Sultan tower and by the Mosque of the Sand, Jamin el-Raml. Like the other two, this building rises over the foundations of a Christian monument, on which the lines of an ancient Latin inscription can still be deciphered: "Master Ebuli Fazie, builder of this chapel, exhorts all who pass this way to pray for the salvation of his soul."

The New Acre

And now for the new part of the city, including its Monument to the Dead and the promenade along the ramparts down by the port. The nearby beaches with their dazzling fine sand are protected by breakwaters, and swimmers may safely swim in the quiet sheltered waters here with no need for the protective presence of a lifeguard.

A new company, which aims at developing Acre's past for presentation to tourists, has started an interesting program called "Nights of Acre." The "Nights" may mean a Druse dance festival, a Hebrew folksong festival, or a night-time cruise along the coast. Hotels and travel agencies are kept posted with schedules during the summer.

Heading north on the main highway, lies a former Turkish *khan* that is now a stud farm. In a magnificently manicured Persian garden on your right stand the last residence and mausoleum of Baha-Ulla, the prophet of the Bahai sect. This is where he came to live in 1892, when he was nominally released after 24 years of confinement in the Acre prison. The impressive aqueduct running parallel to the highway is another of el-Jazzar's works, built over the foundations of an earlier Roman one that conveyed water from the Kabri springs to Acre. The countryside in the distance is the densely cultivated fields of the Hills of Galilee.

PRACTICAL INFORMATION FOR HAIFA AND ACRE

HAIFA

HOTELS. Just as the city is built on three levels, so are the Haifa hotels built into the three tiers—those in the port area (the least expensive), those in Hadar Ha Carmel, and those in the Carmel hills, more expensive and with majestic views of the city, port, Mediterranean and coastline going north to Acre. In the winter, when it rains, the heaters in the hotel rooms come in handy; in the summer, make sure to get an air-conditioned room, or aim for a Carmel hotel, where the breezes bring additional coolness.

Haifa has only one 5-star hotel—the luxurious 220-room **Dan Carmel,** with an immense lobby. The heated pool is next to a promontory that affords a splendid bay view; there's also a health club and sauna. Dome-ceilinged Rondo Room—nightclub, grill room—with its curved glass walls, looks like a flying saucer. Good, live jazz featured in the lobby bar. Many shops. Prices of the rooms vary with the height and the view of the bay; each room has a wall-size picture window opening to a fine balcony, the better to see the panorama picture below. David Ben Gurion always stayed in the Penthouse when in Haifa. Fine shops are here, a beauty parlor, bank, tour office, room TV and piano bar.

The **Shulamit,** 4-star, has 70 rooms with bath, air-conditioning and taped music and a terrace pine garden for drinks and coffee, as well as a glass-enclosed rooftop café for summer drinking and dancing.

Right next door to the Dan is the **Nof,** 100 rooms with bath, rising high for superb views. Air-conditioned, TV in rooms, not as posh as its older neighbor but eager and friendly. *Panorama Café* overlooking bay, plus dining rooms, bank, shops.

Yaarot Hacarmel is nearby on Mt. Carmel. A health resort with 103 rooms with bath, full health club facilities and staff, pool, TV, partial air-conditioning. (*Note:* not graded yet, but listed between 4-star and 3-star.)

In the Hadar area, "Haifa town," the 4-star hotel is the **Zion,** 5 Baerwald Street, the city's oldest first-class hotel, built in 1935. It is next to the Town Hall, two blocks from Herzl Street, the main thoroughfare. Its 94 rooms have Israeli-Oriental flavor; some face the bay, some view the mountains. Also room TV, bank, bar.

In the 3-star class of Carmel hotels, some charge for the rooms with a view, some don't. Good in this class are: **Dvir,** on Mt. Carmel, 39 air-conditioned rooms, and the **Ben Yehuda,** 59 rooms, partly air-conditioned, pool, bank, bar. **Carmelia** is on 35 Herzl St., with 50 rooms with baths; air-conditioning, TV, bar. The 26-room **Marom**, 51 Hapalmach St., **Romema**, opened 1980; not yet graded.

The 3-star **Kibbutz Guest House Beit Oren,** also on Mt. Carmel, has 82 rooms, bar, coffee shop and pool, plus a great friendliness in Israel's "Little Switzerland" mountain region. Other kibbutz guest houses in the area are 3-star **Nir Etzion,** on Carmel Beach, with 75 rooms, pool, bar, TV and coffee shop, self-serve and dining room eateries, sauna, and **Beit Hava,** with 92 air-conditioned rooms, beach, coffee shop, bar, and a fine pool, in nearby Shave Zion. Kibbutz-run **Dor Beach Shore Resort** sports 75 rooms on the Mediterranean coast with kitchenettes plus self-service dining.

Two-star hotels include: **Nesher,** 53 Herzl Street, 15 rooms with shower; **Lev Hacarmel,** 46 rooms partly air-conditioned, with bath or shower, no view, but wonderful tropical gardens; 24-room **Talpioth,** 61 Herzl Street—all on Mt. Carmel.

The 1-star **Lea,** on Mt. Carmel, has 10 rooms.

ISSTA, the Israel Student Travel Association, recommends several budget-priced lodgings, plus the students' Hostel in Technion City.

Carmel Youth Hostel has 400 rooms (singles or families) on Carmel Beach, air-conditioning, sports, 3 daily meals. Between Haifa and Nazareth are two Youth Hostels, both with single and family accommodations, kitchens, 2 served meals daily: 100-room **Tivon** at Kiryat Tivon, and 130-room **Young Judea,** at Ramat Yohanan, which also has swimming. **Tivon Camp** site rents bungalows, tents, has very good facilities, pool, etc. **Newe-Yam** camping at Carmel Beach, offers even more—worth checking.

Nearby **Christian Hospices** include: **Isfiya Sisters,** HaCarmel, Haifa (Evangelical Episcopal); **Sisters of St. Charles** (Order of St. Karl Borromaeus), 105 Jaffa Rd. (Roman Catholic, German), also serves lunches to groups; **Stella Maris Monastery,** Rehov Stella Maris, POB 9047 (Roman Catholic). Best to book all in advance by writing. (See pp. 11, 27.)

RESTAURANTS. Haifa has several first-class restaurants with prices from $10–$20 per person, and up, depending on the hour and your selections. But restaurants here are generally less costly than in other Israeli cities. The **Banker's Tavern,** 2 Habankim St., takes top honors for posh meals and delicacies, but also has a business lunch menu with special prices from 12–6 P.M., plus a well-tended bar and good service.

The **Balfour Cellar,** Balfour St., features Jewish and international cuisine; the **Rondo** in the Dan Carmel Hotel offers grilled and international specialties and the garden-restaurant **Gan Rimon,** 10 Sderot Habroshim (also on the Carmel) features European cuisine (lunch only); **Max & Moritz,** 139 Sd. Hanassi, serves anything from a cold drink to a full meal in a garden setting with a view.

For Chinese treats, the **Pagoda,** at 1 Bat Galim Ave., is often rated "Israel's Best" Chinese restaurant, despite its quite moderate fees for its special Central Chinese dishes; Shanghai cooking is the specialty at **Chin Lung,** 126 Hanassi,

Taiwan is the latest addition, at 59 Ben Gurion Avenue. **Cheung Sang,** 23 Balfour, serves Cantonese specialties.

In the (M) range there is quite a choice. In Hadar, the **1001 Nights;** the **Gan Airmon,** 16 Haneviim St., next to the cinema, serving breakfast, lunch and dinner, with perhaps the widest range of Oriental, European and dairy cuisine in town; the **Mataamim,** 24 Herzl St., for meat and dairy lunches; the **Quick Bar,** 15 Nordau St., really quick with good Viennese fare.

Up in the Merkaz section, two good European-style restaurants specialize in things like Swedish plates, goulash, schnitzel and kebab; the **Carmel,** opposite the Israel Discount Bank and **Café Peer,** Hanassi and Mahanyim Sts., an outdoor café, whose indoor walls are papered with magazine advertisements that show people eating. A good Oriental restaurant up here is the **Finjan,** 4 Mahanyim St., and a new favorite is **Fandu Club,** near Haifa Univ., a restaurant-cum-piano bar at 56 Antwerpen St.

Stella Maris, a cafe-restaurant on Tchernikovsky St. has home-style meals, great cakes and sweets, fabulous views. **London's Pride,** 84 Ha'atzmout, is a new, membership club that welcomes tourists from noon to wee hours. **Ron,** 139 Hanassi, serves exclusive European and Oriental dishes; also has a piano bar.

In Bat Galim, **Misadag** offers fish specialties, as does **Neptune**—19 Margolin Street. The **Iskander,** 8 Zionism Ave., is a popular Oriental eatery; open 7 A.M. to midnight. The **Rimini** (3 addresses: 20 Haneviim, 119 Sd. Hanassi, Romema's Derech Ruppin), serves good Italian food, and **Popolo,** 17 Sd. Ben Gurion, is new, extremely popular, with fine Italian menu. **Pininat HaMizrach,** 35 Sd. Ben Gurion, dishes out good Oriental fare, as does **Amron** and **Benny Ori** (Hadar), 23 Halutz St. Oriental and seafood specialties are found both at **Zvi,** 3 Hameginim, and at **Saleh Bros.,** 5 Hameginim.

Each Thursday evening in summer, folk flock to eat food of all nations at **Dvir Hotel.**

CAFÉS. Café-sitting is as popular in Haifa as it is all over Israel. Haifa's favorite cafés are the **Atara,** Balfour Street, the **Paris,** on a broad terrace overlooking the main intersection, and the **Strauss,** across the street, corner of Herzl and Balfour Streets. The **Ritz,** 5 Haim Street, is favored by artists and intellectuals. Across from the Dan hotel, try the new **Dan Carmel Sabra Coffee Shop.**

NIGHTLIFE. Dan Hotel has Saturday-night dancing in the Rondo Room (very romantic), plus really good jazz in lobby bar. **Exotica** (22 Zionism Ave.) is a restaurant and club, with a live band Fridays and Saturdays; disco other nights. **Max & Moritz** have a weekend piano bar, as does **Lev Hacarmel Hotel.** For students, there's **Technion Club 2.2, Univ. of Haifa,** and the **Academon.** For everyone: "Nights of Wine and Song"—with orchestra, dance troupes, performing artists, wine and cheese sold in booths—at **Gan Ha'em** (Mother's Garden), summer nights only, *free.* In Danya, Hod Hacarmel, **Danva**

Café-Bar and bar gathers good crowds regularly. The **120 Club** bar and disco, in an old Arab building at 120 Panorama St., entertains folks with a singing guitarist nightly. **Pianissimo** Club features fine piano music at 4 Shaar Lebanon St.

 ENTERTAINMENT. The Israel Philharmonic Orchestra, Haifa's Symphony Orchestra and Chamber of Music Ensemble, the Israel Opera, dance and theater groups can be seen at the new **Community Auditorium.** The **International Folklore Festival** usually brings hundreds of dancers, singers and musicians from Israel and abroad to perform in and around Haifa.

There is a theater club in the **Municipal Theater Building,** Joseph St., where entertainment blends East and West, plus strips.

For further details, check with IGTA, (04) 666521/3, the Rothschild Community Center, and the "What's On" 24-hour telephone service, (04) 640840.

 MUSEUMS. National Maritime Museum, 198 Rehov Allenby; Music **Museum & Ami Library,** 23 Rehov Arlosoroff and, in the Gan Ha'em at Rehov Hatishbi, the **Museum for Pre-History, Nature Museum and Zoo.** The **Bahai Shrine,** gold-domed temple in classic gardens, a neo-classic museum, archives. There's a **Museum Center,** 26 Shabtai Levi St.—including the **Museum of Ancient and Modern Art,** and the **Ethnology Museum** (Jewish Middle Eastern Art).

Other interesting museums: **Museum of Japanese Art,** 89 Sderot Hanassi; **Af-al-pi Illegal Immigration Museum,** in a blockade-busting ship now docked on southern slope of Carmel, near beach; the **Manè Katz Museum,** 89 Yafe Nof St., houses works of this famous Israeli painter from Haifa. The **Carmelite Monastery,** Rehov Stella Maris, displays a number of archeological finds. Close by is the **Cave of Elijah the Prophet. The Dagon Silo** has a fascinating museum of exhibits on the history of grains and cereals; guided tours. Sun. through Thurs. at 10.30 A.M.

Note: All Haifa museums are open Saturdays, free. Three-day Haifa tourists receive free pass for all museums.

THE ENVIRONS: Acre is just around the bay. **Ein Hod** artists' colony (bus 123); **Tel Shikmona,** still being excavated, is a site dating to biblical days (bus 43, 45, 47); **Druse villages** of Isfiya and Daliyat el Carmel (bus 52), and Moslem Village **Kababir** (bus 34) founded by India's Ahmadiya sect, 1889. **El-Muhraka,** with its Carmelite Monastery, has beautiful views and a picnic area—where Elijah battled Baal priests. Along the highway, 20 km from Haifa, is **Beit She'arim** ("the House of Gateways"). 1800 years ago the little town of Beit She'arim built on top of a cemetery, was headquarters of the Bet Din, the Jewish Supreme Court then. Buses 74 and 75 from rail station and Herzliya Street.

TOURS. Before you make final plans, we suggest you visit or write the **Haifa Tourism Development Association,** 10 Ahad Ha'am St. (tel. 04 645807). They give away "Haifa At Your Fingertips"—full of all sorts of tourist information, easy to use. Also ask for the "Discover Haifa By Yourself" brochure. And, of course, **IGTA** is also on hand with advice, maps, latest details on Haifa "Walking Tours" (33-language guide), special tours of the environs, etc.

ORGANIZED TOUR OPERATORS here are *Egged Tours, United Tours, Carmel Touring* and *Mitzpa Tours.* Half-day tours include Haifa city, Haifa and Acre, Caesarea and Tel Aviv, Acre with Western Galilee, and Rosh Hanikra. Full-day tours include Lower Galilee, Western Galilee, Upper Galilee and Golan, and Mount Carmel and Caesarea.

AIR TOURS are scheduled by *Kanaf/Arkia,* using 9-seater Islanders starting from Haifa airfield. Book in advance through Haifa Tourism Development Association or direct through *Kanaf/Arkia* (see p. 36).

BOAT TOURS for groups are scheduled regularly by *Open Boat Cruise Co.,* Fisherman's Dock, Kishon Port (bus 58). One covers harbor and bay (great views), another includes visit to Acre, across the bay. Book in advance, between March and September only.

SHOPPING. If *fur's* your thing, don't miss the *Fur Center, Kubnreich Bros.,* Herzl at Arlosoroff. It's a big building, with a branch of *Begged Or* —which also is at Central Carmel Center, the expensive new shopping area, with many tourist items.

Diamonds & Jewelry: *Rosenthal,* on Nordeau; *Haifa Trade and Exhibition Center Ltd.,* Sderot Hahistadruth; *Buxboum Jewelry,* 55 Herzl St., *Big Ben,* 7 Herzl St., *Noga Haifa,* 10 Zahal St.; *Mishkan Jewelry Center* with arts and crafts, too, 3 Balfour St. (*Note:* Diamonds and fine jewelry are particularly good buys in Israel, especially in Haifa.)

Ready-to-wear knit dresses and suits: *Donna,* 21 Herzl St., *Apart,* 2 Balfour St.; *Iwanir,* Dan Carmel Hotel; *Ilka,* 57 Herzl St.; *Ofnat Haifa,* 20 Herzl St.; *Maskit,* 6 Rehov Mahanayim (also arts and crafts). For the men: *K. Yahalomi,* 129 Sderot Hanassi, *Shalfi,* 16 Herzl St., made-to-measure, top workmanship; *Man,* 27 Herzl St.

Arts and crafts, gifts: *Chen,* 74 Haatzmaut St.; *Hetzroni,* 16 Herzl St.; *Venezia,* 10 Herzl St.; *Wizo Arts and Crafts Center,* 9 Nordau St.; *Keshatot,* 6 Nordau St. (also clothing). Antiques: *Goldman Art Gallery,* 93 Sderot Hanassi. *Hamashbir Department Store,* Shmaryahu Levin St., has everything.

Sports shop: *Magen, The Sport,* Bialik St.; *Ziniuk & Michlin,* 55 Haatzmaut. Records: *Blumenthal,* 1 Herzl St. Photography: *Mordehai,* 43 Herzl St. and nearby *Alexander.*

SPORTS. Swimming: Bat-Galim Pool. Hasheket Beach, Kiryat Haim Beach, or Municipal Bathing Beach which is free, near Carmel Beach, south of town.

Sailing: Rent sailboats, lessons free at Carmel Beach Sailing Club. Haifa Yacht Club. Details in *Facts at Your Fingertips* Chapter.

Diving: Scuba diving lessons, rental of gear, and underwater fishing expeditions, departing Tuesdays and Saturdays via Shikmona Diving Center (tel. 233908).

TRANSPORTATION. Intercity, see *Facts At Your Fingertips* Chapter. The **bus station** is new, with good facilities, and clean, located south of central city area, on coast road. **Train station** on Haatzmaut St., Kikar Plumer. **Sherut taxis** nearby and through town: *Aviv,* 666333, 6 Nordau St.; *Arie,* 66395, 15 Baerwald St.; *Kavei Hagalil,* 666450, 7 Rehov Hanaviim; *Mahir,* 664646, 1 Rehov Moshe Aharon.

Egged Buses operate even on Sabbaths (only place in Israel that they do!), give good service all over town and environs: bus for Isfiya and Daliyat el Carmel: 92. Bus for Ein Hod and Caesarea (Haifa-Hadera): 921. Buses for Acre (Akko): 251, 271. **Chauffeur-guides,** per *IGTA,* 666521, or *Dan Carmel,* 89245; *Mitzpa Tours,* 666898. **Taxi services:** *Aviv,* 666333; *Mitzpa,* 662525, 663883; *Carmel,* 82727/6. "Carmelit" funicular **subway,** from Paris Place, 6 stops, 8 minutes (Israel's only subway).

RELIGIOUS SERVICES. Roman Catholic: *Carmelite,* 80 Sderot Hameginim; *Stella Maris Monastery;* **Anglican:** *St. Luke's,* 2 Rehov St. Luke; **Jewish:** *Central Synagogue,* Rehov Herzl, Hadar, *Synagogue Hacarmel,* 10 Rehov Hayam; **Bahai:** *Bahai Temple* (headquarters for Bahai faith). Zionism Ave.

Note: For a complete list of area synagogues, mosques, and churches, check with IGTA.

USEFUL ADDRESSES. Tourist Information: *IGTA,* 18 Herzl St., tel. (04) 666521/3, and at Port Shed 12 (boat arrivals; ISSTA (Student Travel Office), 20 Herzl St., tel. 669139. **Airlines:** *TWA,* 53 Hameginim, tel. 535610; *Arkia* Israel Inland Airlines, 4 Ibn Sinah, tel. 667722; *British Airways,* 3 Rehov Habankim, tel. 535360; *El Al,* 80 Derekh Haatzmaut, tel. 640966. **Car Hire:** *Hertz,* 1 Palmer Square, tel. 665425; *Avis,* 20 Rehov Haatzmaut, tel. 665491; *Hi-Car,* 118 Haatzmaut Rd.; *Sa-Na,* 3 Tel Aviv St. **Useful phone numbers:** Information, 14. First-aid: (Magen David Adom) 101. Police: 100 Coming events tape, "What's On:" 640840.

ACRE (AKKO)

HOTELS. Palm Beach 4-star hotel and country club is big and impressive throughout. Flanked by shops and greenery, it has 136 rooms, heated pool, private beach, tennis, and full health club facilities, plus restaurants, bar, nightclub.

Next door, **Argaman Motel,** at Argaman Beach, features 75 3-room guest cottages, air-conditioned. Built on Israeli "beach village" lines, it also has a restaurant and bar.

Over in the Old City, a recent 120-bed **Acco Hostel** is near the lighthouse; well-equipped, with telephone and good transportation nearby. **Cabri** camping is near with bungalows, trailers, restaurant, good facilities.

RESTAURANTS. Abu Cristo, fine view over the bay; classic Arab dishes, seafood, grilled fish; reasonable. **Achim Ouda** in the souk, meat grilled over woodfires and flavored with Arab parsley (kesbon) delicious, not expensive. **Zor,** in the north of the new city, overlooks the sea and features Eastern and European cuisine. Orchestra in summer, on Fridays from 9 P.M. to 1, and sometimes extra entertainment. Good atmosphere; by day, it's a restaurant-marina.

Migdalor Restaurant, near the lighthouse in the Old City, specializes in well-prepared seafood such as calamari, shrimps, lobster.

WHAT TO SEE. Within the ancient city of Acre, note the **Mosque of Admed-el-Jazzar** (visit inside for IL1.50); the caravanserais, the **Crypt of St. John,** and the ramparts. There is a **concert** in *Knights Hall* every 2 weeks. Gallery situated in ancient stable.

Swimming is at *Argaman Beach* on the southern edge of town.

For **tourist information.** *Municipal Tourist Information Office,* at entrance to Subterranean Crusader City, tel. 04–910251; or through Haifa *IGTA*.

THE GALILEE

A Region of Extremes

Since the beginning of civilization, the Galilee has been a natural trade and migration route between Asia, Africa and Europe. As such, it has been the scene of countless battles for possession of the valuable linking territory. The Egyptians fought here, as did the Canaanites, the tribes of Israel, the Philistines, the Romans, Turks, Crusaders, Moslems as well as armies of both world wars. Scripture also predicts the last world battle will take place in the Galilee, at Megiddo—the ancient fortress also called Armageddon.

Perhaps more than any other territory on earth, the Galilee has been the focal point of events that have drastically affected the course of civilization from the establishment of customs, trade practices, economics, and laws for individuals and nations, to religious and philosophical beliefs and ideas, and even methods of government

278

management and warfare. Abraham first came to the Galilee, beginning the historical trek of monotheism. In two of Judaism's four holy cities (Tiberias and Safad), leading Jewish sages defined codes and calendars and wrote of mysticism. Jesus was born and often preached in the Galilee. Crusaders built chains of forts here and finally were dealt the crushing blow by the Saracen general, Saladin. After generations as a sleepy wasteland, strategic Galilee figured again in world confrontation when large numbers of modern Jewish pioneers came to settle. This area and its boundaries are crucially linked to many of the problems that currently beset not only the Middle East, but the entire world.

Any road you take here leads through sites of past and current significance, from the Jezreel Valley (running southeast of Haifa) all the way to Metulla (northernmost point of this tiny country), and from the Mediterranean's Rosh Hanikra (at the Lebanese border), to the far northern and eastern shores of the Sea of Galilee, under the shadow of the Golan Heights.

The Greening of the Galil

In this land of miracles, it seems that another has taken place just recently: the agricultural reclamation of the Galilee (in Hebrew, the *Galil*). While it remains an obvious feat to make a desert wilderness bloom, tourists to the Galilee might not realize the Herculean effort this involved.

Despite its association with warfare, this region has always been known for its plentiful water and rich fertile soil. Yet, as a result of centuries of neglect, succeeding conquerors, and sparse population, the once-green land became almost barren. Only a handful of small villages cultivated it, and their methods had been out-dated for thousands of years. Countless armies had stripped away the trees of Galilee, allowing top soil to erode and leaving the rolling hills studded with boulders. Water sources choked causing lowlands to become malaria-infested swamps.

In the mid-1800s the first modern Jewish settlers arrived in this desolate region. The land they bought was in such deplorable condition that it couldn't be worked by individual farmers. Nonetheless, the settlers were determined to become farmers, especially after withstanding generations of laws forbidding them to own land in foreign countries. Idealistically, they banded together in communal villages—*kibbutzim*—the first called Degania, on the southern rim of the Sea of Galilee. Then, with collective effort, they set about clearing the rocks and boulders, draining the swamps, irrigating and fertilizing the land with the latest scientific equipment and procedures, and planting crops that eventually thrived. Their careful cultivation and nurturing of the land extended to the re-creation of forests and nature reserves, and to planting soil-grasping shade trees along almost every road, old or new. Today, the Galilee is green again, and a joy to visit.

Some General Sights

Major roads in the region lead to the Sea of Galilee, an inland, fresh-water lake (also known as Yam Kinneret, Lake Tiberias, Genesareth and Gennosar). Its headlands are high in the northern territories of the Lebanon and Dan, where rivers rush down to feed falls and sometimes become mere trickling streams, such as those passing through the Huleh Nature Reserve. Some of these waters are channeled now to Israel's Negev, to irrigate southern deserts and wildernesses, but most finally empty into Lake Kinneret. At the southern tip of the lake, the Jordan River emerges and sweeps southward toward the Dead Sea region, passing along the Jordan Valley, the most disputed *emek* (Hebrew for "valley") of Galilee. The most renowned, lush *emek* is the Jezreel Valley.

Through the Jezreel Valley, a road leads from Haifa, skirting Mt. Carmel and the nearby Druze villages of Isfiya and Daliyat Hacarmel. Passing sleepy villages and prosperous collective farms, the road cuts through wheat and fruit lands toward Megiddo—the ancient stronghold on the caravan trail linking Mesopotamia with Egypt, also called the Via Maris. Here the road branches northeast to Afula, where several major roads cross and lead to a number of sites throughout the Galil. For example, you can go to Beit She'arim, with its Jewish catacombs; Beit Alfa and its old synagogue with delightful mosaics; Beit She'an, location of the country's finest Roman amphitheater ruin and well worth a visit—especially in July and August during the annual Israel Festival. Belvoir, Montfort and the Horns of Hittin are but three of the Crusader sites in Galilee. There are three sites sacred to Christian pilgrims overlooking Lower Galilee: Nazareth, Cana and Mt. Tabor. Near a communal farm called Zippori lies the biblical site of the same name, with interesting ruins of a Crusaders' church. Tabgha, Migdal, the Mount of Beatitudes and Capernaum await visitors to the northern shores of the Sea of Galilee.

The thriving, year-round vacation and spa-resort city of Tiberias retains the name it was dubbed when Herod Antipas rebuilt it as a lavish birthday present for Roman Emperor Tiberias. Situated on the southwestern shore of Lake Tiberias (that many-named mass of water), Tiberias is the Galil's largest city. From here, by land and by boat, you can visit all the shore areas, including Kibbutz Ein Gev on the eastern bank, which holds a music festival each spring. Degania, the first kibbutz, is located near Tiberias, and is but one of the kibbutz settlements you can visit (more kibbutzim are located in Galilee than anywhere else in Israel). It lies near the Jordan River, which welcomes pilgrims for baptism rites, as well as tourists who want to see the bridge over its waters.

In the opposite direction you'll find the mystic town of Safad, the important archeological site of Hatzor, the snow-ski resorts of Mt. Hermon, and many other interesting places to tour. Wherever you wander in the Galil, you will find great beauty and many parks and nature reserves. You'll also note that this is a region of extremes: from river-bank farm settlements to bald, parched hillsides dotted with basalt boulders; from tall mountain peaks often dusted with snow (Mt. Meron, 3,964-feet; Mt. Canaan, 3,150-feet; Mt. Tabor, 1,929-feet) to year-round sunny Tiberias; from sleepy Arab villages to modern, highly industrialized sectors.

Nazareth

This is an Arab town, primarily Christian, but with many Moslems and Jews as well. A sprawling town for its mere 56,000 inhabitants, it enfolds dozens of very important religious sites and establishments, modern hotels and hostels, dwelling places for clergy, an open market *(souk),* graceful Arab villas, grubby city streets, a residential and industrial section where most of its Jewish citizens live—Nazareth Ilit (or Upper Nazareth, or Nazareth Heights)—and a general conglomeration of all things representing each stage of the town's history, from ancient to modern days.

The *souk* has kept its Eastern character. Whether because travelers have already done their shopping in Acre or Jaffa—from the shopkeeper's point of view, Nazareth is badly placed—or because they have come mainly for religious reasons they do little more than stroll through the bazaar or buy religious baubles, blessed or unblessed beads, true or false relics. Many Arabs have kept to their age-old garments; others have adopted total, or at least partial, Western clothing. Outside of water, electricity, TV and modern conveniences, plus tourism, little has changed hereabouts. The same women draw water at Mary's fountain. Housing conditions have improved: Joseph's workshop was in a cave; today it would be in a building or maybe the *souk.*

Since Nazareth is built on hills, nearly all its streets slope up or down. Pious folk should not be taken aback by coming across Casanova Street, one of the more prominent in town. Its name has nothing whatsoever to do with the fabled lover, it's merely a merging of the words *casa* and *nova.*

In the old days, the Franciscans had a hospice in Nazareth, to house pilgrims. When it began to deteriorate, they built another and called it the new house, *casa nova,* to tell it apart from the old. The town has close to a dozen hospices, convents, monasteries, and hostels of varying denominations which lodge pilgrims and, if need be, mere travelers, preferably in groups but sometimes alone.

One thing many tourists note about Nazareth is that, like many other places, it has its own, highly organized, fiercely proprietary, local group of guides, mostly Christian Arabs, who frequently band together against guides from "outside" their hometown. To avoid any union problems or cries of racial or religious discrimination against the local guides, a tourist coming with his own guide from another area usually will be handed over to a local man as soon as he sets foot in town. The hotels in town also operate primarily under Christian Arab owner-management, and do not serve kosher food as almost all hotels in the state are required to do.

Knowing all this may help prepare tourists for the fact that Nazareth —the cradle of Christianity, the religion of brotherly love—has an on-going war raging among members of the different Christian sects represented here, a phenomenom not unique at Holy Land holy sites. However, the Franciscan (Roman Catholic) Order which has been here some 400 years, generally rules. (It was a Franciscan, Father Viand, who made many important archeological discoveries here at the beginning of this century.)

Town of Many Faiths

Nazareth seems to have as many places of worship as it has hills. Maybe more. And they gather in a monotheistic mixture: Jews, Moslems, Christians. Synagogues are in Upper Nazareth, and quite new. Mosques, old and new, are around town, and one worth visiting is the Mosque of Peace. It is the biggest and richest in the Middle East, built at staggering costs largely absorbed by the Israeli government. Christian churches, seminaries, monasteries, chapels and such also abound, with the Basilica of the Annunciation, circa 1965, being the biggest and richest of all—a Franciscan-operated wonder (to be detailed later).

There's also the Roman Catholic Church of St. Joseph, built on the traditional site of Joseph's carpentery shop. The 300-year-old Church of the Annunciation, dedicated to St. Gabriel, is Greek Orthodox. The Melchite community has a Greek Catholic church, near the market-place. The Maronites, some 600 souls, originally from Lebanon, have, in the so-called Latin quarter of *Nabaa,* a Maronite church, where Mass is said in Arabic and Aramaic. An Arab minister holds the services in the Anglican church, near Casanova Street. The Southern Baptist Convention built, about 40 years ago, a Baptist temple, next to the Greek Orthodox church. A small Coptic church was added, in the eastern part of the town, in 1952. The Salesian Order of St. John Bosco built the one Salesian church, also known as the Church of the Boy Jesus, on a hill; it can be seen from far off and is very beautiful, but one has to climb the hill on foot to get to it. Last of all, west of Nazareth, on another summit, stands the Greek Church of St. Joseph.

Today, the synagogue in which Jesus spoke belongs to the Greek Catholics. A chapel was built on a hill south of the town, Our Lady of Fright, belonging to the Franciscan Order of nuns, the Holy Clairs, at the place where Mary was supposed to have been seized with fear for her son's life. And you will be shown, a mile or so from Nazareth, at Djebel-el-Qafse, the hill from which angry townsmen wished to push Jesus. This seems doubtful, since Luke speaks of "the hill whereon their city was built."

The story of Nazareth is the story of the New Testament. The town had a somewhat bad reputation. The people of Galilee looked down on it: "Can any good thing come out of Nazareth?" (JOHN I, 46.) We know that Jesus was called the Nazarene, and that most followers were also from and around Nazareth. Nor should one forget the events surrounding these words, "Verily I say unto you, no prophet is accepted in his own country. . . . "

The Annunciation Sites

According to the New Testament (LUKE I, 26–38), "The angel Gabriel was sent from God into a city of Galilee, named Nazareth, to a virgin . . . and the virgin's name was Mary . . . And the angel said, Hail . . . the Lord is with thee: blessed art thou among women . . . behold, thou shalt conceive in thy womb, and bring forth a son, and shalt call his name Jesus." This event became known to Christianity as The Annunciation, and the cave where it supposedly occurred, a site hallowed by tradition, is under the present Basilica. For 1,600 years, chapels, churches, and basilicas have been built, fallen down, and been rebuilt on an unfounded assumption, supposedly confirmed only a few years ago by an archeological discovery: an inscription, "Hail Mary," in the ruins of the "Christian synagogue." Is this inscription enough to identify the site? The old Greek Orthodox Church of the Annunciation has laid claim for 300 years to the glory of standing on the site of the miracle. So?

So—it is open to question whether these squabbles have any bearing on faith. An age-old dispute has long gone on in Rome, over the remains of a man buried under St. Peter's: are those or aren't those St. Peter's bones? Whether or not they are, the faithful have gone praying there with unabated zeal for over 1,700 years. When faith is strong

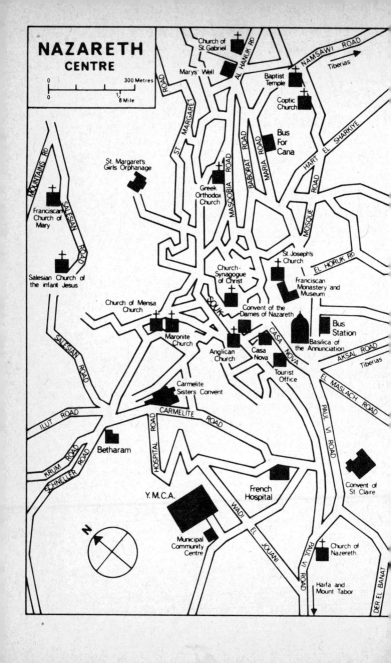

NAZARETH
CENTRE

0 ____ 300 Metres
0 ____ 1/8 Mile

Church of St. Gabriel

AL HANUK RD

NAMSAWI ROAD

Tiberias

Marys' Well

Baptist Temple

Coptic Church

ST MARGARET ROAD

MASQOBIA ROAD

BABORAT ROAD

MARIA ROAD

HART EL SHARKIYE

MOSQUE ROAD

Bus For Cana

St. Margaret's Girls Orphanage

Greek Orthodox Church

MOUNTAINS RD

SALESIAN ROAD

Franciscan Church of Mary

Salesian Church of the infant Jesus

St. Joseph's Church

EL HORUK RD

Church-Synagogue of Christ

Franciscan Monastery and Museum

SOUK

Church of Mensa Church

Convent of the Dames of Nazareth

Bus Station

Maronite Church

Basilica of the Annunciation

SALESIAN ROAD

Anglican Church

Casa Nova

CASA NOVA

AKSAL ROAD

Tiberias

Casa Nova

Tourist Office

EL MASLACH ROAD

Carmelite Sisters Convent

CARMELITE ROAD

PAUL VI ROAD

ILUT ROAD

HOSPITAL ROAD

KRUM ROAD

SCHNELLER ROAD

Betharam

French Hospital

Convent of St Claire

Y.M.C.A.

WADI EL JOUANI

PAUL VI ROAD

N

Municipal Community Centre

Church of Nazereth

Haifa and Mount Tabor

DER EL BANAT

enough to move mountains, it matters little if the place of worship is the actual one or not; it is in himself that the believer carries his shrine.

The present Basilica—lavishly constructed in 1965 and mentioned briefly earlier—was built over a very old altar bearing the words: "And the Word was made flesh" (JOHN I, 14). That alone matters. The early Christians, the Crusaders, generations of pilgrims for the past 2,000 years have knelt here in awe. Four times, in the course of centuries, the Byzantines, the Crusaders, and twice the Franciscans, in 1730 and today, have borne witness to their faith and that of millions by building a church here. Among the faithful of the Middle Ages, the story went around that when Islam, in 1263, was about to turn the church into a mosque, angels appeared who carried off the chapel to Loreto in Italy. Since then, crowds go to pray at the shrine and call Loreto "the Nazareth of Italy."

Environs of Nazareth

Seven miles to the east of Nazareth, on the main road, is Kfar Kana. It was here, in old Cana, that Jesus attended a wedding feast with his mother and turned the water into wine. What happened to the wedding waterpots? A few seem to have withstood the wear and breakage of time. As in Nazareth, two churches lay claim to the spot.

A first chapel had been built in the fourth century by Constantine. Later, the Crusaders built a church on the ruins, and the Franciscan church now stands on the ruins of that. There is a water jar on display, claimed to be one of the originals. On the other hand, the Greek church also claims to stand on the ruins of the old house where the water was changed to wine. As we have said, it makes no difference anyway. Still another tradition places Cana itself elsewhere, eight miles north of Nazareth!

Kfar Kana is an Arab village, drab and dusty, with narrow winding streets, bypassed by travelers and pilgrims alike. The churches are graceless. A blowsy housewife, tagged by her bedraggled child, stops her chores long enough to show us around. We are four miles from Nazareth. The countryside is pleasant, planted with orange trees. Somewhat moved, we think of Jesus and His mother walking to the wedding, all the way from home.

A few miles to the west on a hilltop, lies Zippori, which means "bird." A simple village now, it was the most important town in Galilee in Jesus' time. A foremost spiritual center, the seat of renowned schools, it took pride, among its many scholars, in Rabbi Yehuda Hanassi (the Prince), whose supposed tomb we saw in Beit She'arim. A church, built on the ruins of a Crusaders' church, marks a birthplace holy to Christians: that of Mary in the house of her mother Ann and her father Joachim.

To the north of Kfar Kana lies the plain of Beit Natofi. It is crossed by a dyke built during the last few years to store rainwater and water drained through an underground pipe from the lake of Galilee.

The ruins of Yodefat, the old fortress, lie on the plain. They seem of little interest; but one Ben Mattatia fought the Romans there, at the time of the big Jewish uprising. In the year 69, he was forced to surrender. Taken prisoner, "turning" Roman and taking the name Josephus Flavius (37–95), he wrote a huge book: *De Bello Judaico,* "The Jewish War." This work is one of our sources of information; Jesus is twice mentioned.

Beit She'arim

To the west of Nazareth, along the main road from Haifa, are the Beit She'arim Catacombs, somewhat similar to the Sanhedrin burial tombs in Jerusalem. (Beit She'arim is about 12 miles from Haifa.) Here, along with the tombs where ancient Israel's great wise men were laid to rest, there are gardens, a picnic ground, and a café.

But Beit She'arim is now a ghost town. Long ago, it was a busy and crowded town, famed for its wise man, Rabbi Yehuda Hanassi, called the Prince, and compiler of the *Mishna.* So great was his renown that during his lifetime there was a saying: "To find justice, go to Rabbi Yehuda in Beit She'arim." In the second century, it was the headquarters of the *Sanhedrin,* supreme court of the Jews. It was also the seat of knowledge, moved up from Yavneh, in the south. To make up for the loss of the Mount of Olives burial grounds, barred to the Jews by the Romans, the faithful dug deep into the chalky soil of Beit She'arim. Pious Jews who had the means came from everywhere, as far as the Yemen, or Himyar, to bury their dead. The journey cost a great deal of money; the dead had to be sealed into coffins of earthenware and lead, and transported in camel-drawn caravans. But Beit She'arim was a holy city, deemed worthy by the Sanhedrin and by Rabbi Yehuda.

Of the towns destroyed by the Romans, there is little left beyond the ruins of a second-century synagogue, probably the biggest of its times; an oil press; and that underground cemetery that was discovered by a caretaker, Alexander Zaid. This man is a hero of later-day Jewish history, and a memorial statue of him on horseback was erected on the hilltop overlooking Beit She'arim.

So far, over thirty burial chambers have seen the light of day, and some 200 graves have been unearthed. Unfortunately, most were empty. Like so many Egyptian and Etruscan tombs, they had been looted by vandals: for in the olden days rich Jews were buried with their jewels. Pitted by the stony chalk and crumbling at the touch of air, the bones told archeologists nothing beyond a tale of death. Fortunately, there remained the writings on the tombs, in Hebrew, Aramaic, and Greek; and Jewish and pagan symbols, carved in stone. The Greek influence—Ben She'arim was a center of learning—remains uppermost in the workmanship; there are carvings of the oyster shell, the ox, and even Zeus. In spite of the law forbidding graven images, even the Roman eagle is there, together with the lion of Judah. The emblem of Judaism, the seven-branched candelabrum or *menora*, appears frequently, but the best carving of it is on one of the walls.

One very ornate tomb was of course taken to be that of Rabbi Yehuda, and a scholarly squabble immediately began. One group questioned the grounds, outside of the wealth of workmanship, for such a viewpoint. True enough, the tombs of Gamliel and Simeon, the two sons of *Rabenu Hakadosh* (our holy master) had been identified; but it was known that the Prince had died in Sepphoris, or Zippori, the birthplace of Mary, north of Nazareth. Of course, it could well be that his body had been taken to its last resting place in Beit She'arim. But the wise man had died on Friday at sundown, *erev shabbat*, the eve of the Sabbath, and this belief was not in keeping with the Mosaic law that forbade burial on the weekly day of rest. Travel was slow in those days. As fast as they may have traveled, it seemed unlikely that the remains of Rabbi Hanassi could have arrived in Beit She'arim before the shining of the evening star. The quarrel was cut short by the priesthood: "Yes, the body arrived on time, for the sun stopped in the heavens."

The excavations made in 1960 also unearthed a quantity of glass and earthenware. The finest pieces are on view in the museum, housed within the rounded walls of the old water tank. Take a good look at the stone doorway leading into the burial grounds. It is a wonderful work of art.

Emek Jezreel and Megiddo

South of Beit She'arim we again find the road to Megiddo, one of the most important archeological and historical sites of the Near and Middle East, the key to the valley of Esdraelon, a stronghold that commanded the passage to Africa.

To appreciate the area fully, it is important to know that Emek Jezreel—Esdraelon in Greek—was for a long time a natural battlefield between the people of the valley and its would-be conquerors. One after the other, the people of Galilee held the fortress that barred the passage. Whoever held Megiddo could open or close, at will, the way to Jaffa, as well as to Haifa and to St. John of Acre. Furthermore, the southwest and the coastline have a rich soil; today's cotton plantations yield a crop five times bigger per acre than in Egypt. The northwest was also important for its thriving shipping trade with the Phoenicians from the many ports along the coast.

The road to Megiddo is lined with orchards. Many scholars, chased from Germany by Hitler, settled in Yokneam, and kibbutz Hazorea, next door, in the early 1930s. Both are famous now for raising delicious melons. The waters of the Jordan flow underground nearby, toward the south.

A small mound on the skyline, Megiddo lies along the Old Testament *Derech Hayam,* the way of the sea, also called by the Romans *Via Maris.* In the Bible, the very sound of its name is a trumpet call to war:

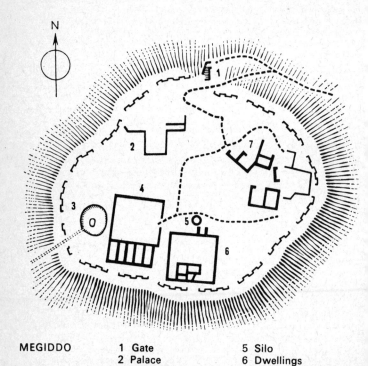

MEGIDDO	1 Gate	5 Silo
	2 Palace	6 Dwellings
	3 Water Tunnel	7 Canaanite Temple and
	4 Royal Stables	Palace

Har Meggido, of which St. John made one thundering word, Armageddon, the ultimate battlefield.

Thutmose III, the proud Pharaoh who took such an interest in the Palestine of old, ordered his victories over Megiddo, in 1478 B.C., to be carved in detail upon stone. Solomon considered it necessary to maintain a garrison there; the tax levied for the walls of Jerusalem also had to finance the fortification of Megiddo. A shrewd soldier, he was also aware that the outcome of battle on a plain depended on the cavalry, and he kept the garrison well stocked with horses and chariots. Josiah, the good king of Israel, was killed here in 610 B.C. trying to stop the advance of Neco, king of Egypt, who had nevertheless told him: "My quarrel is not with thee."

It was here, in 1918, that Allenby broke the back of the Turkish army; and also here, 30 years later, that the men of Mishmar Ha'emek barred the road to Haifa to the Arab troops.

The 20 overlapping strata brought to light by scholars at Megiddo since 1925 cover a period of time from 4,000 to 400 B.C. A movable model, on display at the entrance, gives a very clear layout for anyone with even a dim knowledge of the history of ancient peoples before Moses. At the foot of a wall, the body of a young girl was sealed in as an appeasing offering by the pre-Israelite founders of the city. The most recognizable ruins are those of Solomon's chariot garrison. According to Professor Yigael Yadin, the stables, big enough to house hundreds of horses, date as far back as the ninth century B.C., and were built by King Ahab, Jezebel's husband. The cavalry path, at both ends, can be clearly seen. Also very interesting is the tunnel hollowed into the rock to bring drinking water secretly to the fortress from a spring in the plain. The possibility of a siege had always been kept in mind, and everything had been foreseen to allow the garrison to hold out against the besieger. Together with the water tunnel, a huge silo had been built to store grain. From the top of the hill, a magnificent view of the entire valley can be seen.

The oldest remains uncovered so far are those of the Canaanite temples, built to face the rising sun. A museum, at the foot of the mound, has the unearthed pieces on display, plus a huge, fascinating, moving-parts model of the whole tel. In the same building is a snack bar-souvenir shop; picnic area outside. It's worth noting that finds like Megiddo, and Hatzor, inspired works like the best-seller *The Source.*

The road from Megiddo to Afula has been paved and broadened. Pebbles and bondstones have disappeared. Still, Afula, at the crossroads, is a dismal market town, smaller than its modern suburb Afula Ilit, or Afula Heights, which boasts of three small skyscrapers on a low hilltop. We shall often come across an *Ilit,* which means "Heights" and is now taken to mean "modern," which separates the new town from the old, usually in a hollow. Nowadays, builders buy up hilly land around a low-lying town to use for new quarters.

Afula is supposed to be the garbled Arab name for ancient Ophel, and it was adopted when Jewish pioneers established the town in 1920—mostly Americans. The fame of the neighboring town, Nazareth, has probably stunted its growth. But Afula has a sugar refinery, and flourishes as marketplace for the whole valley of Esdrael-on, being on the crossroad to Haifa, 27 miles; Nazareth, 8 miles; Megiddo, 9 miles; Hadera, 26 miles; Tiberias, 26 miles; and Degania, 20 miles, the oldest of the kibbutzim.

Toward the Jordan Valley—and the Old Testament

About two and a half miles south of Afula lies the kibbutz of Jezreel, on a biblical site of the same name. The First Book of Kings tells the story of King Ahab, who wished to buy Naboth's vineyard.

A little farther on, at the foot of the Gilboa hills, lies another kibbutz: Gidona, which bears the name of Gideon. Nearby, where the kibbutz Ein Harod now stands, flows a small stream; there, in 1050 B.C., for the war against the Midianites, Gideon chose the 300 warriors who, said the Lord, were to save people, for "they lapt the waters from hand to mouth, without bending the knee."

It was at Ein Dor, close to Mount Tabor, that there took place one of the saddest stories in the Old Testament. "The spirit of the Lord departed from Saul," at the end of his life. Jewish tradition has it that the aging king went mad. In his extremity he consulted "the witch of Endor" who conjured up for him the spirit of Samuel. "The Lord had rent the kingdom of Israel from thee this day," cried Samuel, "and hath given it to a neighbor of thine, to David that is better than thou . . . the Lord will deliver thee and thy people unto the Philistines." In the subsequent battle his sons, including Jonathan, whom David loved, were slain. But David had not gone into battle against his people. On hearing of the death of the king who had shown him so much kindness and done him such deep wrong, he burst out into lamentations, among the most beautiful poetry of all times: "Ye mountains of Gilboa. Let there be no dew, nor rain, upon you, nor fields of offerings! . . . How are the mighty fallen! and the weapons of war perished."

At Beit Hashita we turn off to the right. The very old synagogue of Beit Alfa, which dates from the sixth century, is nearby, with the most childlike, touching, and loveliest of mosaics. They were unearthed in 1928, in the simplest of ways, by plumbers putting in water pipes. Carefully restored, this work of art is divided lengthwise into three panels. Above is the Ark of the Covenant, surrounded by animals of all kinds, between two *menoras,* the seven-branched candelabrum which is a Jewish emblem. In the middle are the signs of the Zodiac—with a strong Greek influence though named in Hebrew—around a sunrise depicted by a horse-drawn chariot, and, in the four corners, the seasons of the year. Below is Abraham at the rock, getting ready to offer up Isaac to God.. Writings accompany the picture, and include the names of father and son. A hand reaches out from the cloud to hold back the sword with the word: "Stop." It is difficult to impart how much the simplicity, the awkwardness, and the tremendous good will of the craftsmen have breathed feeling into this small masterpiece. A slightly twisted frieze runs around the three panels; two upside-down animals top a main inscription, in Greek, attributing the workmanship to Marianos and to his son Aninas; then an inscription in Aramaic adds that it was put together during the reign of the Byzantine emperor Justinian I; that is to say, between the years 527 and 565. It is one of the simplest and most peace-filled sights for the traveler to admire in Israel.

Nearby, is Sachne, also called Gan Hashlosha, the Garden of the Three, perhaps the handsomest rest park set up by the National Parks Authority.

The Valley of the Jordan

We go out of the valley of Esdraelon into the valley of the Jordan, which creates almost a straight line from north to south. The road goes downward, almost unnoticeably, until well below sea level. The deep and narrow cleft, beginning a few miles north, encloses the old marshlands of Hula, the Lake of Tiberias, and the Ghor, that flows into the Dead Sea and out beyond.

Beit She'an, four miles from Beit Alfa, is the first stopover. It was here that the postscript to Saul's death occurred. "When the Philistines came to strip the slain, they found Saul and his three sons fallen on Mount Gilboa. And they cut off his head, and stripped off his armor ... and they put his armor in the house of Ashtaroth, and they fastened his body to the wall of Beth-shan (Beit She'an). And ... all the valiant men (of Jabesh-Gilead) arose, and went all night, and took the body of Saul and the bodies of his sons from the wall of Beth-shan, and came to Jabesh, and burnt them there. And they took their bones, and buried them under a tree at Jabesh, and fasted seven days."

Another well-known event took place here. Christian tradition sets in Beit She'an the healing of the leper, as told by the Evangelist, though Luke himself merely wrote "through the midst of Samaria and Galilee."

However, what the traveler has come to see is the Roman theater, admirably cleared free of sand and rock. It was built in the second century, and its restoration, one of the most successful in Israel, clearly shows what a theater was like in those days.

The mound overlaying the old Beit She'an rises straight in front on the bank of the Harod. Called Tel El-Husn, it is the remains of 18 levels of occupation on one site over thousands of years: the ancient cities of Beit She'an. It was excavated from top to bottom by an American expedition that took many of its findings to the United States, but a few were left behind. Jerusalem's Israel Museum houses the basalt slab said to be of Seti I (1313 B.C.). The Rockefeller Museum, Jerusalem, exhibits the slab of "Mekal, Lord of Beth-Shan" (1500 B.C.), and a stone carving showing a fight between a lion and a dog, of the same century. Beit She'an Museum has photos of the first, plaster copies of the other two.

Barely a mile away, there are the remains of the 6th-century Byzantine Monastery of Lady Marie. Lady Marie and her son, Maximus, donated the money for the building and its outstanding mosaics. To see the place obtain permission and key at the Beit She'an Museum, which is located on the northeastern edge of town on the road to Tiberias, only a few minutes walk from King Saul Street, the town's main thoroughfare.

South of Beit She'an is Tirat-Tsevi. The settlement was named after Rabbi Tsevi Kalisher, forerunner of Zionism. Here, we are in the Ghor. In places, the hollow is down to 657 feet below sea level. The Ghor runs its course into the Jordan, through the valley of the Jordan river, flowing down to Jericho and the northern shore of the Dead Sea.

The railroad line that runs northward the length of the valley of the Jordan is no longer in use. The road follows the train tracks up to Gesher—meaning "the bridge"—17 miles from Beit She'an, and crosses the river. On the left, we catch a far-off glimpse of the ruins of a hilltop stronghold of the Crusaders: Fort Belvoir, accessible from the valley of Jezreel through B'nei Brith.

Tiberias

The ancients called the sea Kinneret, because, seen from afar, the lake has the shape of a lute, *Kinnor* in Hebrew. Thirteen miles long and seven miles wide, it lies 686 feet below sea level. Its waters appear calm, but they are deceiving; unexpected, violent storms can whip up from nowhere. The lake is entirely in Israel territory, as is the shoreline.

Like Jerusalem and Nazareth, the sea is linked with the name of Jesus. He walked on its waters (MARK VI, 45-56); He becalmed the storm (MARK IV, 35-41); He filled the empty fishing-net (LUKE V, 4–7); He gathered together His followers: Simon, Andrew, James, and John (MATTHEW IV, 18–22). We meet Him everywhere, in Tabgha, in Migdal, in Capernaum. He avoided the town of Tiberias, governed by Herod, "the fox" to Him. According to tradition, it was there that He heard of John the Baptist's beheading, but there is no word of this in the Gospels.

The official life of Tiberias began with Herod Antipas. After the Romans had destroyed the Temple of Jerusalem and forbidden entry to the Jews, the spiritual home of Judaism was moved to Galilee. We have already spoken of the importance taken on by Beit She'arim and Zippori. Then Tiberias became the seat of the Sanhedrin, and by so doing one of the four holy towns of the Jews, the others being Jerusalem, Safad, and Hebron, the last being southernmost. It was in Tiberias that the writing of the Mishna and of the Talmud of Jerusalem came to an end. The wise Rabbi Meir Ba'al Haness lived and was buried there.

Outside of the Roman occupation forces, the Jews alone lived in Tiberias until the fourth century. Beginning with Constantine, the first emperor to be converted to Christianity, churches went up among the synagogues. Then came the Arabs, and Allah knows they were as fond of mosques as of water. For a time the menora lay down in peace beside the cross and the crescent. Then came the earthquake of 749 and, 400 years later, in 1033, a second fearful one destroyed the town. The survivors moved nearby, settling the "old town." The rest of the story is well known: the Crusaders, the Arabs, the Turks, the English, and, at last, the State of Israel. Tiberias, the first town to be freed, on April 19, 1948, became the capital of Galilee, today it boasts about 27,000 inhabitants.

Water Skiing and the Tombs of Great Men

In 1837, a third earthquake again destroyed the town. The records of the time state "it was rebuilt by the Jews." What Jews? Since the Middle Ages, there were very few in Palestine. But Tiberias indeed had a Jewish colony, whose story is worth telling.

At the time when Columbus set out on his legendary sea voyage, in 1492, the Catholic king and queen of Spain, Ferdinand and Isabella, having conquered the Moors, evicted the Spanish Jews, or *Sephardim*. In the 16th century, the Duchess of Luna, whose son-in-law was a Jew, obtained from Sultan Suleiman the Magnificent a decree allowing Jews to settle in Tiberias. Two hundred years later, Dahr-el-Omar, the Bedouin sheik who rebuilt and repeopled St. John of Acre, called on the Jews to move into the town. Thus the first Zionist settlers of the 19th century were welcomed by fellow Jews.

Let it not be thought that only sufferers from rheumatism go to Tiberias. The landscape is one of the most beautiful in the world. The weather is unbelievably mild. Buffs of water skiing and wind-surfing can spend all year long sporting here. For 20 years, there have been swimming races across the lake and hikes around it.

Take a walk to the excavations of the very old town of Hammat, "the hot." Between town and the spa, a 3-year dig ended in 1976. Just past the new spa, older digs unearthed remains of a first-century synagogue. The beautiful mosaics, restored by skillful craftsmen in 1965, are on view. They are true works of art; though the images are the same as those in Beit Alfa, the workmanship is much finer. The inscriptions are in Greek and in Hebrew. It is thought that the master artisan was Greek, as the signs of the Zodiac show uncircumcised boys.

The tomb of Rabbi Meir Ba'al Haness, one of the town's great men, is nearby; its domes are a few steps from the bath houses. On the way, walk through the ruins of the old Tiberias of the Romans, for a look at the remains of the town and the walls worn away by the passing of time.

Following the shore of the lake northward, don't fail to stop and see, beyond the present synagogue and in front of the post office, the Monastery of St. Peter, kept by the Franciscans. The apse of the old Church of the Crusaders is still shaped like a ship's prow, a reminder of Peter the Fisherman. The Museum of Antiquities, a little further on, will delight the knowledgeable.

The uncommon feature of Tiberias is that the traveler can go everywhere on foot, if he likes to walk. In a few minutes, he can walk to the center of the town and, a few steps from the Town Hall, come upon the Tomb of Maimonides. The great physician and philosopher, Moses ben Maimon, born in Cordova in 1135, lived his last years in Egypt but he wished to be buried in the holy city. By its side is the Tomb of Rabbi Yohanaan Ben Zakai, the wise old man who went to the Roman conquerer Titus to ask him to spare Yavneh, center of learning. His followers are also buried there. The remains of Rabbi Akiva, one of the codifiers of the Talmud, tortured by the Romans in 135, are buried a little farther away.

The Fountain of Mary

In the low-lying quarters of the town, one can still make out the Turkish fortifications, walls of black basalt put up by Dahr-el-Omar. Nearby, the Fountain of Mary has a legend. The All-Powerful put it in the way of His faithful during the seemingly endless 40-year wandering in the desert. The spring, named after Moses' meek sister Miriam or Mary, has since been swallowed up by the lake. In the days of Cabalistic study, mystics were sure that a gulp of its waters would help them unravel the mysteries of Creation.

There are many outings. The traveler is nearly always advised to have lunch at Ein Gev, a kibbutz on the opposite shore of the lake. He can go alone, by car or by coach, or by taking the boat that crosses the Sea of Galilee. Kibbutz Ein Gev operates a guest house, camp site, famous restaurant and the Kinneret Sailing Company, which runs a ferry service between Tiberias and Ein Gev, and organizes outings on the lake, up to Capernaum.

"St. Peter's fish," the specialty of the Ein Gev restaurant, is very good; indeed, enough, in itself, to make the reputation of this corner of Israel. But the kibbutz also has a yearly Music and Folklore Festival, in the spring, and another in the fall. From the very start, the crowds were so big that the kibbutz Ein Gev had to build a concert hall housing 3,000 people. The concerts are first rate. The great take a willing part in the Festival.

In Israel, there is often talk of Karnei Hittin, the "horns of the Hittite." The hill is about seven miles west of Tiberias. Be careful not to mistake it for the village of Kfar Hittim on the way. Of all the warfare of the Middle Ages, the battle that took place there in 1187, between the knights of the West and the lords of the East, the Cross and the Crescent, was to have one of the most far-reaching consequences. Here, Saladin hacked to pieces the Crusaders led by Guy de Lusignan, and it was the defeat at Karnei Hittin that tolled the bell for Christianity in the Holy Land.

At the foot of the hill is a holy place: the Tomb of Jethro, father-in-law of Moses, on whom the Druse have bestowed the title of *nebi*, prophet. Every spring, they go on a pilgrimage to his tomb, and hold a great folklore festival. To go there, one must cross the valley of Arbel. To the right of the road stands the *moshav* Arbel, and the ruins of the old city, with the remains of a third-century synagogue. According to legend, it is in the valley of Arbel that the Messiah will reveal Himself.

In the prehistoric caves of the narrow passes of Nahal Amoud was discovered, in 1925, the skull of a cave-man of Palestine. Scholars have labeled it the Skull of Galilee. It is over 100,000 years old, and belongs to the Paleolithic age.

To the south of Tiberias, a 15-minute drive, is Degania, Israel's first kibbutz (founded in 1909). At its entrance is a small Syrian tank which the settlers stopped in its tracks in 1948 with a hail of Molotov cocktails. It was at Degania that the ideological premise for kibbutz life was first enunciated by A. D. Gordon. The settlement's natural history museum bears his name. The second and third generation of Degania decided to make their own fresh start and launched a new kibbutz next door. They gave it the not very imaginative name of Degania "B." Degania A has 420 members, Degania B has 500—as well as a new museum showing, primarily, the natural history of the region and of Israel.

The Healing Water of Tiberias

Now as in the past, aching men come to Tiberias to be rid of rheumatism, barren women to seek a cure for their problem. It has ever been so since the Deluge, according to legend.

The story goes that one day, King Solomon felt the need of a good hot bath. Some say it was for himself; others insist he wanted it to help and heal the aches and pains of his people, but most agree that masterful Solomon commanded a bunch of young devils to descend into the bowels of the earth to heat water which would gush to the Galilee shore. Whoever bathed in this water felt so much better that its fame spread quickly abroad, bringing flocks of sick people from all lands and areas. Seeing such gladness, Solomon worried what would happen when he died, and the devils stopped heating the water. Being very wise, he finally hit upon a plan to keep them working forever. He afflicted the unlucky devils with deafness, so they never could hear of his death, and therefore would continue their labor endlessly. People vow that the water's strong sulphur smell testifies to the truth of this tale, being a sure sign that hell had a hand in the miracle.

Learned men smile at the folk-tale, pointing out that the springs were hot long before Solomon's time. Some even say cave men stumbled across the water's healing powers for barren women, and when a stone-age woman was slow in begetting offspring, she got tossed in these waters. Joshua knew of the ancient city of Hammat, and its name derives from the Hebrew word for hot: ham (cham).

Evidently, the first grand bath-house was built here by Herod Antipas—the same one who lusted after Salome. He named the spa area Tiberias, in honor of Emperor Tiberias' 60th birthday. Romans loved baths, so it was natural for Herod to build lush facilities. The money minted here during Tiberias' heyday, in the first 200 years of this era, depicts the Emperor's head on one side, and the other side shows Hygeia, goddess of health, sitting on a rock from which gushes a spring, together with the serpent, symbol of healing.

In 749, a terrible earthquake destroyed Herod's fabulous resort area, though excavations have already laid bare a network of clay pipes and chamber areas of those baths, as well as nearby town sites that include an ancient synagogue with fantastically well-preserved mosaic floors. Diggings will undoubtedly reveal even more of the ancient city's secrets. The waters are mentioned several times in Hebrew writings, and the Talmud even has special laws allowing the pious to bathe in these waters on the Sabbath.

Through all the years, the springs have never lost their renown. Succeeding generations of conquerors lolled around here, building bathhouses and assorted facilities for using the water after it cooled sufficiently from its natural heat of 140°F (38°C). Today, visitors can see two ancient Turkish baths. The one built in 1833, considered the more magnificent, now forms the northern wing of the present Bath House and continues in use, partly. The current establishment operates, since 1932, via a concession granted the Tiberias Hot Springs Ltd.

World War II and establishment of the State of Israel, in 1948, preempted building time, but a totally new building was completed in 1955, comparable to international spa facilities and standards. A new hotel went up in the mid-70s, and 1978 saw the opening of a literally beautiful new building by the sea—with pools and massage areas for tourists, plus a computer-run comprehensive Medical Clinic and Health Sanatorium to provide curative and prophylactic treatments, like those given in Dax, Aix-les-Bains, Bad-Gastein, Abano, Baden-Baden. Doctors say advantages here include the choice of active (swimming pool) or passive (bath) treatment; the mud, called Piloma, being non-volcanic and from age-old silt of the Jordan River mouth; and the restful landscape's positive psychosomatic action. Treatments are given for arthritis, degenerative joint disease, spondyloses, fibrositis, cellulitis, neuralgia, traumatic affliction after illness, neurological conditions (paresis), vascular disturbances (hypertonia), gynaecological ailments (sterility and others), bronchial asthma and upper respiratory tract problems (sinusitis). Aside from mud packs, there's physiotherapy, hydrotherapy, electrotherapy, massage and pool exercise, sauna, inhalations, gynaecological treatments, carbon dioxide baths, aerated baths and mineral water baths or pools, public and private. It's year-round, and costs vary depending on treatment. A full medical staff prescribes treatments per your doctor's records or theirs, or helps you use the baths for simple relaxation. See *Facts At Your Fingertips* chapter for other nearby spa areas.

Mount Tabor

The best road to Mount Tabor is from the southern tip of the lake, taking a right turn at kibbutz Kinneret. The road passes the kibbutzim Poriya and Yavne'el and Kfar Kama, settled by Circassians since the Turkish occupation.

A word of warning: the climb up the mount is steep, with hairpin bends. It is so narrow that if two cars meet, one has to back off to a widening in the road to allow the other to pass.

As you drive up the sun beats fiercely down onto the treeless, stony path that winds its way up the mountainside. But, having labored for

1,900 feet up this way, the traveler is rewarded—at the top—by a panorama of almost make-believe tranquility.

Mount Tabor is topped by a tableland, on which stand the Basilica of the Transfiguration and the Hospice Casa Nova, both kept by the Franciscan Order. There is also a Greek church named for St. Elias.

The hill has a historic past. It rose at the meeting-place of the lands granted to three out of the 12 tribes of Israel: Zebulon, Issachar, and Nephtali. Deborah the prophetess preached there, and, at her call, Barak assembled his troops to fight the Canaanites of Sisera. But the place owes its renown to St. Cyril of Jerusalem, who, in the fourth century, named Mount Tabor as the scene of the Transfiguration. The evangelists merely speak of a high mountain, which many thought for a long time was Mount Hermon, in Syria.

The two relevant passages in Luke have served as starting-point for the architects who, through the centuries, were called upon to rebuild the church of the Transfiguration. The latest to date has three triangles on the front, that stand for the three tents. As for the effect of the Transfiguration, it is to be had at sundown, when the rays of the setting sun, falling slantwise through an opening, shine on the golden mosaics of the rounded vault.

The first church to honor the Transfiguration was put up in the fourth century, in the form of three chapels, recalling the three tents. The present altar is said to be on the former site of the biggest chapel, that of Jesus. The two others are today marked by chapels daubed with frescos, of which the best that can be said is that they are artless. One fresco recalls the meeting of Elias with the priests of Baal, mentioned at our visit to Mount Carmel.

From the terrace of the Hospice Casa Nova (64 beds, reasonable rates), there is a breathtaking view over the spreading plain: Megiddo, Upper Galilee crowned by Safad, Mount Gilboa and Mount Samaria. One can clearly make out the town of Na'ine (the old Nain), where Jesus stopped for a miracle and raised a widow's dead son. A crude road leads to Na'ine.

At the foot of the hill lies Ein Dor, famous in the story of Saul, who came to speak with the witch on the eve of the battle that was to cost him his life. Another battle took place thereabouts, 28 centuries later, in 1799, when Bonaparte and Kleber defeated the Turks and Arabs.

In Dabburiya, an Arab village, there are goats, sheep, and children with beautiful eyes. There, 2,000 years ago, nine followers waited for Jesus, with Peter, James, and John, to come down from the "high mountain."

Migdal, Tabgha, Mount of Beatitudes and Capernaum

Heading north from Tiberias via the main lakeside road, you can soon see several New Testament sites. Migdal, the old Magdala, only four miles away, gave its name to that renowned sinner, Mary Magdalen, who was born here. Jesus, having fled Nazareth, stopped near a tower *(migdal)* and met a woman who, through him, was to see the light at last. Of that meeting place, only a small whitewashed dome remains.

When this was a sleepy village, not terribly long ago, its people excelled in salting fish from the Sea of Galilee. Now a mere suburb of Tiberias, its economic base has changed. Some of its people work in the nearby luxurious, 3-star guest house of Kibbutz Ginnosar while others help out sometimes at the youth hostel by the shore, in the nearby camping area, or work in Tiberias.

Four miles further is the site of Jesus's multiplication of the loaves and fishes, Tabgha—now known as Ein Shova. The Benedictine Order has a monastery here built of the grey stone ancient to this area. They make quite a good wine, welcome visitors, and will gladly show you the new church (opened in 1981) as well as the magnificent mosaics from the old Byzantine basilica here. Perhaps the most beautiful in Israel, they picture the "loaves and fishes" story in a wonderful setting of plant and animal life.

The story of the miracle begins when Jesus hears of the death of John the Baptist and departs to a "place apart," which seems to be Tabgha— or Tabigha, the *Heptapegon* (seven springs) of the Greeks. "When the people had heard . . . they followed him on foot." That evening, there was no food for the crowd except "five loaves and two fishes" which Jesus blessed and had the disciples pass about, "and they did all eat, and were filled" . . . the fragments that remained filled 12 baskets. (From MATTHEW XIV, 13–21) This scripture numbers the crowd at 5,000 men; "beside women and children." In JOHN XX, 14, "Jesus saith to Simon Peter . . . Feed my lambs . . . my sheep." In honor of St. Peter, a Franciscan church was built here during World War II, using the black basalt of Tiberias. Such shrines today merge with more modern sights, including nearby pumps that force water towards the far-off, dry Negev.

The Mount of Beatitudes, about 330 feet high, is two and a half miles from Tabgha. On top, there is a hospice kept by an Italian Order of Franciscan nuns, and a round chapel. Here, the sky is wonderfully mild. The Lake of Galilee, spread out below, is a fitting end to the rolling landscape. To the north, Safad, the holy city, shines in the sun on its mountaintop. Farther away, Mount Hermon lifts its snowy peak. Even unbelievers should climb up here, for the view.

The shrine, built in 1937 by the "italica gens" in "the year XV"—of the Fascist era—is perhaps not very beautiful, but at least it has a touching artlessness. Within, the eight sides of the dome list the beatitudes stated by Jesus, in the opening to His Sermon on the Mount. The signs of the seven virtues are inlaid in the floor.

According to tradition, it was on the Mount of Beatitudes that Jesus chose His 12 apostles among His followers. "And He goeth up into a mountain, and calleth unto Him whom He would . . . and He ordained twelve, that they should be with Him." (MARK III, 13.) On going down, Jesus went into Capernaum.

Capernaum is today a graveyard of old stones worked by the hand of man. There are still clear traces of the layout and size of a second- or third-century synagogue, probably built over the one where Jesus preached. For, on coming from Nazareth, He made of Capernaum the "center of His teaching." The "village of Nahoum," on the road from Syria to Egypt, must have been of some importance, since it called for a Roman garrison and a customs house. But, in spite of His prodigies of healing there—Simon's mother, the man possessed of an unclean spirit, the centurion's servant—the people of Capernaum mocked Jesus, who proceeded to lash into them, "And thou, Capernaum which art exalted unto Heaven, shalt be brought down to hell."

Upper Galilee

Nothing is ever very far in Israel. From the northern shore of Lake Kinneret to the farthermost northern boundary of the country, is about 30 miles. From Tiberias, on the west coast, to Metulla, the northernmost Israeli settlement, is 40 miles.

Our first stopover will be at Vered Hagalil, "Rose of the Galilee." It is so named because the American-born horseman who operates this dude ranch is also a horticulturist and raises a dozen different varieties of roses in the garden next to the horses' exercise yard. The restaurant here features American-style pancakes, southern fried chicken, and grilled steaks. Horseback outings can be arranged by the hour, half-day and full day. (See *Facts At Your Fingertips* chapter.)

Higher up, we come to the crossroads of Rosh Pina. To the left is the road to Safad, which we shall take on the way back; to the right, the road to Kfar Hannassi, once a border kibbutz; straight on, the road through Mishmar Hayarden—the guardian of the Jordan—and Ayelet Hashahar, with its pleasant guest house near the bridge over the Jordan.

There has been a great deal of fighting around this bridge: Christians and Moslems during the Crusades, the Turks and the French during the siege of St. John of Acre by Bonaparte; Turks and the English in 1917; the English and the French on both sides during the last war, against the Vichy troops; the Arabs and the Jews in 1948, and again in 1967, when the Jews crossed the bridge under the thunder of Syrian guns. It also saw a big share of action in 1973's October War, when thousands of Syrians, and their allies, invaded and were subsequently pushed back.

For the time being, we go straight on into the former marshlands of the Huleh Nature Reserve, recognized in the 1970s by the International Union of Conservation of Nature as a reserve of world importance. It began with the creation of a seven-mile canal network, finished in 1958, that criss-crossed 775 acres bordering Lake Huleh. The reserve opened in 1964, but closed again and then reopened in 1979 after total replanning and landscaping. Primarily a bird haven today, it also boasts open water areas, swamp meadow, and a reed habitat where water buffalo were reintroduced and now wallow in the mud as in former eras. Throughout the reserve, there is impressive plant life, including papyrus thickets (nowadays scarcely found outside the Sudan). This is a paradise all year for birds of many species, flying to and from Europe, Asia and Africa: storks, pelicans, wild geese, ducks and many migratory birds unfamiliar to Westerners. The waters abound with big carp, catfish and perch, even though fishing, like hunting, is strictly forbidden. The topminnow, an American fish that lives on mosquito eggs, played a big part in helping rid the area of malaria. Tourists can visit here daily, for minimal fees, and the regular free tours are highly recommended.

About six miles from the northern border lies Kiryat Shmona, or Qiryat Shemona, a town of 15,000 named for "the eight"—six men and two women who, in the 1920s, held the Tel Hai (Hill of Life) colony against a band of Arabs, but died there. Among them was former Czarist officer, Joseph Trumpeldor, who had inspired young Russian Jews to settle here. Many others have died for this sliver of land. A sad little cemetery shelters "the eight" as well as men who fell in the War of Independence. The most touching graves, however, date from April, 1974, when three members of the Popular Front for the Liberation of Palestine crossed from Lebanon and murdered 18 people, mostly children and women. Despite its troubled past, the town has new industry, and even a luxury hotel.

Horshat-Tal is nearby, landscaped by the National Parks Authority with a remarkable garden, age-old oaks for shade, and a delightful stream, the Dan, whose source is barely a mile away. This is the country of Kibbutz Dan, Kibbutz Snir and Kfar Giladi, a kibbutz with an excellent guest house (3-star) and tourist facilities, the official Israeli Defense Forces Museum (interesting), and a reconstructed Tel Hai site nearby. This also is the region of Dan of the Bible, and owes its name to one of the twelve tribes of Israel, as does the Jordan tributary winding through the countryside. In the First Book of Kings (XXI, 30), Jeroboam ordered two golden calves to be cast and set up in Bethel and Dan. Jeremiah then prophesied Dan's downfall and, sure enough, Dan fell.

Mount Hermon, rising above Upper Galilee, has snowy crests that delight skiers. The large Israeli Ski Club, complemented by tourists, enjoys holidays at Neve Ativ resort (see *Facts At Your Fingertips* chapter for details).

Metulla, the end of the line, is 1,722 feet below sea level; founded in 1896 with money from the Rothschild family, it has magnificent mountain scenery. The "Good Fence" first-aid station of Israel Defense Forces functions here to give medical help to sick people and battle casualties from Lebanon. Usually, a reserve IDF officer is here and can explain to tourists, even in English, what is happening. A recently erected Observation Platform helps you see the entire region.

The Remains of Hatzor

Retracing toward Safad, the ruins of Hatzor are just opposite Kibbutz Ayelet Hashahar, where there's a specially nice guest house-cum-hotel.

A big new museum, at the entrance of the kibbutz, with explanatory texts in several languages, gives a better understanding of the drama of long ago.

A glance at the map is enough to give an idea of the strategic importance of Hatzor, like that of Megiddo. Here, as there, the great man was Solomon. The Bible speaks of it: "And it came to pass, Joshua took the city of Hatzor." (JOSHUA XI, 10.)

Still farther back, in the 19th century B.C., the name of Hatzor is on the list of cities in rebellion against Egyptian rule—a thorn in the side of the warlike Pharaohs Thutmose III, Amenhotep, and Seti, as the old papyrus bears witness. In the 14th century B.C., the kings of Tyre and of Ashtarot complained of the treachery of the king of Hatzor, Abdi-Tarshi. Finally, Joshua, clearly understanding that Hatzor was the key to the land of Canaan, set it on fire when he captured it.

Later came Solomon, who levied a tax on the people "to build the house of the Lord"—the Temple—"the dwelling-place that was His, and the walls of Jerusalem, Hatzor, Megiddo, and Geser." (1 KINGS IX, 15.) The last three strongholds commanded the valleys of Hulda, Jezreel, and Ayalon. Two hundred years later, the Assyrians took Hatzor.

The first Book of Maccabees tells of a battle waged some 550 years later, between Jonathan, youngest of the Maccabean brothers, and the generals of the Seleucid king, Demetrius II.

Then Hatzor fell into oblivion. Civilizations come and go, the new rising from the old and falling back into dust. At times, as in the case of Hatzor, the very site is abandoned. Nothing is left but a mound, what the Israeli call a *tel*.

Time finally came for the archeologists to take over. Led by famed Yigael Yadin, they discovered exciting finds from 21 different strata covering 2,500 years: early Bronze Age to the Hellenistic second century B.C. The deepest excavation unearthed the Canaanite town burnt down by Joshua 5,000 years ago. By its size, it seems to have been one of the big cities of its time. Conquered, destroyed, rebuilt, and resettled, only to be once more laid waste and its inhabitants put to the sword, it is a tribute to the undying steadfastness of man, who, ever dispossessed, ever remakes his life, doomed to a certain death.

Having overpowered the Canaanites, the Israelites set to work. They were still half nomads, half settlers. It was Solomon who established them. For reasons of safety, only the stronghold was rebuilt. Nonetheless, it was overthrown by Assyrian, Persian and Greek conquerors. Of the passage of time and pride there is nothing left but what archeologists call successive strata. The Mycenean earthenware dug up from the bottom layer show that the battle of Joshua took place in the 12th century B.C.

The ramparts are older, dating from the eighteenth century, and had been built by the Hyksos. The upright stone slabs, set up by the people of the city hundreds of years before the coming of the Israelites, often decorated, are really remarkable. They are now on view to the public.

Before the arrival of Joshua, the Canaanites worshipped the moon goddess, as shown by a shrine unearthed among the ruins. The artistry of the high-relief sculpture in the basalt is admirable. Among others, a shrine to the sun god has also been uncovered.

The walls built by Solomon are strengthened by casemates. The plans of the fortress are the same as those of Megiddo, as recorded in the Bible.

As a rule, the findings in Hatzor bear out the Old Testament stories to the letter: the earthquake that destroyed the city of Jeroboam II (BOOK OF AMOS I, 1); the fire that laid waste the Israelite city in 732 B.C. (II KINGS XV, 29); even the name of King Phaceus, conquered by the Assyrians, was found written on a wine jar. Most of the findings are on show in the Archeological Museum of Jerusalem. Others, as we have seen, are in the museum of Ayelet Hashahar.

Rosh Pina

Six and a half miles from the kibbutz, on the road to Safad, we pass through Rosh Pina, "the corner stone," one of the first Jewish settlements (1882) of the grain-bearing region. The road climbs upward; Rosh Pina is 1,477 feet above sea level. One of the turns is marked by a stone in memory of Shlomo ben Josef, the first Jew to be executed in Palestine since the Roman occupation. He was a *shomer,* that is to say, a sentinel. Revolted by an Arab ambush in which four unarmed men and a woman had been ruthlessly murdered, he took the law into his own hands. Backed by two friends, he attacked a truck full of Arabs. The hand grenade did not go off. The three boys were arrested by the English. On the wall of his condemned cell, Shlomo ben Josef is said to have written: "The way to the heights is strewn with graves." He was barely 20 years old.

On top of the slope, 16 miles from Tiberias, standing proudly on a tableland, is one of Judaism's Four Holy Cities; mystical, with a magic charm, it is one of the strangest and most endearing of towns: Safad.

Safad

It is also written and pronounced: *Sfad, Sefad, Safed, Zefat,* and *Tsefat.* Roughly transcribed from the Hebrew, the spelling is changeable. The town, however, is altogether unchanged, as if under a spell, despite its current 14,600 inhabitants.

The main street, Rehov Jerusalem, runs the length of the town. At one end, there is the usual police station, a reminder of the English. At the other, there is the most blatantly modern building in Safad, the *Yeshiva,* or school of Talmudic learning; in other words, the most conservative establishment. Opposite the Yeshiva lies the Arab quarter, where artists live and preserve its old character, the revival of the past being the most progressive movement of modern art. The fashionable living quarter bears one of the oldest names in the world: Canaan. The first book in Hebrew characters was printed here, in 1578, on the first printing press ever to be seen in Asia.

On the hilltop overlooking the town, the Crusaders had built, in the 12th century, their usual stronghold, Foulques d'Anjou. Today, it is surrounded by a hedge that keeps out the public. However, the town authorities have made of the hilltop around the excavations a terraced garden, with a breathtaking view over the wide open landscape of Upper and Lower Galilee down to the Lake of Tiberias and far beyond, to the Golan Heights and Jordan. We are 2,737 feet above sea level, which, taking into account the 556-foot hollow, amounts to a height of nearly 3,300 feet.

Besides being a holy city, Safad was also the seat of the mystical school, steeped in the word-by-word study of Holy Writ, and known to the rest of the world by hearsay as the *Cabala*. The supposed author of the first work, the *Zohar* ("Book of Splendor"), Rabbi Simon Ben Yochai, is buried nearby, on Mount Meron, 3,964 feet high, the topmost peak of Israel.

Safad owes its fame to the *Zohar,* associated mainly with this town, despite being written in Spain. Its golden age was the chance outcome of a great disaster that overtook the Jews, driven out of Spain by King Ferdinand and Queen Isabella. A man born in exile, in Egypt, Isaac Luria, was so struck by the *Zohar* that he settled in Safad to go on with his studies. Soon, the best Jewish scholars had formed a group around him and a mystical school came into being.

The *Cabala* is a name well known to all men. But the true meaning of the Hebrew word *kabala* is "tradition," that of the inner life; its outward forms are called *masorah*. The key to this tradition is the *Zohar*, or enlightenment, containing both the statement of the Messianic faith and light thrown on its inner meaning. By settling in Safad, Rabbi Luria gave new life to the endlessly subtle and scholarly research begun by Simon Ben Yochai. He was followed by Rabbi Joseph Caro, also a sephardi—that is to say, of the Spanish branch of Jews—who, in turn, expanded and deepened Luria's studies. (His masterpiece, the *Shulchan Aruch*—a codification of Jewish religious practice, printed in Hebrew in Venice in 1565—actually has nothing to do with mysticism, and was completed before his move to Safad.) The cabalistic scholars, usually lost in a maze of thought, made one clear statement of fact. "The clean air of Safad helped them toward "knowledge and wisdom." Rabbi Ben Yochai and his followers held the basic premise that in the five books of Moses every word, every letter, held a hidden and symbolic, but clear meaning. He who could find the key would open the door to the real meaning of Revelation.

Bitter Days, and a Miracle

In 1837, an earthquake shook it to its foundations. Typhoid fever and starvation took a toll of 3,000 people in 1916. An Arab progrom, in 1929, killed hundreds more. In 1948, when the Israeli forces took Safad, it was, or so the people say, only by a miracle. Twelve thousand Arabs held all the key positions, including the police station stocked with firearms left behind by the English. The inhabitants, for the most part elderly God-fearing people, lived in daily dread. A handful of men, a mere 120, were sent to help them; they belonged to the *Palmach,* commando troops of the Israeli army. They crossed the enemy lines by night and took Safad by storm.

This brief summing-up cannot, of course, account for the miracle, which lay in a stroke of luck and in the *davidka*. This tiny handmade mortar, almost a toy, began to boom; it made a hellish noise. Thereupon, God knows why, it began to rain. Scared to death by their own rumors, firmly believing that the Jews had a secret weapon and power over the elements, the Arabs fled, abandoning their positions. So the story is told in Safad, with or without heavenly help, according to whether the storyteller sees the hand of God, or not, in the events of that night. A monument to the dead, topped by the *davidka,* reminds the passer-by of how the town was saved.

We have already spoken of the fortress. Before it was rebuilt by the Crusaders, it served the Jewish rebels as a stronghold against Roman rule in the year 66. At that time, the overseer of the workmen strengthening the fortress was one Ben Mattatia, a man whose name crops up at every turn in the history of Israel. He was in command of the garrison in Yodefat, and was forced to surrender after the fall of Safad. Made prisoner, he became a historian and changed his name to Josephus Flavius, in honor of his patrons Vespasian and Titus, who belonged to the Flavius family.

Formerly, on the summit, this first day of the month was made known throughout the countryside by a bonfire, "that none may be unaware," lit in the fortress of Safad and blazing from hilltop to hilltop. If the traveler should happen to be there at the time of the yearly pilgrimage to Mount Meron, he will see tens of thousands of Israelis and people from abroad walking in procession to the tomb of Rabbi Simon Ben Yochai, to pay homage to the great man who brought glory to their city.

But Mount Meron is also the largest Nature Reserve in Israel, covering about 25,000 acres. A hiking trail has been cleared to the highest peak in Galilee—3,963 feet above sea level. On the way are three observation points whence vistas of beautiful mountain scenery open out, also 14 "stations" from each of which can be seen the rich flora and fauna. These include the Kermes and Cyprus oak, terebinth, hawthorn, Judas tree and arbutus, the round-leafed cyclamen, the coral peony and the Galilee hymatoglossum; the fauna include the wild boar, marten, polecat, salamander and dormouse.

Take a look at the two old synagogues, one *Ashkenazi,* the other *Sephardi.* The Ashkenazi synagogue is somewhat over-ornate and garish. The Sephardi synagogue, older, is moving in its stark simplicity. In it lived, prayed, and worked Rabbi Luria. The visitor is shown a nook built into the thick wall where he used to read and write. Here too was the spiritual home of Rabbi Joseph Caro.

The Torah, carried with great pomp on the day of pilgrimage to the tomb of Simon Ben Yochai, is kept in a third synagogue, that of Rabbi Yossi Bennia, who is buried there.

Two cemeteries, the old and the new, are on the hillside outside the Sephardi temple. Both have their great men. The old graveyard shelters the remains of renowned scholars: Rabbi Luria, Cordoviero, his old teacher; Alkavetz, the composer of "Lecha Dodi," a song that found its way into the prayer books; Joseph Caro; and many others. Unknown ghosts lurk there, and "if the legs of the devout are of a sudden tired, it is from walking over hidden graves."

Artistry and Magic

Artists have managed to keep alive the look and feeling of the old Arab Quarter, now known as the Artists' Quarter. Refurbished, ages-old dwellings have new life and light, and tourists may visit them to watch pottery, paintings and sculpture being made, as well as to buy. On the edge of the quarter stands the renovated 200-year-old Turkish Post Office that's now the enchanting Rimon Inn. Its gardens are different levels of loveliness and fine scents, and its stonework and arches have a timeless atmosphere. The bar here was the postmaster's private apartment; the dining room stabled horses.

In the garden of another hotel, the Herzliya on Rehov Jerusalem, look at two huge, gnarled and twisted olive trees, with knotted roots and branches—said to be some 2,000 years old.

Then, for a touch of magic, visit the town swimming pool that's fed by a spring which—Arabs swear—makes women younger and girls more beautiful. In the old days, brides use to bathe there before their weddings, and it is a fact that men paid twice the usual price for a wife from Safad.

The town still has its small winding streets and alleys, its steep slopes, its stairways, its ruins. It seems, with its high clear air, to bring the seeker to the verge of the Enlightenment. This gathering-place of scholars, living only to find the hidden meaning of life, is haunted by ghosts whose voices we miss and whose heights we long to share.

On Toward Acre (Akko)

Between Safad and Akko, the road, lined with olive groves, runs straight through the plain for 32 miles. If we care to prolong our journey, we can turn right at Rama and drive on the sea road, to enjoy the beautiful view.

Piki'ine, or Pek'in, is a Druse village continuously populated by a few Jewish families for 2,000 years. The synagogue, never profaned, has been, for hundreds of years, supported and kept in repair by the villagers. The new Jewish village, with its shelved hillside fields, is nearby.

The next stop is Ma'alot, a modern town that has appeared like a mirage in the sun-baked rocks. The Rumanian settlers speak Arabic, but the Arabs don't speak Rumanian.

Every cluster of farms is followed by a stretch of olive trees and barren land that calls to mind the former state of the whole country. Then, all of a sudden, in the midst of the rocky hilltops, a television rod lifts its outstretched arms towards the unchanging blue sky.

Fortresses

From Milya, a Christian village built on the ruins of the *Chastiau dou Rei, Castrum Regis,* a bumpy path leads northwards a few miles to *Montfort,* which means "mountain stronghold." An hour away on foot, part of the way can be travled by car, if the driver is sure of his shock-absorbers. From Eilon a one-to-two-mile walk over hill and dale will also bring you to the ruins of this huge Crusader castle.

The fortress of the Knights of the Teutonic Order is in ruins since the onslaught of Baibars, that scourge of the Christians. It had long held out against Moslem attack; but from 1271 on, the eastern kingdom of the Crusaders had slowly begun to crumble. The broken stones of the awesome ramparts, pointing skywards on the hilltop, seem to cry for vengeance against the wrongs done to the Soldiers of Christ. It is one of the most striking reminders of the Crusades in the Holy Land. In the past 700 years, earthquakes have shaken, but not overthrown, these huge blocks of stone.

Less awesome, but just as interesting, are the remains of Metzuda Gadine, or Judine, in Yehi'am, another western fortress fallen in 1291. South of Milya, they can be reached by car, after passing Cabri.

Both strongholds, like the Pilgrim's Castle in Atlit, were part of the Christians' line of defense in Palestine. Much later Great Britain, to keep a grip on the country, was to set up a like network of fortified police stations, several of which you'll see on hillsides throughout the Galilee.

On the road to the west, the last place is Cabri, by the side of the well that fed drinking water to the aqueduct of St. John of Acre. A campsite opened here in 1956. The kibbutz is not remarkable except for its people. True settlers, they first pitched their tents on the shores of the Dead Sea, in Beit-ha-Arava, the "house of the desert." For years, they dug the salt out of the earth to make it tillable. When the Arab Legion occupied the countryside, they had to go. Downcast but not defeated, they went to Galilee and founded Cabri.

PRACTICAL INFORMATION FOR THE GALILEE

NAZARETH

HOTELS. In 3-star category are the **Grand New Hotel,** 90 rooms, and the **Nazareth,** 87 rooms. Both have bath or shower and are fully air-conditioned. **Hagalil,** the only kosher hotel in town, has 90 rooms with bath or shower, partly air-conditioned. All have bars and coffee shops.

YOUTH HOSTELS. About 10 miles out, half-way between Nazareth and Haifa, **Tivon** offers a **Youth Hostel** and **camp area** in an ideal center for trips to Nazareth, Haifa, Beit She'arim and the Oak Forests of Alonim and Carmel area. The hostel has family accommodations as well as dorm facilities; serves breakfast and has kitchen facilities for guests' use; 100 beds; telephone, right on bus line and highway. The camp site rents bungalows or tents; accommodates cars and trailers; has restaurants plus provision store, first aid station, and swimming.

Another youth hostel in the area is **Maayan Harod,** with 200 beds and every facility, even air-conditioning, swimming. The camp site here also has everything-plus.

CHRISTIAN HOSPICES are another good choice for Nazareth accommodations: **St. Charles Borromaeus Monastery,** 316 Rehov 12, German Sisters, Roman Catholic (clergy, pilgrims only); **St. Joseph Theological Seminary,** POB 99, Greek Catholic; **Religieuses de Nazareth,** 306 Casa Nova St., POB 274, Roman Catholic; **Casa Nova,** POB 198, Franciscan, Roman Catholic; **Franciscaines de Marie,** POB 41, Roman Catholic, French, pilgrims only. (See p. 27 for more details.)

RESTAURANTS. The food in Nazareth is less expensive than in larger cities, and equally good, but not as modern in preparation or restaurant atmosphere. Top place in town, for food and friendliness and people-watching, is **Abu Nassar,** Rehov Casanova (also known as the English Bar), European and Middle Eastern food, closed Sunday afternoons. The **Riviera** and the **Israel** both serve oriental specialties; the **Astoria,** Lebanese specialties. Also on Rehov Casanova (Paulous Street) are the **Hope** and the **Hatiqva,** serving Western as well as Jewish food; the **Abu Nowaras,** right next door, has oriental fare; **Abu Alasal** is another one to check. **Nof Nazareth,** on N. Panorama, is a good kosher spot.

TOURS: Cana, 4 miles north-east of Nazareth, where Jesus made his first miracle. Two churches, one Greek Orthodox, the other Franciscan, commemorate the event. Bus No. 353, near Mary's Fountain.

Mount Tabor. Half-way between Nazareth and Tiberias, overlooking the valley of Jezreel, it is the site of the Transfiguration. The Franciscan Basilica was built on remains of the Byzantines' and the Crusaders', from the sixth to the twelfth centuries. A Greek church adjoins the Basilica. Very fine view over the mountains of Gilboa, Samaria, the spurs of Mount Carmel, Galilee, and the Sea of Galilee. Bus No. 357 takes you to Dabburiya at the foot of Mt. Tabor. A taxi from Nazareth will take you to the summit, via the recently repaired road.

You can also take a sherut taxi. Other excursions take in, to the west, Beit She'arim and Megiddo, and, to the east, the base of Mount Gilboa and the Jordan Valley sites.

SHOPPING: In the old *souk* there is a wide range of souvenirs. **Recommended shops:** *Abu Nassar,* in the restaurant, Rehov Casanova; and the shop belonging to the Franciscan Fathers, in the Museum, which sells religious articles. Modern shopping center near the Greek Orthodox church. Lower on Casanova-Paulous Street is a strip of souvenir shops near the Galilee Hotel (Hagalil). It's fun to poke around *Your Souvenir Shop* here, and to wander down for shopping also at the *Holyland Bazaar Olivewood Workshop.* Remember, all closes on Sunday in this town.

CHURCHES AND PLACES OF WORSHIP: The **Basilica of the Annunciation** (RC), built on the site of the angel Gabriel's apparition to Mary and looked upon as the cradle of Christianity. The Franciscans are the guardians of this new building in the Italian style. The small **Church of St. Joseph** (RC), is also known under the name of the *Church of the Holy Family,* and was built on the supposed site of Joseph's carpenter's workshop. At the entrance is a small museum.

The **Salesian Church,** on a hill, is the finest in Nazareth. No public transportation; one has to climb up a steep path. The Greek Orthodox **Church of the Annunciation (St. Gabriel)** is the oldest, built nearly three hundred years ago. The **Greek Catholic Church,** near the market-place, on the site of the old synagogue frequented by Jesus, belongs to the Melchite community. At the Lebanese **Maronite Church,** in the Nabaa quarter, Mass is said in Arabic and Aramaic. The **Anglican Temple,** near Casanova Street, was built a hundred years ago. The **Baptist Temple,** near the Greek Orthodox church, dates from 1924. At the **Copt Church,** built in 1952 in the oriental quarter, Mass is observed according to the Egyptian rite. The Greek Catholic **Church of St. Joseph** adjoins the Seminary, on a hilltop overlooking Nazareth.

Mosques also are in Nazareth for Moslem worship, and **synagogues** with regular services are found in the area called Upper Nazareth.

The local IGTA will be able to supply you with the latest listing of services and events.

USEFUL ADDRESSES: Government Tourist Administration, Rehov Casanova; Tel. (065) 73003, 70555. **The Municipal Cultural Center** organizes musical evenings and other cultural activities.

Travel agencies: *Pilgrimage to Bible Lands,* 303, Rehov Casanova, The *Christian Travel Center,* Rehov Paul VI.

Taxis: tel. (065) 54027, 55105, 54745 or 55554. For sherut service to other towns, call 54412 or 55040.

TIBERIAS

Tiberias is capital of the Galilee region, principal (and only) city on the Sea of Galilee (also called Lake Kinneret). While it is a top Israeli vacation spot, it also attracts tourist masses from abroad, particularly for its year-round warm climate and its hot mineral springs that have lured far-flung travelers since prehistoric days. In winter, Tiberias is a leading resort for internationals, and each year the town facilities expand to meet the pleasurable needs of this ever-growing flock. Summer or winter, Tiberias is a sensible base for trips throughout the Galilee and Golan Heights.

HOTELS. All these establishments are air-conditioned. Some charge half-board, meaning you get breakfast plus either lunch or dinner automatically included in your bill. In the 5-star category, **Galei Kinneret** is at the edge of town, right on the sea; no chrome or modernity, but a definite sedate and distinctive character that have made it popular for decades with diplomats and authors. Private beach, heated pool, 125 rooms with TV.

Newest is the **Tiberias Plaza** located in the central new tourism development area. Posh and 5-star, its 272 rooms have TV and "the works"; there are shops, eateries, pool and nightclub.

Ganei Hamat, 4-star, stands as a triple treat: a beautiful, posh tower-hotel with 174 rooms, all tastefully decorated, in a total-facility building; a hotel and cottage colony next door, shaded by trees and great greenery, is equally well-kept and serviced; and the Tiberias Hot Springs Spa Center is on the same huge grounds. Private beach, tennis courts, nightclub.

On the hilltop above town, is the 4-star **Golan;** each of the 72 rooms has bath and a magnificent view of the sea far below; plus nightclub, bank, etc.

Another 4-star is the **Hartman,** offering 69 rooms with bath or shower; sauna, pool, TV, bar. Around the bend in the road is the 4-star **Ginton;** wonderful panoramic view from each of the 63 rooms; also coffee shop, bar, nightclub.

The 3-star hotels include the 83-room **Chen,** on the hilltop, with health club and nightclub; the **Yahalon** has 72 rooms with bath or shower; most of **Astoria's** 57 rooms have showers, as is in the 56-room **Peer,** where there's also a nightclub. **Daphna's** 73 rooms overlook the sea.

Two-star hotels are all on the hilltop; the 52-room **Eden,** 30-room **Ron,** 58-room **Menora Gardens,** and 33-room **Ariston,** all with bath or shower. The **Garden** has 25 rooms with TV, the **Sara** has 16 rooms, and the **Danny** has 22 rooms.

All the 1-star hotels are on the hilly slopes above town, and include 20-room **Continental,** the 18-room **Eshel;** the 25-room **Polonia,** and the 65-room **Ginossar.**

You can opt for many other types of over-night facilities in and near Tiberias —from thatched huts or camping sites, to luxurious kibbutz guest houses or a Christian hospice that might offer elegant rooms or monks' cells. And check other Galilee listings for an American-style dude ranch, ski villa, national park camp or mystical city caravan inn-cum-post office-cum-hotel.

KIBBUTZ GUEST HOUSES.

An elegant 4-star kibbutz guest house is beautifully situated at the sea's edge, a five-minute drive north of town: the **Nof Ginossar,** with 106 air-conditioned rooms, duty-free shops, private beach, swimming, fishing and water sports, plus interesting folklore evenings.

Also on the Sea of Galilee shore, but reached by boat from Tiberias, the **Ein Gev Holiday Village** is operated by the kibbutz of the same name. It offers 50 rooms, 2 twin-bedroom bungalows with kitchenettes; all air-conditioned; also private beach. Open all year, as is the nearby camping site. This well-known kibbutz, a must-see site in itself, also has a famous seaside restaurant featuring fresh "St. Peter's Fish," and an annual spring festival with national and international performers.

CHRISTIAN HOSPICES flourish in this area, and present tourists with other over-night options. In Tiberias, you'll find these hospices: **Mount of Beatitudes,** Box 87, Franciscan, Roman Catholic, Italian; **Peniel-by-Galilee YMCA,** POB 192 (super high rates); **Church of Scotland Center,** POB 104, British; **Terra Sancta** (Old Town), POB 179, Franciscan, Roman Catholic (bed only); **Franciscan Convent of Transfiguration,** Mount Tabor, Roman Catholic, Italian. See *Facts At Your Fingertips* chapter for more details, and book in advance.

YOUTH HOSTELS in Israel are for all ages, and *Facts At Your Fingertips* chapter gives all details. In mid-town Tiberias, there's the 1978-renovated **Tiberias Youth Hostel,** with 200 beds and every convenience/facility.

Two miles north of Tiberias, in a renovated Turkish building at the edge of the sea, sits the **Tabgha Hostel,** surrounded by palms and eucalyptus. The **Poriah Taiber Hostel** is five miles south of Tiberias, deep in the hills overlooking the southern end of the lake (new family rooms, 1978).

Between here and Safed, 2 more hostels offer good accommodation for all ages, with all facilities: the excellent **Yoram,** at Karë Deshe; **Nature Friends,** at Rosh Pina. At Kiryat Shmuel, **Danny Hotel** has 22 air-conditioned rooms.

CAMPING SITES are also nearby: across the lake are the **Ein Gev, Ha'on** and **Ma'agan** camping areas; a mile south of town is **Kfar Hittim** site; all have assorted, comfortable facilities.

RESTAURANTS. On the quay a variety of fish, European and Oriental meals are served at the seaside cafés—the **Hayam, Nof Kinneret** and **Galei Gil.** The **Quiet Beach** is a floating restaurant specializing in seafood. It is air-conditioned and can seat up to 700 people.

Climbing up into town, in the hotel section, are several café-restaurants: **Hof Gai** is a good food spot, as is **Si Si Bon,** and the **Signonot,** a café and club near the museum lakeside. In the same area try light food at **Gideon Gallery & Bar,** or go all out and splurge at **Donna Grazia**—a fine restaurant, bar, gallery, with dancing at night—or nearby **C'est Si Bon** (which is)—or **Mitzpor**, on the Nazareth Road, overlooking the town and sea. **The House,** opposite Lido Beach, is a Chinese restaurant featuring a Tai chef, Tai and Cantonese food—all inside an interesting, huge old house set high above the street.

Snack spots and cafés are all around, and the Sonol Station sports a **Wimpy** hamburger stand; **Pizzeria Rimini** is here, too. A new strip of small shops, cafés, quick foods, snacks, ice cream and such, can be found on Habanim St., off Hajardin St.

The sea-front public beaches have night-time cafés. The large concrete ship by the road is a steak and grilled fish house: **Shells Beach** 206 on Safed Street has original decoration. For southern fried chicken and grilled steaks try the **Vered Hagalil** restaurant (see Sports below).

WHAT TO SEE: Must-see sites include the hot springs, the tombs of the rabbis, the excavated mosaic floor of a Canaanite synagogue, the kibbutzim Degania and Ein Gev, the various New Testament places (Mt. of Beatitudes, Migdal, Tabgha, Capernaum and Mt. Tabor).

Boat trips organised by the Kinneret Company. Departure from the landing-pier on Hayam Street, toward Capernaum, Ein Gev, and Kibbutz Degania; 2–3 sailings daily.

SHOPPING: *Grety* and *Maskit,* both shops in the Rassco Center; *Souvenir Shop* in the Ginton Hotel; *Galei Kinneret Hotel Gallery; Signonot Art Gallery,* lakeside, old city, near the museum; Art Gallery *Rivka's Fortress,* Donna Gracia Street at Tiberias' old city wall, and the nearby galleries of *I. Nesher* and *Yaskil.* A new Shopping Center is rising midtown near the beach, already boasting several shops, beauty parlor, etc.

SPORTS: The sport here is **water-skiing:** then comes **sailing** and **swimming.** Facilities at several seafront installations: *Blue Beach, Quiet Beach, Shells Beach 206, Lido Beach, Ron Beach* and *Hof Gai.*

Newest popular sport is **horseback riding trips** into the Galilee hills and along the lakefront. From *Vered Hagalil,* a small American-styled dude ranch 15 minutes from Tiberias at Korazim on the Tiberias-Rosh Pina road. Another riding establishment is located on the main, lake-circling road, between the center of Tiberias and the hot springs. *Neot Hakikar* also operates a Crusaders' Trail horseback trip; call their Jerusalem office, or ask *IGTA* for details.

USEFUL ADDRESSES AND NUMBERS. Israel Government Tourism Administration office *(IGTA),* 8 Elhadef St., (Area code 067) 20992; **Egged Bus Station,** Rehov Hayarden, 21082; **Taxis,** 20131, 20353; **Sherut taxis,** 20098; **Boat tours,** 20227; **Police,** 20444; **Ambulance,** 20111.

SAFAD

(Also Zafat)

One of four cities holy to Judaism, it boasts a fine arts colony and it was here that mystical Jewish works were written.

HOTELS. Safad's hotel situation is unique in Israel. Because it sits 2,790 feet high, it is one of the few places in the country that is reasonably pleasant during the intense heat of July and August. As a consequence, Safad's hotels raise their rate 20% during the July-August period. They also raise them during the Passover and during the September Jewish holidays. Furthermore, some charge a minimum rate that includes half-board, giving you a choice of lunch or dinner, as well as breakfast. The hotels are situated in two sections: on Mt. Canaan, above the town, and in Safad itself.

There's a special 4-star hotel here, on the fringe of the Artists' Quarter: **Rimon Inn.** Once, it was a Post Office when the Turks ran the country; today's dining room then stabled horses. Restored in 1967, most of it is some 200 years old, with a new wing following the graceful stone architecture. Fruit grows for guests to pick in a garden of flowers; swimming pool. Timeless atmosphere; a unique "away-from-it-all" place; 36 unique rooms.

Zefat, with 36 rooms, is the latest 4-star hotel, sitting on Mt. Canaan.

The 3-star hotels include the air-conditioned 50-room **Ron,** with nightclub, pool, room TVs; the 26-room **Ruckenstein,** on Mt. Canaan; the **David's** 42 rooms with bath or shower; the **Central,** 54 rooms, and the 55-room **Pisgah,** with a garden and piano bar. All these are partly air-conditioned. Then there's the 84-room **Rakefet** on Ha'ari St., the 36-room **Beit Berinson** which is air-conditioned, the 34-room **Nof Hagalil,** on Mt. Canaan. The **Motel Canaan,** at Beit Shinar, 21 rooms, has kitchenettes, bar, coffee shop.

Hotels with 2-star ratings are the 22-room **Friedman** and the 20-room **Hadar.** There's also a *Youth Hostel* here—**Beit Benjamin**—with 160 beds plus family rooms, kitchens and meal service; on bus line.

RESTAURANTS. Pinati, on Jerusalem Street, looks like nothing much, but has good Middle-Eastern food, and is not expensive. **Milo,** in the artists' quarter, is a gathering-place for the local fraternity, Kosher **Hamifgash** is a top and popular restaurant, on Jerusalem St., not far from non-kosher **Azmon.** There's good food at **Batia** (Oriental/European) on Jerusalem St., and also at the restaurant in the Egged Bus Station.

WHAT TO SEE. Just outside town is a big **swimming pool** that attracts people of all ages, including tourists, in warm weather. For centuries, however, women came here from all over the entire region to bathe in the waters that now feed this pool—waters long fabled to make bathers beautiful.

The **Artists' Quarter** is quite interesting: a colorful conglomerate of old Arab buildings where artists and craftsmen live and work; many galleries and shops;

one entrance ticket gets you into the Printing Museum and Glicenstein Municipal Museum.

Old Synagogues abound in this holy city where thousands of faithful Jews come on pilgrimage each year to the places their revered teachers once lived, worked and died. Some to not miss are: *Ha'ari Hasephardi,* near the cemetery, the only one to have withstood intact the earthquake of 1837. Of more recent date, the *Ha'ari Ashkenazim* has a fine arch, dating from the early nineteenth century. A medieval atmosphere in the synagogue of Rabbi Joseph Caro, who worked there on his *magnum opus,* the *Shulchan Aroch.* The sanctuaries of *Abouhav* and *Alsheikh* are well worth a visit. The Citadel (Metzuda), once a Crusaders' stronghold.

Note: Each spring, thousands of pious Jews hie to Mount Meron, near Safad, for *Lag Ba'omer,* the traditional pilgrimage to the tomb of Rabbi Shimon Bar Yochai, generally considered the author of the mystical "Book of Splendor:" the *Zohar.* On that particular evening (check dates of Jewish calendar with *IGTA*), the pilgrims build a gigantic bonfire, sing, and dance. Mount Meron also is a *Nature Reserve,* Israel's largest, with 25,000 acres and hiking trails, etc.

NIGHTLIFE as such exists only in the summer. **Outdoor dancing** at the *Metzuda,* a pleasant café at the top of Metzuda Park. Several hotels have dancing in the evenings. There are three **nightclubs:** the *Moadon Hashaot Haktanot,* in a vaulted cave, formerly a Turkish hammam. *Leilot Kanaan* ("Nights of Canaan") is in the basement of a medieval house. And don't forget the nightclub at the *Ron* hotel. *Rimon Inn* also has a marvelous little bar room.

USEFUL NUMBERS. IGTA (Area code 067) 30633; **Egged Bus Station,** 31122; **Sherut taxis,** 32577, 30039, 31466; **Police,** 30444; **Ambulance,** 30333.

OTHER SPOTS IN THE GALILEE

AFULA. A large Galilee town, built by immigrants mostly from the USA, it lies between Megiddo and Mt. Tabor, south of Nazareth and southeast of Tiberias. The road through Afula is frequently taken to and from Tiberias, and features a good, clean self-service restaurant, **Doverat,** with a nice gift shop. Run by the Doverat kibbutz, the restaurant is part of a station for car service and petrol. In Afula proper, there are several cafes for meals and refreshments.

VERED-HAGALIL (Korazim). Israel's only "dude ranch" caters to the horse-lover, American-style. Open year-round in the mountains overlooking Kinneret, with charming cottages dotting well-landscaped but natural paths and nooks. A new bunkhouse cottage accommodates families or groups or dorm-dwelling young people, and horseback riding's the big activity. Riding tours cover holy sites and sights. Apartments, junior-suites or cabins, with rates from $15–$35 per person, double occupancy. Restaurant serves U.S. food.

HULEH NATURE RESERVE is an excellent site for picnics and features free, guided tours. Nearby **Kibbutz Gonen** overlooks the Huleh Valley and gives tourists the opportunity of sharing a buffet lunch with kibbutzniks (reasonable prices), touring the settlement, and enjoying informal discussions about life here.

KIRYAT SHMONA. (Also, Kiryat She'mona and Qiryat Shmona.) Near the Lebanese border, this town of relatively new immigrants (mostly from Arab lands) and terrorist disasters has attracted so many tourists that it now has a 90-room, comfortable, air-conditioned 4-star accommodation: **North Hotel,** with room T.V., restaurant, nightclub.

METULLA. A border town where you can visit the "Good Fence"—Israel Defense Forces' medical station set up to help Lebanese sick or war-wounded. Worth it. *IGTA* built an Observation Deck here in 1980. Accommodations are available in two 2-star hotels: **Sheleg Halevanon,** with 31 rooms, tennis courts and a pool, and **Hamavri,** with 18 rooms with baths. Nearby is **Kfar Giladi** 3-star kibbutz guest house. Also not far is **Tel Hai Hostel**—in the pleasant park of the same name, which has an interesting background. Singles and families will find good facilities here.

ROSH PINNA. Near Safad. **Nature Friends' Hostel:** 100 beds, restaurant, family rooms, kitchen, on bus line.

UPPER GALILEE KIBBUTZ GUEST HOUSES/RESORTS. Stretching from Tiberias to Israel's northernmost town, Metulla, some 40 miles distant, this region encompasses the northern shore of Lake Kinneret (Sea of Galilee) and climbs to the heights of Mt. Hermon. Rich in historical and biblical sites, Upper Galilee has few towns, but its interesting scenery is studded with small villages and kibbutz and moshav settlements. Many of these settlements offer accommodations for tourists.

Ayelet Hashahar Kibbutz boasts one of the most posh facilities of the region: a 4-star, 120-room, air-conditioned guest house, plus duty-free shops, fine restaurant, coffee shop, bar and pool. The ruins of Hatzor lie just opposite the kibbutz, and there is a large and interesting museum with findings from and about the ancient city. **Nof Ginossar** also has a 4-star guest house, described in Tiberias information.

Hagoshrim, near the national park, Horshat Tal, is an interesting kibbutz with a 70-room, air-conditioned, 3-star guest house that has tennis courts and a swimming pool. The dining room was converted from an interesting old Arab structure. The kibbutz grounds are riven with the foaming, racing waters that make up the sources of the Jordan River. Hagoshrim has the distinction of being Israel's first *ski resort.* Since the first winter after the Six-Day War, it has been the jumping-off place for skiing on the mile-high slopes of Mt. Hermon. Equipment's for rent here and there's a mountain cable car. Just five miles north, near Metulla, lies **Kfar Giladi**—another kibbutz with a *ski resort,* as well as a guest house with 130 3-star rooms. Well worth a visit, Kfar Giladi is also the home of the official *Museum of the Israeli Defense Forces;* located quite near the *Tel Hai Monument.* The kibbutz offers an interesting tour of its grounds.

Kfar Blum's guest house is also 3-star, with air-conditioning for its 46 rooms, plus pool and tennis. **Kibbutz Lavi,** (quite Orthodox which is more unusual than not, among these settlements) has a lovely 70-room, air-conditioned guest house, also with pool and tennis. Aside from agricultural work, this kibbutz also manufactures synagogue furniture for export.

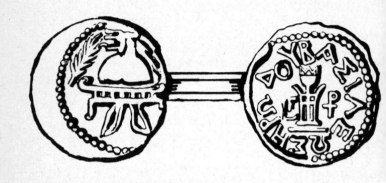

BORDER AREAS

The West Bank, Golan Heights, Gaza, Sinai

The West Bank is the term generally used to describe those parts of Yehuda Shomrom (Samaria and Judea) which lie west of the River Jordan. A part of British-mandated Palestine until 1948, it was occupied by Arab armies (principally Jordan's Arab Legion) in the first Arab-Israeli War and was melded into Jordan in 1950.

The 3,200-square-mile area bulged into Israel like the belly of a fat man, cinched at the waist by a tight belt (the belt buckle being Jerusalem). The northern part of the bulge narrowed Israel's coastal strip between Tel Aviv and Haifa into a slim corridor sometimes no more than ten miles wide. On the first night of 1967's Six-Day War, Tel Aviv itself was shelled by heavy artillery fired from Kalkiliya, less than 15 miles away.

As we go to press, all of the West Bank remains under Israeli administration, along the Six-Day War's ceasefire line, straddling the Jordan River down to, and partly around, the Dead Sea. Of the 639,300 Arabs living here, a large number are Moslem, and about half were refugees or are refugees' children. Some half of these lived in camps before 1967, though almost all are resettled in new homes now. In fact, there's a big building and economy boom here, and West Bankers were virtually inactive during 1973–4 war and terrorism. Many communities even vowed support to Israel then, and almost all announced they preferred not to return to Jordanian rule. Jordan sees it otherwise, naturally, since the West Bank holds half its pre-1967 population and about 10% of its land area.

Today's West Bank has reverted almost totally to its biblical names: Judea (east and south of Jerusalem) and Samaria (north of Jerusalem). Official in Israel, these names seem fitting, as the areas are so "biblical," with largely agricultural economy and many crops being the same as in Bible days—grapes, wheat, olives, barley—and some of the farming methods and husbandry have not changed much since Jesus roamed this very land.

The West Bank—Judea and Samaria—is an integral part of the Holy Land, many of the principal events of the Old and New Testaments having occurred here. The Bible is an indispensable guide to the region and a "must" for its full appreciation.

Later in this chapter, we will also look at the other border areas—the Golan Heights (once part of Syria), the Gaza Strip and Sinai (formerly part of Egypt).

The West Bank

Few people realize that Bethlehem is, figuratively speaking, a stone's throw from Jerusalem. Just about four miles away, it's a 15-minute drive from the center of Jerusalem to the city of the birth of Christ. There's a regular bus service plying the route now (bus No. 30) and sherut taxis going from both East and West Jerusalem.

If you're driving, head south to the Talpiot section of Jerusalem, following the Hebron Road right out of the city. You'll pass Kibbutz Ramat Rachel, the last Jewish outpost on the border with Jordan before the Six-Day War, and then Mar Elias Monastery.

The monastery, on a rise to the left of the Jerusalem-Bethlehem road, was in Jordanian territory and used as the principal bastion south of Jerusalem by the Arab Legion. The ferocity of the battle here is etched in the walls of Ramat Rachel and Mar Elias.

Past the hill, the road descends and a biblical panorama unfolds—there are small orchards and large fields, where sheep and goats graze, tended by black-garbed shepherds.

Rachel's Tomb

On the approach to Bethlehem is Rachel's Tomb, perhaps the most holy of Jewish shrines after the Wailing Wall and the Tomb of the Patriarchs. The tomb is in a small 19th-century domed building put up by the British-Jewish philanthropist, Sir Moses Montefiore. The tall, white sepulcher in the inner room is usually surrounded by worshipers and pilgrims. Rachel was the wife of the Patriarch Jacob and the mother of Benjamin. Her passing is specifically recorded in the Book of Genesis (XXXV, 19)—"And Rachel died and was buried in the way to Ephrath, which is Bethlehem. And Jacob set a pillar upon her grave; that is the pillar of Rachel's grave unto this day." The site is sacred to both Moslems and Jews, and there's usually a long line of the faithful waiting to enter the shrine.

Bethlehem

Just ahead, the road forks—the right side goes to Hebron, the left, up to Bethlehem. The name Bethlehem means "House of Bread" in Hebrew and "House of Meat" in Arabic. It figures prominently in biblical history—it is the setting of the Book of Ruth, and the fields around it are where Ruth and Boaz met and fell in love. (Ruth was the great-grandmother of David, who was born in Bethlehem and was summoned from there to become king.)

But, of course, it is the birth here of the Christ child to the Virgin Mary that has made Bethlehem one of the holiest places in Christendom and a focal point of pilgrimage from all over the world.

On entering the town, to the left, you can look down on Shepherd's Field, where the angel announced the birth of Jesus to the shepherds tending their flock.

The road continues directly to Manger Square, a large open plaza in front of the Church of the Nativity. From the outside, the structure seems more citadel than church, with thick, stone walls and a relatively squat appearance. Even the traditional tall church doors are absent. Instead there is a small opening about four feet high. Appropriately, it is called the *Door of Humility,* as everyone must bow to enter. Even Pope Paul VI, the first reigning pontiff to visit the Holy Land since St. Peter, had to bend low to go through the aperture. (It is said that the door was thus built centuries ago not so much for humility's sake, but to prevent infidels from storming into the church on horseback.)

The first church was erected here by the Emperor Constantine in the fourth century. The original edifice was destroyed and a new church was put up two centuries later by the Emperor Justinian. The present structure is largely the restoration carried out by the Crusaders in the 11th or 12th century.

The length of the church is divided by four rows of columns in reddish limestone. The wooden ceiling is made of stout English oak, a gift of King Edward IV. The vast amount of lead the monarch donated to cover the roof was melted down by the Turks to use as ammunition in their wars against the Venetians.

Three Christian denominations share rights in the Church—Roman Catholic (Franciscan friars), Greek Orthodox and Armenian. Each has its own chapels and altars. Before the central Altar of the Nativity, stairs descend to the Grotto of the Nativity. A star on the floor of the lamp-lit grotto marks the spot where Jesus was born. Next to the grotto is the Chapel of the Manger, where the Virgin Mary placed the new-born Christ child.

Other churches and cloisters of the different denominations are built right up to and connect with the Church of the Nativity.

On the south side of Manger Square is Milk Grotto Street, leading, naturally, to the Milk Grotto. A small Franciscan church stands on the site of the cave where, according to tradition, the Virgin spilled a few drops of milk while nursing her child. These dropped on the dark stones and turned them milky-white. Pilgrims can take little packets of chalky powder made from the stone of the grotto. The powder is said to have the power of increasing the milk flow of nursing mothers.

Near the Milk Grotto, look toward the east for a splendid landscape with the Field of Ruth and the Wilderness of Judah unfolding towards the Dead Sea. Another famous nearby site is King David's Wells—three large cisterns which are identified with the wells from which David "longed to drink" during a battle with the Philistines.

Back in Bethlehem in Manger Square, you'll find, on the south-west corner, a new Government Tourist Office. If you happen to be in Bethlehem in the morning hours, walk up to the market (a few streets west of Manger Square) to see the bustle and color of an Oriental *souk*. It's a good chance to see men and women from villages near Bethlehem in their picturesque traditional garb. Tourists are everywhere, and there are many shops and eateries, even recommended accommodations.

Herodion and Mar Saba

To the east of Bethlehem lie two of the most interesting and least-known sites in the West Bank—Herodion and the Monastery of Mar Saba.

Herodion was one of a string of fortresses built in Judea by King Herod (Masada was another). The huge, circular bastion was among the last to fall to the Romans in the Jewish uprising of A.D. 66–70. It is believed that the defenders here, as at Masada, took their own lives rather than fall captive to Rome.

The fortress was one of Herod's proudest monuments and he himself was buried here. Built on a height 2,500 feet above sea level, it commands the Wilderness of Judah and the Dead Sea. The defensive walls were built over 70 feet high and the great towers over 100 feet from the floor of the fortress. Look to the northwest from here and you'll see Mt. Scopus in Jerusalem.

Closer to the Dead Sea, built on the very wall of a high canyon, is Mar Saba Monastery. The monastery was founded by St. Saba of Cappadocia in the fifth century and was long a center of theological literature and poetry. At one time, as many as 5,000 monks were at Mar Saba . . . today, the monastery is tended by 14 remaining monks.

The isolated monastery was destroyed time and again through the centuries by invading armies and desert marauders. It was sacked for the last time in 1835, and the present fantastic, fortress-like complex was rebuilt by the Imperial Russian Government in 1840. The living quarters are five stories tall and have 110 rooms.

Men are permitted to visit the monastery, but women are strictly forbidden to enter—even female animals, they say. Women, however, may look over the monastery from a special tower to the south of the building.

South of Solomon's Pools

To the west of Bethlehem is the Arab village of Beit Jalla, set among olive groves and vineyards. The friars at the Cremisan Monastery here tend their vines with care and come up with some creditable wines. You can sample and buy Cremisan wines here, though they are available in Jerusalem.

The Hebron Road continues to wind south. A few miles from Bethlehem, on the left, are Solomon's Pools. But most authorities think that the pools date from the Roman period. The Turkish fortress by the watershed was built in the 16th century. The pools, however, still provide a part of Jerusalem's water supply, as they have been doing at least 2,000 years.

After the pools, to the right, you'll catch sight of Kfar Etzion. This group of Jewish farming settlements was destroyed by the Arab armies in the 1948 war and most of the inhabitants killed. For almost 20 years after, it was used as a Jordanian army outpost. Following the Six-Day War, it was resettled as a farming community; some of the new settlers are the descendants of those killed over 30 years ago. Kfar Etzion has built a new youth hostel near the old Jordanian army barracks and opened a kiosk.

Now the road goes through some of the highest country in Judea. A tall tower to the left rises from the Arab village of Halhul, where the locals show what they claim to be the tomb of the prophet Jonah (Nebi Yunes), who is also revered by Moslems.

Hebron

The loftiest (3,050 feet above sea level) of the four Holy Cities of Israel, Hebron has a history of continuous habitation going back 5,000 years. The city is often mentioned in the Bible, beginning with the story of Abraham. It was by Hebron in the Plain of Mamre that Abraham pitched his tents. The Oak of Mamre, or Abraham's Oak, is pointed out today by Hebronites, though the tree seen there is really a relative youngster a few hundred years old. Abraham bought a cave in the Field of Machpelah and buried his wife Sarah here. He, too, was buried here, as were the Patriarchs Isaac and Jacob and their wives Rebecca and Leah. Thus the Cave of Machpelah (*Ma'arat Ha' Machpelah* in Hebrew) became the Tomb of the Patriarchs—the holiest Jewish site after the Wailing Wall. A Jewish legend claims Adam and Eve dwelt here after their expulsion from the Garden of Eden and that they, too, are buried here. Thus the ancient Hebrew name for Hebron: *Kiryat Arba* —The Town of the Four—in honor of the four venerated couples buried here.

Long before David was made king and ruled some eight years from Hebron, Moses sent scouts to spy out the fields in the Valley of Eshkol near Hebron, and they returned bearing huge clusters of grapes, pomegranates and figs, attesting to the richness of the Promised Land.

From the ancient days to the 20th century, Jews had always dwelt in Hebron . . . until 1929. That year, Arabs annihilated the entire Jewish population of the city. In 1968, a handful of Orthodox Jews came back to dwell in the City of the Patriarchs. Today, they live here again, in a large and modern, thriving and very orthodox community that tops the hills: *Kiryat Arba.*

Father Abraham of the Jews is also a saintly prophet revered by Moslems, who call him *al-Khalil er-Rahman,* the Friend of the Lord. The Tomb of the Patriarchs today, in fact, is a mosque.

The high, impressive wall around the mosque was built in the time of Herod, and a few Arabs believe that some of the huge stones came from Solomon's Temple. The wall is about 50 feet high and almost ten feet thick. A basilica was built on the site in the sixth century and a Crusader Church in the 12th, giving the building its present form.

The Mosque of Ibrahim, or *Haram al-Khalil* (Sacred to the Friend), is approached on foot. You leave your car or bus in a parking lot and ascend the road, which is lined with shops and crowded with hucksters. On the way, you see the wares of the city, mainly articles of Hebron glass, sheepskins, goatskins and woodcarvings.

Notice the long flights of stairs leading up to the mosque. Previously, no Jews were permitted access to the shrine, and they were allowed only to ascend to the seventh step.

Rising higher and higher, many people wonder why this is called the Cave of the Machpelah, when it's obviously on top of a hill. The answer is that the tombs, in fact, are in a cave underneath the hill over which the shrine is built.

Inside, the richly-decorated rooms are emblazoned with selections from the Koran. The first cenotaphs are those of Isaac and Rebecca, then Abraham and Sarah, and Jacob and Leah. Note the intricately embroidered green and gold cloths over the cenotaphs. The stained-glass windows through which the light filters are over 700 years old.

There is also a niche in which Moslems believe is the tomb of Joseph, though in Jewish tradition, the bones of Joseph were buried in Shechem, present-day Nablus, in Shomrom (Samaria).

Near the Tomb of the Patriarchs is Birket es-Sultan, the Pool of the Sultans. This is the place thought by some to be the very spot where David meted out justice to the murderers of Saul's son, Ish-Boshet—"And David commanded his young men, and they slew them, cut off their hands and their feet, and hanged them up over the pool in Hebron."

Going through the narrow alleys of the Hebron *casbah* you can see artisans at work, blowing glass, turning pottery and shaping wood in the age-old manner.

The Hebron Road

Favored by private and public transport—especially speedy sheruts —as a short route to Beersheba, the Hebron Road offers tourists an interesting view of the region. Near Hebron, the road will take you to Moshav Elazar (18 km. from Jerusalem): a 1975 Gush-Etzian Jewish settlement. Stop for a short talk and coffee with US, Canadian and UK settlers, visit industries and gift shop. Some 28 families live here now.

As you travel this road, you can't help noticing the bounty of the land, the herds, the people who live here. Always a rich agricultural area (sometimes called the "breadbasket" of the Middle East), this portion of the West Bank recently has become more productive than ever. Though its Arab citizens may have political differences with the Israelis who now administer the region, they seem to see eye-to-eye when it comes to tending land and flocks. Instruction, machinery, plus intensive specialized help from Israeli Ministries of Agriculture and Education have paid off for these local farmers and herdsmen in ways almost shockingly visible to those who have passed this way during the past several years. Today, these fields rarely are worked by hand with ancient wooded tools and methods practiced just a few years ago. Instead, most exhibit neat rows cut by mechanized farm equipment, and bulge with healthy grains, fruits and vegetables—lavishly abundant crops nurtured and protected by the best skills and products modern knowledge can devise. The animals also have multiplied tremendously, and are fat, sleek beasts.

The homes have changed as much as the fields and flocks. While many picturesque old structures still remain, they stand in tandem with the legions of large, new villas, complete with electricity and running water, that have sprouted up throughout the region, always retaining the graceful Arab touches that make these villages and towns such a joy to see. Even the people appear more prosperous, sporting better, brighter clothes and vehicles. Riding through this territory and noting all this, one can hardly help thinking that though these people have suffered from the continuing Middle East political and military fracas, perhaps this balance has been struck—at least in some ways—by their introduction to the 20th century and its ways of making much of daily life easier, safer and more prosperous.

Today, as in the time of Moses, Hebron remains famous for its fruits, figs, and vegetables. Before the Six-Day War, Hebron foods graced the tables of the sheikhs of Araby, being in demand even in Kuwait. Thanks to Israel's Open Bridges policies, the flow of West Bank goods continues—it did not even halt during the 1973 war or other troubled times.

A Trip to Jericho

When starting out for Jericho from Jerusalem, don't fail to take the Bible along. The Old and New Testaments are crammed with references to this ancient city, which may be the oldest in the world. Some archeologists say Jericho was a flourishing city 10,000 years ago.

Damascus, which is generally believed to be the oldest continuously settled city in the world, is around 7,000 years old.

The Jerusalem-Jericho highway is probably the best in the West Bank. Widened and repaved by Israelis, its forerunner (Jordan-built with USA help) can be seen branching off towards Jordan's capital, Amman (though the farthest you will be able to go will be the Jordan River, equidistant between Jerusalem and Amman).

Just a few miles out of Jerusalem, you will come to Bethany—the home of Mary and Martha. It was at Bethany that Jesus raised their brother, Lazarus, from the dead, and where He came with His disciples on the first Palm Sunday.

Off the road, on the left, is a garden leading to the 1953-built Roman Catholic church. Inside, the marble-floored church is decorated with mosaics depicting the story of Lazarus. The large cupola is impressively covered with gold. The floor also reveals some interesting Byzantine mosaics. Behind the church are excavations where remains of the Roman, Byzantine and Crusader periods have been unearthed.

Past the church, going up a hill, is the entrance to the Tomb of Lazarus. The key is with the people running a souvenir stand opposite. For a small fee, you're taken down 24 slippery steps into a dark cave which is deliciously cool no matter how sultry the weather outside. There you may view the tomb. Above: the Greek Orthodox Church of Lazarus.

The Wilderness of Judah

The road to Jericho traverses the Wilderness of Judah, one of the most starkly beautiful landscapes that can be imagined.

On the road, a police-station (hut) marks a road where an ageless caravanserai supposedly tops the Inn of the Good Samaritan. It was around these precincts, too, that John the Baptist preached repentance, "for the Kingdom of Heaven is at hand."

Elevation markers on the side of the road pace your descent. Even after you pass the one saying "Sea Level," you note that there's still a long way down . . . and the only sea you see is the Dead Sea, shimmering far below to your right.

The road forks and Jericho is to your left; the other road continues to the Jordan River and the Dead Sea. A small road to the right leads to Nebi Musa (the Prophet Moses), where Moslems put the site of the prophet's tomb and erected what looks, from the road, like an ancient town. The Bible, though, tells us that Moses' tomb is "unknown to this day" but lies somewhere in the Mountains of Moab.

Riding in the silent, hot valley toward Jericho, what seems to be a mirage emerges on the left. It is a city of low buildings and huts, stretching over acres and acres of ground. This unlikely place was the site of a refugee camp, one of the largest in Jordan. Today, it's deserted, as it has been since the Six-Day War.

Jericho's Highlights

Jericho is a huge oasis, an inviting cluster of green rising out of the parched, dry desert which completely surrounds it. Palm trees and citrus groves seem to be everywhere in lush profusion. An ancient saying reads: "All Palestine is not to be compared to Jericho for sheer luxury."

Go right through the main street and pass the main square, following the signs to the Hisham Palace. This will show you a bit of the opulence that once held sway in Jericho. The enormous palace was built by the Omayyads in the seventh century as a winter resort for the caliphs, who came down from Damascus to enjoy Jericho's balmy weather. A brilliantly colored mosaic, *The Tree of Life,* in the bath house of the palace is a "must."

A little more than a mile away, in the west part of town, is Tel es-Sultan, under which lies ancient Jericho. Here was the Jericho of Joshua, who had the Children of Israel circle the walls of the city seven days. On the seventh day, with the blowing of trumpets and the shout "The Lord has given us the city," the walls came tumbling down.

Look westward from the vantage point of the *tel* and you'll see the Mount of Temptation. This was the place, according to tradition, where Jesus was "led up of the spirit into the wilderness to be tempted of the devil. And he fasted 40 days and 40 nights . . . " (MATTHEW IV, 1-3). Following the slopes of the mount are the crenellated walls of the precarious Monastery of the Temptation.

Across the road opposite the *tel* is Elisha's Fountain. (Known as *Ein es-Sultan,* "the Sultan's Fountain," in Arabic.) In II Kings we read of the prophet Elisha being asked for help by the men of Jericho, as the water of the fountain was bitter and the land barren. He "healed" the waters with salt. Today you may still drink from the fountain, which flows cool and sweet, contributing to the city's heady greenness. Water, too, is just about the only original tourist souvenir to come out of Jericho—"holy water" from the Jordan River is sold to pilgrims by the bottle.

The River Jordan

Six miles east of Jericho, on the Jordan River, is the place where John the Baptist anointed Jesus and proclaimed Him the Savior, or Christ. There are several churches near the spot, the most distinctive being the

Greek Monastery of St. John. A special service of blessing the water is held annually on Epiphany Sunday.

Farther up the river is the Allenby Bridge, which gained fame after the Six-Day War for the refugees crossing over it into Jordan. Later, thousands of refugees returned to the West Bank the same way. Now, West Bankers, with the permission of the Military Government, cross back and forth over the bridge to conduct business or see relatives in Jordan. Israel even permits incoming traffic in the form of students studying in Arab countries (who come from the West Bank), allowing them to visit and vacation at home for the summer.

Though it's not generally publicized, a lot of commercial traffic goes over the bridge, too. Most of it is West Bank fruits, vegetables and tobacco for Arab-world customers; the economic link held up even during the Yom Kippur War.

Returning westward on the Jerusalem-Jericho road, turn east again at the intersection for the Dead Sea. You can't go any further down than the crossroad marker at the lowest spot on earth—1,295 feet below sea level.

Just before you is the Dead Sea. On the far side, to the east, are the Mountains of Moab. Opposite, the hills of Judah come down to the western shore.

At this juncture, you may go swimming in the Dead Sea's bitter, buoyant waters. The *Lido-Kalia* here has changing rooms and showers, the latter a must after a dip in the Dead Sea since you come out, in effect, a human salt lick. You can also fill up on fresh water while you're at it or have coffee or snacks on the terrace overlooking the sea. Note the mural!

The Essenes and Their Scrolls

From here, follow the road west. Minutes later, a turnoff will bring you to Qumram. This is where the Dead Sea Scrolls were found in 1947 and where the ancient Essenes had their center. The area is now under the care of the National Parks Authority.

As you follow the well-marked trail, you may wonder how people ever eked out a living from the barren earth on the edge of the Dead Sea, where a merciless sun beats down the year around. But manage they did, thanks largely to an ingenious water-supply system. The winter floodwaters from the mountains above were caught in channels and carried by an aqueduct to the settlement. Then, the water was parceled out to a network of cisterns to be used as needed.

The excavations reveal in vivid detail the everyday life of the ancient collective community: the kitchen, the long communal dining hall, the vital cisterns, a tower for defense, stables and a scriptorium, or writing room. It is probably in this very scriptorium that the Dead Sea Scrolls were penned.

The cave in which the first of the Scrolls was found is across a deep wadi a bit away from the settlement. It's virtually inaccessible, and it's only because an Arab shepherd followed a stray from his flock and stumbled on the find that it came to light when it did. If the maverick hadn't got lost just there, the Scrolls could easily have remained hidden for another 2,000 years. (The canyons and hills here are riddled with natural caves and Scrolls were found in eleven of them.)

The first settlement on the site was founded about the eighth century B.C. It may even be the "City of Salt" referred to in the Book of Joshua. The Essenes inhabited the place toward the end of the second century B.C. and lived there till the time of King Herod, when Qumram was abandoned. It was resettled again until the period of the Jewish uprising against Rome (A.D. 66–70), when it was finally deserted.

Further south was Ein Fescha Springs, gushing from underground less than 100-feet from the Dead Sea's edge, filling a series of small, clear-water pools before entering the murky sea. Many people come to splash, take mud baths, sun and sip or snack at the modern café. Showers are here, too, and bus service.

A highway now links Ein Fescha with Ein Gedi, Masada and the rest of the Dead Sea region (see *The Negev* chapter). This highway enables you to travel between the two spots in about fifteen or twenty minutes, and it reduces the trip to Eilat by about 50 miles.

North of Jerusalem

As countless travelers before you have done, you may start your journey north from the Damascus Gate going up the Nablus Road. As Jerusalem proper thins out into suburbs, a tall minaret on a high rise can be seen on the left. This is *Nebi Samwil,* "the Prophet Samuel," where the seer and king-maker is said to be buried. From the top of this mosque (which at various times was a church and synagogue, too), one can see the entire breadth of the Holy Land, from the Mediterranean to the Dead Sea and the Mountains of Moab. From this vantage point, over 3,000 feet above sea level, pilgrims in medieval times often caught their first glimpse of their goal—Jerusalem. The height was thus dubbed *Mons Gaudii,* the Mount of Joy.

To the right side, off the Nablus Road, is the site of biblical Gibeah, where King Saul had his capital. King Hussein of Jordan was building a summer palace on the remains of Saul's fortress when the Six-Day War broke out.

Before Ramallah, a side road to the left goes to Jerusalem Airpor (also referred to as Kalandia or Atarot Airport), which connects th capital with Tel Aviv, Eilat and Rosh Pina.

Ramallah means "Height of God" in Arabic. It looks down o Jerusalem from a lofty altitude of 2,930 feet. Its dry, bracing mountai air made it a favourite resort in the Arab world and there are numerou villas here surrounded by beautiful, trim gardens. It is easy to see hov it got its name.

The road west, from Ramallah to Tel Aviv, passes what was th Latrun Bulge, an appendix of land inside Jordan where an old polic station crests a hill near Latrun Monastery. Here, 1948's bloodies battles saw thousands of raw refugee Jews die trying to take the statio and the road, to free Jerusalem's siege. Lush fields hide all that story in this valley where Joshua commanded the sun to stand still.

The Latrun Monastery, built for Italian Trappists some 40 years ago houses silent monks who bottle good red and white wines and sell then here and in cities, via marketing help from nearby kibbutznik buddies

Just a mile or so north of Ramallah, a small road to the right lead to the Arab village of Beit-El, biblical Beth-El (House of God). It i repeatedly mentioned in the Book of Genesis, first as the place by whicl Abraham pitched his tents and built an altar to the Lord in the lan of Canaan, later when Abraham returned here from Egypt with hi nephew, Lot.

Jacob's Ladder

Beit-El is most closely associated, however, with the story of Jaco in Genesis XXVIII when he dreamed of a ladder reaching up to heaven Jacob took the pillow of stone he had rested his head on when he slep and set it up as a pillar. But don't look for the stone at Beit-El; it's sai to be in London under the Coronation Chair in Westminster Abbey— some people believing it to be the famous Stone of Scone!

The road winding through the pastoral hills of Samaria crosses : gorge known as *Wadi el-Haramiye*—The Pass of the Thieves. The Ara village of Sinjal a bit farther on takes its name from the Crusader nam for the spot—St. Giles.

Off the main road to the right is the place where ancient Shiloh stood At Shiloh, the Tabernacle and the Ark of the Covenant rested befor being taken to Jerusalem.

Recent excavations here have unearthed the remains of houses goin; back to biblical times, mosaics from the Byzantine era, and parts of synagogue more than 1,000 years old.

The ancient city of Shechem was located to the north and east of th present-day city of Nablus. Near it, you'll find the 100-foot deep Ja cob's Well, also known as the spot where Jesus spoke with the Samaritan woman (JOHN IV, 5–9). The Well is out of sight, down hut-covered steps in the midst of an unfinished Russian Orthodox basilica, turned over to the Greek Orthodox after World War II. A Byzantine church stood here, and the small Well Chapel is on the site of a chapel built by Constantine the Great's mother, Helena. Rich, worth visiting. A few steps from the Well area is Joseph's Tomb, where his bones were taken by the Children of Israel during the Exodus from Egypt. The small, white-domed building was restored in the last century.

A half-mile from the tomb is the Arab village of Balata and behind the village, Tel Balata, where biblical Shechem once stood. Here, and on the facing mountains of Ebal and Gerizim, were written some of the most dramatic chapters of the Old Testament. Abraham entered the land of Canaan here; Jacob encamped near Shechem; Moses, though he was not to enter the Promised Land, told his people: "And when the Lord will bring you unto the land which you are come to inherit, you shall offer up a blessing on Mt. Gerizim and a curse on Mt. Ebal." (DEUTERONOMY XI, 29.) In response to this command, Joshua divided the tribes of Israel on the two mounts and from the Law of Moses, had the curses therein read toward Mt. Ebal, the blessings toward Mt. Gerizim.

The Samaritans

Mt. Gerizim is the Holy Mountain of the Samaritans. The Samaritans, remembered vaguely by most people in association with some stories in the New Testament, are an interesting Jewish sect whose history goes back to the time of the Babylonian Exile. The Samaritans evolved from those Israelites who had escaped the exile. They held to the letter of the Mosaic Law. When the exiled Jews returned, they considered the Samaritans beyond the pale and would not let them help in the reconstruction of the Temple. This led to a bitter schism. The Samaritans made Mt. Gerizim their spiritual center, eschewing Jerusalem. The Jews were at loggerheads with the Samaritans and looked upon them with contempt, as did the Samaritans on the Jews. The Romans harassed the Samaritans and the Jews harassed them; the Samaritans harassed the Jews, and then harassed the Christians—who did the same to the Samaritans when they had the upper hand.

Though the Samaritans once numbered in the tens and perhaps hundreds of thousands in and around Palestine in the Middle Ages, they became almost extinct by the beginning of the 20th century. Today, their numbers are slowly growing again. There are about 500 all told, half of whom live near Mt. Gerizim and half in Holon, near Tel Aviv.

The Samaritans celebrate the Passover week on top of Mt. Gerizi
following every word of the Mosaic Law literally, up to and includi
the slaughter, roasting and eating of the Pascal lamb on the night
the feast.

The sect recognizes only the Five Books of Moses as Holy Writ.
their synagogue is their ancient Torah, written in Samaritan scri
somewhat akin to Hebrew. They say it was written in Joshua's tim
but authorities believe the scroll to be some ten centuries old.

Samaritans point out a rock on Mt. Gerizim that they say was t
place Abraham prepared to sacrifice Isaac, though Mt. Moriah
Jerusalem is generally believed to be the site where this took plac
They also show twelve rocks Joshua was supposed to have set up the
for the tribes of Israel, though the Bible puts this on Mt. Ebal.

Nablus and Samaria

Nablus is the most populous and modern city on the West Ban
Agriculture and light industries are the mainstays of its economy, ar
the town is renowned for its soap and a sweet pastry called *kenafa.* T
name Nablus is an Arabic variation of the city's Greco-Roman nam
Neapolis, New City.

Approximately ten miles north of Nablus is Sebastia, ancient S
maria. A narrow road leads to the village of Sebastia, where was on
a mighty city, the glory of the region. Crowning a mountain protect
by deep ravines, Samaria was bought by Omri—the sixth king of Isra
—and it became his capital, giving its name to the region. Omri's so
the wicked King Ahab, embellished the city for his pleasure and th
of his wife, the notorious Jezebel.

The city, which became a byword for opulence, was destroyed in t
Assyrian invasion of the eighth century. Rebuilt and destroyed aga
in the intervening centuries, Samaria came to know another "Gold
Age" in the reign of King Herod, who renamed the city Sebastia,
honor of Augustus Caesar (*Sebastos* is Greek for Augustus). Even
ruins, the city inspires awe. Here are the remnants of a huge hipp
drome, a long stately, colonnaded street, a basilica and tribunal, ar
an amphitheater that might be the envy of a 20th-century film directc
There are also remains of the palaces of Omri and Ahab and artifac
of their households.

The summit of Samaria affords excellent panoramas to all points
the compass. The village of Sebastia looks very lackluster in compar
son. The main point of interest here is a fine 12th-century Crusad
cathedral. The walls of the cathedral encompass a mosque. The churc
is said to be built over ancient jails that became tombs of the prophe
Elisha and Obadiah. You can climb down the cramped rock-hew

steps, with a candle-stub from the lock-holding caretaker. Eerie, the weird chamber supposedly holds the head of John the Baptist.

The Golan Heights

From the sea of Galilee northwards for about 40 miles along the course of the Jordan River, the land to the east of the river sweeps precipitously upward, to a height of over 1,000 feet above the valley floor. This cliff-like brow of land forms the western edge of the Golan Heights. Strategically, it dominates all the land in the valleys below, and for 19 years, the Israeli settlements here were sitting ducks for Syrian artillery and snipers. The Golan Heights were also an ideal jumping-off place for the Arabs who harried the settlers—that is, until June 9 and 10, 1967—the last two days of the Six-Day War.

On June 9, Israeli infantry, armor and air force units hit at the heights. It seemed like a suicide mission, for in addition to the bunkers, the heights were sown with hundreds of thousands of mines and ringed by miles of barbed wire. Under a continuous cannonade, the Israelis managed to punch through in two sectors. Casualties were heavy. The Syrians agreed to cease-fire when the Israelis were less than 40 miles from Damascus. The war of 1973 erupted here and in Sinai simultaneously. The death toll for both sides was great. The subsequent battles were followed by peace talks . . . which are still going on.

Though the land in the Golan is very rich—being largely fertile volcanic soil—farming had been neglected in the past years.

At one time, however, the Golan was one of the richest farm areas in the Fertile Crescent. The Golan Heights form a part of biblical Bashan, which was known for its particular breed of "fat cows," great oak forests and succulent fruit (Golan apples, even today, are superb; try some if you're visiting in the fall). The fabled ships of Tyre were built of oak brought from Bashan. But the last of the great forests were cut down 60 years ago.

The Golan is closely linked with Jewish history. The region was given as an inheritance to the tribe of Mannassah, one of the 12 tribes of Israel. It became part of the Kingdom of Israel during the reign of King David (about 1000 B.C.), when its borders extended right to Damascus. Its Jewish population grew, particularly in the time of Alexander Yannai (Jannaeus) and Herod the Great. In the revolt against Rome (A.D. 66–73), the Jews of the Golan fought unstintingly; their heroic stand at Gamla is sometimes likened to the more famous one at Masada.

Jewish population in the Golan remained dense till the sixth century, when Christian persecution thinned its ranks. There are still some remains of second- and third-century synagogues in the area.

The name Golan comes from the chief city of ancient Bashan. Golan was proclaimed one of the Israelites' refuge cities by Moses. It was first used as a regional name for the western part of Bashan in the time of the Second Temple.

The Golan has all natural boundaries: the Sea of Galilee and Jordan River on the west; the slopes of Mt. Hermon on the north; the Yarmuk River to the south, and the Rakkad River to the east. The area's breadth is 15 to 20 miles.

From Mount Hermon to Galilee

There are three natural gateways to the Golan Heights—across the Banias in the north; across the Jordan at Bnot Yaakov (Daughters of Jacob) Bridge, and across the Yarmuk in the south, by El Hama.

Let's assume you've explored the length of the Upper Galilee and find yourselves at Kibbutz Dan, in the extreme north of the country. Heading northeast over a smooth, newly surfaced road, it's less than a five-minute drive to Banias.

The waterfall and fast-running, clear-water springs here feed the Jordan River, and the Banias River is one of the Jordan's three tributaries. Look up and you'll see where the water comes from—the melting snows of Mt. Hermon.

Banias is the Arabic corruption of the Greek name for the site: *Paneas.* Surrounded by sylvan beauty, the Greeks consecrated the place to the rustic god Pan. In the Roman era, it became known as Caesarea Philippi (not to be confused with the Caesarea on the Mediterranean Coast) and is referred to in the first two gospels of the New Testament. In his writings, Josephus Flavius called it *Panium.*

Right by the gushing waters is the former Syrian Officers' Club, where you can stop for a snack—it's now a restaurant.

Farther on, on the slopes of Mt. Hermon, is the Druse village of Majdel Shams (Tower of the Sun). Here Druse farmers sell the produce of their vineyards and orchards. Since the winter of 1967, they've found a new source of income—selling provisions and hot drinks to Israeli skiers. The Israel Ski Club, formed after the Six-Day War was centered here, already has several hundred adherents.

Part of triple-peaked Mt. Hermon is an Israeli-administered territory; the other parts are in Lebanon and Syria. The highest summit in the Israeli part of the mountain is almost 7,000 feet above sea level, but Hermon's highest peaks soar to over 9,000 feet.

Off the secondary road, between Banias and Majdel Shams, you will catch a glimpse of Nimrod's Castle (Kalaat Namrud). This 12th-century Crusader fortress is worth a look (local and tour buses ply the new road right up to its doors). It's in a fine state of preservation despite eight centuries of weather and wars. The view from here is superb, esthetically and strategically. The Crusaders built the castle to fend off Moslem forays from Damascus.

Returning to the main road and following it east, we come to a geological oddity called Birket Ram (Pool of the Height). The height is almost 3,500 feet above sea level and the pool is in reality a volcanic lake, cupped in a crater over a half-mile long.

The crossroads of the Golan is Kuneitra less than 20 miles south of Birket Ram. This was the chief city and headquarters for the Syrian Army in the Heights. The population, mostly Circassian, left when the Syrian Army did. Few inhabitants remain in this ghost-town city. Just outside town, Kibbutz Hagolan takes overnight guests.

Kuneitra to the Dead Sea

Four roads lead out of Kuneitra. One, which we've already followed, goes to Banias; another leads southwest to the Bnot Yaakov Bridge over the Jordan (the heaviest-traveled route across that river); a third curves southward to El Hama Hot Springs *(Hammat Gader),* and a fourth leads northeast toward Damascus, less than 40 miles away.

Around Kuneitra and in other parts of the Golan, you'll come across a number of destroyed, abandoned villages. The scars of battle can be seen too, along the Kuneitra-Bnot Yaakov Bridge road. The land, flat and fertile, was scarcely cultivated and presents a bleakly beautiful picture. Almost the length of the road, Syrian Army installations and barracks appear on either side. As you get closer to the Jordan River, you see more pockmarks, shell holes and mine fields. At the former Syrian Customs House, on a rise just before the river, the full brunt of battle can be seen. A key position, the Customs House bristled with armor and artillery. Russian-made tanks were sunk turret-deep to provide maximum fire power while offering the least target. Some of these tanks, grotesque and burnt-out, can still be seen today.

The road southwest out of Kuneitra runs through empty flatlands for miles. At one point, you'll cross the TAP oil pipeline from Iraq, which goes to Lebanon.

As you approach the Sea of Galilee, the remains of Syrian military outposts begin to crop up again. After the Fik crossroads, you can stop at the former Syrian artillery training post, where, in a bullet-riddled building, you can see a perfectly detailed scale model of the Sea of Galilee and the surrounding Jewish settlements. The artillery ranges have been figured out to the last yard and the tiny model homes bring to mind static targets in a shooting gallery.

Farther on, you'll have a chance to visit some of the Syrian bunkers *(under escort, please, to avoid mines and booby traps!)* dug deep into the escarpment over the Sea of Galilee. Looking through a slit large enough only for the muzzle of the field piece to fire through, you'll wonder anew how these strongpoints were ever taken.

The road begins to curve down from the plateau toward the Yarmuk River basin. After your car or bus has steered round a tight turn, you suddenly see El Hama spread out before you, several hundred feet below. The El Hama hot springs have been known since ancient times and the Romans made use of them 2,000 years ago. There are some remains of Roman structures here including a remnant of a small theater. The mosaic floor of a sixth-century synagogue has been uncovered at El Hama revealing Hebrew-Aramaic inscriptions.

More excavations are underway now, after having been interrupted by the 1973–4 battles. If the zone remains Israeli, you may one day be able to perspire like a pasha in the ancient Turkish bath-house here, due to be reopened by the Tiberias Hot Springs people.

From here on, the road turns west and you find yourself on the southern shore of the Sea of Galilee. There's a small bridge crossing what looks like a stream flowing southward—that's the Jordan River, moving toward the Dead Sea. You're almost 700 feet below sea level here. Look back, and you'll see the Golan Heights towering behind you.

The Gaza Strip

The road you travel on today, from Ashkelon to Gaza, was once part of the ancient *Via Maris*. Gaza is one of the oldest cities of recorded history and dates its origin to more than 4,000 years ago. The name of the city probably stems from the Hebrew word for strong, "Az," and even today, the Hebrew name for the city is "Azza."

Most people associate Gaza with the story of Samson, as related in the Book of Judges. This is where the Philistines brought Samson after he had been shorn of his locks (and thus his strength) by the devious Delilah. But Samson had the last word, toppling the Philistine temple at Gaza—crushing his captors who had blinded and tormented him, and himself perishing under the temple stones. The prophets Amos and Zephania had predicted dire happenings for Gaza, which did come to pass. From being an important way-station for trade between Egypt and Syria, Gaza fell under the sway of all-conquering powers that crossed the area: Greeks, Romans, Moslems, Crusaders and Turks. Napoleon bivouacked here in 1799 and, in World War I, the British took the city from the Turks and Germans—at a cost of 10,000 casualties. Since then, its strategic position has insured its continued participation in what seem perpetual throes of war and fighting.

The Gaza Strip is a tongue of land extending from the northeastern tip of the Sinai Peninsula along the Mediterranean Coast. About 31 miles long and four wide, it marks the northernmost stand of the Egyptian armies in the 1948 Arab-Israeli War. The rectangular strip seems to point to Tel Aviv, less than 50 miles away. The distance seemed even closer after Nasser gave the UN force in the Gaza Strip its walking papers in May, 1967, thus eliminating the buffer that had been keeping that border quiet since 1957. In the 1956 Sinai Campaign, Israel had taken the Gaza Strip and Sinai, but turned them back to Egypt in 1957 on the request of the UN. By the end of May, 1967, there were about 400,000 Arabs in the Gaza Strip, eager to unite with Arab forces for what would be the "Six-Day War." Gaza surrendered to Israeli troops on the second day of this confrontation, becoming part of the territories administered by Israel. The 1973 Yom Kippur War ended with Gaza still under Israel's flag. However, when Israel and Egypt signed and ratified a peace treaty in 1979, this strip of land was named as part of territories whose administration would be altered to some form of autonomy within approximately five years. Special deliberations about the Gaza District (larger than the town, with 441,300 population), the West Bank, and other parcels of land, began in mid-1979 and are continuing as this edition goes to press.

Despite its government upheavals, this area will long be remembered for its light, loosely woven fabric—from which we get the word "gauze."

City and Camps

It's less than a half-hour's drive from Ashkelon to Gaza along the main highway leading south. After passing Yad Mordechai, the well-tended kibbutz fields come to a halt. A fallow area shows where the Erez border point was and then you see row upon row of orange groves. Citrus is the major Strip product. Prior to the Six-Day War, Gaza's second principal activity lay in smuggling duty-free goods into Egypt, but this source of "trade" has now dried up.

Before you reach Gaza, you'll find for sale on either side of the road, two handicraft items of the city—hand-painted pottery in terra cotta or black Sinai clay, and woven rush baskets. All are interesting and cheaply priced and a few could make grand souvenirs.

As you go toward the main street, you'll see that Gaza is a pretty dismal-looking place, quite a disappointment after its long and fabled history. The main street is filled with shops, most of them of little interest. Gaza does produce very nice wicker furniture, but you'll find this pretty hard to stuff into your suitcase. Camel-hair carpets are a very good buy, with a wide variety of striped or solid carpets to choose from. They can be folded up into a neat bundle and sent home by mail. Haggling is *de rigueur*.

After seeing the few sights you can go to the beach to watch the fishermen. If you're here during the December-April citrus season, you can watch Gazaites on the beach loading their fruit onto waiting steamers—lugging the crates on their backs to row-boats, rowing out to the ships and then passing them up to the decks via slings.

Heading further south you'll see the refugee camps of Gaza, where for almost 20 years the Palestinians were practically stripped of all rights and had very little chance to get out of the camps, even if they wanted to. Some 60,000 Gaza folk now commute to work in Israeli towns and cities, bringing home money and new, improved standards for living on many levels. As the money eased their survival strain, education began flourishing along with sanitation, communications and health services.

The Sinai

If you get to Israel, and don't visit Sinai, you'll regret it, certainly. If you do see Sinai, there's no chance you'll ever forget it. Traffic has flowed across here from the two ends of the Fertile Crescent for millennia, camel caravans laden with rich stuffs, perfumes and spices, having made the trek all the way from Araby and Cathay. It seems incredible, when you wander this stark land, but there's been a constant stream of traffic here since time immemorial. In Bible times, Abraham and Sarah traversed Sinai, as did the unwilling Joseph. Miraculously, the Children of Israel—under the rod of Moses and the watchful eye of God—wandered through this wilderness a full 40 years. Then Mary and Joseph, with the infant Jesus, fled across Sinai to escape Herod's wrathful orders.

To this awesome landscape, mystics have come since before recorded history, seeking the revelations and mysteries of deity and monotheism. The harsh country gave birth to monasticism and continues to nourish this discipline. Through the peninsula's depths, pilgrims of many faiths have traveled toward their holy places, carving their holy signs in rocky passages that withstand time, adding to the remnants of countless civilizations that passed through, perhaps remained a while, yet never conquered this unique territory.

Sinai's greatest impact is nature. Throw together every imaginable kind of desert waste—shifting sand dunes, bare rock, hard-baked soil, naked, craggy mountains—punctuated with a few palm groves and oases, and you begin to get an idea of the Sinai Peninsula. Is it superfluous to mention the biting sand storms and searing sun, which can send the mercury up to 120°F. on a summer's day? And the brittle air at night when the stars look as big as table-tennis balls and you shiver under a blanket? Sinai contrasts raw mountains with sea, nomad dwellers with bikini-wearing sun-worshipers, tent communities with modern accommodations and facilities. During the dozen years the peninsula was totally under Israeli administration, the first modern highway was laboriously cleaved along the shoreline, with networks of secondary roads leading into the heart of Sinai. Cleaned, refurbished and studded with kiosks for cool drinks and other tourist facilities, the Sinai coast became a favorite vacation site for locals and internationals, and the chances are that it will remain well-traveled by tourists, regardless of political changes in the land.

Today, Sinai is sliced by Israeli-Egyptian peace treaty lines progressively moving northward until, according to current schedules, the entire triangular peninsula (26,000 square miles with some 30,000 inhabitants—mostly nomadic Bedouin) comes under Egyptian authority on April 25, 1982. Along the Mediterranean it's only some 30 minutes drive south of the Gaza Strip to the Egyptian border at El-Arish—a town Israel handed to Egypt in May, 1979, as part of the treaty agreements. From December, 1979, Egypt's flag could be seen flying over a southern portion of approximately half the Red Sea Gulf coast of Sinai, encompassing several Israeli-built settlements, resorts and military bases, plus some 11,000 Bedouin.

However, tourists still can see enough of Sinai to savor. These jaunts are highly recommended. Check out the many Sinai excursions offered via land, sea and air. Investigate through a travel agent before you leave home, or right after arrival in Israel.

Two-Country Tourism

Both Israel and Egypt declared open borders on May 27, 1979. To visit one country from the other, or visit one after the other, merely apply for visas in the normal way, at consulates or border posts. However, as other Arab lands still do not recognize Israel, tourists planning to travel the Arab world still want a second passport, or should request a separate visa for Israel's entry-exit stamps, rather than have those stamps permanently in passport pages.

After 30 years of armed hostility between Egypt and Israel, citizens hardly can wait to visit each other's lands. A mid-1979 poll revealed almost half Jerusalem's residents planned to see Egypt during 1980, and similar travel hopes are reported from Cairo. Even before treaty ratifications, enterprizing tourism professionals of both countries were meeting in Europe to devise joint programs that would offer tourists the best of both lands. Today, assorted choices are available to individuals and groups wanting to visit back and forth. There still are many formalities, and the costs make the travel prohibitive for many regional pockets, but this two-country tourism is growing rapidly nevertheless.

Foreign tourists must have valid passports and visas, which can be obtained before they leave home or at the Egyptian Embassy, Hilton Hotel, Independence Park, Tel Aviv. For $85 one way, or $170 round-trip, you can fly to Cairo International Airport from Ben-Gurion International Airport at Lod, where there will be a passenger tax of IS30. You may choose either El Al Israel Airlines or Nefertiti Airlines and fly aboard a Boeing 707. There are only four round-trips weekly, but these are so solidly booked the service probably will be expanded soon—however, book early.

Tourists also may go the land route, paying IS23.60 for the regular Egged Bus from Tel Aviv to Neot Sinai, then change to the Egged shuttle that plies the short distance between this Israeli border point and the Egyptian El Arish terminal, where they may board an Egyptian bus. Do be sure to check time schedules carefully, whether going by bus or private passenger car, which also is allowed. The drive from Tel Aviv to El Arish is some 3 hours; Cairo is 6–8 hours further. The ferry at Kantara crosses the Suez Canal only once daily—unfortunately there is no precise time-table (so pack extra food and drinks). Those who drive their own cars (diesel motors are not allowed in Egypt) should check first with the Automobile and Touring Club of Israel (Memsi), 19 Derech Petach Tikva, Tel Aviv, to be sure they meet all requirements such as special fees, licenses, insurance and so forth (still quite complicated). So far (mid-1980) no provisions have been made for rental cars to make this crossing.

Guided package tours, however, cross frequently. Some of the more interesting tours are offered by V.I.P. Travel & Tours, Ltd., 130 Hayarkon St., Tel Aviv and 3 Ben Sira St., Jerusalem. It combines bus, ferry and air tours, with stays in 5-star Cairo hotels for $355 per person double occupancy, and $515 per person single occupancy, including bed and breakfast for an 8-day trip. With lunches and 6 days of comprehensive sightseeing (entire Nile Valley: Cairo, Aswan, Luxor) added in, the prices move up to $690 and $795. There is also a 4–5 day trip, covering historic sites and flying via El Al, with prices ranging from $340 to $430. Arkia, Israel Inland Airlines Ltd., which has branched into international routes, has also jumped on the two-country tourism band-wagon by offering one-day all-inclusive tours of Cairo. These leave Lod each Saturday for a full itinerary that also includes the Nile Valley and return the same evening to Tel Aviv—all for $280 per person. Plans are also in the works for an Arkia day tour to Luxor. American Express also offers comprehensive tours for both countries.

You can visit Sinai and cross borders into Egypt from there, too. All tourism services offered by Israel before Mt. Sinai and Santa Katerina were turned over to Egypt, are still in operation, including Arkia flights, tours by Neot HaKikar, Johnny's Desert Tours and Ya'alat Eilat Tours. Visitors Permits must be obtained (about $3 payable only in foreign currency) at checkpoints along the land route or at Mt. Sinai Airfield, now controlled by Egyptian Civil Aviation Authority. You may go alone or with groups, and there is no limit to how long you may stay. Rooms in the Santa Katerina area may be booked through Mr. Hassan Sadek, Telex 9222, ISIS UN CAIRO. Private aircraft also may land at Mt. Sinai Airfield.

One of the world's most famous diving areas is at Ras Muhammed, Sinai, beyond current Israeli portions of the peninsula. However, divers still may go there from Israel, and several diving firms in Sharm el Shiekh can make all the arrangements. Query IGTA, IGTO or any travel agency for more details.

Tours sail down the Gulf between the Arabian and Sinai peninsulas, sometimes stopping at Crusader ruins to picnic, or at still clear-water coves, or at the unusual coastal retreat built and operated by flamboyant Rafi Nelson. The Gulf water is great for swimming, grand for under-water sightseeing (more than 300 species of marine life in vibrant colors), and challenging for sailors—thanks to strange wind patterns plus miles of coral reefs.

The coastal areas can also be toured by land—in buses and rental cars, or you can opt for the airconditioned, catered luxury of limousines with chauffeur-guides. But a trip to remember forever is the trek through the interior by desert vehicles along ancient routes and amid utterly breathtaking vistas.

In Eilat, look for a ferry plying to and from Hurghada, Egypt. This, and other services, may take you to Israeli tourist sites like Dizihav and Sharm-el-Sheikh (Ofira)—possibly the most beautiful oasis areas anywhere. Also check here for tours to Santa Katerina Monastery—a "must see" Orthodox stronghold dating to the fifth century A.D., set at the base of 7,500-foot Mount Sinai, traditionally the site where Moses received the Ten Commandments.

Mediterranean cruises already operate from Israel to Egyptian ports, and several shipping lines offer cruises to both countries. Again, these tours are being finalized as we go to press, so no details are available, but we can steer your questions to certain shipping firms. The Italian Adriatica Line has proposed including both Haifa and Alexandria in regular weekly sailings from Venice via Piraeus. Then *Arion,* flying the Greek flag and sporting enough room for 550 passengers plus 120 autos, slated service to link the Israeli ports of Haifa and Ashdod to Port Said and Alexandria, Egypt. There's also talk of routing large cruise ships from Israel to Egyptian ports, to act as floating hotels and offset Egypt's shortage of tourist accommodations. Meanwhile, reports flourish about remodeling, refurbishing and enlargment of Egyptian hotels—and one international chain released plans to install Kosher meal service to accommodate the anticipated flood of Orthodox Jewish tourism.

As Moses said when he saw the Golden Calf, "It's all happening!"

PRACTICAL INFORMATION FOR THE WEST BANK, GOLAN HEIGHTS AND SINAI

Information in this section has been arranged to follow the routes outlined in the previous text.

A WORD TO THE WISE

When traveling to the Sinai, don't forget to take a sunhat and sunglasses ... and your bathing suit. It gets cool at night, so take a sweater as well. If you're taking a camera or binoculars (you'll never forgive yourself if you don't), bring along a lens brush. If you have insect-repellent cream or spray (you can buy either in Israel), bring that, too.

Bear in mind that the daytime heat is sweltering from mid-May to mid-October. Plan your trip accordingly, and during the hot season stick to the following precautions:

Get off to an early start; above all, avoid having to hurry.
Never go bare-headed; keep in the shade between noon and 3 P.M.
Drink lots of liquids; eat only light foods and in small amounts.
Take it easy on sun-bathing; sun stroke is the most common tourist affliction in Israel.

WEST BANK

BETHLEHEM welcomes visitors year-round, but is particularly crowded during the Christmas season—especially for the annual Christmas Eve Choir Assembly that brings choirs from all over the world (for more details, contact IGTA and IGTO in Israel and abroad).

HOTELS. While visitors usually elect to stay in Jerusalem hotels, hostels, hospices and camping areas (see both East and West Jerusalem listings), there are overnight accommodations here. **Handel** leads the list as a 3-star hotel with 40 rooms (baths or showers), some with kitchenettes and room tv; also beauty parlor, piano bar, coffee shop; on Jamal Abdel St. The **Palace** offers 25 2-star rooms on Manger Square. Recommended as a pension is **Andalus** Hotel, with 16 rooms on Manger Square, as is the 4-room **Arab Women's Pension,** on Children's St. Excellent nearby bungalows, mobile homes and holiday homes at **Mevo Betar Camping.** (See *Jerusalem Practical Information.*)

SHOPPING. Bethlehem, less than 15 minutes away from the heart of Jerusalem, is full of tourist shops, plying every conceivable souvenir, religious or secular. The town is famous for its production of items in mother-of-pearl and olivewood. Nativity scenes are legion, and priced $10–$100. There is assorted jewelry in silver, gold, mother-of-pearl and stones such as turquoise, jade and tiger-eye, which runs to over $200 on the higher-priced wares. Boxes of Damascened inlaid wood are around $15–$20. Embroidered Arab dresses and men's long Oriental robes begin at $20. Crusader Jackets, with gold and silver embroidery, about the same price. Other good buys here include fur throws, and basketware.

There are two main shopping areas—(1) before the town center as you go by Shepherd's Field and (2) in town, around Manger Square. You might try the **Holy Manger Store** in the former place (on the right side of the road as you ascend) and the **Good Shepherd's Store** on Milk Grotto Street in the latter. Also, handicrafts can be bought at the **Old Bethlehem Museum,** founded in 1972 by the **Arab Union Women,** and exhibiting old furniture and embroideries.

RESTAURANTS. Both shopping centers have snack bars, restaurants and such. On the way to Bethlehem, in front of Rachel's Tomb, two kosher restaurants have opened to serve low-cost meals to pilgrims.

IGTA: Manger Square (02) 742591.

HEBRON. SIGHTS AND SHOPPING. One of 4 Jewish Holy Cities, also sacred to Moslems and Christians. No approved hotels, but within day-trip distance from everywhere; between Jerusalem and Beersheba. The former Jordan Tourist Authority building on the way to the Tomb of the Patriarchs (Cave of Machpelah) has a snack bar.

The uniquely beautiful Hebron **glass** is a favorite purchase. Inexpensive and captivatingly ancient-looking (the special glass-making technique was learned from the Romans), the glass takes the form of necklaces, medallions, glasses, pitchers, vases and lamps. A simple but lovely medal or charm sells for as little as IS5 and a vari-colored lamp for about $15.

Sheepskins—natural, cut or dyed—are also a Hebron specialty. For from IS40 and up, you can get a sheepskin floor mat, which is easy on the eye and a boon for people who hate to step on cold floors. The fleecy skins are also made up into warm, boot-like slippers, which can be had for less than IS25 a pair. The sheepskin jackets—with or without sleeves—have the fleece on the inside and sell for about $20 and up, depending on the quality and your bargaining ability.

JERICHO. SIGHTS AND RESTAURANTS. A few sleepy restaurants range around the town square, but if you go on to Ein Sultan Road, you'll find a more appetizing assortment. They appear one after another and most are garden restaurants, where you can dine shaded by a grape arbor. **Al Khayyam** has a lovely garden and a large menu assortment, starting with *hoummous* and going up to shishkebab, steak, and grilled chicken. The **Green Valley,** up the same road, has a restaurant and bar and even its own pool in the gardens filled with spring water, and diners may take a dip after lunch. The genial management offers a large bill of fare, including the house specialty of *moussakhan.*

Not far from Jericho, on the northern tip of the Dead Sea, there's the **Lido-Kalia,** which has soft drinks, beer, appetizers and sandwiches; you can swim, too: newly remodeled lockers, changing rooms and showers run IS10.

Regular bus service daily to and from Jerusalem. The circle-walled terrace with a fine mural, faces the sea; food is IS3 and up per item, outside or inside café.

RAMALLAH. Almost directly north of Jerusalem, this large Arab town is good for touring, shopping and overnights.

HOTELS. Now recommended is the **Ramallah Grand,** a 3-star hotel on Main St.

RESTAURANTS. *Moussakhan* is a town specialty to look for—delicious! Try it at **Na'oum's** garden restaurant on Mughtaribeen Square, one street from the cenotaph in the middle of town. The *maza* (hors d'oeuvres) here can run to 23 separate dishes. Delightful garden setting. Most main courses here are around $7–$10.

SHOPPING. Arabs and Jews flock here for furniture and local craft work. Excellent for leisurely shopping. Ramallah-made chocolates and sweets are great treats.

IGTA: Call Bethlehem Office, 02–742591 or 742134.

NABLUS. This interesting Arab town was the site of Jacob's Well and biblical events.

HOTELS. Now recommended is the 1-star **Palestine,** with 16 rooms on Shutra St.

RESTAURANTS. Though many visitors satisfy themselves with cold drinks and such, a superb Arab meal is yours at **Jacob's Well Restaurant,** just across from the biblical site. Owner Nazmi Salman Sulaiman is hospitable, also sells gifts, snacks. **Jerusalem Restaurant,** up the hill, is also good, less money; more silent, local men.

OTHER WEST BANK ACCOMMODATIONS recently recommended include: **Normandy,** 9 rooms on Main St. in Beit Jala (no grade yet); **Cleopatra,** with 18 2-star rooms, and **Cliff Hotel,** with 32 2-star rooms, both in Abu Dis; for more information, contact the *Tourism Staff Officer,* Judea and Samaria District, Ministry of Industry, Trade and Tourism, P.O.B. 1018, Jerusalem.

GOLAN HEIGHTS

KUNEITRA. You can get food, and even stay overnight at **Kibbutz Hagolan** near Kuneitra in the "Kuneitra Hilton"—a former Syrian officers' villa turned into a modest hotel.

SINAI

Go for day trips, tours or lengthy stays—but go. For touring information, including tour operators, see *Eilat Practical Information* in the *Negev* chapter, and *Facts At Your Fingertips* chapter; also see Two Country Tourism in *Border Areas* chapter. Three key spots to visit are:

NUEIBA or (Neviot) is about 80 km (50 miles) south of Eilat. It has a service station, a guest house, beach facilities, soft drink counters, a restaurant, and diving equipment to hire. **Neviot Vacation Village** offers desert tours and runs a diving center, and charges $26.50–$36 (half board included) per person; add $8.80 for full board. It has 86 air-conditioned rooms, a private beach, restaurant and nightclub of sorts, tennis courts, water sports, wind surfing and diving center, glass-bottom boats, desert tours.

DAHAB (also called DiZahav) is located some 160 km. (98 miles) south of Eilat. Bedouins own and operate beach resort area; modern with restaurant and showers. It has a service station and similar facilities to Nueiba (see separate entry).

Hotels. Frequently called the most beautiful Sinai oasis, it also has the **DiZahav Holiday Villages** with 42 rooms/bungalows with showers, 5 family houses and a 60-bed hostel. Operates center for diving, sailing, surfing, plus water-skiing, wind-surfing, desert tours. (See *Facts At Your Fingertips* section.)

SHARM-EL-SHEIKH. (Ophira) Truly beautiful settlement; horseshoe-shaped beach; white sands; see-through water; good bathing, a service and repair station, a diving center, restaurants and kiosks, a bank, and *IGTA*.

HOTELS. The **Marina** is big, modern, posh, with fine facilities and restaurants.

The recently built **Field School** has 24 rooms with private showers, and charges minimally for bed and use of kitchen. **Cliff-Top Village** is so new it is not yet graded; but it has 27 air-conditioned rooms with showers.

There are camping areas here, and the 120-room **Louis Price Youth Hostel** offers easy access to fabulous underwater and desert worlds, is also air-conditioned and has restaurant, very good facilities.

You can also stay overnight at the **Santa Katarina Monastery** which has a new row of cell-like rooms just to put up wayfarers, pilgrims and tourists. The stay is a rare experience: all's been refurbished recently, by special reconstruction experts chosen in Greece and flown over. Families, groups or individuals can stay now; write the monastery for all details—MPO 1358, Sinai, Israel.

SUPPLEMENTS

ENGLISH-HEBREW VOCABULARY

Note: h denotes aspirated 'h'.

Generalities

ENGLISH	HEBREW
Do you speak English, French, German?	Ha-im ata m'daber Anglit, Sarfatit, Germanit?
Thank you very much	Toda raba
I don't understand	Ani lo m'veene, (fem., m'veena)
If you please, you're welcome	B'vakasha!
I am a tourist	Ani tayar (fem. tayeret)
Yes—no	Ken—lo
Good morning—good evening	Boker tov—erev tov
Good night	Laila tov
Till we meet again, see you	L'hitra'ot
Hello—goodbye	Shalom
Mr.—Miss or Mrs.	Adon—g'verett
Pardon me	Sliha
This—that	Zeh—zot(f.)
Pleased to meet you	Na'im me'ohd
To life! (toast)	L'hayim
Are you alone?	Ata levad? (fem. At levad?)
May I have this dance?	Ha-mootar li l'hazmeen otach lirkod iti?
Wait for me	Hakeli, (fem. Haki li)
Yesterday—today—tomorrow	Etmol—hayom—mahar

Traveling—Customs

Taxi	Monit
To the station—to the pier—to the airport	Le'tahanat ha'rakehvet—la'namal—Le'sde ha't'oofa
Ticket	Kartis
Porter (redcap)	Sabal
Which road goes to . . . ?	Ech holchim le . . . ?
Ladies—Gentlemen	G'varotte (Nashim)—G'varim
Entrance—exit	Knisa—Ytsia
I am on my vacation	Ani behufsha

In Traffic

Straight ahead	Yeshar (Kadima)
To the right—left	Ye'mina—s'mola

Show me the road to . . .	Na l'har'ot li et ha'derech le . . .
Crossroads	Hitstalvut, tsomet
Where is?	Efo nimtsa?
Bus stop	Ta*h*anat ha'otobus
Stop here, please	Atsor kan, b'vakasha

In the City

Police bureau (station)	Ta*h*anat Ha'mishtara
Would you be good enough to show me . . . ?	Na l'har'ot li . . .
Would you be good enough to conduct me (guide me) . . . ?	Na laka*h*at oti le . . .
Street—square—avenue—highway	Re'*h*ov—kikar—sdera—kvish
American—British Consulate	Shagrirut Americanit, Anglit
Theater—movies	Teatron—Kol-noa
Where is the Tourist Office?	Heichan nimtset lishkat ha'tayaroot
Drugstore	Beth mirka*h*at
Doctor—dentist	Rofe—rofe shinayim

Shopping

I would like to buy	Ani rotse (f. rotsa) liknot
How much does this cost? (What is the price?)	Kama ze ole?
It is too expensive	Ze yakar midai
Do you have sandals?	Ha-im yesh lachem sandalim?
Do you have American, English, newspapers?	Ha-im yesh itonim Americaüm b'Anglit?
Show me that blouse	Na l' har'ot li et ha'*h*ooltsa hazot
Airmail stationery	N'yar ve ma'atefot do'ar avir
Roll of film	Seret le'tsiloom
Cigarettes, matches	Sigariot, gafroorim
Bread—butter	Le*h*em—*h*em'a
Fruit	Peirot

At the Hotel

Do you have a vacancy?	Yesh lachem, *h*eder panooi?
Single—double	*H*eder le'ha*h*id—*h*eder kafool
With a bathroom—shower	Im ambatya—im mikla*h*at
How much per day?	Ma ha'm'*h*ir le'yom?
With a view of the sea	Im mar'e al ha'yam
For one night, two nights	Le'laila e*h*ad, le'shnei leilot
Here is my passport	Hinei ha'darkon
The key, please	Ha'maftea*h*, b'vakasha
Breakfast, lunch, supper	Aroo*h*at boker, aroo*h*at tsohorayim, aroo*h*at erev

The bill, please   Ha'*h*eshbon, b'vakasha
I am leaving tomorrow   Esa Ma*h*ar

At the Restaurant

Where is the restaurant?   Efo Ha'mis'ada
Waiter, the menu, please   Meltsar, ha'tafrit b'vakasha
Soup   Marak
Bread—butter—jam   Le*h*em—*h*em'a—riba
Hors d'oeuvre   Mana rishona
Omelet   *H*avita
Chicken   Ohf
Meat   Basar
Veal cutlet   Umtsat b'sar egel
Salad   Salat tari
Egg   Beitsa
Fish   Dag
Vegetables   Yerakott
Dessert   Mana a*h*rona
Fruit—cheeses   Peirot—g'vinot (singular, g'vina)
Serve the meal on the terrace   Na l'hagish et ha'aroo*h*a al ha'gusoostra
Red—white wine   Yayin adom—yayin lavan
Water, mineral water, fruit juice, beer   Mayim, mayim mineralim, mits, bira
Turkish coffee—tea—ice cream   Cafe turki—tay—gilda
Coffee with cream—milk   Cafe im *h*alav—*h*alav
The bill, please   Ha'*h*eshbon b'vakasha

At the Bank, Post Office

Where is the bank?   Efo ha'bank?
Where is the Post Office?   Efo ha'do'ar?
I wish to cash a check   Ani rotse (f. rotsa) lig'vot hamchaa
I wish to change some money   Ani rotse (f. rotsa) l'ha*h*lif kesef
Stamps, postcard, letter   Boolim (sing., bool), glooya, michtav
Airmail   Do'ar avir
I wish to send a telegram   Ani rotse (f. rotsa) lishloa*h* mivrak

Motoring

Garage—gas (petrol)   Moossach—delek
Gas pump   Mash'evat delek
Oil, please   Shemen, b'vakasha
Change of oil   l'ha*h*lif shemen
Check the tires   Livdok et ha'tsmigim
Wash the car   Lir*h*ots et ha'mechonit

Grease job	La'asot sika
Breakdown	Teker
Towing—repairing	Lig'ror—l'taken
Spark plugs	Slil ha'tsata
Brakes	B'lamin
Gear shift	Ha*h*lafat hiloochim
Carburetor—radiator	me'ayed makren
Headlights	Panasim
Ignition	Ha'tsata
Axle	Seren, Tsir
Springs	Kfitsim
Spare part	*H*elek *h*iloof

Numbers and Days of the Week

1 A*h*at	7 Sheva	30 Sh'loshim	80 Sh'monim
2 Shtayim	8 Sh'moneh	40 Arba'im	90 Tish'im
3 Shaloshe	9 Tesha	50 *H*amishim	100 Mea
4 Arba	10 Esser	60 Shishim	200 Matayim
5 *H*amesh	20 Esrim	70 Shiv'im	300 Sh'losh me'ot
6 Shesh			
			1000 Elef

Sunday	Yom rishon	first day
Monday	Yom sheni	second
Tuesday	Yom sh'lishi	third
Wednesday	Yom revi'i	fourth
Thursday	Yom *h*amishi	fifth
Friday	Yom shishi	sixth
Saturday	Yom shabat	Sabbath

Abbreviated Arabic

Please—Min Fedlak	How much?—B'kam
Thank you—Shukkran	Too much—K'teer
What time is it?—Kahm Saah	One—Wahad
How are you?—Keef *H*alak	Two—T'neyn
Excuse me—Sama*h*mi	Three—Talaati
Yes—Aywah	Four—Arbah
No—La	Five—Hamsa
Hotel—Lukanda, fondok	Six—Sitteh
Left—Shimal	Seven—Sabah
Right—Yamin	Eight—Tamanyeh
Straight—Dugri	Nine—Tisah
Water—Myeh	Ten—Ahshara
Bread—Hoobes	Twenty—Eshreen
Money—Masari	Fifty—Hamseen
Tea—Tchai	One Hundred—Miyeh
Coffee—Kahawah	

INDEX

The letters H and R indicate Hotel and Restaurant listings

(This index also includes useful information from "Facts at your Fingertips." *See also* "Practical Information" sections at the end of each chapter for additional details.)

MAP OF
ISRAEL

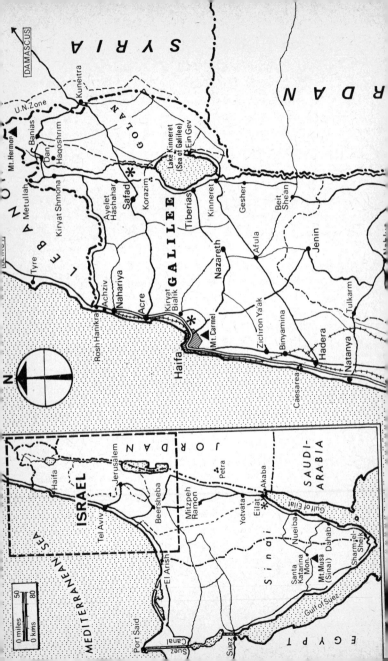

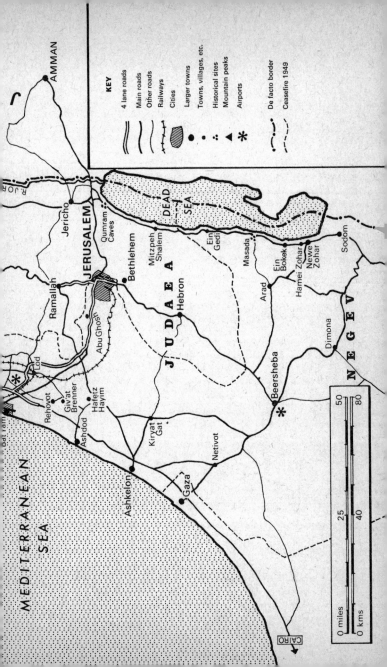

1-1